SRI SRI PARAMAHANSA YOGANANDA
January 5, 1893—March 7, 1952

JOURNEY TO SELF-REALIZATION

COLLECTED TALKS AND ESSAYS ON REALIZING GOD IN DAILY LIFE, VOLUME III

BY

SRI SRI PARAMAHANSA YOGANANDA

Yogoda Satsanga Society of India
FOUNDED 1917
Paramahansa Yogananda

First Indian Hardcover Edition, 2001
Fifth Impression, 2015

 An authorised publication of Yogoda Satsanga
Society of India/Self-Realization Fellowship

The trade dress of this book is a trademark of
Self-Realization Fellowship

Published in India by
YOGODA SATSANGA SOCIETY OF INDIA
Yogoda Satsanga Math
21, U. N. Mukherjee Road
Dakshineswar, Kolkata 700 076

Printed in India by
Srinivas Fine Arts (P) Ltd.
340/3, Keelathiruthangal
Sivakasi 626 130

ISBN 978-81-89535-06-3

Distributed by:

 Jaico Publishing House

Also available from Yogoda Satsanga Society of India, Paramahansa Yogananda Path, Ranchi 834 001, Jharkhand and at Yogoda
Satsanga Ashrams and Dhyana Kendras throughout India.

Dedicated by Yogoda Satsanga Society of India/
Self-Realization Fellowship
to our beloved third president,
SRI SRI DAYA MATA
whose faithful devotion to recording the
words of her Guru for posterity has
preserved for us and for the ages the
liberating wisdom and God-love
of Sri Sri Paramahansa Yogananda

The Spiritual Legacy of Sri Sri Paramahansa Yogananda

A century after the birth of Paramahansa Yogananda, he has come to be recognized as one of the preeminent spiritual figures of our time; and the influence of his life and work continues to grow. Many of the religious and philosophical concepts and methods he introduced decades ago are now finding expression in education, psychology, business, medicine, and other spheres of endeavor — contributing in far-reaching ways to a more integrated, humane, and spiritual vision of human life.

The fact that Paramahansa Yoganandaji's teachings are being interpreted and creatively applied in many different fields, as well as by exponents of diverse philosophical and metaphysical movements, points not only to the great practical utility of what he taught, but also to the need for some means of ensuring that the spiritual legacy he left not be diluted, fragmented, or distorted with the passing of time.

With the increasing variety of sources of information about Paramahansa Yogananda, readers sometimes inquire how they can be certain that a publication accurately presents his life and teachings. In response to these inquiries, we would like to explain that Paramahansaji founded Yogoda Satsanga Society of India/Self-Realization Fellowship to disseminate his teachings and to preserve their purity and integrity for future generations. He personally chose and trained those close disciples who head the Yogoda Satsanga Society/Self-Realization Fellowship Publications Council, and gave them specific guidelines for the preparation and publishing of his lectures, writings, and *Yogoda Satsanga Lessons.* The members of the YSS/SRF Publications Council honor these guidelines as a sacred trust, in order that the universal message of this beloved world teacher may live on in its original power and authenticity.

The Yogoda Satsanga Society of India/Self-Realization Fellowship name and the YSS/SRF emblem (shown above) were originated by Paramahansaji to identify the organization he founded to carry on his worldwide spiritual and humanitarian work. These appear on all YSS/SRF books, audio and video recordings, films, and other publications, assuring the reader that the work originates with the organization founded by Sri Sri Paramahansa Yogananda and faithfully conveys his teachings as he himself intended they be given.

YOGODA SATSANGA SOCIETY OF INDIA /
SELF-REALIZATION FELLOWSHIP

CONTENTS

ILLUSTRATIONS

recorded yesterday. I can even hear inwardly the inflections of Gurudeva's voice in each particular phrase.

The Master seldom made even the slightest preparation for his lectures; if he prepared anything at all, it might consist of a factual note or two, hastily jotted down. Very often, while riding in the car on the way to the temple, he would casually ask one of us: "What is my subject today?" He would put his mind on it, and then give the lecture extemporaneously from an inner reservoir of divine inspiration.

The subjects for Gurudeva's sermons at the temples were set and announced in advance. But sometimes his mind was working in an entirely different vein when he began to speak. Regardless of the "subject for today," the Master would voice the truths engrossing his consciousness at that moment, pouring forth priceless wisdom in a steady stream from the abundance of his own spiritual experience and intuitive perception. Nearly always, at the close of such a service, a number of people would come forward to thank him for having enlightened them on a problem that had been troubling them, or perhaps for having explained some philosophical concept in which they were particularly interested.

Sometimes, while he was lecturing, the Guru's consciousness would be so uplifted that he would momentarily forget the audience and converse directly with God; his whole being would be overflowing with divine joy and intoxicating love. In these high states of consciousness, his mind completely at one with the Divine Consciousness, he inwardly perceived Truth, and described what he saw. On occasion, God appeared to him as the Divine Mother, or in some other aspect; or one of our great Gurus, or other saints, would manifest in vision before him. At such times, even the audience would feel deeply the special blessing bestowed on all present. During such a visitation of Saint Francis of Assisi, whom Gurudeva deeply loved, the Master was inspired to compose the beautiful poem, "God! God! God!"

The Bhagavad Gita describes an enlightened master in these words: "The Self shines forth like a sun in those who have banished ignorance by wisdom" (V:16). One might have been overawed by Paramahansa Yogananda's spiritual radiance, were it not for his warmth and naturalness, and a quiet humility, which put everyone instantly at ease. Each person in the audience felt that Gurudeva's talk was addressed to him personally. Not the least of the Master's endearing qualities was his understanding sense of humor. By some choice phrase, gesture, or facial expression he would bring forth an appreciative response of hearty laughter at just the right moment to drive home a point, or to relax his listeners after long and intense concentration on a particularly deep subject.

One cannot convey in the pages of a book the uniqueness and universality of Paramahansa Yogananda's vivid, loving personality. But it is my humble hope, in giving this brief background, to afford a personal glimpse that will enrich the reader's enjoyment and appreciation of the talks presented in this book.

To have seen my Gurudeva in divine communion; to have heard the profound truths and devotional outpourings of his soul; to have recorded them for the ages; and now to share them with all—what joy is mine! May the Master's sublime words open wider the doors to unshakable faith in God, to deeper love for that One who is our beloved Father, Mother, and Eternal Friend.

DAYA MATA

Los Angeles, California
July 1975

Decades have now passed since Paramahansa Yogananda gave the talks presented in this series of anthologies, in which *Journey to Self-realization* is the third volume. The years have brought recognition of the timelessness in the outreach of his far-sighted, practical wisdom, which penetrates into the deepest realms of spirituality—transcending every boundary of country and creed, speaking universally to the spiritual needs of a newly emerging global civilization.

In one of the discourses in *Man's Eternal Quest*, the first volume in this series, Paramahansaji says: "The one purpose of Self-Realization Fellowship [Yogoda Satsanga Society] is to teach the individual the way to personal contact with God." That personal divine communion, the heartbeat of his spiritual legacy, is the paramount theme in this third anthology as well. As we approach the dawn of a new millennium, it is clear that humankind's truest hope lies in those who take the time to find the tremendous love and understanding awaiting discovery in the presence of God in our souls, directing its flow therefrom as a healing balm toward all the members of our world family.

How tangibly those blessings radiated from the person of my revered Guru. In public, even strangers on the street would be irresistibly drawn to respectfully inquire: "Who is he? Who is that man?" In his presence during periods of deep meditation, we saw him completely enraptured in communion with the Divine. The whole room would be filled with an aura of God's love. Paramahansaji had attained the highest goal of life's journey; his example and words now illumine the path for millions worldwide.

All of us are on the same sacred journey, to a destination as yet perhaps only dimly glimpsed—a journey of discovery that will gradually unfold before us, revealing all along the way new gifts and graces of the soul. In time, it will lead us to the full realization of who we truly are: not the outward form that cloaks us, but an immutable spark of the Infinite Spirit. My prayer is that each reader find in these pages a profoundly empowering vision of that divine destiny, and a new awareness of the joy that is inherent in the journey itself.

DAYA MATA

Los Angeles, California
July 1997

INTRODUCTION

In *Journey to Self-realization,* Sri Sri Paramahansa Yogananda offers enlightening counsel to all who are seeking to better understand themselves and their true purpose in life. To the myriad complexities of human existence, he brings clarity and compassionate wisdom, opening before us a larger, more far-seeing vision of who we are and where we are going.

"Self-realization," Paramahansa Yogananda tells us, "is the knowing—in body, mind, and soul—that we are one with the omnipresence of God; that we do not have to pray that it come to us, that we are not merely near it at all times, but that God's omnipresence is our omnipresence; that we are just as much a part of Him now as we ever will be. All we have to do is improve our knowing."

This book explores *how* to "improve our knowing"—how we can experience the Divine Presence, within us and in all life, not just as a passing inspiration but as a constant inner realization. Through this expanded awareness, we receive the gifts of the soul: peace, love, intuitive guidance, ever new joy— an unfolding understanding that we are indeed "made in the image of God."

This is the third anthology of talks and essays by Paramahansa Yogananda—a sequel to *Man's Eternal Quest* (1975) and *The Divine Romance* (1986). The wisdom in these volumes is not the studied learning of a scholar; it is the empirical testimony of a dynamic spiritual personage whose life was filled with inner joy and outer accomplishment, a world teacher who lived what he taught, a *Premavatar* whose sole desire was to share God's wisdom and love with all.

As a man of God, and as an authority on the ancient divine science of Yoga, Paramahansa Yogananda has received the highest credentials from his spiritual contemporaries, and from readers of his works in all parts of the world—the literary and general public as well as his followers. That he has also received the ultimate commendation from the Supreme Authority is amply attested to by the manifest blessings of God on his exemplary life, and by the infinitely beautiful, uniquely edifying responses given to him by God in vision and divine communion.

This comment in *Review of Religions*, published by Columbia University Press, is typical of the acclaim accorded Paramahansa Yogananda's earlier work, *Autobiography of a Yogi*: "There has been nothing before, written in English or in any other European language, like this presentation of Yoga." The *San Francisco Chronicle* wrote: "Yogananda presents a convincing case for Yoga, and those who 'came to scoff' may remain 'to pray.'" From *Schleswig-Holsteinische Tagespost*, Germany: "We must credit this book with the power to bring about a spiritual revolution."

Of Paramahansa Yogananda himself, Swami Sivananda, founder of the Divine Life Society, Rishikesh, India, said: "A rare gem of inestimable value, the like of whom the world is yet to witness, Paramahansa Yogananda has been an ideal representative of the ancient sages and seers, the glory of India." His Holiness the Shankaracharya of Kanchipuram, revered spiritual leader of millions in South India, wrote of Paramahansaji: "As a bright light shining in the midst of darkness, so was Yogananda's presence in this world. Such a great soul comes on earth only rarely, when there is a real need among men. We are grateful to Yogananda for spreading Hindu philosophy in such a wonderful way in America and the West."

Paramahansa Yogananda was born in Gorakhpur, India, on January 5, 1893. He had a remarkable childhood that clearly indicated his life was marked for a divine destiny. His mother recognized this and encouraged his noble ideals and spiritual aspirations. When he was only eleven, the loss of his mother, whom he loved above all else in this world, made firm his inherent resolve to find God and to receive from the Creator Himself the answers yearned for in every human heart.

He became a disciple of the great *Jnanavatar* (incarnation of wisdom) Sri Sri Swami Sri Yukteswar Giri. Sri Yukteswar was one of a line of exalted gurus, with whom Yoganandaji had been linked from birth: Sri Yogananda's parents were disciples of Sri Sri Lahiri Mahasaya, guru of Sri Yukteswar. When Paramahansaji was an infant in his mother's arms, Lahiri Mahasaya had blessed him and foretold: "Little mother, thy son will be a yogi. As a spiritual engine, he will carry many souls to God's kingdom." Lahiri Mahasaya was a disciple of Sri Sri Mahavatar Babaji, the deathless master who revived in this age the ancient science of *Kriya Yoga*. Praised by Bhagavan Krishna in the Bhagavad Gita, and by Patanjali in the *Yoga Sutras*, *Kriya Yoga* is both a transcendent technique of meditation and an art of living that leads to union of the soul with God. Mahavatar Babaji revealed the sacred *Kriya* to Lahiri Mahasaya, who handed it down to Sri Yukteswar, who taught it to Paramahansa Yogananda.

After graduating from Calcutta University in 1915, Sri Yogananda took formal vows as a monk of India's venerable Swami Order. Two years later, he began his life's work with the founding of a "how-to-live" school—since grown to twenty-one educational institutions throughout India—where traditional academic subjects were offered together with yoga training and instruction in spiritual ideals.

When in 1920 Paramahansa Yogananda was deemed ready to begin his world mission of disseminating the soul-liberating science of Yoga, Mahavatar Babaji told him of the divine responsibility that was to be his: "You are the one I have chosen to spread the message of *Kriya Yoga* in the West. Long ago I met your guru Yukteswar at a *Kumbha Mela*; I told him then I would send you to him for training. *Kriya Yoga*, the scientific technique of God-realization, will ultimately spread in all lands, and aid in harmonizing the nations through man's personal, transcendental perception of the Infinite Father."

Paramahansa Yogananda began his mission in the West as a delegate to the International Congress of Religious Liberals in Boston in 1920. For more than a decade he traveled the length and breadth of the continent, speaking almost daily to capacity audiences in many of the largest auditoriums in the country—from New York's Carnegie Hall to the Los Angeles Philharmonic. On January 28, 1925, the *Los Angeles Times* reported: "The Philharmonic Auditorium presents the extraordinary spectacle of thousands...being turned away an hour before the advertised opening of a lecture with the 3000-seat hall filled to its utmost capacity. Swami Yogananda is the attraction. A Hindu invading the United States to bring God...." It came as no small revelation to the West that Yoga—so eloquently expounded and clearly interpreted by Sri Yogananda—is a universal science, and that as such it is indeed the essence of all true religions.

In 1925, atop Mount Washington in Los Angeles, Paramahansa Yogananda founded the international headquarters for Self-Realization Fellowship, the society he had started in India in 1917 as Yogoda Satsanga Society of India. To this day Sri Yogananda's worldwide work is directed from this location (*see photo facing page 352*), guided and served by monks and nuns of Self-Realization Fellowship, to whom Paramahansaji entrusted the responsibility of carrying on his work and preserving the purity of his teachings.

In the late 1930s Paramahansaji began to withdraw gradually from nationwide public lecturing. "I am not interested in crowds," he said, "but in souls who are in earnest to know God." Thereafter, he concentrated his efforts on classes for serious students, and spoke mostly at his own Self-Realization Fellowship temples and the international headquarters.

Paramahansa Yogananda had often voiced this prediction: "I will not die in bed, but with my boots on, speaking of God and India." On March 7, 1952, the prophecy was fulfilled. At a banquet in honor of the Ambassador of India, Binay R. Sen, Paramahansaji was a guest speaker. He delivered a soul-stirring address, concluding with these words from a poem he had written, "My India": "Where Ganges, woods, Himalayan caves and men dream God—I am hallowed; my body touched that sod!" He then lifted his eyes upward and entered *mahasamadhi*, an advanced yogi's conscious earth-exit. He died as he had lived, exhorting all to know God.

The Guru's talks in the earliest years of his ministry were recorded only spasmodically. But when Daya Mataji became a disciple of Paramahansa Yogananda in 1931, she undertook the sacred task, faithfully recording, for the generations to come, all of her Guru's talks and classes. This volume is but a sampling: under the direction of Paramahansa Yogananda, many transcriptions—particularly those containing private instruction and meditation techniques and principles given to Self-Realization class students—were compiled along with some of his writings into a series of *Yogoda Satsanga Lessons;* other talks appear as a regular feature in *Yogoda Satsanga* Magazine.

Most of the selections in this volume are lectures or classes given at Self-Realization Fellowship temple services or at the international headquarters in Los Angeles. A few of the talks were given at informal gatherings or *satsangas* with small groups of disciples; or at meditation services in which the Guru experienced ecstatic communion with God, affording all present a glimpse of that blissful consciousness. Some inspirational writings are also included in this volume. Paramahansaji was a prolific writer who often used his spare moments to compose a new canticle of love for God or a short article that might help others to better understand a certain facet of truth.

As most of the talks set forth in this book were presented before audiences familiar with Self-Realization [Yogoda Satsanga] teachings, some clarification of terminology and philosophical concepts may be helpful to the general reader. To this end, many footnotes have been included; also a glossary explaining certain Sanskrit words, and other philosophical terms, and giving information about events, persons, and places associated with the life and work of Paramahansa Yogananda. If the reader encounters an unfamiliar term, he or she might wish to consult the glossary. It may also be noted here that quotations from the Bhagavad Gita in this volume are from Paramahansa Yogananda's own translations, which he rendered from the Sanskrit sometimes literally and sometimes in paraphrase, depending on the context of his talk. (Paramahansaji's comprehensive translation of and commentary on the Gita, published by Yogoda Satsanga Society of India/Self-Realization Fellowship, is entitled *God Talks With Arjuna—The Bhagavad Gita: Royal Science of God-Realization.*)

Paramahansa Yogananda honored all religions and their founders, and held in respect all sincere seekers of God. Part of his world mission was to reveal the complete harmony and

basic oneness of original Yoga as taught by Bhagavan Krishna
and original Christianity as taught by Jesus Christ (See *Aims
and Ideals,* page 407.) He showed that the practice of yoga
establishes an inner attunement with God that constitutes
the universal basis of all religions. Abstractions of theoretical
religion pale before actual experience of God. Truth cannot be
wholly proved to any seeker by another; but by the practice of
yoga meditation all of us can prove truth for ourselves through
the irrefutable assurance of our own direct experience. "We are
all part of the One Spirit," Paramahansaji said. "When you
experience the true meaning of religion, which is to know God,
you will realize that He is your Self, and that He exists
equally and impartially in all beings....Do not settle for intellectual satisfaction about truth. Convert truth into experience,
and you will know God through your own Self-realization."

YOGODA SATSANGA SOCIETY OF INDIA/
SELF-REALIZATION FELLOWSHIP

Los Angeles, California
July 1997

JOURNEY TO SELF-REALIZATION

How to Express Everlasting Youthfulness

*First Self-Realization Fellowship Temple
at Encinitas, California,* March 20, 1938*

The kingdom of God is not in the clouds, in some designated point of space; it is right behind the darkness that you perceive with closed eyes. God is Consciousness; God is absolute Existence; God is ever new Joy. This Joy is omnipresent. Feel your oneness with that Joy. It resides within you; and it encompasses infinity. Beyond the gross vibratory boundaries of matter, the Immutable Infinite reigns in all His majesty and vastness. Endlessness—that is the kingdom of God; conscious Bliss, eternal and boundless. When your soul has expanded and feels its presence everywhere, then you are united with Spirit.

We bow to the Infinite on the altar of the horizon where the sky meets the ocean; and we bow to the transcendental Infinite on the altar of peace within us.

In spite of all our demonstrations of ignorance, God continues to give us life by His indwelling presence. He is sleeping in the sod; He is dreaming in the flowers; He awakens in birds and animals; and He knows that He is awake in the human being. In the superman, He finds Himself again.

In ages past, the *rishis* and masters of India, secluded in their hermitages, unraveled the mysteries that hide the Omnipresent Spirit. Their research has given us the valuable techniques and methods that tune the body and mind to the Illimitable Source of life and intelligence residing in every human being. By concentrating within on the Infinite, you can receive this boundless power.

Knowledge acquired from the study of books or from

---

* The Golden Lotus Temple. See footnote on page 251.

learned human beings is limited; but from the Infinite, the unlimited power of wisdom can be had. How to attain that? We teach the method in the weekly lessons sent from our head-quarters at Mt. Washington.* The truths in these lessons have come from God and from the research of the masters of India.

Know the Reason for Your Existence

It is an insult to your Self to be born, live, and die without knowing the answer to the mystery of why you were sent here as a human being in the first place. To forget God is to miss the whole point of existence. Learn to feel God, and to enjoy Him. Make it a habit and you will see in time how much you have gained. Acquiring material possessions and prosperity is no safeguard against sorrow. There will come a day when you will feel totally helpless, a mere pawn of destiny; and then you will begin to realize that God alone is your haven of security. He doesn't want to impose Himself on anyone. You must take the initiative to seek Him through your own fervent desire, pre-ferring Him to all other desires. As the swan can swim through muddy waters with its feathers remaining unsoiled, so should you live in this world. If you coat your mind with the oil of nonattachment, then material desires cannot cling to you.

The dewdrop that separates itself from the lake and floats in isolation on the lotus leaf will be dried up unless it returns to the lake. So, before life evaporates in material desires, bet-ter slip into the consciousness of God. The dewdrop of life will then not have to suffer death but will be eternal. Birth is separation from the Infinite; death is not an end of life but a transition to a higher state. Freedom from birth and death is a return to God. The dewdrop belongs to the sea. Separated, it is vulnerable to the sun and wind and other elements of nature; but when the droplet returns to its source, it becomes magni-fied in oneness with the sea. So it is with your life. United to God you become immortal.

While we are yet separated from the Eternal Sea, our aim should be to manifest as much as possible our essential divine

---

* See information on page 414 about receiving these Lessons from Yogoda Satsanga Society of India.

immortality. On the lotus leaf of material happiness the dewdrop of life must remain untouched and unpolluted until it slips into the vastness of God's presence. How to express our innate immortality in spite of contrary limitations is the purpose of our subject on making youthfulness more lasting.

Youth Is a State of Mind and Soul, As Well As of the Body

Everyone is interested in youthfulness. In one way or another everyone is seeking the fabled "Fountain of Youth." But what is youth? All young people are not necessarily youthful; some are already old and jaded far beyond their years. In contrast, some elderly people remain youthful in spite of their advancing age. They keep their minds young. Their smiles trickle down from their souls into their bodies and faces; their very life blood throbs with the joy of being. And then there are those dull, lifeless persons who are as good as dead before they die—and they don't even know it. They are the "walking dead." You see many people like that—negative, critical, moody, dispirited. There is no excuse for a wrong state of mind. You must be always positive-minded, cheerful, smiling, vibrant. By all means, practice this mental youthfulness that comes from the core of your being.

Thus, the age of the body has no real connection with youthfulness. It is the state of the mind and the expression of the soul that make a person youthful. The definition of youth is that state of body, mind, and soul in which one feels the acme, the zenith, of joy and power. If you want to, you can retain that state indefinitely. Conversely, by carelessness you can lose it very easily.

Let us first approach this subject from the mental standpoint. The mind is the controller; that is, it is at the controls of this body. The body itself is designed by the mind. We are the sum total of the consciousness we ourselves have created over a period of incarnations.* This mind, or consciousness, is the supreme force that governs all voluntary and involuntary activities of this bodily factory with its multifarious outputs.

---

* See *karma* and *reincarnation* in glossary.

The Five Mental States of the Consciousness

We judge our condition as desirable or undesirable by the degree of happiness therein, or by the lack of it. Accordingly, there are five mental states: happiness, sorrow, indifference, peace, and true joy.

Waves whipped up in the middle of the ocean by a storm rise high, recede into a hollow, and then rise again, one after the other, until the storm ceases and the waves dissolve in the sea. Likewise with the mind. The mental peaks are life's alternating joys and sorrows; the hollows in between are indifference or boredom. These are the first three mental states.

You can usually recognize a person's mental state by his face. If you ask a person whose face registers happiness what has made him happy, you will find that some desire had been satisfied—he got a raise, he accomplished something he wanted to do, or was otherwise gratified. A desire fulfilled gives joy.

When you see a person with a glum or sour face, his expression tells you that he has met with some disappointment. A desire contradicted produces unhappiness. The desire for health is contradicted by pain; the desire for money is contradicted by poverty, and so on.

Then there are the people in between. Ask them, "Are you happy?" "No." "Are you sad?" "No." They are in the middle, neither on the crest of the wave of happiness, nor on the clashing wave of sadness; they are in the intermediate hollow. That is the neutral state of indifference.

One cannot remain indefinitely on the crests of either buoyant happiness or turbulent sorrow, or in the dumps of boredom. In this world of competing dualities, the ordinary being is tossed up and down—rising on a wave of joy, sinking into the trough of indifference, and then getting tumbled by a wave of sorrow. They little know anything beyond these states of consciousness. To be thus jostled about is to surrender free will to a seemingly capricious destiny.

What man* needs in order to live a successful and satisfy-

---

* In his talks and lectures, Paramahansa Yogananda generally used the masculine gender, as was the custom of his time. His usage, however, was rooted not in the narrowly exclusive sense of the word *man*, denoting only half of

ing life is evenness of mind. That can be attained only by concentration, mastery of the mental faculties. Even the most terrible sorrow is healed by time; nothing is gained by reliving it every day. Sorrowing for someone who is gone does not help him or yourself, nor does it change that sad fact. Making yourself miserable by nurturing an inferiority complex or punishing yourself for past mistakes or failures will not get you anywhere; it paralyzes your mental faculties. Never allow yourself to get into negative mental ruts. And do not be bored with life either. That is a very uncomfortable state. It slowly stews you. Don't bake yourself and your potentialities in the oven of indifference.

Beyond the first three conditions of the mind—happiness, sorrow, and indifference—is the state of peace. Very few people reach that plane. Those who have money and health and satisfying relationships—everything they really need or want— may say: "I am not happy or unhappy or indifferent. I am contented; I am peaceful." After a period of turbulence, such a condition is welcome. But if for a long time one has peace that is merely the absence of joy and sorrow, he will say, "Please knock me on the head so I can feel if I am still alive!" Such peace, being a negative state in which excitation has been neutralized, is not lastingly satisfying.

So now comes the positive aspect, the last or fifth state of consciousness: the attainment of ever new joy. That state is found only by contacting God in deep meditation, through the practice of such techniques as those given by the masters of India. That all-fulfilling joy will never grow stale. How to describe it? If for ten days you were not permitted to sleep, but were forced to stay awake, and then allowed to fall asleep, the joy you feel at that moment, compounded a million times over, would not begin to express the joy that I am speaking about.

---

the human race, but in its broader original meaning; the word is derived from the same root as Sanskrit *manas*, mind—the uniquely human capacity for rational thought. The science of yoga deals with human consciousness from the point of view of the essentially androgynous Self (*atman*). As there is no other terminology in English that would convey these psychological and spiritual truths without excessive literary awkwardness, the use of *man* and related terms has been retained herein.

Jesus and other divine ones spoke of that joy. Saint Francis and Sri Chaitanya* knew that joy. Why else would saints deprive themselves of material gain, except that they found something greater? This path of Self-Realization doesn't tell you to cast aside everything of this world, but it does urge you to give up lesser, obstructing things for the superior, lastingly fulfilling true joy in life.

The time has come for you to know and understand the purpose of religion: how to contact that supernal Joy, which is God, the great and eternal Comforter. If you can find that Joy, and if you can retain that Joy all the time, no matter what happens in your life, you will stand unshaken amidst the crash of breaking worlds.

So that is the first law of retaining youth: You must have a happy state of mind, a state that is untouched by the events of life. In that joy, not even death can shake you. How could Jesus say, in the face of crucifixion, "Father, forgive them for they know not what they do,"† unless he had that inner joy which even the tortures of the flesh could not take from him? In that steadfast mental foundation, he could, with his dying breath, express love for those who were the instruments of the death of his body. That is the invulnerable state you must strive to cultivate.

Learn to Smile Sincerely in All Circumstances

Seeking God in meditation is the direct way to attain a joyous and youthful state of mind. There are additional practices that will also help to nurture mental youthfulness. First of all, learn to smile—sincere smiles. Wherever you are, no matter how trying the circumstances, smile from your heart. Harbor no form of anger or malice. Try to give genuine smiles to all— friends, family, strangers alike. Half the secret of youthfulness lies in that. If you have a contagious smile that wells up from

---

* A brilliant scholar, Sri Chaitanya in 1508 had a spiritual awakening and became inflamed with love for God, whom he worshiped as the avatar Lord Krishna (see glossary). His fame as a *bhakta* (devotee of God) spread throughout India in the sixteenth century.

† *Luke* 23:34 (Bible).

From the mid-1920s through the mid-1930s, Sri Yogananda traveled all over America giving lectures and classes on the science of yoga meditation and the art of balanced spiritual living to capacity audiences in major cities. (*Top*) Greeted by students upon arrival at train station, Los Angeles; (*center*) one of his classes in Detroit; (*bottom*) at banquet held in his honor in Cincinnati.

(*Left*) Paramahansa Yogananda with his great guru, Swami Sri Yukteswar, 1935. (*Right*) Paramahansaji gestures a warm greeting outside the Self-Realization Fellowship Temple in San Diego, 1949.

Yogoda Satsanga Math, on the Ganges at Dakshineswar near Kolkata. The stately ashram, acquired by Paramahansa Yogananda in 1939, is the headquarters of Yogoda Satsanga Society of India.

your true inner being, you are youthful. I often say that if you can't smile, then stand before a mirror and train yourself to smile by pulling the corners of the mouth up!

The day you make up your mind to smile, you will see that everything seems to conspire to try to make you cry! That is life. The day you make up your mind to be patient and forgiving, it will seem that others suddenly become harder to get along with. That is life. We are often crucified by others, but their meanness should not affect our resolutions to be kind. Let others pursue their way; you be bigger and adhere to your way. It is not the approval of human beings that you want, but the certification of God. Once you find His pleasure, you will be happy. Try to please others insofar as you can, and try not to offend anybody; but don't let that work against your primary duty to please God, first and foremost. It is not worth it.

Practice your smile of mental youthfulness all the time. See how many hours at a time you can keep your balance in spite of your trials. When you can remain cheerfully evenminded always, you will find every cell of your body alive with great joy.

God has blessed me these many years. Whether my smile is seen outwardly or not, divine joy is always with me now. The great River of Joy is flowing beneath the sands of my consciousness. Neither the changefulness of life nor the specter of death can take that away from me. It was hard work to make that state permanent and unchanging, but it was worth it.

So many people have thrown away years upon years and have not found joy. Why imitate them and go after those things that promise happiness and give unhappiness? Contact the Spirit in meditation, and you will know that what I have told you is true. You will possess a joy you will not part with, even if the whole world is offered to you in exchange. Money, sex, wine—nothing can match that supreme joy. It is an ever-burning radiance in your soul.

The Importance of Willingness, and of Being Less Self-centered

Willingness also is important in order to retain youthfulness. When you like someone, you don't mind cooking or doing other forms of service for that person; but if you have to do it for someone you don't like, your unwillingness makes you tired and irritable to do anything for him. This same principle is applicable in every situation: If you are unwilling, then you have no energy or interest. If you are willing, you have the vitality and enthusiasm of youthfulness.

Another key to mental youthfulness is to learn to be less selfish and self-centered, and more giving and caring toward others. To hold on to the joy found in contact with God in meditation, you must practice His quality of loving all, of being just and kind to all. Forgive your enemies. What a wonderful release you will have from the bondage of anger and jealousy. Reach out to help others every day, in whatever way you can— and especially by bringing souls to the spiritual path to seek God. Give to all that same love with which you love your family and dear ones. God gives you loved ones that you might learn to expand self-love to include love for others. And He allows death and other circumstances to take away dear ones that you do not confine your love to only a few, but learn to give it to all. The more universal your love becomes, the more your expanded consciousness will be filled with the joy of His omnipresent Being. The Bhagavad Gita says: "When a man beholds all separate beings as existent in the One that has expanded Itself into the many, he then merges with Brahman (Spirit)."*

Is Eternal Youth of the Body Possible?

Then comes the bodily aspect of youthfulness. Various saints who have remained in secret seclusion, hidden from the skeptical gaze of an unenlightened world, have lived far beyond a normal life span, maintaining youthfulness not only of spirit, but of the body as well. Mahavatar Babaji† is one such. Jesus, in a different way, demonstrated mastery over the elements of his body. He said, and then proved, "Destroy this [bodily] temple and in three days I will raise it up."‡ Such pow-

---

* XIII:30.

† The perennially youthful master who is first in the Yogoda Satsanga Society of India/Self-Realization Fellowship line of Gurus, and who revived the ancient science of *Kriya Yoga* in 1861. (See glossary.)

‡ *John* 2:19 (Bible).

ers have been proven by great masters in India. The higher laws have not been much demonstrated in the West because its culture has concentrated on external material development, whereas the East has devoted itself to an inner research into the realms of Spirit.

Why be astonished that some masters, to fulfill a divine purpose at God's behest, choose to live unusually long lives? We see in nature that there are animals that can live much longer than ordinary human beings. Yet man is supposed to be the superior creature. Why is he less long-lived? Because as human beings we are uniquely gifted with free will, privileged to do anything we like; and by misuse of this endowment, man chooses to do all the things he should not do. His wrong habits of living, thinking, persistence in disunion from God, are passed from generation to generation in the process of evolution, severely limiting the expression of his divine potentiality—physically as well as mentally and spiritually.

When in the mother's womb the human body starts to grow from the division of the first cell—consisting of the union of sperm and ovum—an embryo is formed within four days. The whole potential of the body is there on the fourth day. In the beginning, the formative cells are called germ cells, each one capable of becoming any kind of bodily tissue. According to a specific design, they mysteriously start to specialize to form nerves, bones, skin, blood, organs—all the components of the body. As the body parts are formed, the specializing germ cells become somatic cells, locked into their specific functions and the limitations of those functions. That means they do not always obey the conscious mind, because the evolutionary and individual karmic habits and thoughts of centuries are embedded deep within their composition.

For example, man is able to grow two sets of teeth; so why can't he grow a third set, and a fourth? Because the very cells of our bodies are hypnotized by the evolutionary patterns of generations lodged in our brains and in the cellular makeup. The more we get away from the subconscious hypnosis of the evolutionary state of civilization, the more free we shall be. How to convert somatic cells back into versatile, creative germ cells, which can rebuild and rejuvenate body parts, will be the future endeavor of science.* Our bodies should be able to change in whatever way we will them to do so.

The Greater the Will, the Greater the Flow of Energy

Learn to keep your will strong—a calm will, not a nervous will—and your body will then be full of energy. It is by the power of will that you bring energy into the body and utilize it. The greater the will, the greater the flow of energy. Learn how to draw that energy not only from food and oxygen, but from the Infinite as well, because a time will come when no matter what physical measures you take, your body will be weak. Food and oxygen are useful to the body only when acted upon by the inner life current. If this grows weak from physical and mental abuse, the outer supports of life become ineffective. The methods I teach show you how to recharge every part of your body with life energy coming direct from the omnipresent vibratory power of God that surrounds you and is within you. It is that power which has created your body and which sustains it. By the practice of the Energization Exercises† and especially by *Kriya Yoga* you can enliven your whole being with Divine Life.

Every gram of flesh has within it enough energy to light the city of Chicago for two days. You feel heat and vitality in the flesh generated by that energy, but not the tremendous energy itself within the atoms of the flesh. Each atom is a dynamo of power. You can vitally recharge every cell of the body by *Kriya Yoga* meditation, and by the exercise of will to tap the cosmic source of power. If you keep your will intact, and use that will to perform all your physical and mental actions with cheerful

---

* In recent years scientists have begun to report preliminary successes in achieving this. Robert Becker, M.D., a researcher in orthopedic surgery in New York, has used electrical stimulation to cause somatic cells to revert to the nonspecialized state of germ cells, enabling frogs and rats to regrow lost limbs (even though these animals do not naturally regenerate body parts). Dr. Becker and several other researchers have used this technique on human beings to heal bone fractures that had been diagnosed as irreparable. Further experimentation and research continues to this day.

† Formulated by Paramahansa Yogananda and taught in the *Yogoda Satsanga Lessons*. (See glossary.)

willingness, your body and mind will remain vitally youthful.

Obey the Laws of God Embodied in Cosmic Nature

Nature, cosmic creation, is the embodiment of the laws of God. So you must learn to obey these laws. Disease, mental inharmonies, and all kinds of misery are the consequences of disobedience. By misuse of free will, human beings choose to misbehave; and their actions, being contrary to divine law, later react upon the nervous system and the consciousness, creating inharmonies in body and mind.

When it comes to diet, the laws of health are constantly broken. Most people dig their own graves with their knives and forks. The animals in the zoo are fed more scientifically than the average human being. You should govern your eating habits by what you should eat, and not merely by what pleases your sense of taste. Your diet should include a predominance of fresh fruits and vegetables, and natural whole grains and legumes. Avoid too many refined starches and too many sweets, and greatly limit the intake of fats—these can be very injurious to health. The best candies are nature's sun-dried fruits, unsulphured. Those who eat a lot of meat should break off that habit by strictly avoiding all forms of beef and pork, and eating fish, poultry, or lamb only occasionally. Every piece of meat eaten should be accompanied by a large serving of lettuce. Far more preferable is a totally meatless diet that includes instead some dairy products, eggs, and vegetable protein foods. Unsalted peanuts or almonds or raw garbanzo beans, ground finely and mixed with orange juice, makes a good source of protein as a substitute for meat. Take milk in between meals, not with meals.

Avoid overeating. Ingesting more than the body needs can be as harmful as wrong eating. Don't think you have to eat just because the dinner bell rings. And when you do eat, eat less. Also, learn to fast one day a week and three consecutive days once a month on fresh fruits or unsweetened fruit juices.

Proper elimination is very important. Fresh fruits and vegetables help to clean out your body. When fasting, it is good to take a mild natural laxative in orange juice.

Posture, also, is important to good health. Poor posture

constricts the healthy flow of the life energy in the various body parts and vital organs. The best posture is chest out, shoulders back, stomach and abdomen in, and buttocks tucked under. Don't stand with a swayback or with hunched shoulders. Don't sit in a slumped position with the spine out of alignment, hampering breathing and the free flow of life energy in the spine. Psychologically, a hunched posture suggests a defeatist attitude. Always sit and stand erect. Be master of yourself, with your mind on the infinite power within and around you.

Take regular exercise, such as walking every day. Learn to breathe properly—calmly and deeply, filling the lungs all the way to the lower lobes. When the system is well oxygenated by proper breathing and exercise, the life force therein vitalizes the whole body, including the brain.

Lastly, in connection with the physical aspects of youthfulness, it is extremely important to conserve your power of sex. Overindulgence in sex and misuse of Nature's creative force will bring on disease and old age quicker than anything else. It devitalizes the body and weakens the immune system. Married couples should practice moderation, and single persons should observe abstinence.

By adhering to good-health practices, and by not diminishing the inner life energy through wrong physical and mental actions, you will enhance your ability to retain health and youthfulness. Even bad health karma from past lives can be thus greatly mitigated. No matter what your past is, it is never too late to try to change; it is never too late to correct your bad habits.

The "Fountain of Youth" Is Within the Soul

In the final analysis, the sought-after "Fountain of Youth" is to be found in your soul. Your true Self, being made in the image of God, is immortal. It never undergoes the ravages that affect the body. "No weapon can pierce the soul; no fire can burn it; no water can moisten it; nor can any wind wither it....The soul is immutable, all-permeating, ever calm, and immovable—eternally the same."* Right within your body is this immortality. You are dreaming delusion's dreams of weakness

---

* Bhagavad Gita II:23–24.

and frailty, and thus you do not see that behind you, and within your soul, is the everlasting immutable power of God. You must realize this. If you can once attain that consciousness, then even death cannot disturb you. Those who know God have that consciousness. They know the science of the atomic structure of creation, and its source and essence in the creative thought of God. To know Him is to see the body as a part of Spirit. The miracles of this realization are not to be demonstrated before the staring curiosity of people; but all God-realized saints have in some way quietly manifested that power.

In your dreams, you can make yourself whatever you want to be; you can do whatever you want to do. Sometimes you are sick, and sometimes rich, and so on. Mind can do anything in that dream state. When you learn how to control your mind during the waking state, realizing that its power is a part of the consciousness of God, you can similarly have complete mastery over the body. Meditation upon the soul is the method by which the mind can be made to work its wonders under your control. When you find your true Self, the soul, you shall see that the body is nothing but an emanation of God.

Those who are sincere seekers and follow this path steadfastly shall know the mystery of the everlastingness of the soul. If you can be cheerful and evenminded in all circumstances, and do all things willingly, you can be mentally ever youthful. If, in addition, you obey health laws, and use your will to draw on the infinite cosmic energy, you can promote vital youthfulness in the body. And, above all, if you know that you are immortal, made in the image of God, your whole being will glow with that eternal youthfulness; and if it is the will of God, you will not have to experience so-called death when you cast off this mortal body.* And even if you do undergo the natural transition of death, it will be seen only as a peaceful dream.

Make a solemn resolution to meditate every morning and

---

*In his *Autobiography of a Yogi,* Paramahansaji writes: "Many yogis are known to have retained their self-consciousness without interruption by the dramatic transition to and from 'life' and 'death.'" He himself left the body consciously at the time of his passing in 1952.

before going to bed at night: "First, last, and always, O Spirit, I will keep my engagement with Thee in meditation. You have blessed me to come in contact with this great truth of Self-Realization and its Masters, that through this gateway I may find Thee. Bless me to be steadfast until I find Thee."

Feel your oneness with the Father. Pray to Him that you perfect your body and mind, that in their harmonious instrumentality you may feel His presence within you. May the glory of Spirit abide with you. May His energy charge your body and mind, and His spirit awaken within your soul. Feel His glory registering His Infinite Immortality in your body, mind, and soul.

Remoulding Your Life

Self-Realization Fellowship Temple,
Hollywood, California, January 3, 1943

Today's subject is a very important one. Everything you hear this morning you should strive to remember and put into practice. It is so easy to be inspired momentarily, and then forget much of what you heard. That is why I often employ repetition; for to penetrate the hard core of human consciousness, a truth must be repeated again and again. By such review, it gradually becomes a habitual part of one's thoughts.

There is a vast difference between just listening to a lecture and applying the truths it contains. Everything my guru [Swami Sri Yukteswar*] told me I put into practice. As a result of his training I have always kept my spiritual priorities straight. I never miss three things: my meditations, morning and night; my exercises;† and service to others. These I religiously perform; all else of less importance I somehow manage.

Living in the consciousness of God, I find many things that once seemed necessary have become unnecessary. Last night I felt no need for sleep because my awareness of God was so strong. Once in a while I would see my body asleep, but that subconscious sleep-*samadhi* (*nidra samadhi sthiti*) soon slipped away and my mind and body were filled solely with the consciousness of God.‡

These things that I tell you come from my own direct

---

* See glossary.

† The Energization Exercises.

‡ The unconscious process of withdrawing the mind from the senses and body-identification in sleep is referred to as *nidra samadhi sthiti*. Conscious *samadhi* is attained when the meditator, the process of meditation (by which the mind is withdrawn from the senses by interiorization), and the object of meditation (God) become One. (See *samadhi* in glossary.)

experience; and one day they will be a part of your realization. Through Him whom I perceive within, it is possible to transmit to those who are in tune the light of God that is in me. It is not I, but He who is in me whom I extol. Just as the wealthy man can bestow his fortune on his worthy children, so it is possible for the man of spiritual wealth to bequeath his divine riches to those disciples who follow his example. This is true of all great masters. There are many instances of this transmission of spiritual consciousness, such as the "mantle" of Elijah that fell on Elisha, and the Holy Ghost imparted by Christ to the faithful eleven of his twelve close disciples.

Many come to the spiritual path; but it is those who remain steadfast to the end who will enter the Kingdom of Heaven. True devotees—those who see that the murky paths of this world all lead to disillusionment—steadily pursue God, never doubting Him. It doesn't matter whether He answers or not. The devotee inwardly prays: "Lord, Thou knowest I am coming, so I care not when Thou wilt reply to me. Though I am undeserving of Thy response, yet Thou canst not refuse me when the time is right."

As soon as God is convinced that you are in earnest and nothing can turn you away from Him, then through the guru He gives you the final realization—the guru transmits to you the light of God that flows through him.* Perhaps you thought you would never know such a blessing. That supreme experience I received from my Guru. He gave me by his touch what I could not attain by the power and effort of my meditations alone.

Beginning with this new year, make firm spiritual resolutions. I have made a few myself, and pray with all my heart that with the blessing of the Father and Gurudeva I will carry these through.

Life Is a Matrix of Consciousness

We are made of the matrix of consciousness. All life was spumed out of the one Source of the river of consciousness.

---

* See *guru* in glossary.

Your individualized consciousness is thus the very foundation of your existence. All of your thoughts and actions are bubbles and droplets of the river of consciousness.

The seemingly solid body is actually a mass of electromagnetic currents. Its electrons and protons are condensations of the relative positive and negative creative thoughts projected by God, which I call *thoughtrons*. All creation derives from these thoughtrons, the consciousness of God.

What is the difference between black and white? They are two contrasting thoughts, each frozen into its particular concept, that is all. For example, black horses and white horses in a dream are nothing but different crystallizations, relativities of the dreamer's one stream of thought.

In the ultimate sense, then, all things are made of pure consciousness; their finite appearance is the result of the relativity of consciousness. Therefore, if you want to change anything in yourself, you must change the process of thought that occasions the materialization of consciousness into different forms of matter and action. That is the way, the only way, to remould your life.

The Tenacity of Habits

I can give a directive to my mind and it will at once react or behave accordingly. Most people who make up their minds to stop smoking or to stop eating so many sweets will continue with those actions in spite of themselves. They do not change because their minds, like blotting paper, have soaked up habits of thought. Habit means that the mind believes it cannot get rid of a particular thought.

Habit, indeed, is tenacious. Once you perform an action, it leaves an effect or impression on the consciousness. As a result of this influence, you are likely to repeat that action. After several repetitions, that inclination is so strengthened that the action becomes a habit. In some people, just one act is enough to form a habit, because of a latent predisposition from past lives. The mind may tell you that you cannot free yourself from a particular habit; but habits are nothing but repetitions of your own thoughts, and these you have the capacity to change.

The nature of habit can be understood by this analogy: Clay can be molded into a vase; and while the clay is still soft it is easy to change the form of that vase again and again. But once it is fired in an oven, its shape becomes firmly set. So it is with your consciousness. Your thoughts are molding your actions, and your mental convictions from the repetition of those actions is the fire that hardens the thoughts into unyielding habit patterns.

Why are the faces of all of you different? Because your minds are different. Your habit patterns of thoughts have molded not only your mind but also your body. You have probably noticed that some thin people might eat five meals a day and yet never gain weight. And some heavy people may eat very little and yet become heavier. Why? The former, sometime in a past life, established the thought in their consciousness that they were thin, and in this life they brought that thought and tendency with them. No matter what they do, they never grow fat. It is the same with obese persons. In past lives, they left this world with the consciousness of being fat, and they brought the seed of that thought into their present existence. The whole physiology of the body responds to these karmic seed tendencies. If you want to change your constitution, then you have to say, "It is I who thought myself into being thin (or heavy or sickly). Now I will myself to be robust (or whatever you so desire)." If you get rid of the thought that has made you other than you want to be, you will see the body change. I can maintain my weight, or as easily be thin at will. My trouble as a youth was that I was too thin. Master [Swami Sri Yukteswar] cured me of that consciousness, so ever since I have preferred to be heavier.

"Old Age" Is a State of Mind

Most people are psychological antiques; they never change, year after year always the same. Everyone has self-limiting idiosyncrasies. These were not put into your nature by God, but were created by you. These are what you must change—by remembering that these habits, peculiar to your nature, are nothing but manifestations of your own thoughts.

If you feel that your character is not what you think it

should be, remember that it was molded by none other than yourself. Certainly there are outside influences, but inner acceptance is the determining factor. If everyone says that Johnny is a bad boy, and Johnny accepts that condemnation, he may not make the effort to be good; he adopts that negative thought. But if he had refused to accept it, he could have been different.

One must never give up hope of becoming better. A person is old only when he refuses to make the effort to change. That stagnant state is the only "old age" I recognize. When a person says again and again, "I can't change; this is the way I am," then I have to say, "All right, stay that way, since you have made up your mind to be like that."

Try to be more pliable, like children. However, even some children are old before their time because they have lacked the training and have not been given the incentive to change past-life tendencies; their mental clay is already fired in the oven and they grow up with the same inclinations they had in childhood. On the other hand, there are aged people with whom I have talked, just once, and they have changed for the better. God is not a respecter of age, for the soul is ageless. Those who are always ready to improve and expand themselves are like receptive children. Those who grow in understanding become more childlike. The great masters are like that.

To be childlike doesn't mean one is wishy-washy. I am not afraid of anything in the world; no one can intimidate me. I live for God and truth, and I love everyone. If someone misunderstands me, I try to establish understanding. But if I cannot change that person, neither can I be moved by his bad behavior. If a nonunderstanding person has made up his mind against you, why should you change in order to please or placate him? Stand by your principles when you are right, and be willing instantly to change yourself when you are wrong.

Will Power Is the Instrument of Change

If you have molded clay into a vase and fired it, and now you want to make that object into a tray, you cannot do so. But you can pulverize the vase and add that powder to fresh clay, and then form it into a tray. Likewise, when a bad habit is fixed in your mind and you want to change it, you will have to use your strong will to pulverize that habit and absorb it into fresh, pliable good actions that can be remoulded to the desired image. Strong will means strong conviction. The minute you say to yourself, "I am not bound by this habit," and mean it, the habit will be gone.

Look within and determine your main characteristics. Some love to write, or compose music, or dance; others enjoy finance and economics, and so on. Unfortunately, some love to gossip, and others to fight. Don't try to change in yourself what is good. But those things you do against your will, and that make you unhappy after you have done them, are what you want to get rid of. How? Affirm with conviction, before going to bed and on arising in the morning, "I can change. I have the will to change. I *will* change!" Hold to that thought throughout the day, and carry it with you into the subconscious land of sleep and the superconscious realm of meditation.

Suppose your problem is that you frequently get angry, and afterwards feel very sorry for having lost your temper. Every night and morning make up your mind to avoid anger, and then watch yourself carefully. The first day may be difficult, but the second may be a little easier. The third will be easier still. After a few days you will see that victory is possible. In a year, if you keep up your effort, you will be another person. In my childhood, I used to get angry at injustices. One day I saw how foolish it was: I could not change the world in a minute by a display of wrath. I raised my hands and vowed: "I will never be angry again." Since then, I have never been angry within, though I can be outwardly fiery when necessary.

When I came to America, twenty-some years ago, I saw everyone was drinking coffee; so I tasted it for the first time, and gradually came to like it. Lest it become a habit, I made a rule never to drink coffee by myself. Still, there were so many invitations that I found I was drinking coffee all the time. One day, as I ate alone in a restaurant, I realized I missed the coffee. I thought, "So! You got me! All right: good-bye, coffee habit!" That was the end of it; in the past twenty years I have never touched it. Just last night, some friends served coffee to me. It tasted all right, but it will never again be tempting to me.

Freedom Is to Act for Your Highest Welfare

You must be free—unenslaved by habits, or the wish to please society, or anything else. To be able to do, not what you want to do but what you should do for your own highest welfare, that is freedom.

For example, temperamental people, addicted to their emotions, love to intimidate and "scare the daylights" out of others. I say, "Go ahead, if you must, but remember that *you* will have to pay for that bad behavior—no one else." Every wrong action goes against one's own well-being. It fails to give the peace and happiness expected. Sometimes it seems difficult to be good, while it is easy to be bad; and that to give up the bad things is to miss something. But I say you will not miss anything but sorrow.

Do not be like the naughty child who wants to do the very thing he is told not to do. Everything that the great ones have warned against is like poisoned honey. I say don't taste it. You may argue, "But it is sweet." Well, my reasoning is that after you have tasted the sweetness it will destroy you. Evil was made sweet to delude you. You have to use your discrimination to distinguish between poisoned honey and that which is in your best interest. Avoid those things that will ultimately hurt you, and choose those that will give you freedom and happiness.

In this new year, change your consciousness. Cultivate the right conduct and good habits that lead to freedom. When you can say, "I don't indulge in bad habits because they are against my interest; I choose goodness of my own free will," that is freedom; and that is what I want for you.

Both Discrimination and Will Power Are Necessary

Remoulding your consciousness means exercising free will guided by discrimination and energized by will power. Discrimination is your keen eyesight and will is your power of locomotion. Without will, you may know what is right through discrimination and yet not act on it. It is acting on knowledge that gets you to your goal. So both discrimination and will are necessary.

Will power is easy to develop. Try first for small accomplishments. Gradually you will get rid of tendencies you thought you could not overcome. Watch your consciousness. Develop the habit of self-examination, of watching and analyzing your thoughts and behavior. When there are telltale signs of bad habits or inclinations, that is the time to discriminate and resist with will power.

The first time you succumbed to a temptation, you didn't expect that you would be compelled to repeat it. But after giving in a few times, habit took over. Eventually you felt you could not get rid of that habit. But you can, if you use your God-given discrimination and will power. Habits are simply thoughts grooved deeply into the brain. The needle of the mind plays those records of habits again and again. Even the chemistry of the body responds, as with addiction. Applying mind and will can change those patterns. Don't immediately attempt dramatic changes. Experiment in little things first, to train your inherent power of command. I see that a great many of you here today will be rid of your bad habits as a result of following these suggestions.

Think Away Undesirable Thoughts

Start the new year with the resolve to face your bad habits and conquer them. Take the bull by the horns, so to speak, and tame it. Your bad habits are the satanic influence that has kept God out of your life.

Good habits can be compared to good people. When they look through the window of your mind, they see they cannot get into your life because the chairs of your consciousness are occupied by bad habits. Evict the undesirable occupants and let the noble ones in. You don't need the help of anything or anyone else to change yourself; just change your consciousness. Very simply, all you have to do is to think away the thoughts you want to destroy, by replacing them with constructive thoughts. This is the key to heaven; it is in your hands.

Those people who behave in the same way day in and day out are the ones who refuse to change their thoughts. That is all. There is a saying: "A woman convinced against her will is of the same opinion still." Why say this of woman? Man is the same. Everyone must learn to cut out wrong thoughts with the incisive scalpel of wisdom. Thought is a projection of God's omnipotent light and will. If you make up your mind to change, you can use its power to transform yourself.

We Are What We Think We Are

We are what we *think* we are. The habitual inclination of our thoughts determines our talents and abilities, and our personality. Thus, some *think* they are writers or artists, industrious or lazy, and so on. What if you want to be other than what you presently think you are? You may argue that others have been born with the special talent you lack but desire to have. This is true. But they had to cultivate the habit of that ability some time—if not in this life, then in a previous one. So whatever you want to be, start to develop that pattern now. You can instill any trend in your consciousness right now, provided you inject a strong thought in your mind; then your actions and whole being will obey that thought. Do not settle for a one-track mentality. You should be able to succeed in any profession or do anything you put your mind to. Whenever others told me I would not be able to do a thing, I made up my mind that I could do it, and I did!

Few demonstrations of mind power are more dramatic than the power of thought for good or ill on the health of the body. My Guru told me the following story: He had lost much weight as a result of a serious illness. During convalescence, he visited his guru, Lahiri Mahasaya. The Yogavatar* inquired about his health. Sri Yukteswarji explained the cause of his delicate condition.

"So," Lahiri Mahasaya said, "you made yourself sick and now you think you are thin. But I am sure you will feel better tomorrow."

The next day, Gurudeva went exultantly to Lahiri Mahasaya and proclaimed, "Sir, with your blessings, I feel much better today."

---

* A title given to Lahiri Mahasaya, who is revered as an avatar (divine incarnation) whose life ideally expressed the goals of yoga (science of union with God). (See *Lahiri Mahasaya* and *avatar* in glossary.)

Lahiri Mahasaya responded, "Your condition was indeed quite serious, and you are still frail. Who knows how you might feel tomorrow?"

The next day Sri Yukteswarji was again completely debilitated. He lamented to his Guru, "Sir, I am again ailing. I could hardly drag myself here to you."

Lahiri Mahasaya replied, "So, once more you indispose yourself."

After some days of this alternating health and ill health, which followed exactly the expectation of Sri Yukteswarji's thoughts influenced by Lahiri Mahasaya's suggestions, my Guru realized the powerful lesson Lahiri Mahasaya had been trying to teach him.

The Yogavatar said, "What is this? One day you say to me, 'I am well,' and the next day you say, 'I am sick.' It isn't that I have been healing or indisposing you. It is your own thoughts that have made you alternately weak and strong."

Then Master said, "If I think I am well and that I have regained my former weight, will it be so?"

Lahiri Mahasaya answered, "It is so."

Guruji said, "At that very moment I felt both my strength and weight return. When I reached my mother's home that night, she was startled to see my changed condition and thought that I was swelling from dropsy. Many of my friends were so amazed at my sudden recovery that they became disciples of Lahiri Mahasaya."*

Such phenomenal demonstrations are possible to those who possess the power of realization that everything is thought. When you have yet to attain that realization, you have to keep applying will and positive affirmation until you make thought work for you. *Thought is the matrix of all creation; thought created everything.* If you hold on to that truth with indomitable will, you can materialize any thought. There is nothing that can gainsay it. It was by that kind of powerful thought that Christ rebuilt his crucified body; and it is what he referred to when he said, "Therefore I say unto you, What things soever ye desire,

---

* See also the account of this story in *Autobiography of a Yogi*, chapter 12.

when ye pray, believe that ye receive them, and ye shall have them."*

Let Nothing Weaken the Will Behind Positive Thoughts

Once you have said, "I will," never give in. If you say, "I will never catch cold," and the next morning you have a terrible cold and are discouraged, you are allowing your will to remain weak. You must not get discouraged when you see something happening that is contrary to what you have affirmed. Keep on believing, knowing it will be so. If outwardly you say, "I will," but inwardly think, "I can't," then you neutralize the power of thought and emasculate your will. If your will has become weakened by fighting disease or other reverses, you have to take the help of someone else's will to strengthen you through their prayers and positive affirmations on your behalf. But you must also do your part to change your consciousness. That is my advice to you. Develop your will power and positive thinking, and you will find your body, mind, and soul working to mold everything in your life according to your will.

As thought is the most powerful agent in your life, provided you know how to develop and use it, never let the power of your thought be diluted by mixing with weak-minded or negative people—unless you are very strong-minded and can instead strengthen those persons. Failures should align themselves with successful people. The weak should seek the company of those who are stronger. People who have no self-control should associate with those who are self-disciplined—the greedy man, for example, should eat with the man of self-control; with such an example before him, he will begin to reason, "I also can control my appetite."

Change Your Consciousness From Mortality to Divinity

Just as by the power of thought you can change yourself to be whatever you want to be, so most importantly, you will be able to change your consciousness from that of a mortal to a divine being. The mortal man is he who thinks, "This is the

---

* *Mark* 11:24 (Bible).

way I live and this is the way I'll be until I die." But the divine man says, "I dreamed I was a mortal, but now I am awake and know that I am a child of God, made in the image of the Father." Though it takes time to realize this fully, it can be done.

If when time comes for meditation at night you yield to the thought, "It is so late now to meditate; let me sleep and I will meditate tomorrow," you will be sleeping on into the grave. When the world has surrendered to the drug of slumber, you be awake in God. And throughout the day's activities, think that it is God who is working through you. Give the responsibility to Him. He who thinks of God all the time, can he do wrong? Even if he happens to err, God knows it was his wish to do right. Give everything to God, and you will change because then the human ego can no longer dictate to you.

No matter what comes to you, just say, "God knows best. It is He who is giving me this suffering; it is He who is making me happy." With this attitude, all your nightmares of life will change into a beautiful dream of God.

Darkness is the absence of light. Delusion is darkness; Reality is light. Your eyes of wisdom are closed, so you see only the darkness; and you are suffering in that delusion. Change your consciousness; open your eyes and you will see in the stars the sparkle of that Divine Light. In every atom of space you will see the twinkle of God's light of laughter. Behind every thought you shall feel the ocean of His wisdom.

The dance of life and death, prosperity and failure, have no reality except as dreams of God. Realize this, and you shall see that it is materialized thoughts that are dancing around you, and that you are the ocean of thought. Nothing can stay nor hurt you.

Now I ask you to close your eyes and think of one bad habit you want to get rid of. If you concentrate with me as I say the words in Spirit, and you believe, you shall be free of that habit. Throw away the thought that you cannot give up whatever it is. I am sending a strong thought into your consciousness that right now you are rid of that habit. Affirm with me: "I am free of that habit *now*! I am free!" Hold on to that thought of freedom; forget the bad habit. Many of you will find that the habit you have willed away will never come back again.

Repeat after me: "I shall remould my consciousness. In this new year I am a new person. And I shall change my consciousness again and again until I have driven away all the darkness of ignorance and manifested the shining light of Spirit in whose image I am made."

A World of Cosmic Entertainment

Self-Realization Fellowship Temple,
Hollywood, California, December 9, 1945

The word *world* in the context of our subject today means not only the earth but the entire universe of matter, the material world, whose component parts have been placed in space in a harmonious relationship through the wondrous workings of God's divine laws. It is arrogant to think that our little earth is the only place inhabited by intelligent life. There are many such worlds as this—some more highly evolved, and others in earlier stages of evolution. The orderly manner in which the universe is run shows that it is guided by some form of intelligence that permeates all created things.

When we examine the mechanism of a watch, we know that there was an intelligent being who created that instrument so that it would work according to a mathematical plan. The maker coordinated all the little cogwheels and other parts to produce a certain motion that measures time. Keeping time is a necessity in a universe whose very existence depends on the relativities of time and space.

The entire cosmos is one gigantic watch with myriad cogwheels of galaxies, stars, and planets, sitting in space, measuring the passage of time with the motion of past, present, and future. Just as the man-made watch is the product of human intelligence, so the vast universal watch is the handiwork of a higher Intelligence. We cannot doubt it. In spite of some things that are not to our liking here on earth, we cannot deny that there is a mathematical harmony in the universe.

Why God created this earth is always a very thought-provoking question. From a relative standpoint, we can counter, "Why do we carry a watch?" The answer is to measure time, to measure events and our movements throughout the day. Breakfast, work, dinner, caring for the body, entertainment, sleep—all consist of certain motions in time. So we can say that the watch is required for measuring the passage of our time. Such measuring is necessary because this world in which we have been placed is conditioned by time. Our existence and actions are subject to the divisions of past, present, and future. As human beings, we have to act or we become human vegetables; and our behavior must be in an orderly way that is harmonious with the universal motion of time and its man-made constraints. A watch helps us to do this.

Now, is this cosmic watch a necessity to God? Must He too be circumscribed by past, present, and future? The answer is both yes and no. Time, the orderly ticking of the cosmic clock, is an integral part of *maya*, delusion, "the Magical Measurer," the only way that God could create a variety of forms and events from His one consciousness and display their progression in space for our participation and wonderment.* But no, God Himself is not limited by the relativity of past, present, and future and the changes inherent in the passage of time. In Him there is naught but the eternal now. And though delusion comes from Him, it is not *in* Him.

The World Is God's *Lila*

It is a paradox that if God is not compelled by the relativities of this world as is man, then why did He bring forth creation? If God needed this world, it would imply that He is imperfect, not complete or satisfied within Himself. And on the other hand, if God is perfect, then why did He create such an imperfect world?

The *rishis* of ancient India, having penetrated to the Original Cause of Being, declare that God is perfect; that He needs nothing, for all is contained within Himself; and that this world is God's *lila*, or divine play. The Lord, it seems, like a little child, loves to play, and His *lila* is the endless variety of ever-changing creation.

I used to reason in this way: God was infinite omniscient Bliss; but, being alone, there was no one but Him to enjoy that Bliss. So He said, "Let Me create a universe and divide My-

---

* See *maya* in glossary.

self into many souls that they may play with Me in My unfolding drama." By His magical measuring power of *maya* He became dual: Spirit and Nature, man and woman, positive and negative. But even though He has created the universe out of delusion, He Himself is not deluded by it. He knows that everything is but a diversification of His one Cosmic Consciousness. Experiences of the senses and emotions, the dramas of war and peace, sickness and health, life and death—all are happening in God as the Dreamer-Creator of all things, but He is unaffected by them. One part of His Infinite Being ever remains transcendent, beyond vibratory dualities: there God is inactive. When He vibrates His consciousness with thoughts of diversity, He becomes immanent and omnipresent as the Creator in the finite vibratory realm of infinity: there He is active. Vibration brings forth objects and beings interacting in space in the motions of time—just as vibrations of man's consciousness bring forth dreams in sleep.

God created this dream universe for entertaining Himself and us. The only objection I have to God's *lila* is this: "Lord, why did You permit suffering to be a part of the play?" Pain is so ugly and torturing. Existence then is no longer entertainment, but a tragedy. That is where the intercession of the saints comes in. They remind us that God is all-powerful, and if we unite ourselves with Him, we will no longer be hurt in this playhouse of His. It is we who inflict pain on ourselves if we transgress the divine laws on which He rests the whole universe. Our salvation is to unite with Him. Unless we attune ourselves to God and know thereby that this world is but a cosmic entertainment, we are bound to suffer. It seems that suffering is a necessary discipline to remind us to seek union with God. Then, like Him, we will be entertained by this fantastic play.

It is wondrous to think deeply of these things. I delve in these realms all the time. Even as I speak to you I am seeing these truths. It would indeed be terrible if an Almighty Being had thrown us into this delusive earthly existence without an escape or the ability to realize what He realizes. But this is not the case. There is an outlet. Every night in deep sleep you unconsciously forget this world; it is no more for you. And every time you meditate deeply, you are consciously transcendent; the world doesn't exist for you. Thus do the saints say that to unite ourselves with God is the only way we can understand that this world is not something to which we should give much importance.

Look Upon Life As a Movie

In this world there is a constant repetition of history, of warfare and trouble. If we are objective, we begin to behold events as a sort of continuous cosmic motion picture wherein the same basic story is played over and over again, only in different times and places with different characters. You wouldn't sit through the same movie repeatedly; it would soon lose its interest. So we can grant to the Heavenly Father that He has provided for changes in history and contrasts in good and evil to give variety to the entertainment in this cosmic movie house.

We can say that God should never have created this world in which there is so much trouble. But on the other hand, the saints say that if you knew you were gods,* you wouldn't mind it. If you watch a movie, you like a lot of action rather than something dull, don't you? That is the way you should enjoy this world. Look upon life as a movie, and then you will know why God created it. Our problem is that we forget to see it as God's entertainment.

Through scripture, God has said that we are made in His image. As such, we could behold this world drama as a movie, even as He does, if we but look to that soul perfection within and realize our unity with the Divine. Then this cosmic movie, with its horrors of disease and poverty and atomic bombs, will appear to us only as real as the anomalies we experience in a movie house. When we have finished seeing the motion picture, we know that nobody was killed; nobody was suffering. In fact, that truth is the only answer I see when I look at the drama of life. It is nothing but an electrical shadow-show, a play of light and shadows. Everything is the vibration of God's consciousness condensed into electromagnetic images. The essence of those images cannot be severed by a sword, nor

---

* "Is it not written in your law, I said, Ye are gods?" (*John* 10:34, Bible).

burned, nor drowned, nor suffer pain of any sort. It is not born nor does it die. It only passes through a few changes. If we could watch this world as God watches it, and as the saints do, we would be free from the seeming reality of this dreaming. In that consciousness I can understand that this world was created for entertainment; and that it is not necessary either to God or to us.

Awaken From the Cosmic Dream

You can understand life as God's cosmic dream movie if you analyze the dream movies you create every night in sleep. Sometimes you have nightmares and sometimes you have lovely dreams. How real they seem, not only to you but also to those beings in your dream. But when you wake up you know that they were not real, and you can laugh at that unreality. Of course, everyone prefers beautiful dreams to nightmares. I remind God of this: "If we must participate in Your dreams, Lord, we like beautiful dreams of health and smiles instead of nightmares of disease or mental suffering." But the trouble is, as long as you will love beautiful dreams and fear nightmares, giving reality to any dream happenings, when nightmares come you will suffer. Therefore, the masters say, "Awake from both the beautiful dreams and the nightmares."

If you are attached to human happiness, you are in for a lot of trouble, because nightmares are inevitable along with the beautiful dreams. But if you will think of a dream as a dream, whether it is enjoyable or dreadful, you will have peace. When you realize that life is a dream, then you are free.

That is the philosophy the great masters of India teach— that this world, this creation, is the dream of God. Just as when you are half awake and can see a dream and know you are dreaming, yet apart from it, that is how God feels this universe. On one side He is awake in ever new Bliss, and on another side He is dreaming this universe. That is how you should look upon this world. Then you will know why He created it, and you will not ascribe these dream conditions to your soul. If you pass through a nightmare, you know that it is no more than a bad dream. If you can live in the world in that consciousness, you will not suffer. That is what *Kriya Yoga* will give to you.

That is what *Self-Realization Fellowship [Yogoda Satsanga] Lessons* will do for you if you practice them faithfully. It is on these teachings that you should concentrate, not on my personality or any other personality. And it is not a matter of merely reading these truths, but of practicing them. Reading does not make you wise; realization does.

That is why I don't read much. I keep my mind always here at the Christ Consciousness [*Kutastha Chaitanya*] center.* In the omnipresent light of Cosmic Intelligence how different the world appears! Sometimes I see everything as electrical images; there is no weight or mass to the body. Reading the wonders of science will not make you a sage, for there is so much more to be known. Read from the book of life that is hidden within, in the omniscience of the soul, just behind the darkness of closed eyes. Discover that boundless realm of Reality. Look upon this earth as a dream, and then you will understand that it is all right for you to lie down on the bed of this earth and dream the dream of life. You won't mind then, because you will know you are dreaming.

Western religious teachers preach prosperity, happiness, health, and the promise of a glorious afterlife; but not how to experience Divine Bliss and be untouched by suffering in the here and now. That is where the teachings of the great *rishis* of India go much deeper. Occidentals have accused the masters of propounding a negative philosophy of life—that is, never mind whether you suffer, never mind whether you are happy or not; deny the world. On the contrary, the masters of India ask, "What are you going to do when you are confronted with pain and sorrow? Are you going to cry helplessly, or are you going to practice those techniques that give evenmindedness and transcendence while you are treating the malady?" They urge commonsense remedial action and simultaneous control of the emotions so that if health does go away and pain comes you do not give in to despair. In other words, they stress the importance of enthroning oneself within in the unalloyed happiness of the soul, which cannot be tarnished by the whimsical winds

---

* Located at the point between the eyebrows. (See *Christ [Kutastha] center* in glossary.)

of beautiful dreams of life nor by the corrosive storms of nightmares. Those who habitually cling to material consciousness do not want to make the effort required to reach that state of invulnerability. When suffering comes, they do not learn from it and so repeat the same mistakes.

One man who came to see me boasted how much money he had. I cautioned him, "Don't tell everyone what you have; someone will get hold of you and your money." Soon thereafter, a lady did get hold of him, and after a short while she wanted a divorce and half of his money. By God's grace I helped him get out of the mess. While the divorce was going through, I wrote to him urging him not to get involved again. I knew his temperament. But he came back with another wife. I was astounded by his foolishness. His new wife was a good woman, and had a little money of her own. But now he wanted to get away from her, and she wouldn't let him go. Being a restless man, he had decided he didn't want married life; he wanted his freedom. But I had to advise him, "You lost your freedom willingly, now you must make the best of it." Isn't human nature strange?

In India if the wife dies, you can be pretty sure the husband will not marry again. Usually he lives in her memory. That kind of romance is considered the ideal in India—and yet once in a while we see something there to the contrary. A man came to me crying his head off for his deceased wife. His feeling had given way completely to uncontrolled emotion. He said he wanted to kill himself. I sympathized with his sense of loss, but tried to get him to think rationally. "You can't get her back by carrying on this way," I told him. He sobbed, "I will never marry again." But I saw otherwise, and said, "You will marry in a month from now." He insisted, "Never!" Well, in one month he remarried; but he didn't come to see me because he was embarrassed to remember his strong disavowal of my words.

Sometimes when I am traveling by car I see how many people lived before in the houses that I pass, and how many people will come to reside in them in the future. Once the Lord said to me, "See the human chicken coops and how the occupants come and go. That is the way with human life." Do not pay undue attention to the passing scenes of life. You are the immortal Self, living only temporarily in a dream that is sometimes a nightmare. That is the higher philosophy of the masters of India.

Emotional Sensitivity Is the Cause of Suffering

Do not be so sensitive. Emotional sensitivity is the silent cause of all suffering. To give strength to creation as a reality by emotional involvement in it is foolishness. To not meditate, to not sit still and realize your true soul nature, but to drift along as a part of the eternal motion of creation, is a constant danger to your happiness. Perhaps some day your body will be terribly sick, and though you want to walk or do other things that you used to do in your younger or healthier days, you find you cannot do them; it is a terrible disillusionment for the soul. Before that day comes, make yourself so free that you can look on your body with detachment, caring for it as though it were somebody else's.

One of my students had a very painful condition in her knee in which the bones were decaying. I don't know how many times that leg was operated upon and put back together again. But she talked of it as though it were nothing: "It is a minor operation," she would say casually. Now that is the way to take life. Cultivate that state of mind by which you can live with greater mental strength.

Even when you do not have the opportunity to meditate long or deeply, always think that you are working for God. When your mind can remain anchored in Him, you will not suffer anymore; no amount of disease or illness will be able to touch you inwardly. Sometimes when this body gives trouble, I look within and everything vanishes in the light of God. Just as you see the moving pictures on the screen and enjoy the contrasting conflict between good and evil actions and between the joyful and sorrowful scenarios, so you shall be entertained by this world. You shall say, "Lord, whatever You do is all right." But until you consciously realize that this is all a dream, you will not see why God created this world.

Be Like the Active-Inactive Lord

I think that in bringing forth the universe God wanted to keep busy. Let this be an incentive to spiritual aspirants. Many think that to find God and get away from this dream they have to forsake their responsibilities and seek seclusion in the Himalayas or other such totally solitary places; but that is not so simple. The mind will still be absorbed in its moods and restlessness, and the body will have to be very active just to keep warm and satisfy its hunger and other needs. It is easier to find God in the jungle of civilization if you follow a balance between meditation and constructive, dutiful work. Be like the active-inactive Lord. In creation He is joyously busy; beyond creation He is joyously quiescent in divine bliss. Because I made the effort to find God in meditation, I am enjoying His bliss even in the midst of activity. And thus activity doesn't adversely affect me at all. Even though I may say I don't like this or that in the dualities around me, still within I am calm and like steel: "Calmly active and actively calm; a prince of peace sitting on the throne of poise directing the kingdom of activity."

To all appearances, it seems that out of perfection God created imperfect beings. But in truth, imperfect beings are perfect—souls made in God's image. All God wants you to do is separate your dream imperfections from your perfect Self. When you think about your mortal life and all your troubles and identify with them, you do an injustice to the image of God within you. Affirm and realize, "I am not a mortal being; I am Spirit."

God is ever trying to draw His children back to their inherent perfection. That is why you will see even in evil people there is a search for God, though it may not be pronounced as such. Can you find an evil person who wants to derive misery from his actions? No. He thinks his pursuits are going to give him a good time. The man who drinks or takes dope thinks he will get pleasure from it. Everywhere you will see people, good and evil, searching in their own way for happiness. No one wants to hurt himself. Then why do people behave in an evil way that is bound to cause pain and sorrow? Such actions arise from the greatest of all sins—ignorance. "Wrongdoer" is the right word rather than "sinner." You may condemn wrongdoing but should not condemn the doer. Sins are errors committed under the influence of ignorance, or delusion. But for a different degree of understanding, you might be in the same boat. Jesus said, "He that is without sin among you, let him cast a stone."*

The point is, in everything we do we are seeking happiness. No one can truthfully say he is a materialist, because anyone who is seeking happiness is seeking God. Therefore, in evil as well as in good God is coaxing us back to Him by our search for happiness. The sorrow inflicted by evil will eventually turn the wayward to the joys of virtue. Since life is inherently a medley of good and evil, of beautiful dreams and nightmares, we should seek out and help to create the beautiful dreams and not get caught up in the frightful nightmares.

In the Diversity of Creation There Is an Inherent Unity

From His one consciousness, God created the many. And now He is trying to bring the many back into Oneness again. When the storm is upon the ocean, it creates innumerable waves. When the storm dies down, the waves sink back into the ocean. In the diversity of creation there is an inherent unity— as the ocean is the essence of the waves. Family consciousness bonds groups of souls together. Countries have a leader to unite and direct them. Social groups cohere in a common cause. When you find God, you will see all forces united in Him. "Then life is sweet and death a dream; health is sweet and sickness a dream; praise is sweet and blame a dream—when Thy song flows through me."† You will have a whole different picture of life.

In reacting to life, most people either say, "Praise the Lord," or urge us to be afraid of Him; and some blame or curse Him. I think this is very foolish. What can you say to God that will be praise? He is not moved by praise or flattery, because He has everything. Most prayers are offered by people who are in trouble; some cry out, "Praise the Lord," hoping for some favor thereby. You may curse or praise the Lord; it will not make any difference to Him. But it will make a difference in you. Praise Him—or better still, *love* Him—and you will feel better. Curse Him and it reacts to hurt you. When you go against

---

* *John* 8:7 (Bible).

† From "When Thy Song Flows Through Me" in *Words of Cosmic Chants* by Paramahansa Yogananda (published by Yogoda Satsanga Society of India).

God, you are going against your own true nature, the divine image in which God created you. When you go against that nature, you automatically punish yourself.

From my childhood I was rebellious at life, because I saw so much injustice. But now the only rebellion I feel within me is that people do not know God. The greatest sin is ignorance— not to know what life is all about. And the greatest virtue is wisdom—to know the meaning and purpose of life and its Creator. To know that we are not little human beings, but that we are one with Him, is wisdom.

Every night in sleep God takes away all of your troubles to show you that you are not a mortal being; you are Spirit. God wants you to remember that truth during the conscious state, so that you are not bothered any more by the anomalies of life. If we can very well exist at night in deep sleep without thinking about this world and its troubles, we can very well exist in God's world of activity without being caught up in this dream. Even though dream universes are floating in God's consciousness, He is ever awake and knows He is dreaming. He tells us, "Do not get panicky during this daydream; look to Me as the Reality behind the dream." When there is health and joy, smile in the dream. When there is a nightmare of sickness or sorrow, say, "I am awake in God, merely watching the play of my life." Then you will know that God has created this universe as an entertainment for Himself. And you, being made in His image, have not only the perfect right but also the ability to enjoy this play with its varying dreams even as He does.

Desire is what holds you in mortal bondage. If you want a big home on a hill with a view, a nice income, a good marriage and family, you may wear yourself out striving to get these things; then perhaps your spouse leaves you for somebody else, or you get sick, or your business fails—that is the nature of human happiness. Therefore, I say to God, "Lord, You can keep all of Your earthly baubles. Let only Thy will be done through me. I am willing to follow whatever be Your will. However, Lord, I am not going to thank You for creating me; for I would have been saved lots of trouble if You had not done so. But since You did bring me into being, I know I can be nothing else but Your child." That is the demand you should make of God. No more begging from Him; for you are not a beggar. You are His divine child and inherently have everything He has. Behind the darkness of closed eyes, you have the whole universe rolling in your consciousness. Why present yourself as a beggar before God?

Dismiss this phantasma of disease and health, sorrow and joy. Rise above it. Become the Self. Watch the show of the universe, but do not become absorbed in it. Many times I have seen my body gone from this world. I laugh at death. I am ready anytime. There is nothing to it. Eternal life is mine. I am the ocean of consciousness. Sometimes I become the little wave of the body, but I am never just the wave without the Ocean of God.

Death and darkness cannot cast fear upon us, for we are the very Consciousness out of which this universe has been created by God. In the Bhagavad Gita the Lord says:

> Whoever realizes Me to be the Unborn and Beginningless as well as the Sovereign Lord of Creation—that man has conquered delusion and attained the sinless state even while wearing a mortal body.
>
> I am the Source of everything; from Me all creation emerges. With this realization the wise, awestricken, adore Me. Their thoughts fully on Me, their beings surrendered to Me, enlightening one another, proclaiming Me always, My devotees are contented and joyful.
>
> From sheer compassion I, the Divine Indweller, set alight in them the radiant lamp of wisdom which banishes the darkness that is born of ignorance.
>
> —Bhagavad Gita X:3, 8–9, 11.

Why God Created the World

Self-Realization Fellowship Temple,
San Diego, California, December 16, 1945

No matter how many times you hear me speak on the subject of why God created the world, you will always find something new; through infinite concentration one receives ever
new light on this enigma.

Somehow, God has all the power of the universe at His
command; but why does He have this power? Why is God
God? Why aren't you God? You will rack your brain when you
try to think in this way. That there is a God, an absolute
Intelligence and Power, we cannot rationally deny. The testimony of Jesus, Krishna, Buddha, and the saints cannot be
questioned. From the ideals they exemplified and the miracles
they performed, we know they were speaking truth. They
gave irrefutable testimony that God is; and that He is perfect
and almighty. They have told us that God is Joy, and God is
Love. But if this be so, why did He create such an imperfect
world, and an imperfect body for man? We think that if we
had the power God has, we could create a much better body
than this, and a much better world—at least in our imagination
we think we could!

Jesus said, "He that believeth on me, the works that I do
shall he do also; and greater works than these shall he do."*
How did he know, twenty centuries ago, the "miracles" of
modern science that are commonplace today—we see how by
radar man can determine the presence and location of things
thousands of miles away. A soldier told me that the first time
he believed in God was when he saw radar at work. It is the
wonders of radio, radar, television, and all the other scientific
discoveries that are coming, to which Christ referred when he

---

* *John* 14:12 (Bible).

predicted that we would do even greater things than he had demonstrated. Of course, if each person had radarlike eyes and ears, nobody would have any peace! The thoughts and actions of others thousands of miles away would be impinging on our minds, and there would be no freedom or privacy for anyone. Since there is doubtless some dirt in every home, we have no right to intrude on one another and gossip about our findings. So there is a reason why God threw the cloak of *maya*, the limiting power of delusion, upon man.

Man's Power Is Nothing Compared to God's

It seems that as soon as man gains power, he misuses it. Already they are speaking of push-button war, in which one has only to press a button and atomic bombs will destroy nations. Just imagine, New York City, with all its millions of people, can be finished with one bomb! God has given great power to man that he might use it rightly. Even so, man's power is nothing, compared to God's, because this whole world is an atomic bomb that God holds in His hands. If any individual, or the leader of any nation, thinks he can get away with using bombs, he is very much mistaken, for the words of Christ are still true: "...all they that take the sword shall perish with the sword."* If aggressive countries fight one another, they shall be wiped away, and the meek nations shall inherit the earth.† We must use spiritual force, not atomic bombs, or we are going to perish.

It is evident that in the storehouse of nature are hidden many secrets. Though the atomic bomb is a terrible thing, still it shows that there are inconceivable powers locked in the heart of nature—powers that man has yet to discover. And behind all these is a God. There is an Infinite Intelligence that governs all creation. That Intelligence works through divine law that cooperates with good and punishes evil. Why else is it that Hitler, who first had the secret of building the atomic bomb, lost it, and it came instead into the hands of America? Even

---

* *Matthew* 26:52 (Bible).

† *Matthew* 5:5 (Bible) "Blessed are the meek: for they shall inherit the earth."

though America used it, I don't think she will do so again—I
pray she will not.

Politicians in their blindness start the whole world fighting. But since man didn't create this world, he has no right to
destroy it. Why, then, did God in His almightiness create such
an imperfect world, and give man the power to destroy? If you
were God, you would know exactly what is going on, and why
this universe was created as it is.

When you are reading a very interesting novel, you see good
and evil contradicting each other, and you think it is terrible
when evil is winning. For instance, in one chapter the hero is
about to be killed; but in the next, everything is straightened
out and he is saved. You must understand that each life is a master novel written by God. It is not up to you to try to fathom it;
you will be defeated by the limitations of your *maya*-deluded
intelligence. First conquer delusion and become one with God;
then you will realize why He created this world.

But we do have a right to ask Him why. And there are many,
many reasons. First of all, it could not be that this earth is a necessity to Him, because in that case God would be imperfect; He
would have something to attain from it. But we have the testimony of the saints that He is perfect; and I give testimony from
my own experience, for I have communed with Him. Even
though I had had visions and other spiritual experiences before
I met my guru, Swami Sri Yukteswarji, I told him I wouldn't talk
about God to others unless I knew Him. When I saw those
visions I had experienced coming true, I knew that a Being was
guiding me, and I began to see Him in all things.

This World Is God's Hobby

Since God is perfect and this earth is not a necessity for
His evolution, it is therefore a sort of hobby to God. For example, there are two kinds of artists: one type is the commercial
artist who makes art pay; and the other type is one who creates
gossamer wings of art with no market value, simply for the personal enjoyment of it. Now we cannot think of God as commercial, for He has nothing to gain from His art of creation. Similarly, wealthy people sometimes take up special hobbies that
are expensive, because they can afford them. I met such a man

in Cincinnati; he had a big farm as his hobby. When I visited there as his guest, I said, "Your farm is not paying for itself, is it?" He replied, "That's right. This egg I am eating cost me ninety cents. I could get one in the market for a few pennies."

So this world is God's hobby. But it is not any fun for those who are suffering in it. I often say to the Lord, "If You wanted a hobby, why did You create pain and cancer and terrible emotions as part of it?" Of course, I am not in the world to dictate to the Lord. I know that. But I humbly fight with Him.

He laughs at me, and says, "In the last chapter, all will know the answer to these questions."

Well, I know the answer, but I argue on behalf of those who don't: "It may be a play to You, Lord, but it is misery and death to those who don't know it is just a play. Two people marry and think they have found perfect love, and then one of them dies—what a tragedy! Or someone who has made lots of money thinks he is happy and then sees the stock market crash, and in despair jumps out the window—how terrible! And in the sense traps of sex, wine, and money there is temptation not only from outside, but from within. How is man going to justify all this? And why are there gangsters, and persons who are insane, and all kinds of dreadful goings-on, Lord? Why are there germs that kill so many people every year? If the bones of those who die of disease were heaped together, the pile would be as high as the Himalayas; and yet it is a hobby to You, God. What about those who are victims of Your hobby?"

And the Lord says, "I have made all men in My image. If you know you are a part of Me, you can live in this world and enjoy it as I do."

That is the ultimate answer. We do not see this world as God sees it.

Seeing With the Open Eyes of Wisdom and Calmness

I will give you an example of how things went wrong in creation. If right now in this room I suddenly close my eyes and start dancing wildly, forgetting everything around me and the limitations of my blindness, you will call out to me, "Be careful! You will fall or bump something!" But I insist, "No, I am all right." Then I do stumble and fall and break my leg; and

I cry and ask, "Why did this happen to me?" You will answer, "Well, why did you close your eyes and try to dance in the darkness?" Then I reply, "Oh, my goodness. Why did I dance with my eyes closed?"

Because your eyes are closed, you cannot help thinking this world is terrible. But if you keep open your eyes of wisdom and calmness, you will see there is a lot of enjoyment in this world—just as though you are watching a motion picture.

When you go to a movie, you like to see a happy picture, or one that makes you feel good, because life itself is so troublesome. But according to the cosmic motion-picture theory of this earth drama, the historic revolutions and wars and man's troubles are justified, because if you go to a picture show every day and see only love scenes, you would get tired of them. You would want to see some action, some contrast and excitement. Therefore, God is justified in creating the dualities of this earth. He didn't want this drama to be stale. If there were only angels, it would be a very tiresome play; where there is a villain and a hero, it is more entertaining.

The contrasts were made to help us realize that this drama is only a cosmic movie, and that by translating our consciousness into God's consciousness, we could look upon this earth as He does. But I wouldn't want to be the villain, for crime doesn't pay—especially before the inexorable cosmic law. I would rather be somewhere sitting under a tree, absorbed in meditation on God, or be busy serving others to make them comfortable with true peace and happiness. For although life is governed by a cosmic plan, we have freedom to change our part in the drama.

The point is, if you learn to see this world as a picture show, you will find nothing wrong with it. The only thing I complain about is that pain makes this picture seem so real. You wouldn't mind your hand being taken off if you didn't feel any pain and if you could put it back in place again. Some saints have shown that this is possible. For example, Jesus carried out his prophecy when he said, "Destroy this temple [the body], and in three days I will raise it up."* And when Peter cut off the ear of the centurion, Christ restored it. By

---

* *John* 2:19 (Bible).

knowing the Lord, Jesus had the power to remake the body.

Science concentrates on making more material comforts for man; but when disease comes, and the doctor says, "It is all over," you can't do anything about it. And then how do you feel? Helpless. But the masters say you don't have to feel that way. This world will seem an unjust creation if you keep your eyes of wisdom closed. You must realize that you are God's child, and if you are in tune with Him you will see this earth as a picture—as God's hobby. Then you can live in this world without being affected by it all. It is those who take it too seriously who suffer. And because of that suffering, they don't understand why God created this earth. When a mother hears of the loss of somebody else's baby she feels sympathetic. But when it is her own baby, she suffers great anguish. When you transform your consciousness into divine consciousness so that you feel for everyone else's well-being as you feel for yourself, when all the world becomes your greater self, you will become completely dissociated from the sufferings of your little body. You will behold creation as a sort of dramatic experience in which nothing can hurt you.

Free Choice—God's Greatest Gift

We can say that God made this earth not only as a hobby, but also because He wanted to make perfect souls that would evolve back to Him. He sent them out under the cloak of delusion, or *maya*, but endowed with freedom. That is the greatest gift of God. He has not denied mankind the free choice that He Himself has. He has given man freedom to be good or evil, to do exactly as he pleases—even to deny God. Both good and evil exist, but nobody compels you to be evil unless you choose to practice evil; and nobody can compel you to be good unless you want to be good. God created us with the ability to exercise His gifts of intelligence and free choice, by which we can choose to go back to Him. God certainly means to take us back when we are ready to go. We are like the biblical prodigal son, and God is continuously calling to us to come Home.

The ideal of every human life should be to be good, to be happy, and to find God. You will never be happy unless you do find God. That is why Jesus said, "Seek ye first the kingdom of

God."* That is the purpose of our existence: that we strive to become good, to become perfect, and to use our free will to choose good instead of evil. God has given to us all the power we need to do so. The mind is like an elastic band. The more you pull, the more it stretches. The mind-elastic will never break. Every time you feel limitations, close your eyes and say to yourself, "I am the Infinite," and you will see what power you have.

No joy of the senses, no joy of possession, can match the joy of God. Though He had everything from eternity to eternity, He began to think, "I am all-powerful, and Joy itself, but there is no one else to enjoy Me." And He thought, as He began to create: "I will make souls in My image, and clothe them as human beings with free choice, to see whether they will seek My material gifts and the temptations of money, wine, and sex; or whether they will seek the million million times more intoxicating joy of My consciousness." The point that gives me the most satisfaction is that God is very just and fair. He gave man freedom to accept His love and live in His joy, or to cast it aside and live in delusion, in ignorance of Him.

Though all created things belong to God, there is one thing God hasn't—our love. When He created us, He did have something to attain, and that is our love. We can withhold that love, or give it to Him. And He will wait endlessly until we are ready to offer our love to Him. When we do, when the prodigal son comes Home, the fatted calf of wisdom is killed and there is much rejoicing. When a soul returns to God, there actually is rejoicing among all the saints in heaven. This is the meaning of the parable of the prodigal son as told by Jesus.

Watch Yourself From the Balcony of Introspection

There is so much more to life than what you think. Since everything earthly seems so real, how much more so must be the Reality that creates this unreal reality! But the unreal reality makes you forget the Real. God wants you to remember that you wouldn't mind this earth if it were like a motion picture. Even if the brittle bones of the body break, you would say,

---

* *Matthew* 6:33 (Bible).

"Well, look at those broken bones," and not feel any disturbance or suffering. You can say that when you are anchored in the Divine Consciousness. You will make fun of your habits, and you will be intensely amused at your distinguishing characteristics, as from the balcony of introspection you watch yourself perform in the motion picture of life. I do that all the time. When you know this world to be God's *lila*—His play—then you aren't upset by the contrasts in this drama of good and evil.

In a dream you can behold rich people, poor people, someone strong, someone else groaning with disease, someone dying, and someone being born. But when you wake up, you realize that it was only a dream. This universe is God's dream. And when I ask Him, "Why do You not dream only beautiful dreams? Why must Your play be fraught with nightmares?" He replies, "You must be able to enjoy both the nightmares and the beautiful experiences for what they are—dreams, only dreams. But if you dream only beautiful dreams, you will be drowned in that beauty, and never wish to wake up." That is the answer. So you must not be frightened when nightmares come, but say, "Lord, it is a passing dream. It has no reality." And when you are smiling with health and happiness, say, "Lord, it is a beautiful dream, but do what You like with my dreams of life." When you are neither touched by the nightmares of disease and suffering and worries, nor bound by the beautiful dreams, then God says, "Wake up, now! Come back Home."

So watch this universe like a picture-play, as do the masters who are awake in God. They are very much interested in those souls who try to escape this dream. God wants everyone to get out of this nightmare, and watch this cosmic motion picture as an entertainment. He wants you to know that you are one with Him. That is why from time to time He sends God-realized souls to earth to help mankind. When people get too groggy with nightmares, these souls come to wake us up, to shake us and say, "What is the matter with you? You are dreaming." And you cry, "No, no, my leg is broken," or, "I am suffering with disease," or, "I am drowned in poverty." But when, through the blessings of the great ones, you open your eyes, you see it is a dream.

Separate the Unreal From the Real

As a little boy, I used to dream that a tiger was after me; I would cry out that the tiger had caught my leg. Mother would come and shake me from my dream and say, "See, there is nothing wrong. There is no tiger. Your leg is all right." As a result of that childhood dream I had the first wonderful experience that God gave to me: The last time I had that dream, I said, "That is an old trick. There is no tiger after my leg." And I quickly jumped out of the dream. It went away and never returned. From that time on I was watchful, even in dreams, to separate the unreal from the Real.

Saints are those who are half awake and half dreaming: on one side awake in God, and on the other side dreaming the dream of incarnation. But they can quickly get out of this dream. When my body feels some hurt or pain, I focus my eyes and my mind here at the *Kutastha,* or Christ-consciousness center, between the eyebrows, and then I feel no pain; and in a little while I don't even see or feel the body.

So remember, God is dreaming this world. And if we are in tune with Him, we will live a divinely intoxicated life and nothing will disturb us. We will watch this cosmic picture as we watch the films in a movie house, without being hurt. God created us that we may dream as He does, enjoying this dream, and all its contrasting experiences, as an entertainment, without being affected by it, absorbed in His eternal joy.

How God Is Pulling Us
Back to Him

A compilation from two talks on the same subject delivered,
respectively, at the Self-Realization Fellowship Temples in
Hollywood and San Diego, California, August 4 and 11, 1946

All paths are paths to God, because, ultimately, there is no other place for the soul to go. Everything has come out of God and must go back to Him. Even in evil, man is seeking happiness. Worldly happiness inevitably leads to disillusionment; but those who go on seeking, throwing away one after the other the shining glass-bits of pleasures of the world, will at long last find the diamond of true happiness in God. Satisfaction will never come from anything less than God. Since the various paths of life take you to God eventually in the set course of evolution, if you have self-control and lead a normal, rational life and try to seek true happiness it is all right to keep on in this average way. But it may take you many, many incarnations. It is better to make a conscientious effort to hasten your attainment of God. The saints and ascetics would not go to all of the hard work that they do unless they found inspiration within it—the inspiration of joy. "Unattracted to the sensory world, the yogi experiences the ever new joy inherent in the Self. Engaged in divine union of the soul with Spirit, he attains bliss indestructible."*

Most people are not awakened to the fact that God Himself is what they truly want—first and last. "Bread the men of the world seek after; but seek ye first the kingdom of God." "Bread" means the pleasures and desires for things of the earth for which people pray; but you who are wise, seek God first, and all things else will come to you.

You will be surprised how, by constant prayer, your life will

---

* Bhagavad Gita V:21.

51

change—not the prayer of a beggar, but the loving demand of a
child to his Heavenly Father. God, being your Father, is not
bound by the consciousness of gratuity and pity that motivates
an almsgiver. You have a divine right inherited from God to
demand from Him; and He will respond to you because you are
His own. If you constantly call to Him, He cannot escape the
net of your devotion. If you pray until the ether churns with the
light of your prayer, then you will find God. But if while you are
praying for God to come, you are thinking of something else—
that is, wanting God because you want something from Him—
you won't find Him. Your purpose of seeking God must be
straight, and your efforts intensified by the sense of necessity
for God that you awaken in yourself.

Religious Superstition Has Taught People to Be Afraid of God

You trust yourself more than you trust God, and yet you
know that in the ultimate sense you cannot breathe or walk or
move without the direct impelling force of His presence in the
brain, in the heart, in the cells of the body. Just because you have
become accustomed to dependence on food, air, and sunshine,
you think these externals support your life. It is a delusion to
think so. You are directly dependent on One Power, which is God.

Because He is the All-Supreme, religious superstition has
taught people to be afraid of God. That is not the relationship
you want with your Heavenly Father. I don't give you the
hellfire-and-brimstone gospel. I want to teach you that God is
your own: dearer than the dearest, nearer than the nearest,
more loving than all things that we love. If you would but treat
Him that way! If you would but lift one hand, He would drop
two hands to lift you up. If you are unceasing in grasping for
the hand of Spirit, He will come without fail.

God has put me through the greatest trials; but as often as
I felt He was gone, He came with violent shakings to free me
from my poutings against Him. We pout often, but we should
never doubt. And when we pout, it should be so strongly that
the Mother has to come to look after us.* Of course, I don't pout

---

* See *Divine Mother* in glossary.

for my needs anymore, but for those of the organization. God won't tell me until the last minute that He is coming to my aid; but He does come, without fail. I find that He is with me always. Never has He failed me. If you have that trust and if you love Him more, you shall feel that He has loved you always and that it was you who didn't seek Him. That is why you thought He was away. He is never indifferent to us; we are indifferent to Him.

God is compassionately aware that He has sent us here into this troublesome world; and if He cares for the sparrows that are sold for a farthing,* how much more does He care for us. Only He wants to be sure of our love, so He plays hide-and-seek with us. God has an inferiority complex; He is not sure whether the devotee truly wants Him or something else. I tell Him often, "Lord, if they only knew how wonderful You are, they would seek You. But You keep yourself hidden in the flowers, in the clouds, in the ether." Yet when you look at the beauty and wonders of nature, how can you doubt God? He works in everything, and His tools are life and intelligence. Just as ships at sea can be controlled by radio, so are we controlled by the "radioed" power and intelligence of God. Without His beam of life, we are dead. Why not seek that Power which is the source of our being? Why not seek the Giver instead of the gifts? That is where the real freedom lies. He is working right within your brain cells and your thoughts. If you would but contact Him within, you would find a Friend who is unfailing, a Lover who never lies. It is God alone who is pursuing you with His love, and who is seeking you right within you. If you would seek Him willingly, if you would pursue Him within, you would find Him. It is only the misuse of your free will and the resistance of your karma, the effects of past wrong actions, that prevent the quickening of your footsteps toward the Divine Goal.

The Law of Attraction Inherent in Creation

Setting aside the old superstitious beliefs, we should find out why we should seek God. When we look at the processes

---

* *Matthew* 11:29 (Bible).

of nature, we will see why. So I shall discuss today's subject from an entirely different standpoint—from the standpoint of science and of metaphysics. You will see what a wonderful analogy there is between the descension of the universe from God and the ascension of the universe back to God.

Inherent in creation is the law of attraction. Celestial bodies exert their gravitational attraction on one another; human beings are subject to the pull of good or evil. Many persons take to drink or to various other evil diversions; the saints are intoxicated with God. The man who turns from the church to the bar in the village inn is drinking unhappiness, destruction of health, and loss of keenness of mind; but he who goes into the church within himself and quaffs the inspiration of bliss that flows from the vintage keg of silence is ever happy. So goes the search for the Infinite. When you understand the law of gravitation, you can understand the best way to tune in with the pull of God, and therefore the best way to find Him.

Gravity's effect is seen when two bodies are free to move and they are drawn toward each other. Gravitation, according to physical science, is that attraction which exists between masses of matter—by virtue of which every such mass tends toward every other mass with a force varying directly as the product of the masses, and inversely as the square of their distances apart. That is, if the distance between two masses is one foot, the attraction will be relatively strong; and if the distance is increased to two feet, the attraction will be only one-fourth as powerful.

The law of gravity is universal, the same in the earth as in the sun—and in all objects in space. The sun gravitates the earth and the other solar planets and keeps them whirling around it. The earth gravitates the moon. The attraction of the earth for the bodies on its surface is the same as the earth's attraction toward the moon. The only difference is that the gravitational effect of the earth on the moon is reduced by the square of the distance from the moon to the earth's core.

The mass of both objects, and the distance between them, determines the force of gravity. Gravity is not a one-sided pull, but the pull between two objects. Just follow this analogy. It will come to a beautiful spiritual understanding.

Imagine, for example, that here are two bodies. You pull at

one and it comes toward you, but if that body is pulling away from you with a force equal to your pulling, then there is a balance. The moon, by centrifugal force, is pulling away from the earth; but the gravitational attraction of the earth toward the moon keeps a balance. It is evident that the same force of gravity has given balance to the entire universe, so that the pull exerted by each object on every other maintains an orderly balance; otherwise all things would have flown apart in infinite space. On the other hand, if gravity were the sole force at work in the cosmos, everything would have melted into one mass of matter.

God's Forces of Attraction and Repulsion at Work in Cosmic Creation

With a giant telescope, 6,000 stars were visible in one small part of space; and though they seemed like little dots in the sky, most of them are 100 times bigger than the sun! Just think how immense God is, that the whole universe is contained in only a fragment of His being! The Lord seems to be having a lot of fun playing with these marbles in the sky.

Creation came into being by the power of repulsion by which God sent forth from Himself His creative forces. By this outgoing creative power, God is repulsing us and the world of matter away from Himself, and yet at the same time He has instilled in His creation the force of His pull to draw us back into Himself—which is much greater. If God didn't pull us we would be completely thrown into matter for unending incarnations.

From the study of theogony we learn that many ancient cultures ascribed the beginning of creation to the descent of gods, or celestial creative forces. The ancient Parsis, for example, believed in the gods Ormuzd (or Ahura Mazda) and Ahriman, who evolved themselves out of primordial matter and were the two deities who created, respectively, good and evil. The origin of the material world is illustrated in the Egyptian notion of a cosmic egg, made by the god Ptah, out of which creation issues. According to the Hindu belief, Brahma* is the eternal self-

---

* The Sanskrit rendering of *Brahma* with a short *a* at the end, as in this context, denotes God's all-inclusive Creative Consciousness, not the circumscribed concept of the personal "Brahma-the-Creator" of the Brahma-Vishnu-

existent Being—Spirit, the Immutable Absolute—which un-
folds Itself into creation by condensing a finite portion of Its consciousness into causal, astral, and material objects through the
gradations of subtle creative vibratory elements of ether, air, fire,
water, and earth. Spirit's consciousness as immanent in creation as the Creator is the world Soul out of whom all souls have
come. This Brahma, the transcendental ever-existing Intelligence, emanates a hierarchy of individual creative intelligences.
In the Sankhya doctrine of evolution of matter, we follow the
chain of causes back to the principal creative intelligence, the
unlimited eternal Primordial Nature, or Maha-Prakriti. Out of
this principle, or Original Nature, all existences have issued, and
into it they will return.* This primordial creative Nature is
endowed with its own volition to carry out the development of
creation. Its first emanation as plastic Nature contained the original Soul or deity, Prajapati, out of which all individual souls
have issued—the first physical beings were called Swayambhuva
Manu ("man born of the Creator") and Shatarupa ("having a
hundred images or forms"), just as Adam and Eve are the symbolic first man and woman of the Judeo-Christian tradition.

Though the Hindu concept refers to the creative intelligences as deities, they are understood to be none other than
individualized aspects of the one Spirit. God transforms Himself into these intelligences and then into matter and human
beings, just as our consciousness can transform itself into a
dreamland wherein we can see and experience everything as
though it were real—human beings, earth scenes, plants,
animals, and so on. But when we wake up we see they were
all made of one dreaming consciousness.

Shiva triad (which is rendered with a long *ā* at the end, *Brahmā*). See *Brahma-
Vishnu-Shiva* and *Brahman* in glossary.

* "I am the Source of everything; from Me all creation emerges. With this realization the wise, awestricken, adore Me" (Bhagavad Gita X:8). "At the end of a
cycle (*kalpa*), O Arjuna! all beings return to the unmanifested state of My Cosmic Nature (Prakriti). At the beginning of the next cycle, again I cast them forth.
By revivifying Prakriti, Mine own emanation, again and again I produce this host
of creatures, all subject to the finite laws of Nature" (Bhagavad Gita IX:7–8).
The "Big Bang" theory of modern science provides an interesting parallel to
Hindu cosmology.

The magical power by which God differentiates His infinite consciousness into finite dream images and gives them a dream reality is called *maya,* cosmic delusion. A tug of gravitation exists between God and *maya* and man. God is pulling man and *maya* is pulling man, and man is free to move toward either. God and man, God and cosmic delusion, are all pulling on each other. God is pulling creation, including man, toward Himself; and material man and nature are pulling away from God. Whatever exerts a gravitational pull toward God is "good." Whatever pulls beings away from God is "evil." There is a sort of balance when neither good nor evil predominate. But sometimes that balance is lost, as when man turns toward evil and pulls far away from God so that he feels less and less attraction to the Divine. But no one can pull away from God completely. The stronger gravity of God will gradually draw the soul back to Him again, though it may take innumerable incarnations to do so.

When you shoot an arrow, it travels with its force until that force dissipates and gravity causes it to fall back to earth. In the same way, we were propelled from God, and our desires are the force that keeps us moving away from Him, coursing through the sky of reincarnations. God's gravity may seem to have failed us, but He is constantly pulling us toward an inevitable return to Him. When our desires will be exhausted, then we will be drawn toward God again by the power of His gravity.

How the Thoughts of God Evolve Into Matter

Now, thought is the most elastic of forces because it is the finest vibration of consciousness. You can divide thoughts into smaller and smaller units and you will never be able to reach the end. Conversely, you can increase in size, for example, a mental concept of the earth, expanding it throughout eternity, and still you will never be able to exhaust infinity. So God's first expression of creation is of vibratory consciousness—thoughtrons, or small units of thought. These first thoughts became positive and negative, because no creation is possible at all without duality. Without good and evil, light and shadows, only God's undifferentiated consciousness would remain.

So God projected out of Himself units of positive and negative thoughts from which everything is created, just as a dream is created by units of thought. First, a world of ideas came into being: the causal universe. Then those units of thought became lifetrons, the substance of an astral world of finer-than-atomic forces.* Then lifetrons became condensed into the material creation consisting of positive and negative protons and electrons, atoms, molecules, cells, and so on. Atomic physics demonstrates that all things in the material cosmos are made of atoms that vary in weight, density, power, size, and configuration and have within them the qualities necessary to inform the infinite varieties of matter and life. But science has yet to recognize the lifetronic power and thoughtronic intelligence behind the atomic building blocks that—in accord with God's cosmic laws wielded by Maha-Prakriti, Primordial Nature—combine them to produce mineral, vegetable, animal, and human forms.

Evolution Versus Involution

When God saw that He had driven these elements of creation out of Himself—from the finest to the grossest forms— the process of involution began to work. From the standpoint of our subject today, think of evolution as going away from God and involution as going back to God. For every process of evolution there is a process of involution. As God's creative thoughts assumed their grossest form in matter, then involution began. The process of involution is going on all the time. God's dreaming consciousness manifests first in the stones, or inert minerals. It then begins to stir in the sensitivity of plants, but has no self-consciousness. Then come all forms of sentient life in the animal kingdom. The innate vitality and consciousness then finds expression in man, with his superior intelligent power to reason and discriminate. And finally, in the superman the superconsciousness of God is fully reflected. Thus does creation go away from God, and then come back to Him again. God will give salvation not only to man, but to the planets, the earth, the stars—everything that has worked so hard for billions of years to provide a stage for a cosmic dream drama.

Going back to God by the involutionary procedure of Nature is a very slow process. But the discriminating man eventually

---

* See *astral world* and *causal world* in glossary.

asks, "Why wait millions of years before I can return to God?" He reasons that he didn't ask to be created in the first place—that God created him without his permission and therefore He should release him. He refuses to wait longer. When that desire comes, man has made the first definitive turn back to God.

When you truly want to be released from this earth dream, there is no power that can stop you from attaining liberation. Never doubt it! Your salvation is not to be achieved—it is already yours, because you are made in the image of God; but you have to *know* this. You have forgotten it. The musk deer madly seeks the fragrant musk everywhere, and in its frantic search carelessly slips to its death from the high mountain crags. Had the foolish deer only turned its nose to the musk pouch within itself, it would have found that which it sought. Similarly, we have only to turn within ourselves to find our salvation in the realization that our true Self, the soul, is made in God's image.

Manifesting the Divine Qualities Inherent in the Five Stages of the Soul's Return to God

Man has evolved through aeons. In order to quicken his evolution—his involution back to God—he has to make an effort to stimulate the process of natural evolution. He does this outwardly to better his physical existence. For example, man was created by nature to use his feet for locomotion. The process was too slow and too limited in distance, so he used animals to ride on. Then he invented the car, and the airplane, and so on. Now, why shouldn't we likewise accelerate our soul's evolution? The soul of man has to ascend through the five states, or stages of evolution, previously described, before he gets back to God: mineral, plant, animal, man, and superman. He is to accumulate unto himself the divine qualities inherent in each stage.

1. He must be transparent like the gems, without spots of defective perception. He has to develop their crystalline character, by removing the mental blemishes in his otherwise sparkling mentality. His thinking and perception should have gemlike clarity that will undistortedly reflect

the Divine Mind. This means his sensations must be pure. Misuse or overindulgence of any sense creates flaws in the sensibilities. But if the gem of one's sentient mentality is unclouded, one then develops spiritual sensitivity.

2. The spiritually progressive man is consciously sensitive to life and his surroundings, like the sensitive response of plants to their environment. But as the sensitivity of plants abhors harshness, the spiritually sensitive being shuns the coarseness of material things and finds himself gravitating toward God, as plants turn toward the sun.

3. Then comes the vitality of animals. Though they may have great strength and will power, they do not know how to use these energies intelligently. The progressive man must be full of vitality like the animal, but employ the animal's strong will, not for avaricious purposes, but to govern activity with self-control and to have mastery over the life force. When the vital force is always engaged in something good and worthwhile, and is not dissipated in bad habits or the abuse of sex, then man is going toward God. But as soon as he gives in to plainly indiscriminate animalistic instincts, he is going toward matter. That is the common happening we see everywhere. The yogi, on the other hand, learns how to use vitality and will with wisdom. He is not weak. He is a master of self-control. He knows how to relax and throw the searchlight of vitality within to reveal the presence of Spirit. The reversal of the life force from matter to Spirit is called *pranayama.* By withdrawing the life current from externals through *Kriya Yoga,* the consciousness begins inwardly to awaken to its higher nature in God.

4. The rational man thereby becomes a thoughtful, discriminative being, ever progressive in his power to think and reason clearly. He develops pure reason, or discrimination, in which his rationality is no longer mixed up with doubt and misconception. He learns to reason with wise men and to understand the truths they express and exemplify.

   If you reason with people who are always in doubt and confused—and especially if your own consciousness is not yet firm in true understanding—your brain will also become infected by doubt and confusion. So many people try to win their points by argument, but I let them have a sense of victory right away. There is no use talking to them. "Fools argue, wise men discuss." When we conversed with Master [Swami Sri Yukteswar] it was a communion bound by pure reason and blessed by his wisdom. The masters cling to truth, not theories. But most people are enslaved by emotion and circumscribed by their own opinions. If two people really want to find truth, they can agree very quickly.

It is only by developing both pure reason and pure feeling that you can reach God and truth. In the ordinary man, reason is uppermost and feeling is hidden; in the average woman, feeling is uppermost with reason hidden. If you have too much feeling, it becomes emotion and will take you into the meshes of matter; and too much reason becomes rationalization which also takes you into delusive matter. When you balance reason and feeling by meditation, you will come to God and truth-perceptions. By an interchange of these qualities, man and woman can help to balance in each other pure reason and pure feeling, thus helping each other toward union with God. But marriage is not the only way. By successful meditation one attains this balance within himself, or herself, for it is already there, hidden in the soul.

5. After developing the balanced reason and feeling of the discriminative stage, the last state of involution is to be attained: the pure intuition and omniscience of the superman. He is intuitively progressive in feeling his soul and Spirit. He must then fully lift his consciousness from the body and materiality to his original omnipresent state. The freed soul is back once more with God.

You can develop in yourself all these finer qualities by which God is processing matter once again into Spirit. You can hasten this process in your own body by spiritualizing it through meditation and *Kriya Yoga*. You will see your body changing into a mass of light, atoms of condensed electromagnetic energy.

When you gravitate toward God, those luminous atoms are realized to be naught else than the vibratory thoughts of God— the compressed consciousness of Spirit.

The Paths of Knowledge, Devotion, and Action

Of different prescribed paths that lead to God, I will show you how the law of spiritual gravity is applied to the ways of knowledge, devotion, and action. According to how you apply the principles of these paths, you are pulled either by Spirit or by matter.

The path of knowledge, or reason. If you program yourself with theoretical knowledge, you will become a walking victrola, able to repeat lofty phrases and to be considered a learned being, but your knowledge will be unsupported by your own realization or spiritual attainment. Such intellectualization keeps the ego tied to the physical faculties of mind and its relation to matter. Theoretical knowledge cannot give you realization about God. So don't waste your time on too much theory. Those who do so become lost in the jungle of reason and never get beyond mere theories. In the process of reasoning and reasoning they never perceive truth, for truth is beyond reason. Most intellectualists thus become bound by their own conclusions.

If you use your power of reason only to make money and seek material gain, again you will gravitate toward matter.

So the masters say: Do not use your God-given reason to become more and more mixed up in the labyrinth of matter and in the egoistic limitations of the intellect; with the power of discrimination, study and apply truth until it becomes your own intuitive realization. When you develop your intuition, you will feel the presence of God and His omniscience within you. That is called esoteric reason, or *Jnana Yoga.*

The path of devotion. If you have pure devotion, you will feel the pull of God and will find Him. But again, there are two poles in this path also, two forces pulling you—devotion to God and devotion to matter. Even death tries to remind us that it is foolish to be lured by material attractions. The miser is devoted to objects of matter and remains attached to them to the end, even though he at last has to leave everything behind. Yet, to his final breath, he is just as devoted to material things as the yogi is to God. But the yogi reasons, "Matter is external and possession of its objects is short-lived. Why should I concentrate on the little temporal things and exclude eternity? Devotion to God alone is the only way to everlasting fulfillment."

The consciousness of the worldly man is circumscribed; he is devoted to his body, his surroundings, and his family. His attachment says, "Us four and no more." He should rather use that family affection as a lesson in learning to expand his love. As soon as you love not only your family, but give that love to all, you are going toward God. That is why Jesus said: "Love thy neighbor as thyself." To use family affection for all, to give to the world the same love you have for self and family, is gravitation toward God. Lessen the consciousness of family, property, and all material attachments and begin to reexpress the omnipresence you have lost.

In loving God, do not lose your devotion in emotion. This sometimes happens on the path of devotion. I was surprised to find "holy rollers" in this country. It began with certain sects in India. But when devotion is expressed in physical emotion, the pure quality of love is lost in the external expenditure of the life energy in the muscles. When the body and mind gravitate toward God, they become calm and quiet. The consciousness and life force become interiorized when one is inwardly with God. True devotion is like a plummet that sinks into the sea-bottom of the perception of God. That is *Bhakti Yoga*.

The path of action. Some persons have a natural inclination to be active; they love the motion of working and serving. If you work for your own self you are pulled toward matter. But if you work with the thought of doing everything for God, you are pulled toward God. When your activity centers only on making money for material advantages for yourself and your loved ones, or on any activity with a selfish end, you are going away from God. Thus do most people engage their energies in their attachments and their desires for more and more material acquisitions. But as soon as your active energy is used to seek God, you move toward Him. You see, again, this constant pull from God and from matter. One side says make money for material satisfaction, and the other side says find satisfaction in seeking God, in serving God, and in acquiring monetary success to help God's work of uplifting others spiritually, mentally, and physically.

When you act for material gain you are yielding to the gravitational pull of matter. When you are acting for God, you are linked to the gravitational pull of God. If your desire for material things and for God are even, you will be more or less at a standstill. If your desire for God becomes greater, then your desire for material things will be lessened.

Engaging in spiritual activity consisting of both meditation and working with the thought that everything you do is for God—that is *Karma Yoga*. When in meditation you feel God's bliss eternal, you will no longer feel tied to the body, and you will be filled with enthusiasm to work for Him. You can't be a lover of God and be lazy. One who meditates and loves God is always active for Him and for others.

Work for God, Love God, Be Wise With God, and Realize Him Through *Kriya Yoga*

Seeking union with God by wisdom alone, by devotion alone, or through action alone is one-sided. The far superior way is to take your mind and vital forces and all your desires, and your devotion and wisdom and service, and dissolve them all in God. When by *Kriya Yoga* you can withdraw your life energy and consciousness from the five sense telephones, when you can withdraw your vitality from your body and mind and throw the searchlight of your attention on God, that is the highest way to God. By *Kriya Yoga*, you shut off the senses at will and take your mind and life and vitality and sensibility and plunge into the Infinite. The person within whom the aurora borealis of Spirit is dancing—whether materially he possesses much or no outward glamour at all—he is the real soul.

So, the easiest and best way to God is not to be limited only to *Jnana Yoga*, *Bhakti Yoga*, or *Karma Yoga*, but to combine them. Work for God, love God alone, and be wise with God. Use your reason, not to become an overstuffed intellect, but to find God—gravitating toward intuitive wisdom gained in meditation and avoiding theoretical knowledge and materialistic rationalizing. Use your devotion not for worldly attachment to things or people, but for finding God—absorbing yourself in devotion and ecstasy with God. And work not for yourself under any circumstances, but for God and to help others. The culmination of these lies in following the direct highway to God through practicing *Kriya Yoga*—listening to the cosmic sound of God's voice of *Aum*,* quieting the heart and breath which draw you toward body consciousness, and seeing His great light of omnipresence.

Worshiping in the church or temple is a good habit, provided you learn from that inspiration to go into your own temple of meditation and ecstasy within. In the deepest hours of the night and in the quiet of the dawn, enter your inner cathedral and talk to your thought audiences, rousing all of them to be devoted to the Infinite. And on the grand organ in your temple of peace the great *Aum* will be played.

Start tonight to meditate earnestly. Do not wander aimlessly. Go straight to God. You have closed the gates to Heaven by gravitating toward matter and the body. Gravitate toward Him who is constantly pulling you. Go back to God. Remember, the kingdom of God is within you. If you meditate and seek Him with wisdom, devotion, and good actions, you will surely find Him.

----

* *Aum*, Amen, is the all-pervading sound emanating from the Holy Ghost (Invisible Cosmic Vibration; God in His aspect of Creator); the voice of creation, testifying to the Divine Presence in every atom. Practice of *pranayama* techniques such as *Kriya Yoga* induces a state of deep calmness in heart, breath, and other physiological functions. Freed from distractions of body consciousness, the mind is able inwardly to perceive and commune with the presence of God as *Aum*. (See *Aum* in glossary.)

Acquiring Attunement
With the Source of Success

Self-Realization Fellowship Temple,*
Los Angeles, California, January, 13, 1935

Very few people realize that divine law governs all actions and determines the effects thereof. Thus, the destiny of each individual is directed not by chance, but according to the causes he himself sets into motion. By spiritual realization, every circumstance of one's life can be scientifically traced to a specific cause or pattern of causes. But because the ordinary person does not perceive how the law of action and reaction is governing his life, he believes that what comes to him is in large part a matter of happenstance and fate. He often says: "This was my good luck," or "That's my unfortunate lot." There is no luck that one has not created before, in this or other incarnations; and there is no hapless fate except what has been "predestined" by one's own actions, here in the present or way in the past—sometimes many lives before entering the portals of this life. These self-created causes are why some people are born poor and others rich; some healthy and others sickly; and so on. Otherwise, where is the justice of God if He made all of His children equal, and then consigned some to live in favorable circumstances and others in unfavorable conditions?

The law of cause and effect that governs our lives is what we call karma. *Karma* means action; and it also means the fruits or effects of our actions. These effects, for good or ill, are what make it so hard for people to change themselves or their circumstances. There is no other explanation for the inequalities among humans that does not deny the justice of God. And

---

* Self-Realization Fellowship services were held at this temple, at 711 Seventeenth Street in Los Angeles, from December 1934 to September 1939. The temple property was later taken over by the city for a freeway right-of-way; replaced by a new temple in Hollywood a few years later.

66

without justice, I would say there is no use in living.

If, then, your successes or failures have more or less been determined by yourself in the past, is there no remedy by which you can alter your present conditions? Yes, there is. Reason and will have been given to you. There is no difficulty that cannot be solved, provided you believe you have more power than your troubles, and you use that power to shatter your impediments. You have to make the scientific effort necessary to succeed.

Success Means to Create at Will What You Need

The typical concept of success focuses on having a lot of money. But real success means to have the power to create at will what you need—the power to acquire those things that are truly necessary for your absolute existence and happiness. It is important, therefore, to understand in what lies real necessity—to know the difference between needs and wants. If the perception of "needs" is boiled down, then the necessities for a happy life can be easily met.

The ideal of balanced living is a middle path between the ideas of the East and the West. The East says: "Meditate on God; never mind what you don't have." I think that is too extreme. At the other extreme, the West says: "You must have a nice car and house, and new clothes, and everything that will make you comfortable and keep you entertained; it doesn't matter whether you can afford it or not." Luxury is the goal in the West; it is a habit, and the law of habit makes one bound to his accustomed ways.

Simple living does not mean poverty or poverty consciousness. There are destitute people whose lives are miserable; that is not the ideal of simple living. Simplicity means to be free of desires and attachments, and supremely happy within. It requires a masterful mind and a very strong will to live simply. It entails neither hardship nor deprivation, but the wisdom to work for and be content with what you truly need. To spend money on foolish things, even if you have the means to do so, is weakness. Practice self-control, and reduce your wants to purposeful necessities. And do not live beyond your means; that is the first lesson to learn if you want to be prosperous. Spend less than your income; otherwise, you will never be satisfied and happy. Above all, hold to the thought: "My happiness is unconditional; I can do without anything. But since God has given me a body to look after, I shall do my best to supply it with the proper necessities of life."

How grandly and simply the saints of India live. Possessing little, they are wealthy beyond the riches of kings. All nature begins to synchronize with them. Their complete inner satisfaction is what you should create within yourself—to learn to be happy with whatever you have. Of course, modern living requires more necessities than does residing in a hermit's hut. But instead of carrying with you through life an attachment to a lot of possessions, you should cultivate the power to acquire what you need when you need it. If you haven't that power, you are poor, no matter how much you possess. Even a Henry Ford or a Rockefeller may be said to be poor by that standard, because needs do not consist only of physical necessities. No amount of money can assure health or happiness. Prosperity means uniform fulfillment for body, mind, and soul.

Imagine, George Eastman, who invented the Kodak, had every material thing that anyone could desire. Think of it! He had luxury; but there was something wrong with his prosperity, for which reason his existence was intolerable to himself. Consequently, he ended his life by sending a bullet through his head. Happiness can never come merely from wealth and possessions. Jesus Christ did not have any money. But he had the unlimited prosperity of God at his command. He demonstrated this many times, as on the occasion when he fed five thousand with five loaves of bread. And even when death came, its cruelty could not take away what he had inside. To the end he thought first of others: "Father, forgive them for they know not what they do."

To be all-round prosperous, you must follow the example of Jesus and not that of unscrupulous businessmen. If you learn to apply the divine law of prosperity, it will wait on you. That is the secure way; it is the only condition in which you can be secure in this world. That wealth no robber can steal; it is the security that everyone needs.

Cultivate Prosperity in Order to Help Others

The law of prosperity cannot be manipulated by man for his own selfish advantage. The working of that law is controlled by God, and He doesn't permit His laws to be bent or broken arbitrarily. If man works in harmony with the divine law of success, he receives abundance; if by wrong actions he disrupts its generous flow into his life, he punishes himself.

How are you to work in harmony with the principles of that divine law? First of all, as I said, leave behind desire for and attachment to luxuries; develop your mind power so that it is satisfied with simple things. After that, say: "Well, my needs are only a part of my responsibility. I have dependents and must fulfill my obligations to them also." Provide for your family, but never spoil your children with too much money.

Unless you include the welfare of others in your prosperity you will never be ideally prosperous. I do not mean just a disinterested giving of money to needy persons, but a sincere reaching out to help others help themselves. Then you will see a tremendous law of supply at work in your own life. No matter what your situation might be, that law of reaping the good that you sow will be always with you to help you.

Most people think first and foremost about themselves, and about making money to satisfy their own desires. If you do that, sooner or later you are going to be deceived. Rather, you should start with this thought: "My life's duty is to make others happy." Be motivated by how your actions and plans can be of benefit to others. Then devise the means to accomplish your goals. In order to serve, you must have the necessary resources. If you milk the cow you must feed the cow. The ambition to live well and be prosperous becomes spiritualized if the purpose is to better serve others by being able to include them in your prosperity. In rendering good service, you are bound to get good returns; and when you get good returns, you can improve your own living standard and do even more for others. That is how the divine law works.

Have Faith in the Power of God

You are living directly by the power of God and not by human prosperity. You may argue that unless you have jobs you cannot eat. All right; but even if I put an abundance of food and money before you, and suddenly your heart fails, what good will those material things do you? None. It is God alone who has given you life and the power to work and grow and accomplish. Your very existence is a manifestation of His will, so why shouldn't you depend directly on Him? You must absolutely remember that.

If a need arises, I say, "Well, I must get busy." But I never wish for anything or undertake any action without first seeking God's guidance: "Father, I will reason, I will will, I will act, but guide Thou my reason, will, and activity to the right thing that I should do." Then all the forces of fulfillment work with me. In little things and in big things I have seen that Divine Power work.

I am working for God alone; I have left everything for His cause. I am His child. If you live with the consciousness that you are His child and that He is your Father, and make up your mind to do your best with dogged determination, then in spite of obstacles, and even if you make mistakes, His power will be there to help you out. I live by that law. In that way I was able to acquire our Self-Realization Fellowship headquarters, even though I hadn't the material means in hand to do so. And see, even in this time of depression, still I have bought this temple. I worked the divine law, and this temple is the result. Unless you also live by that law, you cannot know the Power of which I speak.

If you can go through your tests smiling with faith in God, and without harboring any doubts, you will see how God's law works. In San Francisco, I had only $200 in the bank and was about to begin a lecture campaign. I had not enough money even to make a start; and many large bills had to be paid. I said: "God is with me. He has given me this trouble and He will look after me. I am doing His work; I know He will help me." If the whole world forsakes you, but you *know* that He is with you, His law will work its wonders for you.

When my secretary came to me and I told him how much we had in the bank, he literally collapsed on the floor. I said, "Get up." He was shaking: "We are going to jail for not paying our bills!" I said, "We are not going to jail. In seven days we will have all the money we need for the campaign." He was a doubting Thomas, but I had faith. I was not in need of money for any gain of my own, but to spread God's work. I had no fear, even for the enormity of my troubles. Fear is afraid of me. What is there to fear? Nothing should give you fear. Face all troubles with faith in God and you will conquer. Bhagavad Gita says: "With heart absorbed in Me, and by My grace, thou shalt overcome all impediments."* And think of it! I was walking in front of the Palace Hotel when an elderly woman came up to me and said, "Can I talk with you?" We exchanged a few words and then out of the blue she said, "I have money to burn. Can I help you?" I replied, "I don't need your money. Why should you offer money to me when you don't even know me?" She answered, "But I do know you; I have heard so much about you." And right there she wrote out a check for $27,000. I saw in that the hand of God.

In Having God, We Have Everything

But the greatest victory I had was in Phoenix. If only everyone could feel the grace of God as I have felt, they would know, as I do, that in Him they already have everything. That was my experience in Phoenix. I was deeply, deeply praying and meditating, because I had to meet a great need in the morning and someone had failed me. My prayer was not for money, but for freedom. I said to Divine Mother: "Why am I put to such troubles; why do I have to face such a crisis?" But I didn't stop there. I went on meditating; and then I prayed to the Mother: "Talk to me. If You tell me to do so, I will leave everything behind and walk out of the organization, singing Thy name. I do not need anything but You. I ask nothing for myself. Test me. If You will it, I shall at this moment leave everything. In Thy Light I shall walk away."

When Divine Mother saw that I meant what I said, this is what She replied: "I freed thee long ago; but because thou thinkest thou art not free, that is why thou art not free. Dance of life or dance of death, know that these come from Me and as such rejoice. What more dost thou want than that thou hast Me?" From that day I found freedom.

If you have in your consciousness the desire to please God above all else, He will look after you. "...What more dost

---

* XVIII:58.

thou want than that thou hast Me?" Will you remember that? Every one of you? It isn't much to remember. If you will meditate and sincerely pray to God, you will find Him; and He will bring to you all the prosperity you need.

Use the law of meditation. It is the law of all laws, for it brings response from the Power behind all power. I knew, when Divine Mother spoke those words to me, that all would be well. The necessity was met, and I was saved from a catastrophe.

That Power will work for you as it has always worked for me. I speak these truths from my own experiences. It would not be possible for me to talk about them if I hadn't demonstrated them in my own life. I live by faith in God. My power is God. I do not believe in any other power. As I concentrate on that Power, it works through me.

I have been referred to as one of the most successful lecturers in this country. Thousands have been taught by me. Not that I am proud of myself on that account. My success is only because I have believed solely in the power of God. Eventually I gave up all public lecture work—I am giving up everything now for God. I find that I have accomplished that part of what my life's purpose was to be. That purpose is to pick souls from the crowds and help them to know God. I have found such souls all over the country; and I am training them.*

I move by Spirit; there has been no thought of money, but of service to mankind; and because of that, the Lord has opened

---

* By the time Paramahansaji gave this talk in 1935, he had drawn many of the direct disciples who were destined to play important roles in his world mission, including two whom he appointed to be his spiritual successors in leading his work as president of Yogoda Satsanga Socitey of India/Self-Realization Fellowship: Rajarsi Janakananda (see glossary), who met the Guru in Kansas City in 1932; and Sri Daya Mata, who had attended his classes in Salt Lake City the previous year. Among others who were drawn from the lecture-campaign crowds, those who stepped forward to dedicate their lives to Paramahansaji's work and who received his personal spiritual training, were Dr. and Mrs. M. W. Lewis, who met him in Boston in 1920; Gyanamata (Seattle, 1924); Tara Mata (San Francisco, 1924); Durga Mata (Detroit, 1929); Ananda Mata (Salt Lake City, 1931); Sraddha Mata (Tacoma, 1933); and Sailasuta Mata (Santa Barbara, 1933). After withdrawing from nationwide lecturing in the mid-1930s, Paramahansaji concentrated his efforts on classes for serious students, and spoke mostly at his own Self-Realization Fellowship temples and at the international headquarters.

up all channels to support my existence and the existence of this work of Self-Realization Fellowship [Yogoda Satsanga Society of India]. I wish to serve you; that is all. That is why I am here. The minute I need help, it is there—from the Divine. Some money was needed for Christmas. What happens? A student wrote and said, "You have a cash balance in the bank in Detroit. What do you want done with it?" I said, "Send it immediately." My need was fulfilled at the right time.

That power of God is working with you also. You will see it is so if you have faith and know that prosperity comes not from material sources but from God.

Seek God-contact and He Will Guide You

The Lord doesn't tell you that you do not have to think for yourself, nor that you need not use your initiative. You have to do your part. The point is, if you cut yourself off from the Source by wrong actions and desires, and by lack of faith and divine communion, then you cannot receive His all-powerful help. But if you are guided by attunement with God, He will help you to do the right thing, and to avoid mistakes.

The way to start is by deep and regular morning and evening meditation. The more you meditate, the more you will realize there is Something behind the kingdom of ordinary consciousness where a great peace and happiness reign. Practice the presence of this peace and happiness, for it is the first proof of God-contact. It is the conscious realization of Truth within yourself. That is what you need. That is how to worship Truth; for we can worship only what we know.* Most people worship God as Something intangible; but when you begin to worship Him as real, through your own inner perception, you will feel increasingly the presence of His power in your life. No matter what else you might do, nothing will produce that God-contact which comes from deep meditation. Fervent effort to increase the inner peace and happiness born of meditation is the only way to realize God.

The time to pray to God for guidance is after you have med-

---

* "God is a Spirit: and they that worship Him must worship Him in spirit and in truth" (*John* 4:24, Bible).

itated and felt that inner peace and joy; that is when you have made divine contact. If you think you have a need, you can then place it before God and ask whether it is a legitimate prayer. If you feel inwardly that your need is just, then pray: "Lord, you know that this is my need. I will reason, I will be creative, I will do whatever is necessary. All I ask of You is that You guide my will and creative abilities to the right things that I should do."

Be fair with God. Perhaps He has something better for you than what you are praying for. It is a fact that sometimes your most fervent prayers and desires are your greatest enemies. Talk sincerely and justly with God, and let Him decide what is right for you. If you are receptive, He will lead you, He will work with you. Even if you make mistakes, don't be afraid. Have faith. Know that God is with you. Be guided in everything by that Power. It is unfailing. This truth is applicable to every one of you.

By practice of ever deeper meditation, you can eventually go into the superconscious state of inner realization and remain therein while performing on the conscious plane all of your activities. When you learn to work from the state of superconsciousness, and to work with divine inner happiness no matter what you are doing, you will feel with you always the presence and power of God.

"As I Perceive, May You Perceive"

I have delivered His message to you, and I see His great light in you all. In that Light I bless you. The ethereal power of God flows through me: through my speech, my brain, my cells, every wisp of my consciousness—every thought is a channel through which His divine light is passing. Open your hearts and realize that the Divine Light is also passing through you. As I perceive, may you perceive; as I behold, may you behold.

Business, Balance, and Inner Peace

Restoring Equilibrium to the Work Week

In the 1920s, American industrialist Henry Ford introduced the idea of a five-day work week. The proposal, heartily endorsed by Paramahansaji, brought forth the response in this article.

The word holiday sprang from two words, "holy day." A holy day should be a time for introspective thinking and for man to nurture his sacred soul qualities. One of the Ten Commandments is "Remember the sabbath day, to keep it holy"— a day of rest and spiritual renewal. Christians observe the sabbath on *Sun*day—a day for basking in the *sun*light of wisdom. The Hindus reserve a number of days in the year for spiritual purposes. Easter, Thanksgiving, and Christmas correspond to some of the sacred days of the Hindus. The Durga Puja festival is as widely observed in India as is Christmas in the West.

Man is a spiritual and a material being. He should develop himself spiritually by inner discipline, and become materially efficient by developing his business faculties. Primitive man kept all his mental faculties busy satisfying the needs of the material life. His time was spent in hunting, eating, and sleeping. Modern man tries scientifically to meet the present material conditions of life. What primitive man did unmethodically, modern man does methodically. This method in modern man's efforts for material success has indirectly improved his inner faculties.

The masters of India counsel direct development of the inner faculties, such as will power to fight temptation, feeling for serving fellow beings, and intuition for directly realizing truth.

Crime and Violence Are the Bitter Fruits of an Imbalanced Civilization

If making money to secure material comforts is necessary for man, then making happiness is supremely necessary.

Possession of material riches without inner peace is like dying of thirst while bathing in a lake.

People crave different things—money, or fame, or spirituality—as a result of early habits and specific environmental influences. That is why the people of both the East and the West lead one-sided lives. The East is generally more spiritually inclined and the West more materially inclined. But we cannot live happily by spiritual doctrines only or by riches only. To bring a balance into the lives of men of East and West, both should adopt a method of developing an equilibrated life.

People in general spend six days of the week in making money, and even the seventh in thinking about it; but they spend hardly any time on self-development. One reason the West has so much crime, so many murders and robberies in spite of its developed civilization, is that people are too busy securing the commodities of material comfort and have no time to reflect on the practical value of following moral and spiritual principles.

If material poverty is to be avoided, spiritual poverty is to be abhorred; for the latter is the underlying cause of all human suffering. A practical spiritual man is a happy man, and only a happy man is a successful man. One hundred percent material prosperity among the inhabitants of a city will not prevent murders and crime. Following the universal principles of mutual service, spontaneous cooperation, love for the spiritual life, and disciplining the human sense cravings is wholly necessary for the harmonious, happy, healthy, prosperous life of any community.

Official records annually show that almost one billion dollars are stolen by young men and women ranging in age from fifteen to thirty. We have the New York newspapers' report that 400,000 more meals were served in the jails this year than last year. Why is all this? Because the ordinary man's attention is not yet fixed on the vital problems of the art of living. Why not use some of the money spent for erecting and maintaining jails to create How-to-Live schools, which will prevent children from becoming criminals? Criminal offenders grown worse in jails are let loose in healthy society for further spread of the bacteria of crime.

Most persons will say, "Oh, I am too busy with my business to think about the art of living. We all know about that. Someday we will come to it, but what we are interested in right now is money." But what purpose would money serve if one succeeds in making millions at the cost of a complete nervous breakdown and loss of poise and happiness?

Spiritualizing Ambition With the Ideal of Service

Since God has given us hunger, and since we have a physical body to look after, we must have money and we should earn it honestly and scientifically, by serving the right needs of our fellow beings. Business life need not be a material life. Business ambition can be spiritualized. Business is nothing but serving others materially in the best possible way. Those stores that start out with the idea of only making money are readily recognized as commercial money-making dens. But stores that concentrate on serving customers with the best articles at the minimum cost will succeed and will also advance the moral development of the world.

I have never forgotten the remark of a fine salesman in a large shop where I was selecting an overcoat for myself. "Sir," he said, "I am not trying just to sell you something; I am trying to find out exactly what you need." He did not try to sell me the most expensive overcoat; he showed me a less expensive one that exactly suited me in every way. I was pleased to get what I needed at a reasonable price. Thus he secured in me a permanent customer for his company.

People should spiritualize their business ambitions by starting out with the idea of serving the proper needs of their fellow beings. Not only should man make money by serving, and thereby get something for himself in return, but should also work for the sake of acquiring money to use in creating institutions that will serve public needs. When one has made a great deal of money, and simultaneously helped his workers and associates to become more prosperous, and then uses his wealth for helping others to help themselves, that is spiritualizing ambition. Wealthy parents who leave too much money for their children choke the evolutional development of self-created, self-earned success and happiness in their offspring. Even the "brainy" man must exercise ambition or he does injustice to himself by crippling his faculties. By injuring himself he sets a bad example and thus hinders the progress of humanity.

That is why I agree with Mr. Henry Ford in helping people to help themselves, and not in humiliating, slave-breeding charity. It is only by having ambition and crowning it with the ideal of service that materially ambitious people will find a spiritual reason for making money.

A Balance of Oriental and Occidental Traits Is Needed

Oriental peoples have, as a rule, been spiritually inclined, taking life philosophically and cultivating a natural tendency toward contemplation. Of course, many Orientals have used their leisure for indulging in laziness instead of working for spiritual realization; but on the whole, they have an awakened spiritual perception.

Our Western brothers have devoted their time predominantly to developing the material and intellectual sides of life. But they are often too busy even to enjoy the fruits of their labor, or to know the taste of peace, relaxation, and the bliss of meditation. They become enslaved by less important engagements and forget their highest engagement with the blissful ideal life of God-contact.

Because of the extensive use of machinery, Westerners have this advantage over their Eastern brethren: they can use the time thus saved to advance more in the deeper studies of life. Business activities and money are meant for the comfort and betterment of man; he should not allow blind greed for them to rob him of his happiness and the achievement of higher goals.

Six full days and nights of machine-like existence, and part of one day (Sunday) for the cultivation of one's inner self, is not a balanced way of life. The week should be allotted to work, amusement, and spiritual culture: five days for money-making, one day for rest and amusement, and at least one day for introspection and inner realization.* In the Western world,

---

* For the spiritually sincere and eager, Paramahansaji encouraged a routine of morning and evening meditation every day (before and after one's active duties), and one day a week devoted to silence, introspection, spiritual study, and a period of meditation of at least four hours or longer.

life is altogether too fast; the Orient tends to go to the other extreme. A balance needs to be struck. Every man must have some free time to find himself. One day a week—Sunday—is not enough, because it is his only holiday and he wants it for rest and is too tired to meditate.

With a five-day working week, as proposed by Henry Ford, people could use Friday night, Saturday, and Sunday for getting away from the noisy city environment, and thus increase their longevity. The Chicago Chief of Police reported a study that says man's longevity could be increased by eleven years if the city noises were cut out and man's nervous system calmed down thereby. Almost every family in America can afford an automobile of some kind, and with it they can get out of the cities on weekends and refresh themselves in the peaceful retreats of nature, living the double life of a hermit in the woods and a warrior in the field of worldly activity.

Learn the Art of Living Rightly

Since ultimate wisdom—knowing everything that can be known by the maximum use of human reason—is the human goal, then why not learn the art of living rightly?

People lose their balance and suffer from money madness and business mania only because they never had the opportunity of culturing habits of a balanced life. It is not our passing thoughts or brilliant ideas but our everyday habits that control our lives. There are some very conscientious businessmen who make millions without being irregular or nervous, but there are others who become so engrossed in making money that they cannot think of anything else and do not wake up from their obsession until something terrible happens to them, as sickness or loss of all happiness.

We must begin with the children as well as with the adults. The plastic mind of the child can be molded into any shape with the cooperation of self-disciplined, reformed adults. Desired habits can easily be created in children because the will to perform is mostly free except for a few innate tendencies. Adults have to battle and expel old habits in order to lodge new good ones. But all habits, whether in children or adults, must be cultivated through the medium of spontaneous willingness. In training children in a balanced life or in habits of paying equal attention to the earning of money and to the acquisition of spiritual happiness, the time and method of training has to be considered.

Many psychologists say that the later periods of life are but the repetitions of the training one received between the ages of two to ten or fifteen.

Spiritual sermons inspire the minds of children to better action, but that is all. Actual practical discipline is necessary for roasting the seeds of past-life prenatal habits lodged in the subconscious and superconscious minds. This can only be done by directing inwardly the cauterizing power of the electricity of concentration.

Children ought to be brought up with a spiritual ambition to make money only for the sake of service. Modern children are mostly reared in a wrong atmosphere where money-making is the goal, so they try to "get rich quick," even by the hold-up method. Their reason argues that if making money by any means is the goal, then why shouldn't hold-up methods prevail?

It lies in the hands of today's adults to uplift the citizens of tomorrow by educating the children into a balanced life. As long as the adults will remain intoxicated with a one-sided material life, so long will the children follow that example and their hopes will remain unfulfilled. To save the future of the world by saving the children, the modern adult must wake up and cultivate a balanced life of spiritual as well as material habits.

Leading a Balanced Life

Many heads of concerns manage to work only five days a week from nine in the morning to three in the afternoon and generally take Saturdays and Sundays off. They have some poise, more home life, but they spend most of their free time in playing golf and going dancing and to the movies, instead of giving some time to spiritual culture.

In order to lead a balanced life, adults must educate themselves to realize that business ambitions should be only for making ourselves and others happy. Without this ideal, over-strenuous business activity produces nervousness, lack of harmonious social qualities, miserliness, greed, and disrespect for all good principles. By realizing the true purpose of business activity—service for the benefit of others as well as oneself— life can be really happy.

I think Mr. Henry Ford has inaugurated a new era in spiritualizing business life by proposing a five-day work week. "The sabbath was made for man, and not man for the sabbath: therefore the Son of man is Lord also of the sabbath."* Jesus wanted people to have Sundays as the Son's day, or wisdom's day, to culture soul knowledge; but when people are so busy all week, they want Sundays for relaxation and amusement, instead of giving it to God and introspection. The clergymen and priests who are opposed to having movies and diversions on Sundays ought to sympathize and cooperate with Henry Ford's plan. The hardworking man could utilize Saturday for relaxation, gardening, wholesome amusement; then he would feel free and glad to use Sunday wholly and solely for attending religious services and for spiritual self-discipline through practicing the techniques of concentration and meditation for attaining inner peace and God-communion.†

I know many prominent, intelligent businessmen who in their heart of hearts are discontented and are craving for God and wisdom, but they are helplessly carried away by their work habits and by too many social engagements. Their highest engagement with God, Truth, higher studies, and more home life is sacrificed for money-making or useless socializing.

So it is extremely necessary that truth-loving real world patriots should cooperate for making Saturday a day for amusement and relaxation, and Sunday a day exclusively for culturing habits of meditation, association with good persons, good principles, and the highest good—God-Bliss within.

As certain training is needed for engaging in the art of war, so does our engagement in battling with active life. Untrained warriors are soon killed on the battlefield; so also persons untrained in the art of preserving their inner peace are quickly

---

* *Mark* 2:27–28 (Bible).

† Those whose spiritual tradition it is to observe Saturday as their holy day would instead use Sunday as their day of rest and relaxation.

riddled by the bullets of worry and restlessness in active life.*

Man's great need is to find more time to enjoy nature, to simplify his life and his imaginary necessities, to enjoy the true needs of his existence, to learn to know his children and friends better, and most of all, to know *himself* and the God who made him.

---

* Sixty-five years after Paramahansa Yogananda's publication of this article, a 1991 study by Harvard economist Juliet B. Schor showed that the principles advocated by Paramahansaji are as timely now as they were in the 1920s. Professor Schor discovered that the average American now works the equivalent of a whole month more per year than did his or her counterpart in 1970. Modern Americans, she found, are working longer hours than people at any time in history other than the Industrial Revolution—spending even more time on the job than did medieval serfs!

Increased efficiency of production can result in either more earnings or more leisure time, states Schor. Ever since Henry Ford and other industrialists revolutionized workforce habits in the first two decades of this century, America as a whole has typically opted for the money. Greater income and an exceptionally high standard of living have resulted. Yet, despite most Americans' ability to purchase fancy cars and homes that overflow with sought-after creature comforts, Professor Schor found that they are no happier as a result. As she writes in *The Overworked American: The Unexpected Decline of Leisure* (New York: Basic Books, 1991): "If our desires keep pace with our incomes...getting richer doesn't make us more satisfied....According to a recent review of existing findings, Americans are literally working themselves to death—as jobs contribute to heart disease, hypertension, gastric problems, depression, exhaustion....Studies point to a 'sleep deficit' among Americans, a majority of whom are getting between 60 and 90 minutes less a night than they should for optimum health and performance....Parents are devoting less attention to their children. Stress is on the rise, partly owing to the 'balancing act' of reconciling the demands of work and family life."

"If we are to have a chance at leisure," Schor concludes, "we'll need to resurrect the public debate that ended in the 1920s."

Probing the Core of Nervousness

Self-Realization Fellowship Temple,
San Diego, California, June 15, 1947

Everyone has at times been nervous, more or less, without knowing why. I may shake this piece of cloth and say it is nervous, but what is making the cloth move? When I cease moving my hand, the cloth lies limp. You always blame other things for making you nervous, but never accuse yourself. Yet it is you who make yourself nervous; ninety-nine percent is your own fault. Restlessness, emotional excitement, concentrates too much energy in the nerves so that they begin to wear out. After years and years, the adverse effects of that nervousness begin to show. The nerves are very tough—God made them so, because they have to last a lifetime—but it is necessary to give them proper care. When you stop overloading the nervous system, as when you are in deep sleep or a state of calmness in meditation, you are not nervous at all. In meditative ecstasy the nerves become highly rested and rejuvenated.

Healthy Nerves Essential for a Healthy Body

Nerves are like wires connecting all parts of a factory. If the wires become worn or burned out, then the whole factory or certain affected areas of it cannot function. Similarly, the nervous system enlivens all parts of the body, including the perceptive, cognitive, and responsive functions of the five senses. If the nerves are destroyed, then transaction with the world is also destroyed.

There are two systems of nerves: the central nervous system in the brain, medulla, and spinal cord; and out of that the peripheral system, which connects the nerve centers to the different organs of the body and carries energy to them. The nervous system sends sensations to the brain, enables the brain to process them, and then reacts upon the brain's interpretation of those stimuli.

During the primitive growth of the embryonic brain, the first formative stage of the nerves is like liquid, which then gradually becomes fibers that eventually grow into nerves—tough super-highways for conducting energy from the brain to all parts of the body. The brain is the house of government; the twenty-seven thousand billion cells are the subjects. The nervous system that connects them all must be kept in proper working order. You may recall the paralyzing effect of the recent telephone strike. That is what can happen in your body. When the nerve "telephones" are paralyzed, they cannot convey their vital messages. For example, if the optical center in the brain is impaired, owing to wrong eating, disease, or strain, the nerves of the eyes are affected, and the eyes begin to grow weak.

Examine Yourself to See What Makes You Nervous

Most nervous diseases are due to overexcitation of the mind. These arise from many causes. Examine yourself to see if you are nervous, and then determine what it is that makes you nervous. When you get mad, for instance, you send tremendous volts of energy into the brain and the heart. Emotions such as anger and fear can so overload the nerves that they cause the body to malfunction, sometimes even stopping the heart and causing death. If you pass a million volts of current through a small wire that can stand only a few volts, the wire will be burned out. Excitement means you are directing too much energy to a certain area and depriving other nerves of that life force. The man of calmness, on the contrary, keeps his nerves well fed with a balanced flow of energy so that no part of the body is detrimentally overloaded or depleted.

Nervousness is the disease of civilization. I remember when some of us were driving up Pikes Peak in Colorado. Other cars were speeding past us on the steep, winding grade. I thought they were hurrying to get to the mountaintop in time to see the sunrise. To my great amazement, when we arrived we were the only ones outside to enjoy the view. All the others were in the restaurant drinking coffee and eating doughnuts. Imagine! They rushed to the top and then rushed back, just for the thrill of being able to say when they got home that they had been there, and had coffee and doughnuts on Pikes Peak. That is what nervousness does. We should take time to enjoy things—the beauties of God's creation, the many blessings of life—but avoid undue excitement, restlessness, and sudden emotions, which burn up the nervous system.

Talking too much, including the habit of engaging in long conversations on the telephone, creates nervousness. Habitual twitching—such as drumming the fingers or moving the toes —burns energy in the nerves. Another cause of nervousness, though you may not be aware of it, is the noise of the radio or television going on for hours at a time. All sounds cause the nerves to react.* A study conducted in the police department in Chicago showed that if human beings were not subjected to the bombardment of the sounds of modern living, which are especially harsh in cities, they could live years longer. Learn to enjoy silence; don't listen to the radio or television for hours on end, or have them blaring mindlessly in the background all the time. There is enough "television" of saints and music of the spheres going on throughout the cosmos that you don't need to listen to canned music or watch canned pictures. Through the calmness of inner silence, learn to tune in to God's wondrous cosmic programs.

Learn to Control Your Emotions

Another major cause of nervousness is unkind speech. Never gossip or talk against others. Be busy reforming yourself. Practice kind speech. Don't be quarrelsome. If your husband or wife gets angry and rouses your ire, take a little walk and cool off before responding. If he or she speaks sharply, don't retort in the same way. It is better to remain quiet until the temper has cooled down. Avoid being stubborn or patronizing;

---

* Many researchers have described the adverse effects of noise on human health, including Dr. Samuel Rosen, clinical professor of otolaryngology at Columbia University, who wrote: "It is known that loud noises cause effects which the recipient cannot control. The blood vessels constrict, the skin pales, the voluntary and involuntary muscles tense, and adrenaline is suddenly injected into the blood stream, which increases neuromuscular tension, nervousness, irritability, and anxiety."

but at the same time, refrain from involving yourself in a quarrel. Wait until you both have regained calm reason. Never let anyone rob you of your peace; and do not steal away the peace of others by your verbal misbehavior. The misuse of speech is one of the most injurious of all weapons. You may say something in anger or high emotion that you do not really mean, and then feel sorry afterward; but for twenty years or longer the other person remembers it. (In this respect, memory is a bad thing. The power to remember is a blessing if used in the right way, but harmful if used as a repository of the bad things that have been done to us.) If your wife screeches at you and you shout back, you will suffer twice as much— once from her harsh words and again from your own. You primarily harm yourself. By the time you get through, you will feel that there is nothing left of you. This is why there are so many divorces.

Frankly, people should not marry until they have learned to have some control of their emotions. The schools should educate young students in this art, and in how to develop calmness and concentration. The American home is breaking up because these things are not taught—neither at home nor in the schools. How can two people who are habituated to nervous activity live together without almost destroying each other with their nervousness? In the beginning of a marriage, the bride and groom are carried along on the emotions of excitement and passion. But after a while, when these inevitably start to wane, the true natures of the couple begin to come out and the quarreling and disillusionments set in.

The heart requires true love, friendship, and, above all, peace. When through emotion peace is destroyed, it is a desecration of the bodily temple. A healthy nervous system is what will maintain in proper order all the bodily organs and feelings. And to keep the nervous system healthy, it is important to remain free from devastating emotions such as fear, anger, greed, jealousy.

Cast off fear. What is there to be afraid of? Even a little bit of fear, such as senseless apprehension of the dark or worrying about things that "might" happen, affects the nerves more than you can imagine. Why dread even death? God allows it to happen to everybody, so it cannot be bad. That is a very consoling thought to hold on to. Death is just like a refreshing sleep; and you are not afraid of sleep, are you? Death is complete rest. God gives you death to release you from all of your troubles here, and then to provide you with a fresh start in a new incarnation.

To Be Caught Up in Emotion Is to Forget God

To be caught up in fear, anger, greed, or any violent or impulsive emotion is to forget God. If your senses, which govern your emotions, are under your control, you are a saint. No one knows better than yourself whether you are a master of your senses or a slave to them. Remember, anything that overrules your self-control leads your nervous system to destruction. The greedy man eats, and the man of self-control eats. One eats for the well-being of his body, and the other overeats for sensual gratification. If one's love is concentrated more on God and less on the senses, then all sensory abuse will be overcome. When tempted, pray to the Lord, "Make Thyself more tempting than temptation. No matter how You test me, Lord, I shall cling to You." When your nervous system is filled with peaceful, loving thoughts of God, your nerves become recharged with His power. Krishna said: "When the feeling (chitta) is absolutely subjugated and is calmly established in the Self (the soul), the yogi, thus devoid of attachment to all desires, is spoken of as the God-united."*

Movie stars and other professional entertainers are considered the beautiful people of America. But why are their personal lives so often in a shambles of unhappiness and multiple divorces? Most of them live too much on nervous energy concentrated in the senses. Overeating, promiscuous sex, the intoxication of wine and drugs—all produce a pseudo happiness. In God alone one finds fulfillment of all desires. In God alone one finds ever new joy, which can never be attained through the instrumentality of any of the senses. If you are in the grip of any abuse of the senses—and this means any one of them—contin-

---

* Bhagavad Gita VI:18.

uously affirm your freedom: "I am not enslaved by this habit; my love for God is supreme, greater than for anything else."

Desire and Attachment Feed Nervousness

Desire and attachment feed the disease of nervousness. By the time you have acquired the things you crave, you are worn out. Desireless nonattachment is freedom from the tyranny of enslavement to possessions. Everyone says how beautiful Encinitas is.* I like it because on the altar of the horizon of the ocean and blue sky I see God. When the Hermitage was given to me, for seven days I delighted in it. Then I gave it to God, inwardly freeing myself from all sense of possession. Now I enjoy it through the joy of others.

All the things that India sadly lacked, and that I had wished for her, I see you have here in America; but still you are not happy. Now I pray that India does not become too westernized. Both India and America express extremes. There needs to be balance—American civilization modified with the spirituality of India. Every nation wants the material advantages that America has. And the spiritual consciousness that every nation needs is found in India. I think that life in America is becoming more simplified, which is good. It takes too much time and energy to keep too many possessions in good order. The truth of the matter is that the more unnecessary "necessities" you have, the less peace you have; and the less you are possessed by possessions, the more happiness you have. The way to develop spiritually is to live simply, live quietly, study good books (never read cheap novels), practice calmness through control of the senses and emotions, and meditate much of the time. California with its equable climate and natural endowments is an ideal place to lead a simple life; and here will be a great spiritual resurgence.

Right Attitude Toward Wealth

People shy away from the idea of renunciation, yet they renounce so many things of true value—not the least of which

---

* The SRF Ashram Center in Encinitas, California. (See *Encinitas* in glossary.)

are peace of mind and even sometimes their very lives—for the sake of money, which is perishable. Wealth may be taken away from you, or you may be taken away from it by death; you cannot take it with you. The only value of money is to do good for the well-being and true happiness of self and others. Those who think only of their own security and comforts, forgetful of others in need, are courting poverty; it will be forced upon them sometime. Those who cling selfishly to their wealth instead of doing good with it do not attract prosperity in their next life. They are born poor, but with all the desires of the wealthy. But those who share their good fortune attract wealth and abundance wherever they go. Jesus spoke of this principle when he said, "Sell all that thou hast, and distribute unto the poor, and thou shalt have treasure in heaven."*

If you learn to share with others, you will see that God is ever with you; He will never leave you, and you will never go without. Depend upon Him, and He will look after you. Do not forget that your very life is directly sustained by the power of God. When you remember that your reason, will, and activity are dependent upon Him, you will be guided by God, and you will realize that your life is one with His Infinite Life.

He who is motivated by selfish desires neglects his assigned role in helping the drama of God's creation. He who lives only for himself, creating webs of desires, becomes entangled in those webs. But he who acts and works for God is free. You do not know why you are here on earth, or why you are a man or a woman, or why you are the way you are. You are not here merely to have your own way. You are here to do God's will. To work for yourself is to be bound by life. To work for God is to be free.

Learn to be very active in this world, doing constructive work; but when you are through with your duties, turn off your nervous motor. Retire to the center of your being, which is calmness. Mentally affirm to yourself: "I am calm. I am not a mere nervous mechanism; I am Spirit. Though I dwell in this body, I am untouched by it." If you have a calm nervous sys-

---

* *Luke* 18:22 (Bible).

tem, you will have success in everything you undertake; and, above all, you will succeed with God.

The Nervous System Connects You to the World and to God

The nervous system has two duties. The nerves allow you to interact with the world; and, as the yogis of ancient times discovered, the nerves also serve to connect you with God. The life force in man's body ordinarily flows outward from the brain and spine through the nerves to the senses and their external experiences. When in yoga meditation that energy is reversed to flow inward, it draws the consciousness to the subtle spiritual cerebrospinal centers of divine perception and God-realization. *

Nervousness, the overstimulation of the nerves, ties the consciousness to the body; calmness conduces to God-communion. When you turn off external nervous energy and calm yourself in meditation, and the life force retires from the senses to the cerebrospinal centers of spiritual perception, your nervous system is then connected with superconsciousness, and you have God. You are in the land of light, which is beyond the subconscious realm of sleep. Sleep is an unconscious way of turning off life energy from the nerves. You therefore get some rest during slumber, but you do not have the conscious experience of bliss that the superconscious state produces. When you awaken from sleep, you are just the same as you were before sleep. But if you can cross the subconscious realm into the superconscious land of light, you will have the most wonderful experiences, and these produce lasting spiritual changes in the con-

---

* Yoga teaches that within man's brain and spine are seven subtle centers of life and consciousness. Yoga treatises refer to these centers as *muladhara* (coccygeal); *svadhisthana* (sacral), *manipura* (lumbar), *anahata* (dorsal), *vishuddha* (cervical), *ajna* (medulla and Christ (*Kutastha*) center between the eyebrows), and *sahasrara* (thousand-petaled lotus in the cerebrum). Without the specialized powers lodged therein and flowing outward into the physical organs and senses, the body would be an inert mass of clay. Conversely, when the energy and consciousness are focused inward, the wondrous source and sustaining power of life is revealed, evolving from the supreme consciousness of the soul and Spirit. (See *chakras* in glossary.)

sciousness. The more you can remain in that interiorized state of bliss in meditation, the more you will feel that joy with you all the time, even in the midst of activities.

The Spiritual Physiology That Makes Man Unique

There is a spiritual physiology underlying the nervous system that makes man a unique vehicle for the highest stages of the evolution of consciousness. Man's brain, being larger than that of most animals, with the exception of the elephant and the whale, and being more complex, contains the greatest capacity for thought. This makes the human brain a proper instrument for man, whose consciousness is the most highly evolved of all creatures. Man alone is capable of advanced levels of discrimination; and ultimately, of God-realization. The greater the amount of thought (for example, in man as contrasted with animals), the greater the complexity of the cerebral convolutions. The fissures of these convolutions are about one inch deep in the adult brain. The gray matter of the convoluted surface of the brain is where our sensory-motor thought processes are lodged. In early stages of the developing fetus, the brain is more like a marble dome. The awareness and responses of the fetus increase with the developing complexity of the convolutions. The mind, the source of thought and discrimination, is a process of consciousness, not physiology; it triggers the physiology.*

Now, you will find very interesting how God has made this physical body. It is a deep and vast subject; so just a few points I will touch on. The gray matter on the surface of the brain is the receptacle of nerve impulses. This is where all the nerve cells

---

* In yoga science, the mind is conceived of as a conglomerate of interacting components: *chitta* (consciousness; intuitive feeling), *manas* (the sensory mind), *buddhi* (discriminative intelligence), and *ahamkara* (egoity). Yoga teaches that the physical body, including the brain, is a product of consciousness—not the other way around, as is held by some Western theorists. Yoga points out, however, that in man's usual state of consciousness the mind is so identified with the physical body that biochemical changes have a tremendous influence on the mind, which in turn reacts on the body through the mediums of the endocrine and nervous systems. This complex reciprocal interaction between body and mind is the major factor in man's physical and mental health.

and electrical vibrations are located. When you decide to move any part of your body—your hands, fingers, eyes, for example—this creates electrical impulses in the cells of the gray matter, which are transmitted through the motor nerves to the body part that you want to move. As that part moves, another electrical current is sent back to the brain via the sensory nerves. These electrical impulses stimulate the nerve cells in the gray matter, and more energy-giving oxygen is drawn from the blood vessels in the membrane surrounding the brain. An exercise that is very good to stimulate the energy in the brain is to rap the head gently but firmly with the knuckles. This is especially helpful if done in the morning as you begin your day—or anytime you feel brain lag.

The Spiritual Eye: Epitome of Creation

Underlying the gray matter in the brain is white matter, which is spoken of as passive. The construction of the brain has a correspondence with the single or spiritual eye* in man. In fact, this eye of astral light, which can be seen in meditation, is an epitome of the creative energy and consciousness of which man's body is formed and by which it is enlivened. Jesus said, "The light of the body is the eye: if therefore thine eye be single, thy whole body shall be full of light."† The spiritual eye is perceived as a golden aura surrounding a sphere of blue, in the middle of which is a five-pointed star of white light.

When you look in a mirror at your two eyes, you see they are patterned after the spiritual eye: the outer "aura" or white of the eye; the inner circle or iris; and the central "star" or pupil. The point of origin of the single eye is in a subtle spiritual center in the medulla oblongata (at the base of the brain, where it joins the spine).‡ The energy from this single eye divides at the medulla and pours through the brain into the two physical eyes, through which the world of duality is perceived. The spiritual eye with its three lights, or three different rays—one within the other like an extending telescopic lens—has all-seeing spherical vision. Through the gold ray,

---

* See glossary.   † *Matthew* 6:22 (Bible).   ‡ See *medulla* in glossary.

the deeply meditating yogi beholds all matter and the mass of radiation (the vibratory cosmic energy) permeating the universe. Penetrating the blue light, the yogi will realize the Christ or Krishna Consciousness—the *Kutastha* or infinite intelligence of God, the "only-begotten son" or reflection of God—which is present in all creation. Piercing the tiny five-pointed white star, the yogi experiences Cosmic Consciousness—the transcendent consciousness of God that underlies all creation and that is also beyond the realms of manifestation in Infinitude. The yogi in Cosmic Consciousness perceives that all creation, including the microcosm of his body, is a projection of the fivefold rays of God's Cosmic Consciousness.*

The Divine Creator's Cosmic Consciousness, His pure reflected intelligence in creation as Christ or Krishna Consciousness, and His active creative power as Cosmic Vibration are thus the very Essence of all manifestations.† Gold, blue, and white—the colours of the radiations of this Holy Trinity of God in creation—are therefore the most spiritual of all colours: white reflecting the transcendent God-Consciousness, blue reflecting the Christ or Krishna Consciousness, and gold (or red, a transformation of gold) reflecting the radiation or energy present in the cosmos. Throughout history, man has instinctively associated white with purity and spirituality; blue with tranquil omnipresence, as in the blue sky or heavens; and gold or red with energy.

How the Intricate Human Body Evolves From Spirit

The tricoloured rays of the spiritual eye, through a complex transformation known to yogis, form the physical body of man the microcosm. The golden rays of cosmic energy, for example, are strongly inherent in the vital red blood, and are

---

* Yoga defines the five elemental vibrations of matter as earth, water, fire, air, and ether—thoughts of God that manifest as the universe and its beings through God's intricate laws of nature. These elemental vibrations evolve from five original magnetic forces of Spirit. A discourse on this is given in *The Holy Science* by Swami Sri Yukteswar, published by Yogoda Satsanga Society of India. (See *elements* in glossary.)

† See *Trinity* in glossary.

manifested in the electric current that flows through the nerves. The blue rays are a predominant factor in the gray matter of the brain, which provides a medium for the expression of thoughts through sensory-motor activity—just as on the universal scale Christ Consciousness [*Kutastha Chaitanya*] provides the medium that upholds all of nature's activities. And the white rays are the predominant factor in the white matter of the brain, in which God's transcendent Cosmic Consciousness is insulated.

The nerve tissues are cylindrical in form. If you see a diagram of the nervous system, it is like a web of projecting rays, pathways of electrical energy without which there is no life in the body. The underlying spiritual physiology relates to the projected thoughts of God. The first manifestation of God the Creator is thought, Intelligence itself. When God began to "think" the body of man, it produced tentacles of thought—a thought is a linear projection. These became rays; the rays became fibers; and the fibers became nerves through which energy is conducted throughout the nervous system to the twenty-seven thousand billion bodily cells.

I became aware of these various corollaries as I read a little bit of physiology; God was showing me at the same time His deeper science. It is so interesting to see the marvelous evolution of complex matter from the singular consciousness of Spirit. How intricate it is, and yet so simple, when you see that everything is God. It is all upheld by the power of His thought. "On a little piece of thought rests the cosmic lot."

Colour Is Important in Your Life

In the creation of the body of man, the rays of the spiritual eye first formed the astral body, the rainbow-hued body of life energy that is the blueprint and enlivening power of the material body. Because the material body is a condensation of the multicoloured rays of light of the life-giving astral body, colour is important in your life. The point is, you are affected by colour because colours are manifestations of specific vibrations. You should always try to wear, and to surround yourself with, colours that are harmonious to your nature. And for the reasons I have mentioned, gold, blue, and white are good for the nervous system. Of course, for a change you should use other colours as well. But generally, it is good to have some of these particularly beneficial colours around you. You will find your nervous system will be much calmer. Though it is quite all right now and then, for variety, to vary the colours you use, and that you feel harmonious with, radical changes can affect you. You wouldn't want to paint the rooms in your home black, for example.*

The Best Diet for the Nerves

Even foods, which also are material condensations of astral rays of life, have effects that are correlated to their colour. Various kinds of natural white foods are good for the nervous system; they benefit the white matter of the brain. Berries are good for the gray matter of the brain—that is, blueberries or blackberries (which are really purple). Most fruits are gold in colour (or variants of gold, such as red and orange). As gold is the colour of the creative vibratory energy in matter, such fruits help the muscles, the blood, and the tissues. Goat's milk, unbleached almonds, and raisins are very good for the nervous system. But all forms of meat of higher animals, especially beef and pork, are harmful to the nervous system; they are hyperstimulating and cause aggressiveness.

Avoid too much starch, especially foods made from refined flour. Eat whole grains, cottage cheese, and plenty of fruits, fruit juices, and fresh vegetables—these are important. Needless to say, alcoholic beverages and drugs destroy the nervous system; stay away from them.

A yogic drink that is very good for the nervous system is made by adding crushed rock candy and fresh lime juice to a glass of water. It should be thoroughly mixed and evenly blended so that the taste is equally sweet and sour. I have recommended

---

* Modern science has found interesting confirmation of this ancient yogic discovery. Research at the University of Delaware by Roger Ulrich, Ph.D., showed that the predominant colours in one's environment have a measurable influence on the frequency and strength of one's brain waves. "Studies show that blues and greens have a calming influence," said Dr. Ulrich. "Oranges and reds activate or increase arousal."

this to many people with excellent results.

Another beneficial practice when you are very nervous is to take a cold bath. I once told this to a newspaperman. He said, "Well, if I did that every time I was nervous, I would have to carry a bathtub with me all the time!" I said, "Not necessary. Take a large piece of ice and rub it all over the body, especially over all the openings of the body. With this yoga technique, you will find that your nerves will become much calmer."

Attunement With God: Greatest Cure for Nervousness

Remember that the greatest healing of nervousness takes place when we attune our lives to God. The highest commandments given to man are to love God with all your heart, and with all your soul, and with all your mind, and with all your strength; and secondly, to love your neighbor as yourself.* If you follow these, everything will come in its own way, and in the right way. It is not enough just to be a strict moralist—stones and goats do not break moral laws; still, they do not know God. But when you love God deeply enough, even if you are the greatest of sinners, you will be transformed and redeemed. The great saint Mirabai† said, "To find the Divine One, the only indispensable is love." That truth touched me deeply.

All the prophets observe these two foremost commandments. Loving God with all your heart means to love Him with the love that you feel for the person who is dearest to you— with the love of the mother or father for the child, or the lover for the beloved. Give that kind of unconditional love to God. Loving God with all your soul means you can truly love Him when through deep meditation you know yourself as a soul, a child of God, made in His image. Loving God with all your mind means that when you are praying, your whole attention is on Him, not distracted by restless thoughts. In meditation, think only of God; don't let the mind wander to everything else but God. That is why yoga is important; it enables you to con-

---

* *Mark* 12:28–31 (Bible).

† A medieval Rajputani princess who renounced her royalty and became a renowned devotee of God. She composed many devotional songs that are a treasured part of India's spiritual lore.

centrate. When by yoga you withdraw the restless life force from the sense nerves and become interiorized in the thought of God, then you are loving Him with all of your strength— the whole of your being is concentrated in Him.

Live Like a God, and You Will Attract Godly Friends

Lastly, learn to love your neighbor as yourself. Remember, you are here on earth in this lifetime for just a little while. You have come here before in numerous incarnations, interacting with many different souls. Who are your real relatives? To the wise man, everyone is his relative; everyone is his "neighbor." Of course, the wise man discriminates, knowing that though the sun shines equally on the diamond and the charcoal, it is the diamond that beautifully reflects the sunlight. One should seek and associate with the highest diamondlike mentalities. Take time to find true friends. Good souls attract good souls. Live like gods, and you will attract godly friends. Live like animals on the sensual plane, and you will attract animalistic companions. Do not mix closely with those who lower your ideals and create materialistic nervousness in you; but at the same time do not exclude anyone from your love.

In addition, be not only a giver of love, but also a peacemaker, that wherever you go you bring harmony, calmness, and upliftment. No one wants to be around a skunk; everyone avoids it. The nervous man—he who is always restless, irritable, emotional—similarly repulses others. We do not want to be human skunks. We want to be like the rose, which even if crushed exudes its sweet fragrance. Be a human rose, spreading the essence of peace wherever you go.

Kriya Yoga Gives the True Experience of Religion

Your life will reflect spiritual consciousness if you meditate. Since the publication of my book [Autobiography of a Yogi], everyone is asking about Kriya Yoga. That is my purpose. I didn't come to give theological abstractions, but a technique whereby those who are sincere can truly know God, not just theorize about Him. I want you all to develop on this path of Self-Realization [Yogoda Satsanga]; and draw others to this highway of *Kriya Yoga*. The practice of *Kriya* gives the true experience of religion, which cannot be had by just talking about God. Jesus said: "Why call ye me, Lord, Lord, and do not the things which I say?"*

When by *Kriya Yoga* I open my spiritual eye, the whole world drops away from my consciousness, and God is with me. And why not? I am His child. St. Ignatius said, "God seeks willing hearts that He may give His bounties to them...."† That is most beautiful, and that is what I believe. God seeks willing hearts for the bestowal of His gifts. He is willing to give us everything, but we are not willing to make the effort to be receptive. He looks in our hearts, and if they are filled with something else, He does not come. But when you can truthfully say to Him, "Lord, there is nothing in my heart but Thee," He will come. For a while He will play hide-and-seek with you; but if you are persistent, you will begin to see wonderful things happening, mysteriously, that you know come from God. In time, you will receive His clear response in the form of direct answers to your prayers, or in visions of the saints. Then at last He will come to you openly. You will be able to talk to Him; you will be able to commune with Him. Nervousness will never again be able to touch you once you are permanently anchored in the realization of God's Presence.

---

* *Luke* 6:46 (Bible).

† Paraphrased from *Colossians* 3:23–24 (Bible).

What Is Truth?

*First Self-Realization Fellowship Temple at
Encinitas, California, February 13, 1938*

Truth is a very ambiguous word; it is a difficult concept to explain. Everyone has convictions they swear to as truth. But among countless differing ideas, what is really true?

Truth is relative, and truth is absolute. It passes through many evolutions in the relative stages before it reaches the absolute state. For example, two people are discussing a business venture. One makes a proposal that is sure to bring success, and the other person makes a counterproposal that accomplishes the same goal but has additional advantages. But then a third person comes along and has an even better idea. Each method was "true" in its own right, but in a relative sense.

Truth Is That Which Gives Permanent Happiness

In the absolute sense, anything that contradicts true happiness is untruth; and that which gives permanent happiness is truth. Permanent happiness refers not to the temporary thrill that comes with material success and pleasure, but to the joy found in the soul's attunement with God. By this standard, you can judge any action you perform as to its projected end result— whether or not that action will promote lasting happiness.

The ultimate Truth is God; and God is the ultimate Truth. The universe is upheld by this Truth through the operation of the Lord's cosmic laws. These laws are basic truths that are eternal and not subject to man's manipulation. For instance, the absolute truth is that since God is templed in every creature, it is wrong to kill or to harm another. In the relative sense, however, the lesser of two evils may be to use force to protect the innocent from an evil person, or to kill a lower form of life to save a higher form of life. But to destroy anything just for the sake of killing is wrong. The universal law is unity through love, necessitating the practice of tolerance and amity. If you want to find truth, your thoughts and actions must be true—physically, morally, and spiritually in accord with the eternal divine principles.

Truth is the ultimate Substance. Let me first explain where the presence of that Substance is to be found. Everything is linked with Cosmic Intelligence—the tree, the sky, a bird, man. That link is called Substance, the essential nature of all phenomena. It is the connecting link that makes of all manifestations one Essence. This Substance or Truth is hidden; what you see are only phenomenal appearances arising out of Substance by the power of cosmic delusion, or *maya*.

The Three Ways of Arriving at Truth

Now, there are three ways of arriving at truth: through sense perception, through inference, and through intuition.

If your sense perception is wrong, your inference is wrong. Looking at the horizon you may think there is a fire, because you see smoke; but as you approach the site, you find it was just a cloud of dust. In order to apprehend the truth of anything, you depend on your sight, hearing, smell, taste, or touch, plus the power of the mind. These, however, could not be ultimate proof of the truth; because if the senses lie, the mind will lie. Your mind draws its conclusions from what the senses perceive, and the senses are extremely limited. Jesus therefore conveyed truth to the masses in parables "because they seeing see not; and hearing they hear not, neither do they understand."*

The ears are tuned only to certain rates of vibration. The highest and lowest sounds your ears cannot catch. If the power of your hearing were sufficiently increased, you would hear the magnificent sound that the universe is making as it rolls along through space. Everything is in motion and that motion is accompanied by sound. Nothing is at rest, except in that transcendental sphere of Spirit where there is no vibration. Right within your body you can hear those vibratory sounds of creation, manifestations of the omnipresent *Aum* or Amen. But being of a higher rate of vibration, those finer sounds are audible

---

* *Matthew* 13:13 (Bible).

only to your astral ear—the subtle power that provides the gross sense of hearing to your physical body.

Similarly, if the power of your eyes were increased, you would see all kinds of different lights. Your physical eyes show you only a very limited scope of light, but your spiritual (astral) eye sees the true nature of all things as images composed of God's creative light. Your whole body, which you perceive as solid flesh, is nothing but electromagnetic waves. Dr. Crile has shown that the brain of a dead calf, and also that of a dead human being, emanates a great amount of electric rays.* Ordinarily, when you close your eyes, you see only darkness; but with spiritual development, you will see wondrous lights. The Bible says: "The light shineth in darkness; and the darkness comprehended it not."† These are fundamental truths that you do not perceive because your senses are all tuned only to a limited range of certain gross vibrations.

Intuition: All-Knowing Power of the Soul

So how are you going to find the truth, the reality that lies behind what the senses perceive? You cannot do it by your rationalizing mind, because your mind falls victim to the senses; it only infers about what the senses tell it. The mind therefore does not comprehend the infinite forces that are dancing all around. Only by the development of intuition can you know what is truth. Intuition is direct perception. It is the all-knowing pure comprehension of the soul.

You have an inkling of the nature of intuition through those unexplained feelings called hunches. A hunch is undeveloped intuition, something you know without the medium of the senses or inference, some truth that comes of itself. You may be sitting quietly, and for no reason you think of someone you

---

* Dr. George Washington Crile (1864–1943) was an army surgeon who devoted his career to discovering a better understanding of the phenomena of life. Unsatisfied by the conventional explanations then to be found in physiology and biochemistry, he established the Cleveland Clinic Foundation, where for twenty-two years he conducted biophysical research that led him to formulate in 1936 his "radio-electric" theory of the life processes.

† *John* 1:5 (Bible).

haven't seen or had contact with for a long time; and then suddenly he arrives, or you hear from him. Now, how did you
know? It was through a momentary flash of intuition. That
kind of spontaneous intuition all of you have had at some time.

Errors in judgment are a result of not having developed
intuition. Most of you have had the feeling that you could be
great, and do great things; but because you have lacked intuitive power, that potential has, for the most part, remained dormant. To progress and to avoid the misery of mistakes, you
have to find what is the truth in everything. This is possible
only if you develop your intuition. That is the practical truth
of the matter. That is why I am asking you to cultivate and
use intuitive power in everything. In your relationships with
others, in your business, in your married life, in every part of
your life, intuition is essential.

By not developing the faculty of intuition, you make wrong
decisions, pick up the wrong business associates, and get caught
up in wrong personal relationships. Since the judgment of your
mind is conditioned by the information fed to it by the senses, if
your senses become deluded you may think a person is wonderful without knowing what he truly is inside. You may think you
have found your soul mate, so you enter into matrimony; and
then end up in the divorce court. But intuition will never make
such a mistake. It will not look at the magnetic power of the eyes
or at the attractive face or personality of a person, but will feel
and perceive accurately in the heart what that person is really
like.

By the power of intuition, which I learned to develop from
my guru, Sri Yukteswarji, I have never made a mistake about
human nature. Intuition has been very helpful to me in that
regard. But I do not try to see the wrong side of people; to help
others I give them unconditional love, even when I know they
may misuse my trust.

Many people, lacking intuition, put a lot of money into
financial prospects that do not produce anything, and consequently they lose everything. I have been successful in every
decision I have made through intuitive power. It never fails.

As you develop, intuition comes as a certain feeling or a
still voice. Because ladies are more receptive to feeling than are

men, they usually have more intuition—except when they become emotional. Men are generally ruled more by reason than by feeling; but if they have fine intelligence balanced with feeling, that leads to intuition.

Through Intuition, Know the Purpose of Your Existence

If you use your intuition, you will know the very purpose for which you exist in this world; and when you find that, you find happiness. This earth is a stage, and God is the Stage Manager. If everyone insisted on being kings and queens, an unfolding drama would be impossible. The servant and the hero as well as the royalty must perform their parts well for the play to become successful. The villains are those who upset the righteous drama of the Lord. Those who choose such a role must pay dearly for their blundering disregard of divine direction. No matter what material position one possesses or fortune one has amassed, he cannot be called successful if it was gained by evil means. True happiness is possible only if one plays his part *rightly*, and not otherwise. The one who is playing the millionaire, and the one who is playing the role of a small businessman—both are the same to God. On the last day, God shears every person of all possessions and titles. What you have acquired in your soul is all that you take with you.

Great ones like Jesus know truth because of their intuitive power. They perceive not only through the eyes and the mind, but through intuition that is so developed that they know everything. Jesus, who lived such a pure life, knew he would nevertheless be betrayed and crucified. But he knew also he would be ultimately in the arms of immortal God. So are we all the children of God, sent here to play our part; it is not the part, but how we play it, that concerns God. Never be discouraged when your role is difficult. When you will be through with your acting, you will be received as a child of God. Until then, you will not be wholly free.

Intuition Develops Through Meditation

The only way to know and to live in truth is to develop the power of intuition. Then you will see that life has a meaning, and that no matter what you are doing the inner voice is guiding you. That voice has long been drowned in the mire of untrue thoughts. The surest way to liberate the expression of intuition is by meditation, early in the morning and before going to bed at night. As you keep your engagements for business, and for everything else that you think of as important, so should you not forget your engagement with God. You may think you are too busy, but suppose God were too busy to give you life? You would drop in your tracks! To keep your daily appointment with God you must reserve the time for Him. Meditate and pray deeply; and wait for His response. If you repeatedly call on Him with ever deeper concentration, He will answer your prayer. A joy and peace will strike your heart. When that comes, you know that you are communing with God. If you make the effort, you shall contact that Power. Give yourself that opportunity. You cannot succeed unless you try.

If you spend your life in constant excitement, you will never know true happiness. Live simply and take life more easily. Happiness lies in giving yourself time to think and to introspect. Be alone once in a while, and remain more in silence. If the radio is going all the time, or other stimuli are constantly bombarding the senses, it truly affects the nerves and creates nervousness.

And don't think so much about reforming others; reform yourself first. The greatest field of victory is your own home. If you are an angel at home, you can be an angel everywhere. The sweetness of your voice, the peace of your behavior, is needed in your own household more than anywhere else.

Attain the Power That Never Fails

When you contact God, intuitive perception of truth will guide you in everything you do. Seven years ago I came in a housecar to this site overlooking the ocean [Encinitas] and said, "I feel there will be a great place here one day." And today we have here our temple and hermitage—the nucleus of an ideal center for God.

The purpose of this center is that it be a place where you can come to contact God, to experience God. Why not consciously attain that Power which never fails you? Realize that Power within yourself. Make it a habit to come here regularly.

I don't want curiosity seekers. I am keeping my engagement with God, and I seek only those true devotees of God who will come here in these beautiful surroundings to recharge themselves in His power.

You will find that Power works in everything to make your life complete, your health vibrant with cosmic energy, and your mind keen with the focused clarity of concentration. You will realize that your soul is a receptacle of God's unfailing, ever-guiding truth and wisdom.

God is the Fountain of health, prosperity, wisdom, and eternal joy. We make our life complete by contact with God. Without Him, life is not complete. Give your attention to the Almighty Power that is giving you life and strength and wisdom. Pray that unceasing truth flow into your mind, unceasing strength flow into your body, and unceasing joy flow into your soul. Right behind the darkness of closed eyes are the wondrous forces of the universe, and all the great saints; and the endlessness of the Infinite. Meditate, and you will realize the omnipresent Absolute Truth and see Its mysterious workings in your life and in all the glories of creation. "O Arjuna, understand that knowledge to be sattvic (pure truth) by which the one indestructible Spirit is perceived in all beings, undivided in the divided."*

---

* Bhagavad Gita XVIII:20.

The Omnipresent Consciousness of Christ and Krishna

First Self-Realization Fellowship Temple at
Encinitas, California, December 18, 1939

With the coming of Christmas and the New Year, resolve to follow a new mode of life. Seek communion with the Lord every day. The best way to find God is through technique. There is a method to everything we study, and religion is just as much a scientific discipline as are medicine and mathematics. So also is yoga ("union" with God) a science of spiritual techniques. India's divine teachings were sent here by God-realized masters in communion with the great saints and Christ. On the universal path of Self-Realization [Yogoda Satsanga] there is no reason and no room for prejudice and division, for through one's own Self-realization we come to know that there is but one God and that we are all His children.

The war that is coming will more and more testify to the folly of man. Let us pray that all nations cease from useless and senseless war and work instead to pave the way for a United World. You can save America only by being spiritual, and save yourself above all by meditation. Once in a while you must get away from the world and meditate. Make use of your time to seek God. I am telling you today of the omnipresent Christ or Krishna Consciousness through which He may be found.

An ordinary man is conscious chiefly of sensory impressions. He sees through his eyes and hears through his ears and gradually he expands his mind by reasoning about the reports of the senses. Man has great mental powers, if he would develop them. Although he is tied to his body, by his intelligence he can stretch his imagination to the heavens. He can discover that the light of a star which has been dead millions of years is still traveling to reach the earth.

But no matter how he develops mentally, man is still subject to the limitations of his physical body. If a stone hits him, he is finished. Jesus proved by spiritual development a great scientific truth: the body is indestructible energy. It is not the physical solid that it seems.*

By modern definition the physical vehicle of man is essentially an electromagnetic wave. If the body of a 180-pound man were placed in certain acids, it would dissolve completely. Where would it have gone? Seemingly evaporated, that body would have become a mass of gases. Its total atomic weight would still be 180 pounds. The only difference, when a body has been broken up into its component atoms, is that you cannot see it anymore with the physical eyes; only scientific instruments can detect its presence as atomic vapors. The disappearance of the body does not mean that it has become nonexistent; it has merely changed form, remaining hidden somewhere in the ether.

Metaphysically, the body may be viewed as a thought in the mind of God. It exists in His consciousness in much the same way that it exists in our consciousness when we behold it during the dream state. Our dreaming consciousness creates a body form out of concentrated thought and energy. It vanishes when our consciousness reenters the turbulent waking state.

Jesus had attained that consciousness wherein he knew by direct realization that the body is only a mass of energy. Because he had realized this, and not merely imagined it, he was able to resurrect his body after its crucifixion. Earlier, when one of his followers had cut off the ear of a servant of the high priest, Jesus put his hand on the wound and made the ear whole again.† Modern science has yet to discover how this is done. The ultimate goal is to realize that the body, and all else in this universe, is essentially Spirit. The ordinary man is not aware of this. Jesus the Christ was.

One needs to understand Jesus in the light of his spiritual experience of the Cosmic Consciousness of the Heavenly Father present in all creation. His name was Jesus; his title was "Christ"— an ancient term that corresponds to the Sanskrit *kutastha* ("the

---

* A truth also demonstrated throughout the ages by great yogis of India.

† "And Jesus answered and said, Suffer ye thus far. And he touched his ear, and healed him" (*Luke* 22:51, Bible).

consciousness that is in every atom"). He was Jesus the Christ.

More than three thousand years ago, before the time of Jesus, there was born in India a great avatar whose family name was Jadava. "Krishna" (or "Christ-na") was his spiritual title, and it means the same as "Christ": the divine consciousness that is omnipresent in creation. He was Jadava the Krishna.*

The scriptures tell of the wonderful powers of Christ and Krishna, showing that their consciousness was not tied to the body like the ordinary man's. Jesus and Jadava had expanded their consciousness beyond the confines of the fleshly human form to include the universe—their cosmic body. They were attuned to the divine consciousness that is simultaneously present in every atom. It was not imagination; they had become one in consciousness with the Heavenly Father who is omnipresent and omniscient. That expansion of consciousness which Jesus and Jadava experienced had to be learned. All men can similarly expand their consciousness to infinity, through devotion and scientific meditation on the Lord. "God is a Spirit: and they that worship Him must worship Him in spirit."†

So "Jesus Christ" means "Jesus whose consciousness fills the entire universe." When his friend Lazarus died in Bethany, and Jesus, in another place, said to his disciples, "Lazarus sleepeth,"‡ he didn't know this through any human informant. It was the universal Christ Consciousness manifesting in him that enabled him to feel himself present not only in his own body but in the body of Lazarus. He referred to this omnipresent Intelligence when he said: "Are not two sparrows sold for a farthing? and one of them shall not fall on the ground without [the sight of] your Father."§

If you close your eyes and ask ten people to touch you, you know exactly when and where each touch falls. God similarly feels and sees everywhere in His great cosmos. Jesus Christ and Jadava Krishna had attained that omnipresent consciousness. Jesus therefore realized that his body was a creation of God's mind and, being in tune with that Cosmic Consciousness,

---

* Reverentially referred to as Bhagavan ("Lord") Krishna.

† *John* 4:24 (Bible).   ‡*John* 11:11 (Bible).   § *Matthew* 10:29 (Bible).

was able to re-create his body three days after it had been crucified and laid away in a tomb. Krishna had the same power and performed many similar spiritual feats. On one occasion he held a mountain aloft over the village where he was. Many such miracles are thought to be merely legends, but most of them are true. Krishna was one of the greatest yogis of India. Yoga teaches that body control by which you can understand that the flesh is simply condensed energy. And what is energy but the product of God's thought? He concentrated, or thought, and there was energy.

The Universe Consists of Materialized Thoughts

Suppose I dream that I have created man and water and earth and when I wake up I find that I have not created anything except ideas. Similarly, the difference between solids, liquids, and gases is only a difference in God's thought. Jesus understood this, and because he was attuned to the divine consciousness, he could walk on water and change water into wine. He beheld the body and the water as projected thoughts of God and realized that it was a simple matter for one thought (the water) to uphold another thought (his body).

If you fall asleep and dream, you might see yourself walking on the water as Jesus did. Why doesn't the body in the dream drown in the dream ocean? Because both are merely thoughts. So once you realize, as Jesus did, that there is essentially nothing in the universe but mind or consciousness, you can do anything. The body is a materialized thought and the ocean is a materialized thought and you can put one thought on another.

Jesus and Krishna can appear to you in response to the call of your heartfelt devotion. The invisible will become visible, just as steam vapor can by a process of condensation be frozen into a solid piece of ice. The intangible God can be similarly "frozen" by your devotion into the visible form of Krishna or Jesus or any saint whom you yearn to behold.

It is not necessary to see Christ in form when you meditate on him, though he can be seen in form. My theme today is the spiritual Christ. In order to know that Jesus you must know his spirit. His body was like any other man's but his spirit was in the whole universe. If you can't imagine this, close your eyes for a moment. You do not see your body anymore. Yet in your mind you can travel millions of miles in any direction without the use of your body. Mind is the creator of everything. When you know the nature of the mind, you have control of everything, for all is mind. These beautiful buildings and grounds sprang from thought. Nothing exists but that it came out of the Cosmic Mind. Therefore remember Christ as the universal consciousness that beholds us from the stars, that is aware of even the tiniest grain of sand on the shore. I hear His song in the bird and in the voice of the wind; I see His beauteous form in the sky and in the mountains and the ocean. Every thought I think comes from the consciousness of Christ.

During each cosmic cycle of creation, Spirit divides Itself into the Trinity. In the role of the Father, Spirit is the Creator of the universe. As He thought, there came into being the electrons and atoms, and they began to condense into vapor, and the vapor into water, and the water into solids. Thus Spirit projected out of Itself the cosmic creation. This is His form, His body.

The Intelligence throughout the cosmos is called Christ Intelligence or *Kutastha Chaitanya.* This is the "only begotten Son,"* or reflection of the Father's Intelligence present in all creation. Jesus and Krishna were in tune with that Consciousness.

Correspondence of the Trinity in Hindu and Christian Scriptures

The Holy Trinity of the Christian scriptures, Father, Son, and Holy Ghost, corresponds with the Trinity of the Hindu scriptures: *Aum, Tat, Sat.* God the Father is *Sat,* Spirit beyond all creation. The Son is *Tat,* the *Kutastha Chaitanya* or Christ Intelligence present in all creation. The Holy Ghost is *Aum,* or Amen, the Word or Cosmic Vibration that structures creation.

When at the end of a creative cycle God dissolves everything within Himself, there is only one principle, Spirit: everexisting, ever-conscious, ever-new Bliss. But in each new creative cycle Spirit again projects Itself as the Trinity—Father, Son, and Holy Ghost.†

Man is an epitome of the whole creation. The material uni-

---

* *John* 1:18 (Bible).   † See *Trinity* in glossary.

verse is the vast body of God, the cosmic electrical energy is the astral form of God, and the soul or life in everything is the essence of God. Everything has life; even a stone can feel pain. The consciousness in a piece of tin can be deadened with chloroform. These seemingly inanimate objects feel pleasure and pain, and the life in them can be killed.*

Expand Your Consciousness and Know the Real Christ

To find the real Christ you must expand your consciousness as Jesus did. When you learn to feel for others as you do for yourself, you grow spiritually. When you share with all families the same kindred spirit that you feel with the family in which you were born, you are growing. When you are proud of all nations as you are of your own country, you are growing. And when you are ready to sacrifice self-love for the greater love of all mankind, then you have grown. That is what God wants you to do. Every nation that goes against the principle of love for mankind will suffer terribly. The Father is trying to establish oneness in the universe and that can come only through love for all. We must grow spiritually. We must love all nations as our own.

I feel you all as my own. I would do as much for you all as I would do for India. And if it were necessary for me to go to war for you, in a righteous war, I would do it. You should banish all prejudice from your mind. Remember, God has taken the form of every race and nationality. He is in the Negro and the Hindu and the Jews and all others. Real Christianity means that you become Christlike, loving all impartially.

Let this coming Christmas be your greatest. Make it a religious Christmas. That is what we do. Self-Realization Fellowship [Yogoda Satsanga Society of India] members around the world observe the 24th of December† as a day of meditation, of communing with the Christ. Get away from everyone else and pray with all your soul. See what happens to you when you go deep and meditate long. That is the way to worship Jesus in spirit.

---

* These truths were conclusively demonstrated by the great Indian scientist, Jagadis Chandra Bose, as described in *Autobiography of a Yogi*, chapter 8.

† Or any of the several days preceding Christmas Day.

The physical way of practicing what Christ taught is to behave toward all as the children of your own Father, and the spiritual way is to meditate until you feel the vast joy of God through the Christ Consciousness. Universal brotherhood will not come until, by deepest concentration and devotion, you stand aside from all your restless thoughts and feelings and sit in the temple of your soul, wherein the vast joy of God expands and engulfs this world, and you realize there is naught else but That. Then you will say: "I am one with the eternal light of God, the eternal joy of Christ. All the waves of creation are tumbling within me. I have dissolved my body-wave in the ocean of Spirit. I am the ocean of Spirit. No longer am I the body. My spirit is sleeping in the stones. I am dreaming in the flowers, and I am singing in the birds. I am thinking in man, and in the superman I know that *I am*." In this state you realize that fire cannot destroy you; that earth and grass and sky are all your blood relations. Then like a spirit you walk on earth, no more afraid of the tumultuous waves of creation.

This is my message to you: Meditate every night until you can banish all your mundane thoughts and desires. "Know ye not that ye are the temple of God, and that the Spirit of God dwelleth in you?"* God made you all blessed, created in His image. You have forgotten that, and have identified yourself with your body. But Jesus came to tell mankind: "Don't be afraid of the frailty of your body. Rise above it by meditation and be one with the Spirit."

My greatest wish for you is this: may the love and perception of Christ come within your consciousness. He waits to receive but one Christmas present—the gift of your love. Tie it with golden strings of your devotion and on Christmas Day you will find Christ himself has come to receive it from you. Once he accepts your love, he gives himself unto you. That gift shall be everlasting. And if you receive him as the Christ Consciousness, even when all the gifts of this earth are gone, you shall be immortal, safe in the bosom of Christ and Krishna.

[After a brief meditation, Paramahansaji led the congregation in

---

* I *Corinthians* 3:16 (Bible).

the following prayer:]

"I will adorn the tree of life with the stars of my good thoughts, and I shall lay at Christ's feet my best gift of love tied with golden threads of devotion. May Christ receive it, and may I receive His love this Christmastide. I will try my utmost to make myself ready, that Christ may be born within my consciousness. During this Christmas and in the New Year I make a solemn resolution to change my life that it may become more Christlike. I will try to rise above all prejudices and love the people of all nations as Christ and Krishna loved them, as children of God.

"Heavenly Father, bless my life. Bless all nations. May they desist from war and come together in a United World, with Truth guiding us.

"Heavenly Father, Jesus Christ, Jadava Krishna, Mahavatar Babaji, Lahiri Mahasaya, Swami Sri Yukteswarji, Guru-Preceptor, we surrender our bodies, minds, and souls unto Thee. Make us like Christ. *Aum.* Peace. Amen."

Spiritual Selfishness
Versus Evil Selfishness

Self-Realization Fellowship Hermitage,
Encinitas, California, June 15, 1937

The soul is the true Self, the pure manifestation of Spirit within you. The ego is the pseudo-self, the soul responding to the world of duality while in a state of identification with the limited instruments of the physical body and mind. For the purpose of discussion, let us say that anything you do for the benefit of your self, either as the soul or the ego, may be called selfishness. In this usage, evil selfishness is that which you think you are doing for the good of yourself, but which goes against the interest of your true Self. Good selfishness, spiritual selfishness, consists of those actions by which the pure Self within you can be realized; it helps you continuously to manifest the perfection of that innate image of Spirit.

Selfishness is characterized by different gradations. The actions of a child are performed more or less unthinkingly. When he sees somebody else playing with different toys, he wants to possess them. He wants to eat this thing or to do that thing because he sees someone else enjoying it. This is unconscious selfishness. I watched this reaction in my own childhood. When I was very little and saw others playing with something, my first thought was to possess it. But soon I found that whenever I wanted something, there was always somebody else trying to get it or hold on to it. So I began to exert my strong will to possess what I wanted. But when this brought about fights with others, I wondered if it was right to assume such an attitude.

My mother used to say, when giving some special treat of food to me, "Share this with somebody else." Initially, my reaction was that she was trying to give me less. But immediately I began to picture in my mind, "Well, if I like this food so much, maybe somebody else would also like it." So I decided I should share. Then came the thought, "If I share with everybody, there will be nothing at all left for me." That began to puzzle me. But my experience was that if I shared with others, then I enjoyed more—the joy received from sharing was even greater than the joy I got from the thing I had shared. That is why I have always parted with whatever I have loved. Whenever some possession was wanted or needed by somebody else, my mind would say, "Well, he is 'sick' with this desire; you were healed of your wish for it, so now let him have that benefit." One by one I gave away everything that came to me— and my joy was multiplied. When I wanted something and got it, I enjoyed; and when I gave it to somebody else, I enjoyed it again. No desire has ever been permitted to take possession of my soul; that would be contrary to the ideal of spiritual selfishness for the welfare of my true Self. Never love anything so much that it possesses you.

The Idea of Possession Is a False Notion

Whatever you give out, you will attract in kind. What you are will show in your countenance and actions, and others will feel the underlying vibration and respond accordingly. If you set an example of evil selfishness, others will want to take everything from you. But if you are the opposite, you will find everybody inclined to be generous toward you. Suppose you give me your favorite walking stick, and in return I want to give you something. But my mind says, "You can't part with your umbrella, even though you know he has admired it." Then I reason, "He loved his stick, yet he gave it to me; so I wish to give him something I value." That is the spirit which predominates when a person shows unselfishness.

You cannot own anything. You are only given temporary use of things on this earth. Sometime you will have to part with them—either by accident or theft or deterioration or death. So when you try to hold on to or save anything just for the sake of possessing, you are fooling yourself.

Even this bodily house that you have lived in for so many years must one day be relinquished. So it is wrong to impose on the soul a conviction that you own something you cannot ever own. When something is given to you, know that it is yours only for a little while, and be willing to share it with others.

Great trouble lies in coveting more than you need. The Gita says: "That person realizes peace who, relinquishing all desires, exists without craving and is unidentified with the mortal ego and its sense of 'mine-ness.'"* No doubt you must have necessary necessities such as food, clothing, and some material security; but in aspiring after these, omit unnecessary "necessities"—the nagging desires that crave more and more.

The World Family Is Your Greater Self

Always have in your mind the ideal that while you are laboring for your own needs you will help others acquire what they need, and will share with those less fortunate what you receive. Remember that you are a part of the world family, and you cannot exist without it. What would life be like without the carpenter or inventor or farmer? Through interchange God wants us to think of others. It is a grave error to live only for oneself.

Whenever you think of your own happiness, think also of giving happiness to others. You are not asked to give away everything for the welfare of your world family. That is impossible. But you should have consideration for others even as you have for yourself.

God intended that man should thereby be truly spiritually selfish, serving his greater Self in others. But the first, and often the last, thought of the ordinary man is for himself. Self-preservation is a strong instinct. The world creates in us that delusion of self-preservation by which we limit ourselves to our own bodies and those things we consider our own. However, everybody is our own; for God is our Father, and we are all His children.

God gave man intelligence and imagination that he might remember when he is cold or hungry that there are others around him who also know what it is to be cold or hungry. So in seeking your own comfort, reach out to provide comfort for

---

* Bhagavad Gita II:71.

others also. Since you yourself do not like misery, you should assist those around you in order to allay their misery. They suffer just like you—and some even more so. If you say about your family and close friends, "Well, these people are mine, and I include in my happiness only them and no more," then you limit yourself and your misery starts to increase.

Keep yourself ready to help others, and find happiness in giving happiness to whoever crosses your path. Do not think of it as having to practice unselfishness. That makes it seem something hard to do. Rather, feel that what you are doing is for your own pleasure—the joy you find in removing the unhappiness of others, physically, mentally, or spiritually.

Without Evil Selfishness the World Would Be Heaven

The whole world would be heaven today if it had given up evil selfishness and followed spiritual selfishness. In the error of evil selfishness lies the cause of all wars. First came stone clubs and then bows and arrows to protect one's own selfishness against the selfishness of others. Then guns were invented, then machine guns, and now bombs and poisonous gases—all to protect the selfishness of one group of people against the selfishness of another group. Man's potential destructive power has grown much more than his constructive power. The boil of evil selfishness must eventually come to a head. But more bodies will have to be broken before man comes to the realization that national selfishness is just as evil as personal selfishness. A nation is built of small communities, and they are built of individuals. The right ideals must begin with the individuals; and you must begin with yourself.

See what happened because of evil selfishness: wars in Spain and China, and the Depression. This country [America] first had national selfishness in which for years she enjoyed prosperity. Similarly, India in her golden age was extremely prosperous. But the karmic consequences of selfishness and pride, resulting in the misuse of the caste system, caused India to lose her freedom.* America must not abuse her freedom nor forget

---

* Reference to the long period of foreign domination that ended ten years after this talk was given, when India gained her independence in 1947.

her spiritual ideals of equality or she could suffer a similar karmic fate. Prejudice based on race and skin color is one of the worst forms of selfishness. Climatic conditions will change, so that in the distant future much of the Western populace could well become dark-skinned, and those of the East become the "white race."

The boundaries and governments of the world are everlastingly subject to change. This country, for example, belonged to the native Indians before you claimed it; and in the ages to come, many, many others will yet hold title to it. Great Britain was once ruled by Rome. Genghis Khan conquered most of Asia; but where is he now? This is the paradox of the earthly drama. It is God's creation and we own nothing in it! What a great error it is to propagate misery through the evil selfishness of a false sense of possessiveness.

Selfishness that seeks happiness with no consideration for the happiness of others, or that tramples on and destroys the rightful interests of others for its own ends, proliferates unhappiness. That is what is happening in America today. Everybody had good jobs and there was plenty. But now the big industries are taking prosperity from the little ones and the little ones are trying to undercut the big ones. Profiteering is a great mistake. Communism, which on the surface expounds the good of the masses, will not work because it is based on suppression and force. But what Jesus and all truly great ones teach is unselfishness based on spiritual willingness to share. That method avoids evil individual selfishness in business and communities. When your neighbors and your nation will be your own self, then you will have spiritual selfishness.

If you look only to the welfare of the hands and feet and do not look after your head, your brain will not work to guide your motor skills. You must harmonize the working of the entire body. Similarly, the brains (executives) of the nations must work harmoniously with the hands and feet (labor). When they are divided in their interests, there is bound to be disorder and suffering.

You do not want labor to take control, for then you will have communism; and you do not want the capitalists to have sole rule, for then you will have dictatorship. There must be a balance, and that equilibrium will never be perfect without individual unselfishness.

The Joy in Being Unselfish

Jesus Christ gave up his body for all, but he is enjoying eternal life. In being unselfish he was looking after his spiritual selfishness. You also must be able to give up your evil selfishness for a higher selfishness. Use your imagination! Materially you will not lose anything, mentally you will not lose anything; but by evil selfishness you will lose everything.

In this world there are two teachers. If you take God as your mentor, you will have a wonderful time; but if you choose the devil as your guide, you will have bullets of misery. The key word for most people as they go through life is "myself." The spiritual man, on the other hand, thinks equally of others. Those who think only of themselves attract enmity from their associates. But those who are thoughtful find others wanting to be thoughtful of them. If there are one hundred people in a town and each one is trying to take from the other, each one has ninety-nine enemies. But if each one is trying to help the other, each one has ninety-nine friends.

I have lived that way. I haven't lost anything by giving up everything. I have gained. The words of Jesus are wonderful: "Everyone that hath forsaken all for my name's sake shall receive a hundredfold, and shall inherit everlasting life."* No matter what I have given up, much more has been given to me. I want nothing now, because what I have is far greater than anything the world can give to me. Everything man wants is for the purpose of acquiring happiness; so when you have true happiness with you all the time, you do not want or need the conditions of happiness.

As regards material things, I have no bank account of my own. My security in this world lies in the goodwill of men. I do not believe in any other earthly security. If one is enthroned in the hearts of his fellow beings, that is the greatest kingship.

By being unselfish, wholly unattached, you will be truly happy. If you set that example, others in your family or neigh-

---

* Paraphrased from *Matthew* 19:29 (Bible).

borhood or business will follow you. Start with that spiritual selfishness in your life; do away with evil selfishness, which is the root cause of all trouble, whether individual or national.

Unselfishness Expands the Consciousness

As soon as you think kindly of somebody else, your consciousness has expanded. When you think of your neighbor, a part of your being goes forth with that thought. And it is not only thinking that is necessary, but being prepared to act on that thought. Even if you have an enemy, he is your neighbor. Do not exclude anyone's happiness from the vision of your mind.

In marriage is a lesson in unselfishness. Two individuals learn to share with each other. Then children come and the parents share with them. But it again becomes selfish if they think only of their own little family: "Us four and no more." In time, loved ones will be taken away; it is a reminder that the purpose of human relationships is to stretch the consciousness by sacrificing for others and sharing with others.

There is so much happiness in being unselfish. It is the greatest happiness, for in unselfishness you guard your own happiness. My goal is the happiness of others for the happiness of myself. You can never know the joy of that achievement unless by unselfishness you include others when you think of your own happiness—not only those who are related to you, but all.

Look at Gandhi. He had money, position; but he gave up everything. And his wife followed him, not even demanding a few bonds for the security of herself and her sons. They gave up all and lived for others; having nothing, they have everything. Gandhi has set a supreme example of humility and unselfishness in this age.

Jesus said: "Whosoever shall exalt himself shall be abased."* Egotism and selfishness must be destroyed out and out. These two kindred evils have driven from the earth the kingdom of God. The world got away from spiritual selfishness, which takes care of the entire man properly, and fell victim to evil selfishness. But you can help to reestablish that divine kingdom again, pro-

---

* *Matthew* 23:12 (Bible).

vided you make the effort. Every one of you, start by applying the rule of selflessness. Live it. Don't be afraid for yourself. Suffer a little if it is necessary; but don't give up that ideal of unselfishness. Live for others; don't think first of yourself. Show the example by giving to others. This doesn't mean that you are to reduce yourself to poverty; it means to be caring and sharing.

Serve Others With Truth Through Your Example

Live the principles of truth in your life; and by your example and deeds share those ideals. You cannot teach unselfishness to others unless you yourself are unselfish. Start it yourself, then others will follow suit.

I have given my life to serving others with truth. I used to travel and speak before huge audiences. But I know I can better serve all through my writings. Crowds can be drawn, but they do not necessarily come to find God; rather, they come for a period of spiritual relaxation and inspiration. I am seeking souls who have a real desire for God. That is why I have always emphasized the necessity of communing with God. This is of the utmost importance. All those on this path of Self-Realization who will seek God in earnestness, with serious attention and continuity of devotion, and with steadiness of meditation, will find Him. Meditate. Meditate and meditate! That is your watchword. God drown Self-Realization if ever it becomes an organization that is only eager to fill halls and draw crowds of people without having, foremost, the desire to give them Self-realization. I have done all this organizational work because it was the wish of the Masters.* I am not personally seeking anything from anybody. When I leave this earth and this body, nothing will belong to me. Therefore, I have mentally and materially renounced everything now for God. All I want from you is that you live the life of God.

---

* In his *Autobiography of a Yogi,* Paramahansa Yogananda wrote: "The founding in the West of a Self-Realization Fellowship organization, a 'hive for the spiritual honey,' was a duty enjoined on me by Sri Yukteswar and Mahavatar Babaji." In chapters 27 and 36 of that book, he recounts the events that led up to the establishment of Yogoda Satsanga Society of India/Self-Realization Fellowship. (See also *Gurus* in glossary.)

Learn to love God with all your heart, mind, soul, and strength; and to love your neighbor as yourself. You do not need any other commandments if you follow those two. What is the meaning of loving God with all your heart, and with all your mind, soul, and strength? Heart means what you feel; mind means concentration; soul means divine communion in meditation; and strength means to place all your energy on God. Therefore, love God with all your feeling and with all your concentration in meditation, reversing the searchlights of your energy and attention from the body and the world back to God. You cannot love God truly without meditation, because only by meditating can you know yourself as the soul, in which lies your true eternal relationship with God.

Create in your hearts a throne of supreme love for God. There is naught else for which I live, no other ambition, but to love Him, to talk of Him, and to teach others the way to know Him. I want nothing; I ask nothing else of you. Whenever God brings me here to these meetings, it is my privilege to be with you, to speak of Him, and to love Him with you.

It is so wonderful to love God and to love all as a part of God. To find Him you must feel His love in all. There is no greater force than love. If at any time you clash with others, give love to them mentally. I love my enemies because I feel them as my friends. By feeling God, you cannot hate anybody. What would happen to us if God became angry at our misdeeds? If you remain calm when others try to hurt you, then you are a god.

The great God whom I worship on the altar of the sky and ocean, and on the altar of my own consciousness—He is manifest everywhere and in everyone. Him I embrace in all of His infinite forms.

Did We Meet Before?

Self-Realization Fellowship Temple,
Hollywood, California, January 10, 1943

Did we meet before? Certainly. Long ago, in the bosom of the ether where we were created as souls, we all were sleeping beneath the shroud of God's wisdom. When He awoke us, we wandered away from Him, like the prodigal son in the Bible story, and forgot our divine kinship with one another. We became strangers. Having left our home in God, we are lone travelers of destiny on this earth. Do you realize how far away you have roamed, and that you have been wandering for many incarnations? How many, it is hard to tell. Yet now and then, certain experiences, places, and faces awaken in you an inner feeling of familiarity that whispers of past knowing.

Each soul is omniscient; but its external, body-identified ego-nature becomes limited to its present name, family, and environment. On that day when your soul shall remember its divine origin, your consciousness will live again in the great mansion of Spirit, and you will know everything that is in Spirit, just as you now know your little earthly home and family.

It is a most wonderful experience to meet and recognize someone you knew before—someone with whom you have traveled the same pathway of life in former incarnations. All those in my family I knew from past lives. And every now and then I meet others who were known to me in previous incarnations, such as friends of my childhood. Though they have nothing in common with my present life, they are souls I had known before.

Even before I had left India to come to this country, and later, when I first arrived in Boston, I was aware that there were many true friends of past lives that I would meet again here. I recognize distinctly those whom I have known before when I meet them in this life. To some of them I have said, "At last I have found you again, because we have been together before. Why have you waited so long?" I look for those who were to come here to be with me in God's work. Every day I call for them, "Where are you who were walking with me before?" Suddenly I see a face in the crowd, and I say to myself, "There is one who has heard my call."

Even now, as I look at your faces I cannot but think that sometime, somewhere, in the dim distant past, you heard my voice. And the call of that voice has brought you here. Why else, out of millions, were you prompted to come, if not that God has picked you?* Some souls—those who are slightly awakened from the slumber of ignorance that veils memories of past lives—will stop and think: "Yes, I know what he is saying. Somewhere I have heard his voice before. It is not unfamiliar to me."

I never saw my usually reserved guru, Swami Sri Yukteswarji, as excited as when we first met. He knew that I instantly knew who he was; and he knew more than I knew. As Krishna said to his beloved disciple: "O Arjuna, many births have been experienced by Me and by thee. I am acquainted with them all, whereas thou rememberest them not."† I can never forget the joy of recognizing Master at that first meeting. Never in my life have I met anyone as great as he. He lived the spirit of God.

Sri Yukteswarji was very humble and also very stern. If you associated with him as a friend, you would never have cause to be timid around him. But if you came to him as a disciple, woe unto you if you couldn't take incisive discipline! He never dealt with your words; he worked with your thoughts. Many couldn't take his strictness. But I rejoiced when I saw that he was clearing all wrong thoughts from my mind and filling me with divine wisdom. Such a wonderful fount of wisdom he was; for when you love God truly, you know all that He knows. Master was a true lover of God.

---

* An allusion to the divine law that God ordains the guru and the path the devotee will follow to return to Him. Once that guru-disciple relationship is formed, through God's blessing, it continues for as many incarnations as necessary, until the devotee reaches God. (See *guru* in glossary.)

† Bhagavad Gita IV:5.

Many Lives Needed to Build the Mansion of Friendship

So, in one sense you are a stranger traveling alone through this world. Not one whom you think yours is yours. Isn't that true? No one is owned by another. Our karmic destinies have each their individual course, and no one can own or control anyone else.

But in a different sense, you are not alone in this world. There are some close relationships that endure, and from which we draw support and joy. Who are these souls who are close to you? They are not always those born in your family, but those with whom you feel an inner tie of deep friendship. For instance, there are those around me here in the ashrams. I have nurtured them with my ideals. They reflect my thoughts and my perceptions. They are considerate of me, and I of them. I have planted my life in them, and the divine friendship we share is an eternal bond in God.

The foundation of friendship is not secured in one life; many lives are needed to build the mansion of friendship. It is built with souls you have known before, life after life. That is why, from among the throngs, Jesus called his disciples to him one by one—those whom he had known before. They met again in the bosom of eternal friendship.

Recognizing Those You Knew Before

How can you recognize those you knew before? In a crowd of strangers, sometimes there is one whom you feel at first meeting you have known long ago. Others you never feel close to, no matter how much you associate with them. If you are unhampered by prejudices and not deluded by sexual attraction, and you find souls whose faces and personalities draw you much more strongly than others, it is likely that you knew those souls before.

A little test will also help to determine which ones are true friends of the past. You may have a lot of so-called friends; and they will tell you that you are wonderful, and agree with everything you say. Such persons want you for something for their own benefit. True friends want nothing from you except the joy of your presence. Sometimes the test of friends is in how they behave toward you when you have done something that happens to rouse or contradict them. Those who are your own will never be vengeful or forsake you, even though there may be disagreements. Those who were your true friends in other lives will have an unconditional love for you. No matter what you do, they will always be your friends. Anyone who loves you unconditionally is someone you knew before. That kind of friend you should be, also.

In analyzing who are your friends of past lives, you can also tell by the attunement you share with one another. As you gradually concentrate your consciousness on developing true friendship with another, you find that you begin to know how that person will feel or respond, even before he reacts. If you can do this after only a short acquaintance, certainly you knew that person before. These are some of the signs by which we know who our past friends are.

Be a friend to all, but don't expect all to be your friends, unless they have passed these tests. To those who fail, give your love and consideration, but remember that they are not ready for your friendship. You should not allow your heart or feelings to be hurt by them. The mansion of friendship must have a solid foundation. If you think differently from your friends, and lose their friendship because of it, then you know they were not really your friends. You should not try to build the mansion of friendship on the sand of those relationships.

Most people are self-centered. They want to please others for what they can get from them. Such persons are "yes" people, led by the expediency of the moment. Never give up your freedom of will or compromise your conscience and ideals for self-gain. Hold fast to right principles.

Sincerity Plus Thoughtfulness

Be true, be sincere, and friendship will steadily grow. I remember a discussion with Master about sincerity. I had said, "Sincerity is everything."

"No," he responded, "sincerity plus thoughtfulness is everything." He went on: "Suppose you are sitting in the parlor in your home, and there is a beautiful new carpet on the floor. It is raining outside. A friend you haven't seen in many years flings open the door and rushes into the room to greet you."

"That is all right," I said. But Master had yet to make his point.

"You were sincerely happy to see each other," he said, "but wouldn't you have liked it better if he had been thoughtful enough to take off his muddy boots before he came in and ruined the carpet?"

I had to agree he was right.

No matter how well you think of someone, or how close you are to that person, it is important to sweeten that relationship with good manners and thoughtfulness. Then friendship becomes truly wonderful and enduring. Familiarity that leads you to be inconsiderate is very harmful to friendship.

Sincerity is one of the things I prize most. Do not mix with people who flatter you, for someday such friendships will be torn asunder; you will find that you have wasted your time on them. Always beware of flattery. It is good to encourage others with wholehearted praise and appreciation, but the insincerity of flattery is a poison that destroys the soul of both the giver and the receiver. If anyone prefers flattery to love, he doesn't deserve friendship. Those who give love do not give flattery. And those who give flattery do not give love.

If you mix with people with real sincerity, thoughtfulness, and love, then you will attract those whom you knew before. Otherwise, you will never find your real friends. You have to be rid of all hypocrisy and insincerity. And never willfully hurt anyone. Never antagonize your friends, or give them cause to be angry. Never abuse or take advantage of a friend. Never give counsel unless asked for; and when you do give it, do so with sincerity and kindness, unafraid of the consequences. Friends help each other with constructive criticism.

To be able to stand criticism is one of the greatest virtues. I learned that from my guru. I have always appreciated constructive criticism. And I have never sought revenge on those who have unjustly criticized me; nor have I felt unkindly toward them, because I realize that even through our enemies God tests us. Isn't this so? When Jesus said, "Father, forgive them, for they know not what they do," he was exercising divine compassion and understanding. Through such a life and example we know how kind and loving is the Heavenly Father. Great ones reflect the nature of God.

Earn the Friendship of God

The great man doesn't think he is great. Those who say they are great are not. And those who are great are too busy being great to think about their greatness. Besides, no matter how wonderful you think you are, as soon as you proclaim it, everyone wants to prove you otherwise. The point is: be sincere. Live it in your life. Never try to deceive others. A fake rose can never be a real rose. And a real rose will shed its fragrance no matter how much it is crushed. So never pretend to be what you are not. If you egotistically display yourself before others, the world will eventually cast you aside. And don't try in any way to deceive God, for in the false notion that you can fool Him you only deceive yourself. He is just behind your thoughts. If you are not sincere with Him, He will fly away. He comes only to those who are humble and true devotees. When you love Him, you will know Him; and you will know He is fully present in every soul. It doesn't matter whether that soul is covered by a charcoal or a diamond personality; God is equally present in both. But the diamond mentality of the saint more fully reflects God.

There is no joy comparable to that joy which comes when you have earned the friendship of God. And it is most wonderful to share that joy with others. When a cup is filled with milk, and you pour more into it, it overflows. You can't help it.

When Friendship Becomes Divine, You Will Love All

When you love God, you can truly love others. Your perception of souls is pure—like a crystal-clear mirror. Whoever comes before you will be reflected there as he really is.

Many years ago I met George Eastman, the inventor of the Kodak. Outwardly, he appeared cold, like steel. He was well known for his philanthropies, and, like other men of great wealth, no doubt had cause to wonder about the motives of others he met; he didn't know what I was after. Without preliminary, he asked, "Do you accept my invitation to come to my home?" To which I replied, "I will be glad to, if you accept my invitation also." He agreed.

Later, when he came to my apartment and saw me cooking the meal of curries, he said, "You know, I like to cook, also." We became a little more friendly. Then I remarked casually, "Mr. Eastman, isn't it true that most rich men have no real friends? I want to meet you as a friend, not as a man of wealth." He smiled.

From that moment, and during our two-hour visit, I saw a different Eastman, the real Eastman,* because I understood him and met him on the plane of sincere friendship. The next day he sent me a camera, which I have to this day.

When you unconditionally love your friends, you will see that divine friendship in them. In my earthly father, and in so many souls on this path, I found that kind of friendship. When we develop friendship with true souls, one day the Friend of all will come and reside in that mansion of friendship. And as you develop true divine friendship, one day you will love all as Christ was the friend of all.

Please pray with me: "O Lord, in the noble character of true friends is Thy wisdom. In their laughter is Thy great smile. In the twinkle in their eyes Thou art looking at me. In their voices Thou art speaking to me. And in their love Thou art loving me. *Aum.* Peace. Amen."

---

* "Behind an austere exterior there is an emotional and a carefully cloaked spiritual nature, very much the servant of his will power." —Carl W. Ackerman in *George Eastman* (Boston: Houghton Mifflin, 1930).

The Art of Getting Along in This World

*First Self-Realization Fellowship Temple at
Encinitas, California, November 3, 1940*

With the dawning of each experience as we pass along the pathway of life, we must learn to live more consciously, more understandingly, if we are to get along in a better way in this world.

As we survey world civilizations and explore the deep nooks of past civilizations, we have a very large outlook before us. We find that man is both an individual and a gregarious animal. Every human being is endowed with the desire for an individual life and a social life; he has individualistic tendencies as well as tendencies to form into clans—even in the earliest savages there was the idea of gathering together as a group. In ordinary life, too much social interaction does not give much happiness, and neither does too much individual exclusiveness. God wants us to maintain evenness in balancing our individual and our social life.

The individualistic and collective principles in man come from God. He is very individualistic: Apart from the stars and the universes and the thoughts of men, beyond all sensations and dreams, transcending all perceptions of matter, the Lord exists by Himself—alone, having no other company; complete within Himself; satisfied in His own Self. "Where no sun or moon or fire shines, that is My Supreme Abode."* It is said that the omnipotent God so loves His eternal silence that He does not want even a little ray of light or tremor of vibration to disturb Him there. In that region of darkless dark and soundless sound, the uncreated nothingness, the Absolute Essence of

---

* Bhagavad Gita XV:6.

everything, He exists by Himself—all-sufficient unto Himself. No doubt it is easy for Him to get along with Himself; He has no one with whom He can disagree.

But at the same time, one part of God is not secluded at all: He is collectively active in the flowers and in the birds and fishes and in all forms of life on this planet—in the millions of human beings and in every creature—and He is very busy in the electromagnetic laws of the universe, and in the copious laws He has set forth to govern the sphere of manifestation. So in this sense He is not individualistic; and He has to get along with the diversity in His creation—this vast variety in which He Himself is contradicting Himself. He is the Uncreated and the Created, the Brahma of which the Hindu sings.

In the ultimate perception, there is no difference at all amongst God's diverse creations; though there seems to be contrary dissimilarity, as between man and beast and tiger and its prey, still God is able to get along with all experiences in the material, delusive panorama of this world. He is harmony in eclectic activity as well as harmony within Himself as an individual. He wants us, similarly, to learn to get along with our own self and with others.

Importance of Getting Along With Yourself

To be able to get along with yourself is marvelous. Most people know how difficult it is to get along with others. But have you ever given thought to getting along with yourself? That is most difficult. Separate your psychological perceptions from yourself and you will see how you are constantly fighting with yourself. You do not like anyone or anything if you do not like yourself. If one does not get along with himself, how could he be expected to get along with others? Getting along with self is the most important point in getting along in this world. So first and foremost you must learn truly to appreciate and love yourself. But when I say love yourself, I do not mean love for your egotism, selfishness, and self-interest. (It is instinct, of course, in man to save himself in the face of danger; self-preservation is the law of life.) Love yourself because you are a child of God with divine potentials; it is your love and concern for this potential self that inspires and inspirits unfoldment of your true soul-nature.

You cannot get away from yourself, even if you fly away from civilization to the farthest corner of the earth. That is why God wants you to correct yourself where you are. Some people live in the worst circumstances and are wonderful in their ability to get along with themselves. Others have every opportunity in the world, but they cannot get along with themselves; they are constantly at war within.

You must not wait for your circumstances to change. If you wait for that, you will never make any progress. Say to yourself, "I am all right in spite of my environment. If I want to meditate, I will find a way to meditate in spite of my surroundings. If I want to study to improve my mind, I will do so regardless of outer conditions." I knew a remarkable man in India who was versed in eighteen languages; yet he was so poor that he couldn't even afford a lamp to read by. So he used to go to the street corner and read under the streetlight. "Where there is a will, there is a way." There is no excuse that you cannot correct yourself despite any outer conditions.

You are the only one who knows whether you can get along with yourself, for you hide yourself very cleverly from others. That is why it is up to you to strive every day to find out whether you are at peace with yourself.

Master [Swami Sri Yukteswar] used to say, "Learn to behave." In that lies great inner peace and happiness. When you learn to get along with yourself, you will know how to get along with everybody. That is what I learned. That is what Jesus demonstrated: He could say, "Father, forgive them," for he had found that peace within himself.

Your Conscience Will Help You Get Along With Yourself

There are several practices that are necessary in order to know how to get along with yourself. One: Anyone who is extremely emotional or is restless with bad habits can never get along with himself. If your conscience tells you all the time that you are doing wrong, how on earth can you expect to get along with yourself? And when you meet others you will find that they will not extend their trust and their goodwill toward you, because a person who goes against his conscience mistrusts himself and that reflects in his character. Man's conscience speaks to him all the time and is constantly prodding him to change and to behave rightly. It is true, of course, that you can blunt your conscience. But it will not remain blunt forever. If nothing else, the laws of one's country will disturb the complacency of those whose conscience becomes completely dulled through misuse of free will. Criminals find out that their conscienceless acts did not pay.

So always listen to your conscience, the voice of your inner self; it is there to help you get along with yourself.

Evenmindedness: The Right Foundation for One's Existence

Secondly, evenness of mind must be practiced. No matter what experiences you face in life, do so with an even mind. Evenness of mind, evenness of disposition, brings great happiness, not only to yourself but to others. That does not mean you should be spineless or without enthusiasm; it means you should practice calmness. It is all right to enjoy the good things of this world, but do not become overexcited by them. And when sorrows come, accept them manfully; and think how to overcome them instead of permitting yourself to become distressed and restless, losing your calmness within. Some people are always restless; only a few are most of the time calm and evenminded regardless of circumstances. But evenness must remain constant that it may serve as a foundation of your existence. That is what Swami Shankara* taught: "Be thou always of even mind if thou dost want the evenminded Lord to adorn the altar of your soul." Without that evenmindedness one can never find God.

Just stop and think how well Jesus Christ got along with himself. That is how he could get along so well with the diversity in the multitudes. He behaved toward everyone and under all circumstances with the same evenness of mind, even during his greatest trial of crucifixion. "The relativities of existence (birth and death, pleasure and pain) have been overcome, even here in this world, by those of fixed equal-mindedness. Thereby

---

* Regarded as India's greatest philosopher; reorganizer of the ancient Swami Order. (See *Shankara* and *swami* in glossary.)

are they enthroned in Spirit—verily, the taintless, the perfectly balanced Spirit."* We should study the lives of truly great ones. When we understand them, we will know how similarly to pattern our lives.

Deep Thinking: A Corridor to God and Intuitive Perception

The next point in getting along with yourself is control of your thoughts. Learn to practice deep thinking. Learn the art of concentration so that when you put your mind on a particular thought your attention does not become restless, hopping from one idea to another. Most people live on the surface of life. But it is by deep-sea diving in the ocean of thought that you receive the pearls of knowledge. Deep thinkers are happy people because they can get away mentally from the disturbances of their environment. The average person has no escape. He is always living on the surface like the fish that is easily caught by the fisherman.

By practice, cultivate the habit of deep thinking. Take a difficult problem and ponder it. Go as deep into thought about that subject as you can. If you go deep enough, a solution will be forthcoming. And in that inner depth, a sense of peace will come over your soul. Why? Because in every deep-thinking state is a corridor to the kingdom of God. Without deep thinking, concentration of the mind, one will never find the way to God. Even profound thinkers who do not know God are nevertheless happy within themselves because they have made a deep inroad into intuitive perception and to God without consciously doing so. Those who are capable of thinking very deeply about different subjects, yet do not consciously connect with God, may fail in divine perception because they became hidebound in their thought. No one can find God without consciously seeking Him. But deep thinkers are at least nearer to God than those who live superficially in ignorance. There is no sin greater than ignorance. That is why I say, do not pass your time in idleness. Do something useful in life, something worthwhile, constructive, that will deepen and broaden your consciousness; and you will be nearer to God.

---

* Bhagavad Gita V:19.

Those who think deeply get along better with themselves and with others; because of their ability to explore the depths of thought, they know how to act when confronted with a difficult circumstance. Deep thinking is a mental preparedness by which you can surmount circumstances in a divine way.

Common Sense Puts Deep Thinking Into Action

Along with deep thinking, you have to develop common sense—that is, sense that is common to all, an intuitive sense. "Well, my husband was very sick, so I began to think very deeply about it. And by the time I had concluded my deep thinking and decided to call the doctor, my husband had passed on." That kind of thinking is not helpful! One must use common sense. It is essential that you know how to put your deep thinking into action. And no one can teach you common sense. It is an intuitive feeling that readily tells you what to do. Common sense is present in every soul, but very few people know how to develop their ability to tap that source of discrimination. You need to cultivate that power by which you can find out the right course of action in any given situation.

Control Desires and the Habit of Wasting Time

Lastly, in order to get along with yourself, you must control desires. So-called merriment means burning all candles at once. No one has to chastise such people; they punish themselves by their overindulgences, which create nervousness and anger and moods. They have no joy in anything because they are controlled by their insatiable senses. The true master is one who controls his senses. When he says *no* to temptations, he means *no*. And when he says *yes* to right action, he means *yes*.

Never kill time. It is too valuable to waste on useless things. I never learned to play cards or checkers or any such thing because I saw they are just a means of killing time. Life is too precious to squander. God-consciousness has to be cultivated. Always be busy with God, then nothing and nobody will be able to distract you. How wonderful it is to lead a simple life—a life of inner contentment is a heaven you know not. Even if I go to the movies once in a while to get away from organizational demands, I am not entranced with the scenes on

the screen, but rather with God-consciousness. I am not seeing the movies, but the cosmic movies within.

The consummate purpose of life is to find God. So do not
waste your time in uselessness.

Getting Along With Others Begins at Home

While learning to get along with yourself, you should also
practice the art of getting along with others—a great but difficult art.

Begin in your own home with the persons with whom you
live. There is a saying: a street angel and a house devil. If you
learn to get along with those in your own home, you will be better equipped to get along with the rest of the world. You need to
correct your own behavior and attitude. If you instead try to escape from those who rile you, your temper and passions will
nevertheless cling to you; wherever you go, you will continue to
have difficulties. Why not cure your difficulties here and now?

First of all, whenever you have problems with others look
to yourself; blame yourself if that is where the fault lies. Do
deep thinking and see if your behavior is right; see if you
deserve the criticism of others. And remember, example speaks
louder than words. If you want to change someone else, change
yourself first. If you want to teach someone else to get along
with others, set the example. Getting along with human beings
means getting along with God, provided those human beings
are not behaving unjustly toward you. Jesus was unjustly per-
secuted. But if persons *justly* criticize you, that means you
have yet to make greater effort to correct yourself.

Do Not Sacrifice Your Ideals to Please Others

Getting along with people does not mean agreeing with
everybody; and it does not mean that you should sacrifice your
ideals for their sake. That is not the kind of getting along that
I mean. But you can maintain your ideals without being offen-
sive. In fact, from that standpoint, Jesus Christ did not get along
with many during his time. But he maintained his ideals without being repugnant. He certainly got along with himself, for he
knew that what he was doing was right. And he said, "To this
end was I born, and for this cause came I into the world, that I

should bear witness unto the truth."*

So above everything else, please God and live up to your own ideals; never compromise your ideals, and never harbor an ulterior motive. If you can live loving God and meaning no harm to anyone, and still the world wants to hurt you, that is all right. It is better to be cursed by the whole world and be a favorite child of God than to be loved by all and forsaken by God. Getting along with others means getting along first with your conscience and with God, and then with people.

That realization is one of the great blessings I received from my Master. There is nothing in the world that measures up to the joy that I received from his company. When you have the security of true joy, you have everything. You do not need the world.

During my earliest years in this country, I was once invited as a guest of honor to a large party. I didn't know what an "elite cocktail party" was, so I didn't know what I was getting into. But I never before, or after, attended such a gathering. Everyone was drinking heavily. Late into the evening, they asked me to speak; so I gave them a talk that I think they never forgot. I did not speak in anger, but in truth: "Is this your natural way of life? Are you really happy embalming yourself in drink? This is not fun, getting dead drunk and talking in an evil way. What is this?" I know many of those present made an inner promise never to go to such parties again. I was not mad, for I kept myself inwardly aloof. In that way, I can get along fine with others. I do not have to follow their ways; rather I would try in a kind way to influence them to follow my ways. With God in your breast, joy in your heart, wisdom in your mind, and all the power of heaven in your soul, you are in the joy of the Eternal Father. That is the power which I see and feel all the time.

Behave in a truthful way that is not hurtful to others. If you cannot get along with others because of your ideals, then it is best to get away from those naysayers. If your goodness becomes a torture to others, stay away from them. You should not feel you have to beat others over the head with a club to make them follow. If they do not want to follow you, let them go their way. But always be willing to share your understanding

---

* *John* 18:37 (Bible).

with those who are seeking and who are thirsty for the nectar of the soul. Make them happy.

Smile From the Soul

Develop the habit of being pleasant. I do not mean that you should smile always like a Cheshire cat. Such a smile means nothing; it is shallow. But a smile that registers deep in the heart and expresses itself in the face is marvelous. It comes from being sincere. Sometimes those who are much in the public smile in a lifeless, practiced way, while inside they are thinking of something else. There is nothing inside to make their smile real. But the smile that reflects from the soul is very attractive; few people can resist an individual with such a sincere smile.

There are some persons who are chronic sourpusses. And many are hard-boiled, rigid in their reactions toward others. How to get along with such persons? First, make sure that no matter what the provocation nobody will be able to get you mad. That is one of the primary steps in learning how to get along with others. No matter what happens, let no one get your goat. It is difficult for those who have no self-control, but it is the easiest thing to do if you make up your mind. Do not boast that you never get angry, just practice it to the best of your ability. If you proclaim it, people have a tendency to take advantage of you. And do not be outwardly docile while seething dangerously inside. Under no circumstances let anyone make you angry enough to do something that you will rue later on. Most people who lose their temper regret afterward what they have done. Affirm with conviction: "I have perfect possession of my emotions." Persons who do not have their emotions under control are their own worst enemies. Every unfulfilled desire rouses their ire. When anyone can make you mad, it is because some desire within you has been contradicted. Otherwise, no one could make you angry.

There Is a Time to Remain Quiet but Firm

In your efforts to get along with others, do not be a doormat or everyone will want to run your life for you. If they cannot dominate you, they get angry; and if you listen to them and do their bidding, you become spineless. Then how are you to behave? When you find resistance to your ideals, the best way is to just remain quiet but firm. Say nothing. Do not get angry. Verbal punch after punch you may get, but do not permit it to provoke you. Refuse to quarrel. Eventually those persons will understand that you do not mean to anger them, but at the same time you have your own good reasons for not wanting to do what they request of you.

When people lose their tempers, get away from them until they are calmer. If you can get together and talk out your problems, it is wonderful. Communication is vital. But if anyone just wants to fight, simply say, "I am going to take a little walk." Then return and be prepared to discuss. But if the person still wants to fight, go out again and take a longer walk. Refuse to fight. No one can quarrel with you if you noncooperate. Never supply more fuel to anyone's anger. The angry person is satisfied only if he can make you angry too.

I can work with anyone, though I don't care to be with those who don't know how to live in harmony. When someone has made up his mind to win a point, let him have the victory—it is a hollow victory. Don't argue. Great men seldom argue; they smile and say, "I don't think so," but they don't fight.

Use Tact; Persons Are Not Unfeeling Stones

Learn to use tact with people. That does not mean you should be a hypocrite; it means consideration of others. You are not a stone; you are a thinking, conscious being, and you do not want to treat others as though they were unfeeling stones. Do not openly resist the desires of others. The person who always busies himself with the affairs of others is both a cause and an object of difficulties. If a person can take it, and if it will do some good, then speak out. But sometimes the recipient does not like it and will defiantly do exactly what you don't want him to do.

When you can get along with others, you are like a fragrant flower. As you pass by a garden, sometimes you smell the fragrance of roses or orange blossoms and you think, "Oh, how sweet they are." That is how great souls are. When you come into their company, the perfume of their lives touches you; it is a fragrance that uplifts your soul. But when you are around a foul odor, you do not like to remain there. When someone has a malodorous temperament of anger and quarrelsomeness, you don't want to be around that person. Those who are always inharmonious are of that type. They are like human skunks exuding an obnoxious odor.

In a religious organization, two classes of people are clearly distinguishable—those who are trying to change themselves for the better, and those who are quarrelsome and start trouble by trying to change everybody but themselves. The latter seem to take pleasure in trying to make others uncomfortable.

I remember in the early days in Boston we were planning a banquet. Two middle-aged ladies were real crackerjacks in gossiping. Unsuspectingly, I had given them charge of the banquet. But someone said to me, "Beware of these two. They have caused much trouble for other teachers." That put me on guard to watch their behavior. As banquet arrangements proceeded, my secretary put place cards on the head table designating certain persons to sit there. These two ladies started fireworks: "Why should these persons be on the platform and not us?" To restore peace, these guests were seated down at the other tables.

One day, these two ladies started disrupting organizational plans of the center. Their intention was to be the leaders of the work in Boston. So I called them aside: "Do you accept me as your spiritual teacher?" They said, "Yes." I said, "Will you listen to me?" They said, "Absolutely." They thought I was going to place them in positions of importance. After a little while I saw them separately, and I told each of them what I described as a secret and asked them to promise they would not divulge that information. They agreed. After a few days each one had "secretly" told many others what I had told her. When they realized what was happening, a feud broke out between the two of them. I then distanced myself from them. But they sought me out. I was in the Boston Plaza Hotel. They called me on the phone and wanted to see and talk with me. I said, "I will see you provided you speak very calmly; the minute you raise your voices, I will leave."

When I came down to the lobby, they were trying hard to control themselves. They said, "What is the idea of telling the 'secret' to each of us?" I answered, "To show you that you cannot be trusted; that you are disloyal, and that you love to fight and to gossip. By this means I have convinced you about your wrong behavior. I told you something that was of no importance, just to see if you were capable of keeping a confidence or if you would give in to your habit of stirring up trouble with your gossiping. The fault did not lie in the teachers who have come to this town and whom you have criticized so freely. The fault is in your own natures. I asked one thing of you and you could not keep your word. Do you realize how your reputation makes you disliked in this city? Now the trouble you give to others has come back to hurt only you. If you cannot keep one promise of confidence given to your spiritual teacher, how can you expect others to have confidence in you? If you don't keep faith with me, you won't keep faith with anybody else. Are you truly at peace and happy within your own souls?"

I was sincere with them, but I gave them that day a very honest and earnest appraisal of their behavior. After doing so, I said, "Now, I am not going to shut you out of my classes. But you must promise me that you will not talk against anyone during the class series. Do not think of yourselves as teachers. As long as there is prideful desire to teach, you are not qualified to teach. First you yourself must live it. If you do that, others will follow your example." And do you know that hour after hour they attended the classes and didn't once disturb anyone. They were the meekest of students. You see, I got along with them all right because I did not get angry. I used tact to bring them to the sudden realization of their mental weaknesses.

But getting along with others cannot be done only by tact. It also requires example, calmness, evenness of mind, sincerity, joy, doing everything in an honorable way; not clinging to pride and egotism; and not governing your actions by what everybody else does, but doing those things that please God. Find your peace by meditating regularly and deeply, and you will be surprised to see how your relationships with others improve.

Also develop your power of usefulness. That is love. Think about that. Learn to be serviceful to others—useful with positive thoughts; useful with your speech; useful with constructive suggestions. But do not give advice where it is not wanted; if your suggestions are unwelcome, have the control to remain silent. And when sometimes you do good to others and then can no longer help them in a material way, if they become inimical because they continue to expect from you, never mind; go on doing what is right. Do the best you can and forget it.

Be Sincere; Never Resort to Flattery

Be sincere with everyone. You can get along with most people if you flatter them. But that destroys the character of both the giver and the receiver. Praise is not harmful if it is sincerely meant. Everyone likes encouragement and to be praised for one's good qualities and actions, if that recognition is sincere. But when someone gives flattery in order to get something in return, that is wrong. If my love is not sufficient, I shall not bribe anybody with flattery.

There was once a wealthy student from Milwaukee, a Mr. R——, who came to stay at Mt. Washington. This was during a difficult early period when we had very little money to support the work. He came to learn, but soon developed the habit of trying to teach everybody else instead. I called him to my study and said, "I prohibit you from giving any more money to the organization. I gave you my love, but you want flattery from me. You came here to learn, but now you want to teach us." He became angry. I said, "Don't think you have fooled me because I have remained quiet. All you need is a good dose of flattery and then you think you are all right. But I will not give you flattery."

Tears came in his eyes and he said, "But everything here will go to pieces. The magazine* will be stopped and Mount Washington will not last unless you take money from me." I replied, "What of it?" He was angry for a long time, predicting that everything would fall apart without him. But I said, "Maybe not." Then I cautioned him, "Beware, you are making dire predictions; but I say unto you that if you go on in this way all your money will be taken away from you." He left Mount Washington and later joined another society; they flattered him and

---

* *Yogoda Satsanga* Magazine (see glossary).

gave him an important position, and then divested him of all his money. He had to go back to where he started. What would we have been if we had accepted money from that man? I would have had to close my eyes to his evil ways—and this I could never have done.

Right after that experience, one of the greatest friends and devotees came into the organization. That was St. Lynn.*

I have seen great things in my life. Everything that you give up for God, He knows. What is it if by flattery you gain friends and followers if God is not there? You are forsaken by the world for insincerity and forsaken by God as well, going at death into the depths of the astral world without any assurance from your conscience nor from God nor from man.

Relationships that are based on an exchange of sincerity and respect are wonderful. Do not sully friendship by becoming too familiar with anyone; familiarity breeds contempt. No one has been able to be overfamiliar with me. Disrespect and taking someone for granted severely jeopardize a relationship. Whenever you mix with people, mix respectfully with love and sincerity.

When you feel like being alone, get away from people; be by yourself. Do not keep company with people unless you are prepared to give them your full attention. In that regard, when I am with others I mix with concentration, with attention, with love. But when I am alone, I am alone with my God. Do not make a habit of associating with people uselessly. When it is worthwhile, it is all right. I like to be with people in worthwhile activities and uplifting exchanges of friendship, but not in anything that is a source of inharmony. Keep your distance from whatever or whoever creates inharmony.

Come for Truth That Flows From My Soul

I wish these truths were taught in childhood. They should be dinned into the ears of your children. Lessons learned early

---

* Mr. James J. Lynn, later known as Rajarsi Janakananda (see glossary). A highly successful business magnate when he met Paramahansaji in 1932, he attained an exalted state of divine illumination through practice of the Yogoda Satsanga Society of India/Self-Realization Fellowship teachings. Through the years, he was an exemplary spiritual influence as well as benefactor in the support and growth of Paramahansaji's work.

in life make lasting impressions. In my own childhood, one day I made up my mind that I would never get angry; and I have never broken that vow. Sometimes I have talked sharply, but inwardly I am never angry with anyone. I don't like to speak forcefully, but I do it sometimes because an individual may better remember what is said to him with firmness. I have great peace within myself. If you are a man of peace, no one can steal that tranquility from you unless you yourself carelessly relinquish it. From that inner center of peace, I teach with the principle of love and kindness; it is the better way. If that is misunderstood by anyone, I leave that person alone; I remain silent.

You come here for pure truth that flows from my soul. And if even one person receives this truth and is changed, I shall have done more good than if thousands came rocking with emotion.

I seek nothing of you but your joy in God. And you seek nothing from me but God's wisdom and joy. A spiritual man will get along with everybody—even if they may not always get along with him—because he will understand and sympathize and try to bring them to God.

Jesus said: "Heaven and earth shall pass away: but my words shall not pass away."* Prepare yourselves now to be instruments of truth. I used to tell the students in my school in India that they must not only speak truth and expect forgiveness, but that they must speak truth and willingly accept any unpleasant consequences. Make the effort to get along with others through kindness, love, and compassion; but whenever untruth comes, stand firmly against it. Never cooperate with untruth.

Ask Yourself If You Are Getting Along With God

My Master was a great soul—such souls you will read about when I have completed my book.† He never brought his ideals down to the level of his disciples. He was firm and uncompromising. But he used to tell me that my ways were softer than his. I understood him. And what he did for me, no words of this world can ever possibly describe. I would rather be trampled by

---

* *Luke* 21:33 (Bible).

† *Autobiography of a Yogi* (Available from Yogoda Satsanga Society of India).

his scoldings than be enthroned in a castle without God. I always told him my foremost craving was to get along with God.

Every day you should ask yourself, "Have I gotten along with God?" Do you know what are the signs that you have not gotten along with God? They are restlessness, unhappiness, and an uneasy conscience. But if you are getting along with God, your conscience is at rest; and you are drunk with inner happiness and contentment all the time. I have no other desire but to be in that happiness and to give those living waters of joy to whoever comes to me.

The more you get along with God, the more you will be able to get along with the world. The world may forsake you for a little while, but it will come back to you. And when you are gone from this earth, those who had turned away will say, "He has left footprints, following which we too will reach our home of eternal contentment."

So strive always to keep your thoughts tuned to the Absolute. There is no happiness in any pursuit like the happiness you find in seeking God. Surround yourself with good thoughts, that those thoughts may help you to be closer to God.

This truth has come here to last forever, because it has been transplanted into some great souls. What we build in the souls of men is eternal. It is to your advantage to follow this truth, for you will see in it such freedom that no tongue can describe. Spiritual things are intangible in the beginning, but they become more tangible than all things else as you go along the path.

I am interested in your soul; and if you try to develop yourself, you will find here an infinite treasure of truth. If you study these teachings, you will know that they are not the result of imagination; they are the direct perception of truth, which has come through me and my great Gurus. And remember to spread this message wherever you go. The greatest way that you can spread it is by your example. And then help others with good thoughts of truth. Those who will persevere to the end will find freedom in God.

To meet God at the end of the trail is a great consolation. It does not matter whether we go through trials or disappointments in life if at last we all meet Him. We belong to Him, and in Him we will find the fulfillment of all our dreams. So we must never be discouraged no matter how life treats us. Repeat with me: "Lord, Thy joy alone is mine; that only is mine."

Now let us pray together: "Heavenly Father, teach me how to get along with Thee. And with Thine understanding, may I get along with all. Bless me that wherever I am I may exemplify Thy message. Teach me to do every day—with sincerity and strict adherence to Thy laws—the things that please Thee and that help others with Thy peace, harmony, and understanding. *Aum.* Peace. Amen."

The Psychology of Touchiness

Self-Realization Fellowship International Headquarters,
Los Angeles, August 4, 1934

Mastering the art of not being touchy, of avoiding over-sensitivity, is important in the development of spiritual consciousness. An analysis of the psychology of touchiness shows that it is the result of misunderstanding, inferiority complex, and an ungoverned ego. Sensitiveness expresses itself in a lack of control over the nervous system. A thought of being offended runs through the mind and the nerves rebel against it. In reacting, some persons seethe inwardly with anger or hurt feelings and show no irritation outwardly. Others express their emotions in an obvious and instant reaction in the muscles of their eyes and face—and often in a sharp retort of their tongue as well. In either case, to be touchy is to make oneself miserable, and to create a negative vibration that also adversely affects others. To be able always to spread an aura of goodness and peace should be the motive of life. Even if there is good reason for being excited because of mistreatment, one who instead controls himself in such a situation is master of himself.

It is a common trait of human beings to be touchy. And when this irrational emotion comes, it blinds the eyes of wisdom. Even though the touchy person may be in the wrong, he perceives himself as thinking rightly, acting rightly, feeling rightly. It is when the scales of ignorance fall away from the inner sight that one is able to measure exactly the good points and the weak points of oneself and others without the prejudice and intolerance of the emotional ego. One then worships only what is good, and remains transcendentally indifferent to what is psychologically unwholesome.

Many persons think that they should pity themselves when criticized, and that sensitiveness brings a little relief. But such people are like the opium addict; every time he takes the drug he becomes more steeped in the habit. Be as firm as steel against sensitiveness. Never be touchy or harbor self-pity.

An oversensitive person frequently suffers in vain: generally nobody has any idea that he has a grievance, much less what it is. So he feels further hurt in his self-created isolation. Nothing is accomplished by silently brooding over some perceived offense. It is best to remove by self-mastery the cause that produces such sensitiveness.

In my youth I was very sensitive; and consequently the one who suffered most was myself—it was a process of self-torture. Because I was so sensitive, others seemed to delight in "getting my goat." Your "goat" is your peace; let nobody take away your peace. My discomfiture was not wholly the fault of the taunting of others; it was also the result of my own sensitiveness to their remarks. I found that the more I argued with people who criticized me, the more satisfaction they got. At last, I made up my mind that no one would be able to destroy my peace. I decided, "Let them criticize all they want to." I remained indifferent to their unjust barbs, as untouched as if I were dead. They soon lost their enthusiasm to pick on me; and many became my friends and followed me. It is futile to demand kindness and respect from others; you must rather learn to merit it. If you are sincerely kind and respectful to others, and return any courtesy they show to you, you will always be treated respectfully. And do not paralyze the goodwill of others by being touchy when they offer constructive criticism. Cooperate whenever anybody tries to help you.

My master, Swami Sri Yukteswarji, was very strict with me. He watched every nuance of my thoughts and freely corrected me. He was harsh at times, but it was always for my highest good. Many did not survive his sharp discipline; but I did, and words cannot thank him enough for undertaking the task of molding my life with his wisdom. Persons with well developed spirituality can clearly see the faults in others. When a clear-sighted well-wisher tries sincerely to help you, that person should not be looked upon as one who wants to exercise lordship over you, but rather as one who is trying to give you understanding and strength to see and conquer your weaknesses. You should cooperate. Be courteous and kind; and if you start to sink into the mood of touchiness, immediately control yourself. Intelligent people, those who possess true understanding, always leave nonunderstanding persons alone. They do not want to waste their time and effort in dissembling with those who have no ears or willingness to hear.

Within my inner heart, I never let myself become touchy. I am at peace with myself. It is when you are not at peace with yourself that you become touchy. This is to be small. To be great is to be big-hearted no matter how others hurt you. That is the way to live. Do not wait until tomorrow; begin today.

One should be able to control his moods instantly. To let the fire of sensitiveness eat into one's heart, and to keep it smoldering there, will burn away the fibers of inner peace. A wise person controls his sensitivity, knowing that it is nothing but an agency of metaphysical Satan* trying to destroy the soul's peace.

When anything distresses you, no matter how you justify your unhappiness, know that you are succumbing to undue sensitivity, and that you must not indulge in it. Sensitiveness is an unspiritual habit, a nervous habit, a peace-destroying habit that takes away your control over yourself and robs you of your happiness. Whenever a mood of sensitiveness visits the heart, its static prevents you from hearing the divine song of healing peace that plays within through the radio of the soul. Whenever sensitiveness appears, try immediately to conquer that emotion.

There is a difference between emotional sensitiveness and spiritual sensitivity. Those who are spiritually sensitive are discriminatingly watchful of their own feelings and are keenly perceptive of the feelings of others, but they remain aloof from the disturbances of psychological impulses—just as butter can float in water and remain unchanged, undiluted, by its surroundings. But touchy sensitiveness is like a ghost that haunts you. It tortures your nervous system and makes you feel that the whole world is full of enemies. The person of extreme sensitivity often foolishly blames others for the hurt he feels; he should try to understand that his hurt is self-inflicted. It is

---

* See glossary.

better to blame oneself for being oversensitive than to be angry with others.

Nobody should catch you in a touchy mood. Quietly correct yourself. If necessary, hide yourself in a room away from others until the fever of sensitiveness is gone. The face is the reflector of your inner self; the heart, the source of feelings, is the basis of that reflection. Your face should be an inspiring sermon. Your countenance should be a beacon for others to follow, a lighthouse by which shipwrecked souls can find the way to safety in the harbor of peace.

Your face should be an altar where peace reigns, where God reigns—where all the votaries of psychological goodness assemble to invoke the almighty God of peace and love: "Heavenly Father, bless us that we establish the temple of purity in ourselves—within our hearts, our thoughts, our feelings—that our countenance may be an illuminated altar of Thy peace and love."

Why Love Succeeds
Where Jealousy Fails

First Self-Realization Fellowship Temple at
Encinitas, California, April 10, 1938

Jealousy, anger, fear, all the negative physical and mental impulses that impel human beings to do wrong—where do they come from? Many say these are of psychological origin. But I say they come from the Evil Force. There are two forces in this world—good and evil. Wherever there is good, there is also evil. Man, endowed with independence and free will, suffers the consequences of his wrong actions, but he is not the creator of the agents that influenced those errors. Plants commit no evil, and yet they succumb to diseases. The animals, which are governed by instinct with no consciousness of evil, similarly suffer. Side by side with every good there is a corresponding evil. God creates the sunshine and the Evil Force creates destructive storms and droughts. The beautiful flower blooms and is destroyed by insects. God says to love; the Evil Force says be jealous, you are justified to hurt and enfeeble an opponent. Don't listen to that dark power. It isn't you. Jealousy, anger, fear, are creations of the Evil Force. Recognizing this force as a conscious power, Jesus said, "Get thee behind me, Satan."*

Any time the voice of jealousy, fear, or anger speaks, remember that it is not your voice, and command that it be gone. But you will not be able to expel that evil, no matter how you try, so long as you give that negative feeling a safe harbor in your mind. Eradicate jealousy, fear, and anger from within, so that every time an evil impulse tells you to hate and to hurt, another stronger voice within tells you to love and to forgive. Listen to *that* voice.

---

* *Luke* 4:8 (Bible).

Just imagine, if we could take away from the world self-ishness, jealousy, and anger, there would be no wars. But these destructive perpetrators are tenacious, and constantly fight with goodness for supremacy. God speaks of peace and the Evil Force urges restlessness and discord. God is trying to coax you into actions of love; the Evil Force is trying to lure you to fight. You are a free agent; you can choose as you please. Whenever you are jealous, you are in collusion with the cosmic delusion of Satan. Whenever you are angry, Satan is guiding you. The voice of fear is his evil voice. But whenever you are filled with love and forgiveness, God is with you. Help Him to work through you; He cannot do so unless you help Him.

All Relationships Should Be Grounded in Friendship

The followers of Satan have but one reward: misery. The followers of God have blissful peace. "He finds peace who knows Me... as the Infinite Lord of Creation, and as the Good Friend of all creatures."* Heed the voice of Love within. Live love; practice it within and without; wherever you go, give love and understanding. Become like a flower whose fragrance overpowers the noxious vapors of jealousy, fear, and anger. Spread the fragrance of divine love and friendship to all with whom you come in contact.

Those who refine their spiritual sensitiveness will feel the awakening of universal Christ Consciousness [Kutastha Chaitanya] in their expanding love. Cultivate it by first practicing godliness with the people around you. Always think of others before yourself. Be a selfless friend to all—to your spouse, your children, your close associates, everyone you meet. Requisite to friendship is the acceptance of each one's individuality—two souls, different in character, pulling together the chariot of life to a common goal.† Truth must be the standard upon which a relationship is based. And no matter what one says, even if it must be to discipline or dissent, it should be said with love, never with harshness or meanness. The duty of friends is to con-

---

* Bhagavad Gita V:29.

† See "Friendship" in Songs of the Soul by Paramahansa Yogananda (published by Self-Realization Fellowship).

tinuously help each other to develop themselves. When souls seek progress together in God, then divine friendship flowers. If the qualities of the heart are spiritualized and perfected with sincere friends, and that circle of love is expanded until it is all-inclusive, then one finds the Friend of all friends, the Divine Friend, behind all relationships.

Jealousy Foreshadows the End of Happiness

Whereas the love of God unites, the negative impulses of the Evil Force divide and destroy. Great havoc is wrought by jealousy and its cohorts of fear, anger, and hatred. Human relationships are devastated, homes are broken up, lives are destroyed. Jealousy foreshadows the end of happiness, first in the one who harbors it, and then in others who are objects of its vengeance—even innocent bystanders, such as the children of broken homes.

Jealousy exists everywhere; it is an ever present danger to all human relationships. I have so many times seen it at work in this world. Everybody wants the "good position," but few want to make the effort to merit it or to assume the inherent responsibility. The divisive nature of jealousy transforms a heaven of harmony into a hades of discord. One jealous person can generate so much trouble! When possible, try to avoid giving anyone cause for jealousy. Go out of your way, if necessary, to create understanding.

Jealousy Comes From an Inferiority Complex

Jealousy comes from an inferiority complex, and expresses itself through suspicion and fear. It signifies that a person is afraid he cannot hold his own in his relationships with others, be they conjugal, filial, social. If you feel you have cause to be jealous of someone—for example, if you are afraid that the one you love is transferring his or her attention to another—first strive to understand if there is something lacking within yourself. Improve yourself; develop yourself. The only way to hold on to the affection or respect of another is to apply the law of love and to merit that recognition by self-improvement.

Love and its counterparts can never be acquired or preserved by demands or begging or bribes. I have observed how some people behave around those who are wealthy or influential. I once said to a prince in India, "Do you think these people who court your favor really love you?" He replied, "Yes." But I had seen them in a different light, and I cautioned him, "Stop giving them money and gifts and you will find that they are not sincere. They mock you with their flattery."

True love cannot be bought. To receive love, one must give it freely, without any condition. But instead of following this rule, the insecure person resorts to jealousy. This makes the loved one angry, and thus defeats its very purpose. Jealousy then responds to the anger with a desire to strike back. But anytime one wants thus to harm another, he ultimately hurts himself even more. Evil acts have their source in evil thoughts; these caustic mental parasites eat away the very fiber of one's being. They burn and destroy inner peace—one's greatest wealth.

"Whatever Is Not Mine, Let It Go!"

Why be jealous? If you give someone your love and it is not appreciated, if that person does not want you, or gives to another the recognition you think you deserve, jealousy certainly will not hold that person or cure the strain in the relationship. Making prisoners of one another with jealousy and demands will certainly not produce happiness. Successful relationships can grow only in trust and love. Love survives in respect, usefulness, and freedom from possessiveness.

So what is the remedy? Any time jealousy tries to bind you, make strong affirmations: "I am free from the bondage of jealousy and fear. Whatever is mine will be mine; whatever is not mine, let it go!" When you will be free from all jealousy and fear, your life will be wonderful. You *can* be free. What is yours will be yours, and what is not meant for you would not make you happy. Fulfillment lies in constantly improving yourself so that instead of your seeking others, others will seek you. Give love and friendship without expecting or demanding anything in return. Expectation will make you a victim of misery.

Even while striving to improve yourself, learn to stand alone, secure in your own virtues and self-worth. If you want others to believe in you, remember, it isn't only your words that have an effect, but what you are and what you feel within—

what is in your soul. Always strive to be an angel within, no matter how others behave. Be sincere, kind, loving, and understanding. Anyone who does not respond to goodness is not worthy of your attention. Even if you have to lose a loved one, it is better to let him go thinking of you as an angel rather than as a green-eyed monster of jealousy. Leave with that person a beautiful thought of your love, and that love will ever remain in his heart.

Thoughts Can Be More Effective Than Words

Never speak harshly under the fire of jealousy. The mouth can be like a cannon, and speech more damaging than any exploding shell. Be discriminate in your use of words. People do not like to be told their faults. If guidance or constructive criticism isn't welcome, withhold your words. Otherwise, the more you say, the worse you may make the situation.

Thoughts can sometimes be more effective than words. The human mind is the most powerful broadcasting machine there is. If you constantly broadcast positive thoughts with love, those thoughts will have an effect on others. (Similarly, if you broadcast jealousy or hatred, others receive those thoughts and respond accordingly.) Ask God to put His power behind your efforts. If, for instance, it is the husband that is going astray, the wife should pray to God: "Lord, help me to help my husband. Keep all taint of jealousy and resentment out of my heart. I only pray that he realize his error and change. Lord, be with him; and bless me that I do my part." If your communion with God is deep, you will see that person change. The more errant a person is, the greater kindness you should give. Instead of succumbing to jealousy and fear of losing a loved one, strive for right attitude and behavior, keep yourself physically attractive, and be strong mentally and spiritually.

God Is the Ultimate Answer

Never forget that God is the answer to all the questions life places before your soul. God is love, and love is the panacea for human suffering. There is nothing greater than love— God's quality of attraction and unity that is manifested in the soul of every being. This love, when expressed under all circumstances—in family, social, and national life—expands to embrace the whole world. Such universal love is the pure love of God. When you have achieved that love, then and then alone are you a citizen of the kingdom of God. Always be proud that you are a child of God; for just a little while you have been an alien in the kingdom of matter. Develop God's divine love inherent in you, and you will reclaim your citizenship in His kingdom of omnipresence.

When you learn to go within in meditation, you will find His kingdom. It is within you; God is within you. It is His power that is behind your ability to talk, move, and feel. Without Him you can do nothing. Though He is transcendent, beyond all things, He is also immanent; you can commune with Him right within you. If you remove the dust of restlessness from the mirror of inner silence, you will see Him reflected there.

Never miss your daily engagement with God in meditation. Those who are wise make it their business to contact Him. If you are sincere, you shall know God in this life; and to know Him is to be free.

Diamond Mentalities Reflect the Light of God

You know in your heart that you are not happy with the present state of your life. There is only one direct route to happiness, and that is to contact God. "Naught shelters thee, who wilt not shelter Me." * God is the one who will never forsake you. The way to find Him is to follow someone who knows Him. Attune yourself with the great ones who commune with Him; only they can show you God. I searched for many, many years in India, where they specialize in the science of God-realization, until at last I found my Guru [Swami Sri Yukteswar] who had attained the contact of God.

The law of cause and effect governs all human beings. Just by the act of coming here to these services, see how much you change. Study the [Yogoda Satsanga] Lessons, and you will find the answers you are seeking. That new understanding will change your whole life. Those who are not yet on the path, but

---

* "The Hound of Heaven," by Francis Thompson.

who want to know more, should apply for these instructions and learn to meditate. Then meditate regularly. Have the determination and perseverance to follow the path of Self-Realization absolutely and completely. You will find emancipation; and the influence of your life will show others the way to emancipate themselves. Every day, do something to help another person materially, mentally, and spiritually; and try to awaken some soul to follow the path to God.

Every one of you who comes here should resolve never to miss your daily meditation. You could be taken away from this earth at any minute. Use the time you have to make the effort to know God, who is the only one who will be with you forever. "As many as received him, to them gave he power to become the sons of God."* The sun shines equally on a piece of charcoal and a diamond placed side by side in the sunlight, but the diamond reflects the light while the charcoal does not. Those who have become spiritual diamonds reflect the sunlight of God's consciousness; they become sons of God. The Great Masters† are the diamond mentalities after whom we should pattern our lives. To follow them is to find quick and direct exit to divine liberation.

The Effectiveness of Single-hearted Devotion

Most of you here today were born Americans. You do not know what you were before this incarnation or what nationality you may be in the next life; but you have always been and always will be the child of God. The time has come to merge our differences and unite in God. Break the ramparts of His silence. He remains hidden because He knows most people don't want Him. But if you make up your mind to contact Him, He will respond. If you are determined to find Him, you will know Him. No one can give Him to you, just as no one else can eat your food for you. You must make the effort. Jesus said, "The harvest truly is plenteous, but the laborers are few."‡

---

* *John* 1:12 (Bible).

† Reference to the Gurus of Yogoda Satsanga Society of India/Self-Realization Fellowship (see glossary).

‡ *Matthew* 9:37 (Bible).

In the early morning and before going to bed at night, talk to God, again and again, in the language of your heart: "Reveal Thyself, reveal Thyself. Why do You hide from me?" Go on praying to Him, with determination and devotion, until you lose yourself in the thought of God. Refuse to become discouraged or impatient. Then during the day's activities, keep the thought of Him in the depths of your consciousness. You know how sometimes, no matter what you are doing, there is one thought revolving in your mind like a dynamo—its power generating the desired result. That is the way you should ceaselessly think of God. As Krishna says in the Bhagavad Gita: "I am easily reached by that yogi who is single-hearted, who remembers Me daily, continually, his mind intensely focused only on Me."*

Very early in my life I learned the effectiveness of that single-heartedness. When I was a small child, I wrote a letter to God and dropped it in the postbox. Every day I waited anxiously, with tear-filled eyes, for His answer. No reply came through the mail. But I never gave up the thought that He must answer that letter. Then one night, in a great light, I received His response, written in letters of gold, that He will ever protect me and be with me.

When you contact God, you will see that in all departments of your life a silent Friend is helping. We love anyone who is useful to us; therefore we should love God supremely, because He is useful as nobody else is. We love our parents and friends because of what they do for us. But no one can be as useful to us as God, for He can resurrect our souls and free us from all human bondage.

[With the following words, Paramahansaji led the congregation in a period of chanting and meditation:]

Mentally call to God with all the fervor and sincerity of your hearts. Consciously invoke Him in the temple of silence; and in deeper meditation, find Him in the temple of ecstasy and bliss.† Chant with the consciousness that God is here.

---

* VIII:14.

† Reference to the chant "In the Temple of Silence" in *Words of Cosmic Chants* by Paramahansa Yogananda (published by Yogoda Satsanga Society of India).

Through your thoughts and feelings, send Him your love with all your heart, mind, soul, and strength. Through the intuition of your soul feel the manifestation of God bursting through the clouds of your restlessness as great peace and joy. Peace and joy are the voices of God that have long slumbered beneath your ignorance, ignored and forgotten in the din of human passions.

The kingdom of God is just behind the darkness of closed eyes, and the first gate that opens to it is your peace. Exhale and relax, and feel this peace spread everywhere, within and without. Immerse yourself in that peace.

Inhale deeply. Exhale. Now forget your breath. Repeat after me: "Father, hushed are the sounds of the world and the heavens. I am in the temple of quietness. Thine eternal kingdom of peace is spread tier upon tier before my gaze. May this infinite kingdom, long hidden behind the darkness, remain manifest within me. Peace fills my body; peace fills my heart and dwells within my love; peace within, without, everywhere. God is peace. I am His child. I am peace. God and I are one. Infinite peace surrounds my life and permeates all the moments of my existence. Peace unto myself; peace unto my family; peace unto my nation; peace unto my world; peace unto my cosmos. Goodwill to all nations, goodwill to all creatures; for all are my brothers and God is our common Father. We live in the United States of the World with God and Truth as our leaders. Heavenly Father, may Thy kingdom of peace come on earth as it is in heaven, that we all be freed from divisive inharmonies and become perfect citizens, in body, mind, and soul, of Thy world. *Aum.* Amen."

Invite the Christ Consciousness Within You

Self-Realization Fellowship International Headquarters,
Los Angeles, December 23, 1934

"Heavenly Father, bless us this morning with the consciousness of Jesus, that we too might experience Thy universal presence as the Christ Consciousness inborn in every pore and atom of space. O Father, we thank Thee for sending unto us Thy great son in the form of Jesus, a resplendent light, a beacon to guide this world on the path of spirituality. We bow to Christ Jesus. May we enshrine him forevermore on the altar of our hearts. May his spirit be manifest within us.

"We invoke the spirit of Jesus, the omnipresent Christ Consciousness, to descend upon our consciousness and bestow the realization of Infinity. May that Infinite Christ, cradled in space, in blossoms, in all beings, and in our hearts—everywhere—be manifest to us evermore. *Aum, Aum, Aum.*"

Inflame your heart with the fire of devotion, that the light of Christ may blaze within you. Purity, peace, happiness beyond dreams, are sparkling and dancing within your soul. Let that peace within join the transcendent, infinite peace without. You are immersed in that eternal light. Your whole being is filled with that omnipresent blessed effulgence of Christ. Beyond body and breath, you are that ever-living light of Christ peace and joy.

This is a blessed morning in that it so closely precedes the spiritual and festive celebrations of Jesus' birth.* In honoring his nativity, do not think of Christ as limited to the tiny

_____

* Many years ago, Paramahansaji started the custom of celebrating the birth of Christ by having an all-day meditation one or two days before Christmas, followed by the traditional festive celebration on December 25.

body of a helpless baby. The Christ Spirit was born on earth in the physical vehicle of the infant Jesus; within his consciousness was omnipresent God. Behind the nascent brain of the little boy was the wisdom of Spirit. How else could he, as a young child, startle wise and learned men with his precocious words? Even though the spirit of God becomes incarnate in the birth of great souls, still those divine ones play the drama of infancy, youth, and all other phases of life and death. But it is to be remembered that behind their mortal consciousness is the immutable Christ Consciousness, the ever pure reflection of Spirit—which the sages in India call *Kutastha Chaitanya* or Krishna Consciousness. This conception of Jesus very few people have. If you know Christ in reality, you will know how to bring his universal spirit into your own consciousness.

The Proper Observance of Christmas

What is the significance of celebrating the sacred birth of Christ on a certain day? It is not just to provide an opportunity for festivity and gift-giving. It is especially and distinctly to revive in our thoughts the inspiration of his perfect qualities. If you hold a portrait before you, the image reminds you of the salient characteristics of that person; so is a day of remembrance, when properly observed.

It is sad when people forget the purpose of Christmas. Millions are thinking only of the material side of this holy season. We shall not be among them. Tomorrow, we are going to have our meditation day. From ten to six o'clock we will be meditating on Christ. To feel his presence and his consciousness is our purpose. Christ has remained unknown to men. They have kept the gates of their devotion closed, locked with material desires, so that Christ cannot enter. When those portals are opened with love for Christ, he will come. I want everyone to take the spiritual celebration of Christmas seriously. Our aim is nothing less than to bring Christ into our consciousness.

The Justice of God

St. John said, "But as many as received him, to them gave he power to become the sons of God, even to them that believe on his name: which were born, not of blood, nor of the will of the flesh, nor of the will of man, but of God."* These sacred words reveal the justice of God. What would be our position and our hope if the Lord made and equipped only one man, Jesus Christ, with the insight and will power necessary to conquer temptation and attain God-union? Jesus was both human and divine, as are we all. If this were not so, then his trials and the pain he endured in crucifixion were just a farce. Rather, he was a perfect type and an ideal model that all God-seekers may follow in shouldering their own crosses. How could we be expected to overcome the myriad temptations of *maya* unless we too are made in the image of God and are as much chosen and loved by Him as was Jesus? The primary difference between Jesus and most other beings is that he conquered the tests that they have yet to go through. He attained the divinity of Christ Consciousness by continuous effort and will power to overcóme all mortal temptations and attachments. That Jesus was like us gives us courage and the desire to be like him.

What an extreme test Jesus faced in surrendering himself to be crucified. Patanjali points out that even great saints feel attachment to the body on the last day, and are loath to leave it. My Guru [Swami Sri Yukteswar] explained that the hesitancy to leave the body at death is comparable to the experience of a long-caged bird that fears to soar out of its prison into the skyey vastness. By his words on the Cross, Jesus revealed that he had to struggle to destroy the last shred of attachment to the body.† He fought his human nature and won; that is why I see him as an ideal exemplar for all mankind.

Millions of persons in this world have a charcoal mentality, unable to reflect the divine consciousness that is in their souls. You must become like the diamond, radiant with the sunlight of Christ Consciousness. If even one soul out of this gathering becomes enlightened, that is far better than if I were to speak to audiences of thousands who come just to hear an inspirational discourse. I know that some of you here have

---

* *John* 1:12–13 (Bible).

† "My God, my God, why hast Thou forsaken me? (*Matthew* 27:46, Bible)....Father, into Thy hands I commend my spirit: and having said thus, he gave up the ghost" (*Luke* 23:46, Bible).

real communion with Christ. That pleases me most.

There is a vast difference between imagination and Self-realization. If you only imagine, you may have subconscious dreams and inner "visions" of Christ every day. But that does not mean that you are truly in touch with him. The real visitation of Jesus is the communion with Christ Consciousness. If you are in tune with that Christ, your whole life will change.

The Universality of Christ Consciousness

The love of God uplifts and enlarges us. I can never think of myself anymore as exclusively in this body; I feel that I am present in all bodies. I have no awareness of race or other distinctions at all. In my perceptions, just as I feel my own consciousness in every part of my physical form, I feel you all to be a part of me. Everything that is living I feel within this body. I know the sensations of all. It is not imagination; it is Self-realization. This consciousness is far beyond telepathy. It is awareness of the perceptions of every being. That is the meaning of Christ Consciousness.

When that Christ comes within you, you lose your ego; the "I" is demolished. In humbleness you find a valley of dreams redolent with blossoms of Self-realization, nurtured by the waters of the Infinite Christ that gather and inundate all arid boundaries within you. You feel all things pervaded by One Life.

Infinite Oneness: That is what God is; that is what Christ is. If you would be like Christ, you must follow his ways. God could be cruel and destroy evildoers; in an instant He could destroy the whole world. But instead, He is using love to bring errant creation back to Him. Thus did Jesus teach: "Love your enemies," for God "maketh His sun to rise on the evil and on the good, and sendeth rain on the just and on the unjust."* Bhagavan Krishna similarly said: "He is a supreme yogi who regards with equal-mindedness...friends, enemies...the virtuous and the ungodly."†

Why should you hate anyone? To do so is against your own interest. Even though someone may hate you, if you give love

---

* *Matthew* 5:44, 45 (Bible).   † Bhagavad Gita VI:9.

in return you will feel wonderful. I am a friend to all. If I try to dislike anyone it burns me within. Do not abhor your enemies; to love them is the best way to conquer them. If you find the infection of hate spreading around you, why increase that epidemic by contracting the disease? Make yourself immune with the antidote of love.

Remember, your enemies, too, are children of God, and are loved by Him as dearly as you are. The Lord is like a mother; no matter how a child behaves, the mother loves it just the same. Those who do evil have gone astray, and God wants intensely to bring them back to His fold.

Another reason you should love your enemies is that transgressors for the most part are ignorant of their erroneous doings, feeling fully justified in their behavior. No thinking person *wants* to do wrong; most people simply do not realize the error of their ways. They act on impulse, with no clear vision or power of reflection. That is why they "know not what they do."* Such persons actually do great harm to themselves, and therefore should be objects of our sympathy.

It generally requires far more strength and purity of mind to love than to hate. But a sage finds it easier to love than to hate, because he "beholds his Self (Spirit-united) in all creatures and all creatures in the Spirit."† He sees all beings as a part of his greater Self, indissolubly bound together by the universal Christ Consciousness.

To bring divine awareness into our human consciousness we must outgrow the limited conventional conception of Christ. To me, Christmas is a thought of spiritual grandeur— a realization that our minds are an altar of Christ, the Universal Intelligence in all creation.

Who is the devotee that really knows what Christ is? To human vision he is the little babe born in Bethlehem, and the savior who healed the sick and raised the dead. To divine vision he is the Christ-awareness in all space and in every atom. You should aspire to know that Christ within you. Banish every prejudice and love all beings. See Christ in them, because they

---

* *Luke* 23:34 (Bible).   † Bhagavad Gita VI:29.

are a part of your real Self. How can you hate your own Self dwelling in any form? If you do, it shows that you do not know Christ—the Christ Consciousness that is just behind your human mind and feelings. When you hold a wrong thought about anybody, you obliterate Christ from your inner vision.

Christ is born in the cradle of tenderness. Greater than the destructive force of hate is the compassionate power of love. Whatever you say or do to others, let it be with love. Harm no one. Judge not others. Hate none, love all; behold Christ in all. Whatever blessings you have, desire that all should have.

The things you own are not really yours; they are given for your use temporarily. When death comes, they will be taken from you. Banish the consciousness of possession. Share with all; then you naturally attract good to yourself. Give and you shall receive. Many times I have been left without a cent, but I always rely on the Bank of God; His prosperity and His power are with me. That is the utmost security. First, you must carefully prepare your consciousness in order to bring Christ into your body-temple. Then, wherever you go, whatever be your need, the universal law will work with you.

Love All Countries and All Races

Think of everything in terms of universality. Do not be interested only in your own country. Love all nations. Mankind cannot afford warring and fighting within itself; there should be a common striving to establish the consciousness of Christ love and unity in the hearts of all. It is foolish to create divisions among nationalities and races and religions. Every church is a church of God, every place of worship is a temple of God, and every human being is a child of God. If you believe in Christ and in what he stood for, how can you feel differently?

Christ must be invited through devotional meditation into a cathedral of inner silence. The newborn Christ Consciousness must be awakened in the cradle of each heart. So instead of taking this coming Christmas as just an occasion for material happiness, make your own heart a cradle wherein Christ can be born.

If you want really to feel Christ and know him, meditate. Christ is within you, and you can realize this truth by using the ancient yoga techniques of meditation. There is no instrument other than deep meditation that can detect the presence of that almighty Grace within. Still the body, withdraw energy from the senses into the brain, calm the heart: Christ will be there; you will feel the divine joy of the Infinite Christ. If that joy is lacking, there is some spiritual kink in your mental frame of mind that you must straighten out. Make the effort.

Have greater zeal! Buddha sat eight years under a banyan tree until he realized the Universal Consciousness. It can be attained by anyone who makes the effort. Buddha, Christ, Krishna, great prophets of all climes and ages, had that consciousness. All who so aspire can achieve it. Self-Realization Fellowship [Yogoda Satsanga Society of India] has come to show the way. That is the true Second Coming of Christ. Seclude yourself at night and in silence follow the spiritual techniques; practice *Kriya Yoga*. Meditate! What are you waiting for? Bring Christ to the altar of your consciousness now, that you may have him still when you pass from this world to the next. Tarry no longer among those who yet wonder, "Where is Christ now?"

May Christ Have a Second Coming Within You

May Christ have a Second Coming, within your own consciousness! That is my humble prayer for you today. And I am giving this special blessing to you all, that if you will meditate deeply during the Christmas period, you will feel the presence of Christ. The perception of Christ in your hearts is the greatest gift I could give to you. But you must have open hands to receive it—you must meditate.

At this time, the angels in the ether celebrate Christmas. An Infinite Light shone on the earth on that first Christmas day, and each year at this holy time the ether is filled with that Light. To honor Christ in meditation is the real celebration. May we start a new era on earth by celebrating spiritual Christmas everywhere! Tell your friends wherever you go, as long as you live, to pass a day in meditation during the Christmas season. Then within their hearts December 25 will be a real birth of Christ.

Christ *is* the joy of meditation. It is his perception you feel in the deepest hours of silence. And this is my wish for you, that you may bring that Christ into your heart every day, every hour.

Meditate whenever you can. Practice *Kriya Yoga.* Any time that you have leisure and can be calm, meditate. Jesus said he would send the Comforter—the Holy Ghost. When you are in tune with its vibration—the *Aum* or Amen—you feel great joy, the bliss of God as omnipresent Christ Consciousness.

The eternal consciousness behind all creation is that of God the Father. The Son or Christ Intelligence (the *Kutastha Chaitanya* or Krishna Consciousness of India) is hidden in the womb of Mother Nature, the Holy Ghost or invisible creative power of *Aum.* Any time your consciousness is attuned to divine realization, Christ will take birth anew in the cradle of your awakened soul perceptions. Coming out of the secret fastnesses of Nature, the Omnipresent Christ reveals to you the wonders of infinite love and wisdom.

Spread this message of Christ-realization, the true Second Coming. Wherever we go we shall establish temples of God— not edifices of stone, but living temples of realization in the souls of men.

At this moment I perceive the light of the Infinite Christ, the light of Eternal Spirit. In that light I bless you and baptize you. May your life, forever awake in Christ Consciousness, be a true messenger of that Light.

"Lord, we pray that the Universal Consciousness of Christ be manifested in the minds of all. Heavenly Father, make us one with Thee. Let the heart of every member of Self-Realization Fellowship [Yogoda Satsanga Society of India] and every member of our world-home and every living creature on all planets be a perfect cradle to hold the Christ Consciousness. May the celestial joy that comes through awareness of Thee be awakened in the hearts of all our brothers. O Christ, make us diamonds of spirituality sparkling in the ornament of thy Being!"

What Is the True Equality of Man?

Circa 1938

Truth is neither Eastern nor Western—it is the inalienable property of every soul that draws the breath of life. Likewise, the true equality of man lies not in the social nor political nor economic equality that people wrongly imagine will arrive someday, but in the equality of every soul before God, and in their equality to seek Him and to know Him.

Without intelligence, it is impossible to understand anything properly. Everything should be judged intelligently on its own merits, and not on baseless assertions or secondhand opinions. If one does not make an effort to discover truth beneath any and all perplexing veils, then one will never even know his own real nature and will remain the sport of outside forces and the slave of circumstance. Contempt for anything, without investigation, is the sign of a deluded man who will come to grief.

One stipulation of Eastern teachings that should be stressed is that enlightening instructions can be wholly comprehended only if one practices them regularly in his daily life after receiving them from a true guru, one who possesses actual God-realization. The wondrous light of truth that leads from the dark world of matter into the celestial powers of divinity is neither casually bestowed nor effortlessly embraced; and no endeavor should be considered too arduous to find that light and to follow it.

All the world's great religions are based on common universal truths, which reinforce rather than conflict with one another. Practically all forms of religion and the basic systems of philosophy everywhere have drawn their inspiration from ancient scriptures. Every modern spiritual message of any power or vitality is a restatement in a new form of the truths pronounced ages ago by God-knowing sages of India. These illumined *rishis* devoted themselves exclusively to investigating spiritual laws and man's supernal potentialities, and in outlining paths of discipline for various natures to follow in order to bring out their soul's divinity and to achieve a reciprocal harmony with the cosmic forces of the universe.

Mankind has only one real enemy—ignorance. Let us all work together for its annihilation, helping and cheering one another along the way. Stripped of ignorance, all souls stand in equal blessedness before our One Father-Mother-Friend-Beloved God.

The Need for Universal Religious Principles

Reply to Questions of a Truth-Seeker

The following questions were put before Paramahansa Yogananda in 1951 by Professor Bhagwat S. Upadhyaya of Rajputana University in Rajasthan State, distinguished author and historian of Indian culture. The professor met with Paramahansaji at Self-Realization Fellowship International Headquarters in Los Angeles.

Paramahansaji, do you belong to a particular spiritual order?

Yes, to the ancient Swami Order of India reorganized centuries ago into its present form by Swami Shankara, Adi Shankaracharya. I belong to the Giri ("mountain") branch, one of the ten subdivisions of the Order, as did my guru Swami Sri Yukteswar from whom I received initiation.

You are a man of religion; but don't you think that religion has been a cause of division, bloodshed, and evil in the world?

The existence of imitation gold does not decrease the value of pure gold. Similarly, spurious religion does not diminish the worth of true religion. Those who abuse the power of religion or who only pretend to follow religious practices for their own self-promotion become hypocrites and are sometimes perpetrators of evil; they are the wrongdoers, not religion. Those who exemplify true religion, or *dharma*,* are a source of upliftment to the world; and they themselves become forever free from sorrow. True religion consists of those principles by which body,

---

* See glossary.

mind, and soul can be united to God. It is ultimately the only savior that can rescue man from all the evils of the earth.

Is religion per se really necessary for the upliftment of man? When he joins a particular faith or order, does he not rather circumscribe himself and thus create barriers between himself and those of other creeds?

Dogmatic religions are bypaths, sometimes blind alleys leading nowhere; but even so, a fairly good dogmatic religion can lead the sincere seeker to the highway of true religion, which in turn leads to God. That highway is yoga, the scientific process by which every soul reunites with Spirit. In the Bhagavad Gita, yoga is proclaimed greater than all other paths —greater than those of devotion, wisdom, and righteous action. Yoga is the science of how man descended from Spirit into flesh and became identified with the body and its senses and possessions; and how he can reascend to God. The experience, or realization, of truth that comes from yoga practice provides proof of the underlying unity of all religions found in the perception of their one common denominator—God.

Should religion take the form of an organized entity, such as Buddhism or Christianity, or should it rather be one of individual intuitive faith?

Organized religion is the hive; realization is the honey. Both are necessary. But it often happens that when organized religion concentrates on the outward tenets and ceremonial aspects it becomes a dogmatic empty hive. At the opposite extreme, some yogis in the Himalayas gather the honey of God-realization in their hearts without providing hives of organized religion through which others might share that divine nectar. That is selfish. If organized religion is backed by great savants, it does much good in the world. If it is promoted only by egotistical, bigoted, or commercial people, it does little good and often much harm to people in general.

If faith be intuitive, will it even then need a guru?

God does not talk openly to novitiate spiritual seekers; their intuition is not yet developed, and so inner guidance is not infallible. God therefore guides through the instructions of a guru who communes with Him. The preceptor must have divine attunement or we have "the blind leading the blind."

Does not religion take the form of a dogma after it is organized and defined by symbols and conventions?

Just as the nut is hidden within the shell, so is true religion hidden in the distorting dogmatic formalities of religion. But as a nutshell can be opened by a nutcracker and the meat found inside, so deep spiritual seekers, by the nutcracker of intuitive meditation on religious ideals, can break the dogmatic shell and get at the inner hidden truth. A crow may peck vainly at a hard walnut shell and never get at the meat; similarly, shallow spiritual seekers bite unsuccessfully at the dogmatic shell of religion without ever getting to the kernel of truth.

You believe there is a fundamental unity of all religions. If that be so, why is there jealousy and conflict between the followers of one creed and those of other persuasions?

We read of such conflicts even in the ancient scriptures. The disciples of the great god Shiva extol him as supreme; the Vaishnavites consider Vishnu and his incarnations as Rama or Krishna to be the highest.* Worshipers within the divisions of religion have not the full realization of those whose lives have inspired true paths. I have often said that if Jesus, Krishna, Buddha, and other true emissaries of God came together, they would not quarrel, but would drink from the same one cup of God-communion.

The varying views of religionists are akin to the story told in India about six blind brothers who were washing an elephant. The first brother proclaimed that the elephant is like a huge wall; he had been washing the sides of the pachyderm. Hearing this, the second brother disagreed, asserting that the elephant is like a flexible bamboo pole; he had been washing the trunk. The third, thinking those two brothers were fools, insisted that the elephant is like two banana leaves; he had been

---

* See *Brahma-Vishnu-Shiva* in glossary.

washing the ears. Hearing these absurd pronouncements, the fourth brother corrected them with his definition that the elephant is like a large fleshy roof supported by four pillars; he had been washing the legs. The fifth brother laughed derisively, for to him the elephant was just two pieces of bone; he had been washing the tusks. Now the sixth brother knew they were all crazy and declared definitely that the elephant was only a piece of rope hanging from heaven; he had washed the tail and, being the youngest and smallest, he couldn't reach the top of the tail and so assumed it descended from the celestial regions of the gods. At the height of the quarrel, their sighted father arrived and explained, "You are all right, and you are all wrong. Right, because you correctly described what you experienced, but wrong because each of you experienced only a part of the whole. The elephant is an aggregate of all of these parts."

Man's consciousness evolves through incarnations and gradually experiences more and more of the nectar-ocean of truth. Each person can absorb only to the degree of his individual experience. These differences in perception are the cause of arguments and controversies, each seeing only a part of the whole truth. An exchange of differing views is constructive if done with openness and respect; but destructive, ending in quarrels, if there is bigotry and fanaticism.

Do you find similarities between the Hindu and Christian faiths?

The Bhagavad Gita and the Christian Bible, especially the New Testament, I consider the greatest of all scriptures because they both point out the same yoga highway to God. The Bhagavad Gita teaches: "He is a man of realization who sees Spirit equally in all."* And the Bible says: "Know ye not that ye are the temple of God, and that the Spirit of God dwelleth in you?"† The Revelation of St. John in the Bible is an allegory of the same principles of yoga cited in the Gita. My Guru sent me to the West especially to show the underlying yoga highway to God

---

* "He sees truly who perceives the Supreme Lord present equally in all creatures, the Imperishable amidst the perishing" (Bhagavad Gita XIII:27).
† *I Corinthians* 3:16 (Bible).

to be found in both the Bible and the Bhagavad Gita.

Do you think Americans are God-fearing people? Can they indeed have faith in God, the unknown Infinite, in view of their emphasis on material living?

I find the Americans, who have achieved the most in material accomplishments, are reaching out more to real spiritual ideals; whereas in some European and Asiatic countries, due to famine, disease, and lack of necessities, people are inclining more toward materialism.

Do Westerners really understand the Indian philosophy you teach? How was it that you chose America, of all places, as the base of your organizational activities?

Yoga is scientific, and Americans respond to that approach to God. They have had plenty of materialism and dogmatism. America and other countries in the West are ready and eager for proven methods that provide a practical experience of God. When I met my Guru in Banaras, he told me that my destiny was to show the people of the West the unity of their religion with that of India. My mission in India is also progressing.

Do you promote the yoga system of Patanjali* or that of the Bhagavad Gita?

If we had the time now, I could show you how all the warriors mentioned in the Bhagavad Gita are allegorical representations of the same yogic principles mentioned in Patanjali's *Yoga Sutras*. For example, the Pandava twins, Nakula and Sahadeva, represent *yama* and *niyama* (the proscriptive and prescriptive rules to be followed). Arjuna represents fiery self-control. Bhima represents *pranayama* (control of life and breath), and Yudhisthira ("he who is calm in battle") represents calmness or intuitive discrimination. The opposing Kurus, who stole the kingdom of the righteous Pandavas, represent the negative qualities and forces to be overcome by the aspiring yogi. The Gita truths, having been written earlier, were eluci-

---

* Ancient exponent of Yoga, whose *Yoga Sutras* outline the principles of the yogic path. (See glossary.)

dated in concise *sutras* by Patanjali. His work is a masterful condensation of the yoga science.*

Do you think that in the attainment of the Ultimate, Hatha Yoga *plays an important role? Do you advocate* Hatha Yoga *practices?*

Hatha Yoga postures, or *asanas,* are very beneficial for young people. If they start at an early age, when they grow up they can sit in one posture and go deep into meditation for a long time without the body's causing discomfort or disturbance. All the gymnastics of the postures, however, cannot be practiced by most adults, whose bodies are no longer supple. Older persons who lack discrimination in trying to practice the *asanas* may injure themselves; and if they try to meditate in a difficult, painful posture, the mind will be more on the pain than on God. So, as far as the *asanas* themselves are concerned, I advocate them for all who are young. The *asanas* help them to remain exceptionally youthful and healthy, as can be seen in the boys and young monks and nuns who reside in our ashrams. But they are taught, in addition, *Kriya Yoga* for God-communion. *Kriya Yoga,* introduced in this present age by Sri Shyamacharan Lahiri Mahasaya, is the highest of all techniques of *Raja Yoga.*† You can read about *Kriya Yoga,* which I have explained in some detail, in my *Autobiography of a Yogi.*

Do you think that Hatha Yoga *practices in themselves engender spiritual powers and realization?*

No; *Hatha Yoga* only disciplines the body and keeps it healthy and ready for spiritual advancement by *Raja Yoga,* meditation for God-communion.

Do you approve of the various orders of saktas *and* tantrikas *(or of any of them)?*‡

They all originally had some good in them, when correctly

---

* The foregoing points are elaborated in detail in Paramahansaji's commentary of the Bhagavad Gita, *God Talks With Arjuna,* chapter 1.

† The "royal" or highest path to God-union. (See glossary.)

‡ *Saktas (shaktas)* are worshipers of God in the aspect of Shakti, the mani-

understood in their pure scriptural form; but as practiced today they are mostly bad, because they advocate fantastic methods that are not suitable to the common man. Some *tantrikas* who know the spiritual seed-words, vibratory mantras, by which they can attune their consciousness to see visions of deities (personifications of God's divine powers), and thence ultimately commune with God, are very good; but *tantrikas* who indulge in sex, wine, and evil practices are not good.*

The tantrikas *say that not suppression but satiety of the senses leads to bliss. Do you agree with this idea?*

The *tantrikas* do not say that. Certain followers of *Tantra* try to develop self-mastery by engaging in sex, eating meat, and drinking wine while remaining mentally unattached to those actions. Persons who are licentious in their habits might find some good in the basic aspects of practicing moderation and mental control. But yogis usually condemn this path, for most seekers merely find in it an excuse to indulge their baser instincts and lusts rather than to attain self-control.

The path of inner renunciation and scientific meditation for contact of God as Bliss advocated by the Bhagavad Gita is the supreme path. It enables even the weak seeker of truth to withdraw from the tempting scenes of his weakness, and gives him a taste of the inner divine Bliss, which, by comparison, he will find far more satisfying than the pleasures of material indulgences.

---

fested energy or power of Spirit that is active in creation. *Tantrikas* are those who follow the various practices described in the *Tantras,* one of the main categories of *shastras* or scriptures of Hinduism.

Tantra deals primarily with ritualistic worship and the use of mantras. The purpose is to reunite the individual soul with Spirit, the Creator, by gaining knowledge of and mastery over the forces active in creation. Its scriptures present profound truths under the veil of detailed esoteric symbolism; *Tantra* in its pure form is understood only by an enlightened few. There have been many degenerate offshoots, including those whose followers seek after phenomenal powers and experiences, and those who wrongly employ various sensual practices.

* Paramahansaji is here referring to *Vamachara,* "left-handed" tantric rituals that were outlawed in India when their practice was perverted into hedonism. ("Right-handed" *Tantra* advocates many forms of systematic yoga practice and self-discipline.)

Is there really a God, personal or infinite, that creates and destroys the universe? Has not man in his fear and greed created such a Being after his own image, rather than that a Divine Creator formed man after His image? The presence of so much evil and suffering in the world would seem to support this view.

Man's view of the universe is perversely limited by the circumscriptions of his limited mind and senses. Thus he sees created things, but not their essence nor their Creator. In a motion picture, we see the villain and the hero projected on the screen by the same beam of light. The movie villain was created that by contrast we may love and be inspired by the hero. By analyzing the movie, that both the villain and the hero and the events that revolve around them are created by the same principle, we understand that no harm has taken place—everything was a portrayal of shadows and light. The same is true about God's ever-changing motion picture of creation.

Savants who realize their oneness with God see creation as a motion picture of forces emanating from Him. Man, though created in the image of God (a soul that is an individualized part of Him), has become identified with the light-and-shadow relativities of cosmic delusion, or *maya*. When he uses his free choice to adopt those actions by which he frees himself from attachment to *maya*, he understands the true nature of creation and its Creator. In his deluded state, however, man's consciousness of God is limited or expanded according to the greater or lesser degree of his delusion. The man of full realization knows God as ever-existing, ever-conscious, ever-new Bliss; and that all contrasting illusions evolved from this one underlying Cosmic Consciousness.

God created the various kinds of faculties and potentialities at work in man and in all creation, but man as an individualized part of God endowed with free will becomes engrossed in delusion by misuse of those faculties. In doing so, he himself creates the good or evil role he plays in the cosmic drama, and thereby influences the trend of good or evil events. When man ceases to identify himself with the body and matter, he realizes he is made in the image of God—not before. The enlightened man works with God for the strengthening of good in the world, and for the divine upliftment of others.

Is it essential that there be a God?

Something cannot come out of nothing. There has to be Something that is the cause and source of being. That Something is Spirit, Eternal Consciousness, God the Father-Mother of Creation. As the waves of the ocean cannot exist without the ocean, so soul-waves, or individualized expressions of being, could not exist without the ocean of God's presence. So long as soul-waves play with the storm of delusion, they rise out of the sea and are shattered and broken. That is why it is essential to return to the calm deeps of the oceanic bosom of God.

What is Bliss, the final emancipation? Is not man born once and his individuality lost forever in death?

Man lives in one body and with one name only once. He never reincarnates again with the same form and identity. A person may wear a garment for some time and then discard it, never to use it again. Similarly, the soul wears a different body in each of many lifetimes until, through reincarnation and spiritual evolution, it ascends back to Spirit. Thus you live only once as any particular person, but the soul, the eternal you, lives through numerous reincarnations, carrying with it the cumulative personality and karmic tendencies of its past existences.

The mind, or sentient consciousness in man, is subject to alternating waves that agitate the soul and keep it separate from God: the wave of sorrow; the wave of pleasure; and the wave of indifference or boredom. When these waves, created by the storm of delusion, have been dispelled by yoga, man experiences the negative state of peace, or the absence of these agitations. By deeper yoga practice and meditation, he goes beyond the vale of peace and experiences the positive state of ever new Bliss. Sorrow, pleasure, and indifference are transitory experiences of the incarnate soul; but the state of Bliss is an integral part of the Self, and as such is eternal. It is ever new; it never grows stale. Having once attained this Bliss, man never again seeks anything else. When he reidentifies with his soul as individualized ever-existing, ever-conscious, ever-new Bliss, he then merges with the all-pervading ever-existing, ever-conscious, ever-new Bliss of Spirit—even as a droplet returns to the sea. Still, that individuality is never lost; that portion of Spirit eternally retains its "memory" of that individualized existence.

From what I have seen of your work, I feel that you have a good and devoted following. Have you had to make an effort to create it?

Does a magnet make an effort to draw the iron? There is a natural attraction according to the affinity of the iron and the power of the magnet. Of course, the iron must be near enough to the magnet to be drawn. So is the relationship between guru and disciple. It is a question of the recipiency of the disciple and the spiritual power of the preceptor to inspire and draw him to God.

Jesus said, "No man can come to me, except the Father which hath sent me draw him."* The omniscient God brings shallow seekers in contact with lesser teachings and spiritual books; from these they derive some benefit commensurate with their degree of spiritual desire and understanding. But deep seekers of God are brought by Him into contact with fully realized gurus who are able to commune with God and to serve as channels in imparting divine guidance. It is their duty to introduce the devotee to God. So it is ultimately God who brings together guru and disciple, but there is also a desire on their part to come together. Through earnest spiritual longing the disciple, perhaps unconsciously at first, seeks the guru—one who can lead him to God. And the true guru, when he intuitively knows a disciple sent by God, makes an effort to draw him, and goes out of his way to help him. The true disciple, finding a true guru, becomes magnetically attracted to him and recognizes him as the one sent by God. This is the law.

Perhaps you will agree that the world is facing a crisis. What is the cause of it, and what is the remedy?

All nations have to follow the influence of the ascending

---

* *John* 6:44 (Bible).

and descending *yugas*.* The present world crisis is due to the upward climb of Dwapara Yuga; in order for the world to become better, evil must be expunged. The forces of evil will cause their own destruction, thus assuring survival of the righteous nations. The conflict between good and evil has been going on since the dawn of history. But as the world is moving upward through the Dwapara Yuga, the electrical or atomic age, there is greater potential not only for good, but also for destruction through the misuse of technology by those who are greedy and desire power. In keeping with the influence of Dwapara Yuga, technology is rapidly moving the general populace to higher levels of achievement. But this progress also creates a greater gap between the achievers and nonachievers. This foments jealousies and social, economic, and political troubles.

Do you think, then, that Communism with its philosophy of equality and its policy of leveling the strata of society to some smooth surface is doing a humanitarian work, and easing God's concern, if you please, about the needs of all His children?

I believe in the brotherhood of man created by mutual love and understanding and cooperation. All worthwhile goals and ennobling ideals should be introduced to the world by spiritual example and good methods, not by brute force and war. Political power without spiritual principles is dangerous. By spiritual principles I do not refer to doctrines of specific religions— which may also be divisive—but to *dharma* or universal principles of righteousness applicable to the well-being of all humanity. To prevent the spread of evil, sometimes righteous war is even necessary. You cannot preach nonviolence and cooperation to a wild tiger, for he will destroy you even before you can

---

* The Hindu scriptures teach that the earth goes through repeated cycles of evolution and devolution. These world cycles consist of 24,000 years each, and are divided into four *yugas* or ages—12,000 years of ascending through these *yugas* to increasing enlightenment, and then 12,000 years of descending through the *yugas* to increasing ignorance and materialism. Each half-cycle consists of Kali Yuga, the dark or materialistic age; Dwapara Yuga, the electrical or atomic age; Treta Yuga, the mental age; and Satya Yuga, the age of truth or enlightenment. (See *yuga* in glossary.)

expound your philosophy. Some human perpetrators of evil are similarly unresponsive to reason. Any wagers of aggressive war, as was Hitler, will lose. Those who are compelled to fight a righteous war against evil will win. Whether or not a war is righteous is judged by God.

Do you think that America needs to change its character?

America represents the highest in material development, which is much needed in the world; and India represents, through her great masters and prophets, the acme of spiritual realization. In the course of the evolution of civilization, God has brought about these exemplars to show that midway between these two antipodes lies the ideal civilization: a balance between materiality and spirituality. All the world needs to adopt some of the more beautiful aspects of the material progressiveness of America, and also the spiritual idealism of India. America is already embracing a great part of the spiritual civilization of India, as evidenced by the phenomenal growth of Self-Realization Fellowship, and by the widespread interest in Hindu thought in general. India, on the other hand, needs a great deal of the scientific know-how of America to fight disease and poverty and provincialism, which are stains on the name of India's high spiritual heritage. The East should take the best constructive methods of the West, and the West should follow the East's emphasis on God as the supreme goal of life.

Would you like to give a message to the world?

My brothers and sisters of the world: Please remember that God is our Father and He is One. We are all His children, and as such we should adopt constructive means to help each other become physically, mentally, financially, and spiritually ideal citizens of a United States of the World. If in a community of one thousand persons each individual tries by graft, fighting, and chicanery to enrich himself at the expense of others, each person will have nine hundred and ninety-nine enemies; whereas, if each person cooperates with the others—physically, mentally, financially, and spiritually—each one will have nine hundred and ninety-nine friends. If all nations helped one another through love, the whole earth would live in peace with ample opportunity for promoting the well-being of all.

Man seems to forget his spiritual nature and reverts instead to his primal animal instincts. God created man as a potentially spiritual being; so as long as he will give vent to his animal nature, he will have trouble, wars, famine, poverty, and disease. When he will realize the necessity of universal brotherhood, he will create a world of great prosperity and happiness.

It is saddening to see leaders of nations foster untold misery because of greed and hate, instead of getting together in goodwill and harmony to work out their differences. Because of ambitious and evil politicians, the earth has suffered two world wars, and faces the prospect of a third world conflict. If the money spent on destruction were instead collected in an international fund, it could remove the slums of the world, eradicate hunger, and greatly advance medical science, giving every man, woman, and child a better chance to live in the peace of a God-centered life.

History shows that from the dawn of civilization hate and selfishness in man have created innumerable wars, with their ever-increasing snowball of misery. A third world war would enlarge this snowball until it would freeze the earth with misery, poverty, and death. The only way to melt the snowball of misery is through brotherhood, love, and divine attunement that comes from God-uniting methods of meditation. When every soul will rise above petty divisions in true spiritual understanding, world misery will be consumed in the fire of the realization of the universality of God and the brotherhood of man.

Such media as radio and television and air travel have brought us all together as never before. We must learn that it can no longer be Asia for Asiatics, Europe for Europeans, America for Americans, and so on, but a United States of the World under God, in which each human being can be an ideal citizen of the globe with every opportunity for fulfillment in body, mind, and soul.

That would be my message, my plea, to the world.

Mahatma Gandhi: Apostle of Peace

In 1935, Paramahansaji visited Mahatma Gandhi at his hermitage in Wardha, India. At that time, the Mahatma requested initiation into *Kriya Yoga*. Ten years earlier, Gandhiji had paid a visit to Paramahansaji's Yogoda Satsanga school for boys in Ranchi. Expressing keen interest in the balanced curriculum of the Yogoda program, he inscribed in the guest book a gracious tribute.

This talk was given in 1948 at a dinner sponsored by the Chinese Culture Society in honor of Mahatma Gandhi, India's freedom, and the cause of peace. On this occasion Paramahansaji and Dr. Hugh E. MacBeth were speakers. Following are highlights from Paramahansaji's tribute.

Two kinds of prophets come into the world. There are qualitative prophets, who mold their faithful disciples into great souls. And there are quantitative prophets, who influence the masses, so that vast multitudes are inspired and receive some light from the presence of such a master. Some masters do both; but by these qualitative and quantitative standards we may judge all the prophets of the world.

Qualitatively speaking, I have met many great, Christlike masters, with whom I have lived, and about whom I have written in my book, *Autobiography of a Yogi*. But quantitatively speaking, I think that since the time of Christ there has been no single individual whose life and ideals have influenced the masses more than Mahatma Gandhi's. Christ's teaching of loving enemies was never better demonstrated in the life of one individual in modern times than in the life of Mahatma Gandhi.

By ordinary standards, he was considered very homely, but when you looked into his eyes, you could see the universality of his soul*—then a vast concourse of spiritual thoughts over-

---

* "In those who have banished ignorance by Self-knowledge, their wisdom, like the illuminating sun, makes manifest the Supreme Self" (Bhagavad Gita V:16).

powered you. He was shrewd; he was joyous; he had great faith in God. Though he did not develop qualitative Christ-like souls as did some of the masters of India, God sent him into the world as a prophet who for the first time (unlike other great spiritual leaders of the world) went beyond his flock and influenced the great masses of people politically—even thick-headed politicians who had always believed that violence and brute force can conquer.

Brute force destroys itself. Originally, when men clashed with each other, it was because one clan had more than another, so they fought for each other's property. In this way, from prehistoric days down through the Christian era, the karma of thousands of wars gathered like a snowball into the first World War. And what did it accomplish? It only accumu-lated in its wake more trouble, more disaster. The second World War came; and now, when we analyze the results, don't we wish that we had the world as it was before this devasta-tion occurred? As Jesus Christ and Gandhi said, "If you use the sword, you will fall by the sword."*

Man's Use of the Atom

The snowball of bad karma is growing bigger and bigger, and now the politicians are speaking again of war! Why? They should know very well they will not be safe—not even in the White House or the Kremlin—because the atomic bomb has spread the threat of devastation everywhere, affecting combat-ants and noncombatants alike. On the other hand, we can see that the Lord has given unto man—through the great scien-tists—the use of atoms; and we know now that the latent power in droplets of water could furnish the city of Chicago with enough electricity to keep it running for three days! If con-structively used, this atomic energy could bring the millen-nium. It could eradicate all the slums of the world. Man would not have to work more than two hours a day. But remember, nothing can bring about that constructive use of atom-power unless man realizes that he is not a brute, entitled to use brute

---

* Paraphrase of *Matthew* 26:52 (Bible).

violence, and concentrates instead on brotherhood.

Only brotherhood, the warmth of brotherhood, can melt the colossal ever-increasing snowball of war karma. So this is the time to preach brotherhood. No matter how dark you think the picture is, do not be too discouraged. I know there is a God who gives to the nations of the world what is for their good. They reap good or bad results according to their karma; and very few realize that the good karma of America and the good karma of India are on the ascendant. Let me remind you that no power on earth can destroy the idealism of India and the spiritual democracy of America. I know that the atomic bomb is a very bad thing; but I know also that it is better in the hands of America than in the hands of anybody else. I wish, and pray, that America will never again use the atomic bomb, but will destroy the need for all bombs and thus stop the growing snowball of bad karma—war karma—that is destroying the fraternal warmth of the world. Only by love, by adhering to the principles of Christ and Mahatma Gandhi, can this be done.

Gandhi's Treasure

Mahatma Gandhi was laughed at by his enemies, scoffed at by ignorant people. Many cartoons have been drawn to ridicule him. And still in his life he had shown that evil travels with the wind, but the power of Truth travels against the wind. He demonstrated that.

I was talking once to a band of students who criticized Mahatma Gandhi because he did not provide any financial security in the form of bonds for his wife or children; and his son recently announced: "Father has not left us anything." I am going to write to him: "Your father has left to you, to us, to all the millions of people in India, and to every nation, the riches of the spiritual truth he proved: that political freedom can come to four hundred million not by the sword, nor by the firing of a single shot, but by the power of love." Mahatma Gandhi's son has received freedom; all India has received freedom, by spiritual means through Gandhi.

Mahatma Gandhi has left a richer world today, a world in which the practical power of these spiritual truths of love and understanding, which was laughed at before, has been effectively demonstrated before the mouths of cannons.

Once, in Bombay, the native soldiers of the Indian army revolted and were firing on and killing English people. It is alleged that Churchill threatened to send an army to bomb India out of existence. Then Mahatma Gandhi wrote to him, saying, "You don't need to do that. I will stop them." And he went to them, amidst the shots that were being fired. They stopped firing, and he said, "Peace unto you. You will not gain freedom by killing a few British people. Conquer them by the greater force of love." They remained peaceful, and Mahatma Gandhi by his appeal got the British to forgive the native insurrectionists.

I said that after the war, India would be free; it was predicted in our magazine, *East-West*.* I was laughed at for saying this, and for declaring that this World War II was being fought for the freedom of India and all downtrodden nations. Yet it has come true. India would never have been free if this war had not come about. *God* did not bring about this war; but because people believe in war and create karmic causes, there is war. God does not need to use atomic bombs and miracles to destroy the devil. The devils kill themselves by using power wrongly. But we find that Mahatma Gandhi conquered by the literal application of the methods of Jesus Christ.

Facing Death

Never has any religious or political leader been so honored at his death as Gandhi. He is even more powerful today than when he was alive. He retained his powers and exemplified his teachings to the very end. Only one week before his death, he was the target of a bomb, which barely missed him, but he asked his followers not to be hard on the traitors! He said that God was keeping him there to do a little more work; and that when it was done, God would take him away. The night before his death, he told his grandniece, "Abha, Abha, bring the important letters. I'll sign them. Tomorrow it may be too late." He knew his time had come.

Such a man is Gandhi, who has freed India, who has

* In 1948 Paramahansaji changed the name of the magazine to *Self-Realization* (see glossary).

brought the nonviolent method before all bull-headed politicians, and proved it an effective method.

Mahatma Gandhi was of God. He may not have been as great as Christ, or the masters I knew, but he knew God. When he was shot, he had a smile on his lips, and made a sign of forgiveness with his hand. With that gesture, Gandhi was asking the Father's forgiveness for his assassin. This was as inspiring as Jesus' words on the cross: "Father, forgive them; for they know not what they do."

What of the Future?

Gandhi is living today in the hearts of men, to remind them that violence is the law of the brute. When brutes such as the big saber-toothed tiger infested the earth, they didn't *rule* the earth. Man, by superior intellectual power, overcame larger, more powerful creatures, even without being equipped with machine guns. The President and Stalin should remember that if the strong destroy each other, the meek shall inherit the earth. The spiritually meek shall never be destroyed. Their weapon is Christ's method: loving the enemy, and conquering the enemy by love.

This is a time when God is bumping the heads of Communism, Imperialism, Capitalism—all isms that believe in the power of force. I make one prediction now: *The world is not going down to destruction.* So don't be frightened. Believe in your Father. He will protect you if you remember His ideals, if you keep faith in Him. We are moving upward. The twelve hundred years of the material cycle have passed, and three hundred of the twenty-four hundred years of the atomic age are gone. Then there will be the mental and the spiritual ages.* We are not going down. No matter what happens, the Spirit will win. I predict this; and that America's democracy and practical material power combined with India's spiritual power will prevail and conquer the world. Anybody who uses the bomb, motivated by aggression, will fall by the bomb; but I know that in the hearts of America and India there is no love of violence.

---

* See *yuga* in glossary.

As Hitler with all his power fell, so any dictator, wherever he is, shall be downed. This I predict.

Publisher's Note

The following words of Paramahansa Yogananda's, written in 1951, put into perspective the Master's view of war:

Wars of aggression and suppression are heinous crimes against the heritage of humanity as freeborn children of God. A war thus motivated is unrighteous action by the aggressor, and it is not unrighteousness to defend ourselves against such evil. To protect one's country and its helpless citizens against evil is righteous action. Spiritual power is the greatest force; it should be the bulwark behind every form of resistance and defense. The first line of action should be to use all spiritual and moral power possible to counter evil; and to strive to change the world's inclination to war and violence by removing the causes that strengthen evil—poverty and hunger, disease, injustice, greed, and selfish interests. If, in the last, evil force has to be met with righteous force, the Bhagavad Gita advises the Kshatriya, the soldier, to not waver but fulfill bravely his God-given duty.

Nations, Beware!

1937

Why do world suffering and world misery arise? When people all over the earth are happy and prosperous they are in tune with God, and the entire vibrations of the earth in relation with the planets are harmonious. But as soon as one nation starts fighting with another, or selfish industrial gourmands try to devour all prosperity for themselves, it brings depression. And when depression starts in one place, it begins to spread everywhere, owing to the vibrations that travel through the ether. The last world war [World War I] created wrong vibrations in Europe first, which then spread all over the earth; and where there was no war, influenza appeared. The agonies of the people who died in the world war created the subtle cause of the epidemic of Spanish influenza, which immediately followed the war and killed 20 million people while the war itself killed about 10 million only.

In the present Spanish Civil War, vibrations of the death struggles of thousands of men, women, and children are floating in the ether—causing floods in America, storms in England and Portugal, and earthquakes in India. And so the peoples of the world, instead of creating more conflicts and getting into wars, should try their utmost to use peaceful means and non-cooperation—for example, blockades—to stop war.

The murder of thousands of Ethiopians* (who didn't want war) and the vibrations of injustice done to them, has upset the equilibrium of the world. For no one can get away with disturbing one part of the world without the disturbance moving through the ether waves to other parts of the earth. If people in one part of a house are disturbed, then the entire household is

---

* Reference to the 1936 invasion of Ethiopia by Italy.

bound to be disturbed. After the Ethiopian conquest, the dread of war left as an aftermath of the last world war vanished. Many nations are again enthused for wars of aggression. The Ethiopian war was a war of aggression. The war in Spain is a war of aggression. According to the League of Nations, a war of aggression is untenable. But since the world ignored the divine mandate and divine rule of outlawing wars of aggression (which came as a great lesson from the last world war), the world is again headed towards the self-created, Satan-influenced possibility of a greater world war and greater destruction.

The Depression is caused by the sins of the last war; and if another world war is started there will be very little for the population of the world to eat. So it is better that the nations of Europe do everything possible to avert any wars.*

Right Patriotism

Another thing, patriotism can be evil when it doesn't mind its own business. When, instead of being used to keep intact the prosperity and happiness of its parent nation, it gets into international complications by wanting to spread its territorial influence, it destroys its own national well-being—the very thing for which patriotism stands. On the other hand, those patriots are foolish who think that they would lose national advantages by espousing international patriotism; for international good includes the national good, and partial national good should be sacrificed for international good. But if the national good acts against the interest of international good, it will defeat its own purpose. National selfishness that disregards the international well-being brings national as well as international disaster.

Ye nations of the world, beware! Use your patriotism to protect your own country and do not get mixed up with any other nation that advocates aggression. All nations should unite

---

* The 1940s saw the fulfillment of Paramahansaji's warning. During and after World War II, food was scarce in most of the world, owing to war-time conditions and to crop failure caused by plant diseases, inadequate irrigation, flooding, and severe storms. Millions of people, especially in Europe and Asia, starved during this unfortunate decade.

to noncooperate in every way with those nations that want to start wars of aggression. Nations of the earth should get together to find ways to mitigate the causes and effects of such nature-created calamities as disease, floods, droughts, sickness, earthquakes. Man should not add to the natural catastrophes by the avoidable self-created tragedies of poverty, lack, suffering, and death due to wars; for it is evident that self-created calamities and wrong vibrations of war and industrial selfishness bring about natural calamities.* The state of Texas in America could produce enough wheat and corn to supply the whole world; why is there any starvation in the world today? Because of man's political and industrial selfishness, which is against the divine laws of cooperation, mutual service, and sharing God-given prosperity properly among the nations of the world. If people would follow the laws laid down by Christ, "Love thy neighbor" and "Give all ye have," then there would be no poverty-suffering on earth today.

The politicians are blinded by their patriotism, selfishness, and love of fame. Disregarding the divine laws laid down by God and voiced by great saints, they are bringing an avalanche of miseries upon the nations of the earth. Follow the dictums of saints who are the true children of God, and not the dictums of Satan. We wish every true child of God of every nation would noncooperate with Satan and war, and work in every way to establish constructive, international peace and prosperity and spiritual happiness in their own nation and in all nations. Let us eradicate all wrong misery-producing sense

---

* "The sudden cataclysms that occur in nature, creating havoc and mass injury, are not 'acts of God.' Such disasters result from the thoughts and actions of man. Whenever the world's vibratory balance of good and evil is disturbed by an accumulation of harmful vibrations, the result of man's wrong thinking and wrong doing, you will see devastation....

"The world will continue to have warfare and natural calamities until all people correct their wrong thoughts and behavior....When materiality predominates in man's consciousness, there is an emission of subtle negative rays; their cumulative power disturbs the electrical balance of nature, and that is when earthquakes, floods, and other disasters happen. God is not responsible for them! Man's thoughts have to be controlled before nature can be controlled."—Paramahansa Yogananda, in *Man's Eternal Quest*

of false patriotism and establish in every world-citizen the true international patriotism of brotherhood, peace, mutual goodwill, and mutual mental, hygienic, industrial, social, scientific, philosophical, moral, and spiritual progress and happiness.

A United World
With God As President

Condensed from a talk during dedication ceremonies held in India Hall, one of several newly completed constructions on the site of the Self-Realization Fellowship Temple in Hollywood, April 8, 1951

I am so very happy that all of you are here today. I wish the dais were large enough so that all who have helped to make India House* a reality could be up here with us. It is a day of rejoicing, made possible by my boys [the monks of Self-Realization Fellowship], who have built this place. Here the people of East and West can have a cultural exchange of intellectual and philosophical experiences.

Now, Orientwise, we will meditate. Please sit upright. Exhale your breath twice; remain calm. Do not concentrate on respiration or muscular movement; relax completely. Bid adieu to the world of sensations—sight, hearing, smell, taste, and touch—and go within, where our soul expresses itself. From the factory of the soul emerge all experiences of our inner life. The body means nothing when the soul, the intellect, and the life have flown. So let us concentrate on That from which our being emerges: Know thy soul.

Dismiss all sensations of the body; dismiss all restless thoughts. Concentrate on the thought of peace and joy. Behind closed eyes you are beholding a mass of darkness, a sphere of darkness. Expand this ball of darkness until it surrounds this hall. Go on expanding it more and more, until it encompasses the city of Los Angeles; beloved America and all its states. See the whole world in this sphere, floating like a bubble. Now, visualize the expanding ball shimmering with a subdued light and joy. In this luminous joy see the planetary system, the

---

* The name was subsequently changed to India Hall, after the discovery of the prior use of India House by a firm in San Francisco.

Milky Way, the roaming universes, and the oceans of electrons and protons that surround them—all floating in this great sphere of light and joy. Thou art this boundless ball of light and joy. Affirm within, "In me the worlds are bubbles." Let us all say together, "In me the worlds are bubbles."

Meditate on the thought that in this ball of light and joy are all churches, temples, mosques; all nations of the earth; all worlds of God. In that universal consciousness we want God to guide us to establish here on earth a United States of the World, through brotherhood and peace, so that here and in the hereafter we shall realize we are one with God, made in His image. We are no longer the little human beings we see through our physical eyes; our inner eye of intuition is open.

"Heavenly Father, in this meditation we find Thine omnipresence. Though Thou hast limited us in this cage of the body, still with closed eyes we behold, through the eye of intuition, infinitude above, infinitude below, infinitude on the left and the right, everywhere. Therein we know that we are made in Thine image, even as Jesus Christ and the great masters realized this."

Expand Your Love to All Nations

The great ones are the models. Though their bodies were finite, they realized within that they were a part of the Infinite Ocean; that all individualized forms are the waves of the Cosmic Sea. In this world we circumscribe ourselves within a little family. When we love our neighbors, we become bigger. When we love our country, we become bigger still. When we love all nations, we become even bigger. And when we are one with God in the hereafter, or by deep meditation while we are still here in the body, we realize truly that the Ocean is the wave, and the wave is the Ocean.

I love India, because it was there I learned to love God and all beautiful things. But that love I do not keep for one nation alone, for this whole world is my India now. I love America as I love India, for she has been my second home. India and America represent the best of the East and the West. I believe a cultural exchange between the people of India and America will bring about a solution to the unsolved problems of the world;

all mankind will become true citizens of the globe, with a United States of the World established in every heart, and God as President. This statement may be Utopian, but what have most politicians done? They have brought wars, and wars, and more wars. I have no boundaries. I know God is our Father and we are all His children. The true spirit of America, and the true democracy, is that in which all nations find unity, as in India all religions find unity.

Not long after I came to America, I asked a Hindu college student, "What do you think of the Americans?" Evidently he considered himself on a very high seat above them, for he told me, "You know, they are like little children." "Oh," I replied, "then I am going to get along with them very well; for of such is the kingdom of God, as Jesus said."

Become a "Smile Millionaire"

I believe in America, because I know America does not institute a single war just for selfishness. America has given generously to the whole world. I have watched this very carefully. All the things I wanted for India I find that American people have. But one thing I noticed, even in the villages in India where people had perhaps only a little handful of rice to eat: those people had smiles in them that many American millionaires don't have. As I pass along the streets of America I look into the thoughts of the people, and all I see—dollar bills swirling in their brains: "If I had a few more dollars, I'd be happy." Money is necessary; there hasn't been a saint who didn't use it in some manner, for the necessities of life, or for the well-being of others. But money alone isn't enough.

I have met many millionaires, but I found they were not happy. Happiness lies in first becoming a "smile millionaire." Against all odds, you must try to smile from within. That will do you good! The time to smile is not only when everything goes right, but also when everything goes wrong. That is what the East teaches. And if you can't smile, stand before a mirror and pull on your cheeks so that the corners of the mouth will turn up. When I hear, "Oh, he was a millionaire and a very successful man, but he died of heart failure," I want to be an Easterner and sit on the banks of the Ganges and meditate. But when I see the poverty of India, then I want to be an American and get busy with science and machines to alleviate human suffering. Being made in the image of God, we have the power to use our individuality and our will to do great things—this is a wonderful ability God has given us.

Every time you look at your body of flesh and bones, you see yourself as small and limited. If even a little thing happens to your body—if you start sneezing, or if you hit your hand hard and break it—you realize your smallness. But when you close your eyes in meditation, you see the vastness of your consciousness—you see that you are in the center of eternity. Concentrate there; take a little time in the morning and the evening just to close your eyes and say, "I am the Infinite; I am His child. The wave is a bulge of the ocean; my consciousness is a bulge of the great Cosmic Consciousness. I am afraid of nothing. I am Spirit." That is the teaching of the East. You need that realization.

Finding God Gives Great Comfort and Happiness

If you keep a little time for God, it will give you great comfort and happiness. That is why Jesus said, "Love the Lord thy God with all thy heart."* If you are saying the Lord's Prayer, but thinking of a chicken dinner or a duck roast, the Lord knows that you don't want Him, so He doesn't come. Concentrate on God alone, without whose power you cannot move. Just as ships at sea can be moved by radio-activated power, so God moves us by His power, which flows into the medulla oblongata.† When the divine power leaves the body, you are dead. Why don't you think of the Source of that power? God does not deny you comforts. Jesus said: "But seek ye first the kingdom of God..."‡ Why? Because the nest of all happiness lies there. "...and all these things shall be added unto you."§ "Neither be ye of doubtful mind."**

---

* *Matthew* 22:37 (Bible).

† The "mouth of God." "Man shall not live by bread alone, but by every word that proceedeth out of the mouth of God" (*Matthew* 4:4, Bible). (See *medulla* in glossary.)

‡ *Matthew* 6:33 (Bible).   §Ibid.   ***Luke* 12:29 (Bible)

I own nothing, yet I have everything. Sometimes I have given away my last dollar. But I was never left out. God has always provided for me. I am very rich in that respect, even though poor outside—poor, not by compulsion, but of my own willingness. If I have my Father with me, what riches more can I want? That is the teaching of the East. That is what all Americans need to remember. Behind the dollar, behind all your efforts, is that great Power. And if that Power wishes you to have the right job, the right anything, you will have it tomorrow, if you are in tune with God. Everything was given to me that way. And I gave it all away to the cause, that I be not a slave to anyone or anything.

I never call myself a preceptor or a master or a guru. I only know that I killed my "self," and I find none else within me but the Heavenly Father. When you will kill your ego, you will find the same Being within you. As all lamps of a city are lighted by one dynamo, so all of us are lighted by God. "Know ye not that ye are the temple of God, and that the Spirit of God dwelleth in you?"* Why do you think that Jesus Christ was recognized as a son of God? Because he was our example, as the great masters were. Unless you become like Christ there is no meaning to these words: "But as many as received him, to them gave he power to become the sons of God."†

The diamond and the charcoal are both made of carbon. But the diamond receives the light and reflects it; the charcoal doesn't. Charcoal mentalities are those who are always complaining: "The world is bad, I have a headache, I want this, I don't have that, I can't succeed"—always the negative spirit. But the brilliant diamond mentality affirms: "It doesn't matter what happens to me; I shall make my way, for God is with me." Such a one receives the light; and ultimately, through material, mental, and spiritual evolution, he becomes like the Father.

Do not in any way minimize the power of the little wave that has been battered by the big waves. Somebody needs to say to it, "Little wave, what's the matter with you? Don't you see that the whole ocean is behind you? You are a bulge of the great

---

* *I Corinthians* 3:16 (Bible).   † *John* 1:12 (Bible).

ocean." Don't look to your little body; look within. The meditation that I gave you is of utmost importance. You will see how vast you are—you are everywhere in Spirit.

So, my friends, remember this: the East should be your preceptor in spiritual things, not minor superstitions. And the Easterner should realize that God has not spared the East suffering just because of its spirituality. The Orientals should consider the wonderful Americans, who have succeeded in driving away malaria and many other diseases, as their preceptor in material things. By the constructive exchange of the best of East and West, we shall build a United States of the World, with God as our President.

Is God a Dictator?

Self-Realization Fellowship International Headquarters,
Los Angeles, California, April 20, 1941

The question that is today's subject has perhaps never before been the topic of a spiritual lecture. I ask God all kinds of questions; He is never dismayed. And no matter what the question is, the Divine Being always gives me the most wonderful answer. You, too, can speak openly to God. If you will remember that, you will find great satisfaction in the understanding you will receive from Him about the anomalies of life that have mystified you.

Man came on earth uniquely endowed with individuality and free will. He was put here to evolve his intelligence, and thereby rediscover and express his true nature, the soul: a reflection of Spirit. He was to gradually develop his innate intelligence, not merely through books or lectures and sermons, but also through his own efforts to exercise his mind and improve the quality of his thoughts and actions.

The Bible tells us that we are made in the image of God.* But that image is certainly not apparent in all men. Though the light of God is in all equally, we cannot deny that it is more manifest in some than in others. If the light of God were fully manifest in all people, then human beings would remain constantly in their native state of perfection. But we see that in most people there is room for improvement; they have yet to evolve to a higher level of intelligence.

The flexibility of human life shows that there is a divine power lodged in all. That some show greater development than their fellow beings simply indicates that they have made more effort. You may ask, "Well, if divine intelligence is in all, why are

---

* *Genesis* 1:26–27 (Bible).

some people born morons?" To answer that fully we would have to look into their past incarnations for those unwise actions that brought about this sad result. But there is no question that every man is made in the image of omniscient God. And if the "hopeless" condition in the brain of a moron were corrected, his soul would be able to manifest more of its native intelligence.

The History of Leadership

Looking back through history, we see that as some individuals developed more intelligence than others, they stood out from the crowd and became leaders. Their leadership was gained and secured through demonstration of physical prowess; the strongest and cleverest of the tribe became the leader. In this way different clans developed. Gradually, to become stronger in order to accomplish common purposes, several clans united under one leader. Those leaders became kings, elected according to their demonstration of physical power and intelligence. But some of them abused their position and became tyrants. They further established that their descendants were to be the successors to the crown. The right to rule by virtue of birth, rather than capacity, vitiated this form of leadership. The evil crept in because even if the kingly offspring was physically, mentally, or otherwise unqualified, he nevertheless inherited, and usually insisted on exercising, the right to rule. In some cases, incompetent heirs were manipulated by scheming ministers in their service.

So we see that the system based on inheritance was defective. Some nations eventually became weary of this kind of tyranny and rebelled against their rulers. Many kings were slain, and others dethroned.

Then came the idea of a republic. Countries such as France and America chose to have presidents elected by the people. George Washington qualified himself for this position by all he did to help bring freedom to this land. He loved this country and had its highest interest at heart; he was a real president. Under his able leadership, this great land took its first important steps as a new nation. Lincoln, too, was an exceptional leader.

But what crept in to obstruct the perfect ideal of "government of the people, by the people, and for the people"? Though presidents are elected by the citizens' vote, the system is flawed by graft and other inequities. Often, the best talker gets elected. We all know how people love to eulogize their own good qualities. Such a person can also talk against others for hours, and never think of the time; but he will not talk about his own faults and doesn't like to be reminded of them. Those who feel qualified to castigate others for their failings should be willing to stand up and confess their own shortcomings, too. But politicians know they won't get elected that way. So sometimes they get the vote simply because of their shrewdness in putting themselves over through their speeches. Then, after they get to the top, they do just as they please, in spite of all their promises to the people.

Voters don't really know a candidate. Usually they are not in a position to make a personal judgment of his character. They know only what they read or hear about him. If he is said to be capable and a nice person, they feel inclined to vote for him. But where is the ground for judgment? Where is the standard of truth with which to measure each politician? None has been established. Thus the masses too often are swayed by propaganda and sentiment, without really knowing what is going on. Even an unworthy candidate can get votes if he has the money for a good publicity program. But it is wrong to advertise how good he is if he hasn't the qualities to back it up. The system of voting for candidates is spoiled when money, rather than merit, can make the difference in getting someone elected president; and politicians, unfortunately, have a reputation for seeking out the moneyed people for help. Worthy candidates without such contacts may remain too little known to attract the voters. Of course, to be wealthy is not necessarily to be involved in influencing elections! I have always admired Henry Ford because he has done much good with his money for worthwhile causes in this country, and throughout the world as well. Proven merit through good works should be one of the criteria for the election of leaders.

To a large degree, voters are dependent on, and hence controlled by, what is printed in the newspapers; but I think people are getting away from that kind of influence. It used to be a common attitude in India that if someone said, "I read it in the paper," people automatically took it for granted that it must be false. Newspapers are often biased, and this makes people skeptical. Truth and sympathetic justice, not expediency and exploitation, will restore integrity to news reporting and reestablish people's faith.

So we find that though democracy is the best ideal, the present system of voting is extremely inefficient because the decision too often has to be made on what the candidate says about himself or against others who are running on the ticket. Too little attention is paid to the real character of the candidates. If only saints and others who are truly capable of analyzing character went to vote for our leaders, we would be assured of a good president in the White House; we would always have worthy ones to guide us. A truly great president is one who looks to the good of the nation first, and includes in that the well-being of the whole world.

So, because of the discrepancies in the voting system, we get some good presidents and some bad ones. Still, this democratic system is certainly far better than any other present-day alternatives. Inept kings and those who rule by force cannot be demoted without violence, but the people can lawfully replace presidents who prove unworthy.

Now we come to the modern-age form of dictatorship. Dictators are a classic example of politicians who make promises and then break them after they get in office. Dictators usually start out with the desire to help their people, but while they may be loyal to their own country, their self-interest makes them very disloyal to all other nations. Through jealousy and overzealousness, they bring trouble to the whole world as they rise to power. When they get to the top, they begin to rule by force to prevent anyone else from taking their position. Right or wrong, their word is law. This is the flaw of dictatorships. In the beginning, the dictator gains power by doing some good for his people. He stirs their faith in him, because he rules by merit. But when he gets to the top, he rules by force.

In One Sense, God Is a Dictator

Now comes the question: Is God a dictator? Certainly not in the context we have just discussed; but in one sense He is, because He created us against our will. Isn't this true? We did not ask to be created. Who told Him to create us? That is the one question God does not answer. I often tell Him He had no business to create us and put us in a body so susceptible to disease and suffering. Even a car has parts that can be easily replaced from time to time, but not this human machine. You have a right to say to God, "Lord, since You created me, redeem me." This is the way you should pray to Him. You are His responsibility.

The Pattern of Creation Is Set by God

Why did God create women, men, and animals, and identify the soul with the particular limitations of consciousness peculiar to the form in which it is encased? It is in this sense that God is a dictator. Animals have no chance to improve themselves; they remain just as they are, bound by instinct. And human beings take advantage of the poor creatures. We don't wear shoes made of human skin because humans would resist that idea. But we feel free to take the flesh and skins of animals because in the God-created order of the world they cannot defend themselves against man. I say that in these ways God is a dictator. But just the same, He is responsible for us, because we are thrust into this world without being asked if we want to come, and without being told why we are here.

Yet we can see that His purpose must be good. This whole creation shows that it is the work of some great Intelligence. There are the senses through which we perceive and relate to this world. There is food to satisfy our hunger, and we have been given the ability to look after this body and fill its other needs. Each life form follows a more or less set pattern. The average life of man is less than a hundred years; the redwood tree lives up to four thousand years. After a relatively short time, the ordinary house plant dies, no matter how carefully you look after it. Some insects live only a few hours. All this shows that there is a Dictator who has ordered things as they should be. He has set the standards by which all living things are governed.

Spiritual Dictatorship

Now the difference between the leadership of Joseph Stalin and Mahatma Gandhi is an important one. They both rule millions of people, but Gandhi is a spiritual dictator. He leads through love, not force; and people follow him out of love, not fear. Similarly, I think God can be said to be a spiritual dictator. If He were to come on earth in human form with all His wondrous qualities unmasked, which He could very well do, everyone would follow Him without question. He does come, but in the guise of His avatars, in whom He keeps His powers partially hidden so that He might play a specific human role for the good of man.

Thus God was born as Jesus, who let himself be crucified even though he could have destroyed the world with a glance. He who could raise the dead could certainly have annihilated his enemies by the command of Spirit within him. The followers of Jesus expected him to be an emperor of this world. But instead he wore a crown of thorns, and by so doing he became a real emperor, ruling the hearts of millions through the ages. Where are Napoleon and Genghis Khan today? They are mere chapters in history books. But in every nation there are those who love and follow Jesus.

The life of Jesus shows that God is not like the ordinary dictator. He is almighty, yet He does not use His power to destroy His enemies. You can curse God, deny Him, and call Him all the evil names you want; He will never punish you for those insults. But because you have filled your mind with evil thoughts, you won't be at peace with yourself.

God Refuses to Dictate to His Children

God has created this universe to run according to law; if we break one of the cosmic principles, we punish ourselves. Jump from the top floor of a high building, and your bones will be broken. You can't ignore the law of gravity without experiencing the consequences. So in this world man can act freely only within a limited scope. If he goes against divine laws he will punish or destroy himself. In the sense that God has established inexorable laws, He does seem to be a dictator. But the fact that He Himself remains absolutely silent, and calls us only through love, proves that He doesn't like that role. If God spoke to us directly, we would in that instant lose our free choice, because we would immediately feel impelled to obey Him; we couldn't resist His wise and loving influence.

For the same reason, no saint has been permitted by God to exert spiritual force to change the world. Great saints have tremendous power. My Master could raise the dead, but he never used his power to force the world to change. If people are shown miracles, they will be attracted by phenomena instead of being drawn to God out of the soul's spontaneous love for Him. So God does not allow any saint to draw souls to Him by the use of spiritual power in a way that imposes on the free choice of those souls.

Down through the ages, in fiery speeches prophets have warned that God Himself will come out of the clouds to destroy the wicked. But God has never done that. When people are evil—when they break His divine laws—they set in motion the cosmic forces that produce the inevitable consequences of their wrong actions; thus they punish themselves. I don't think God Himself has ever come down to chastise anyone. If that were His way, He would be punishing wrongdoers right now, for He knows who is right and who is wrong in this terrible war* that is going on.

God is humble and has hidden Himself. He doesn't want to come and say to mankind, "I am God. You have to obey Me." But He does try to keep us from harming ourselves by speaking to us through His laws and through great souls. Christ said: "He that is least among you all, the same shall be great."† He who is truly humble in the eyes of God is like God Himself.

Man Should Be Taught Universal Patriotism

Through the misuse of our freedom we have made our earth what it is.‡ Once we understand this, we have the explanation of everything that takes place here. There is always

---

* World War II.   † *Luke* 9:48 (Bible).

‡ The cumulative actions of human beings within communities, nations, or the world as a whole constitute mass karma, which produces local or far-ranging effects according to the degree and preponderance of good or evil. The thoughts and actions of every man, therefore, contribute to the good or ill of this world and all peoples in it. (See footnote on page 191.)

plenty of money for war, but there is never enough to rid the
world of slums. Do you see the false reasoning?

If all world leaders were educated to be like Gandhi, or
Lincoln, or Christ, there would be no more wars. For this reason, I submit that an important advancement toward peace
would be the creation of world cities where orphans of all nations could be taken and raised together. They should be given
not only academic education, but also the highest education in
cultivating soul qualities and spreading by example the brotherhood of man.

National patriotism based on selfishness has been the cause
of many disasters and untold suffering all over the earth. Therefore we must teach, along with patriotism, the brotherhood of
man. When the seeds of brotherly love take root in the hearts of
people, wars will cease.

Consider how much discrimination there is in the world;
we have an example in America's citizenship laws. People from
European countries can become citizens, even though they
sometimes turn out to be gangsters; but souls like Mahatma
Gandhi and other great men could not become citizens because
they happen to come from disbarred nations.* I never feel self-
conscious about such laws; wherever God places me, that is my
country. And in loving that nation I include the whole world.
This is the ideal to be taught to all.

Some Worthwhile Ideas From Francis Bacon

Francis Bacon wrote a perceptive treatise† that gives us
stimulating food for thought. He tells of a party of voyagers who
had been blown off course by strong winds, and found themselves in a new and unfamiliar region. They came to a wonderful island, on which was cradled a beautiful city. An official,
wearing silken robes of azure blue, came out to the ship and
invited the lost travelers to stay for a time with their people.
The city was a scientific Utopia. Marvelous discoveries and
inventions were disseminated to the citizens from a place called

---

* With the urging of President Truman, a bill was finally passed in 1946 making it possible for emigrants from India to become citizens of the United States.
† *New Atlantis.*

Solomon's House, whose members consisted of exceptionally learned men—the "shooting stars" of the arts and sciences. All were of noble and scientific mind, interested in truth alone. The foremost purpose of their research was to reveal for the benefit of man the wonders immanent in God's creation. The progress and well-being of this Utopia were thus dependent on and guided by the finest people of the community.

India, in its Golden Age, went even deeper than this, holding to the ideal that leaders of the people should be not only scientists, but saints; because scientists without spiritual realization can be blind to the true highest good of the people. In those ancient times in India, wise saints advised the ruling kings. Leaders of men *should* be guided by great souls. The earth's problems would then be solved, because saints who love God look to the good of all, and would not institute in any country unjust laws that would foment troubles. Great saints look upon the whole world as their kingdom. Therefore the saints have always advised kings to keep harmony not only in their own country, but to help promote it in other countries as well. This requires the broadness of spiritual patriotism, which opens the borderlines of nationality to embrace all. Gandhi has said that his India consists not only of Hindus, but whoever loves India and follows Truth—no matter what his nationality or religion.

And when we think of Lincoln, we think of another wise and understanding man. There may be more like him today: "many a flower is born to blush unseen."* Man's worthiness and desire for trustworthy leadership must be there to encourage such noble souls; then gradually they will reveal themselves.

To come back to the Utopia of Francis Bacon's story—he had a royal imagination!—the people of that land had an excellent practice: Representative scientists were sent at twelve-year intervals to different countries all over the globe. Their mission was to learn the language and study the constructive laws, the newest discoveries, and the best customs of those nations. When they returned to their island, the highest of what they had learned was introduced into their own culture.

---

* Gray's *Elegy in a Country Churchyard.*

Everyone lived in peace and harmony, willingly obeying the just laws of that land.

We Have to Make a Start Somewhere

People have not been educated into this kind of unselfish thinking. That is why it is not possible yet to have a Utopia on earth. True happiness for all can come only under the spiritual government of the soul.

We have to make a start somewhere. In governments there should be a standard and exchange of highest wisdom. It is starting even now. In the government of India there are certain chairs for philosophers. But this is not enough. Ordinary exchange of trade between governments has created wars. Merchants of wisdom would bring such understanding between nations that all participating countries would learn how to exchange and share material commodities without fighting. This must come to pass. Don't think that the world is going backwards. We will gradually come to this state. The war will help to clean out politics. It will bring to light many of the causes of the ills of the world. Just think, in peacetime, anyone who bombs a house is put in prison. But in war, the person who destroys masses of homes gets a medal for it. What a wonderful concept!

We must begin now to put into effect new concepts, spiritual ones. Don't minimize your own abilities, for the almighty Father is within you. The minute you recognize that Power within, you will be able to do great things. The ocean consists of drops of water. If the drops were taken away, there would be no ocean. And there would be no works of God in this world without us. Think in terms of the whole world when you think of what service you can render. You are made in the image of God, and must not look upon yourself as a frail human being.

Develop your love, that you can give it to your nation and to all nations of the world. God wants you to know that you are sent here to develop love for your world family. Incarnation after incarnation death takes you away, that you may not become too clannish and too identified with only one nationality and a few loved ones. Jesus showed us the way. He loved his mother dearly, but he loved all other people of the world too.

It Is God Who Animates All Beings

Two boys were watching some potatoes boiling in a pot. One said, "Look, brother, the potatoes are jumping up and down." The wiser boy said, "But it is the fire that makes them jump." God is the fire that animates all beings. You think you are doing everything; you forget that it is God who is working through you. It is God who loves through you; it is His love alone that expresses through all forms of love on earth. Friendship is the purest love of all; in that love lies the potential to love the whole world, for true friendship is unconditional. Loving your family is just the first lesson in learning to love all mankind.

The world has come to the state wherein it is essential that we be schooled not only in patriotism, but also in divine brotherhood. Jesus said: "Love thy neighbor as thyself."* Every nation must love every other nation as its neighbor.

A Dictator Wouldn't Give Us the Right to Throw Him Out

So we may say that in creating us without our consent, God is a dictator. But on the other hand, He is not a dictator because He has given us complete freedom to throw Him out and never think of Him. That is why some good people who never even think of God seem to get along all right. If God were a dictator, He would say: "Oh, there is that man. I will fix him so that he will have to think of Me." But God doesn't do that. You will not suffer so long as you follow His laws, even though you have totally forgotten Him. It is only when you break His laws that you punish yourself with suffering. But God's laws are subtle: It is difficult to avoid breaking them without seeking His help. So, even though God has all physical, mental, and spiritual power, He doesn't use it when we go against Him. You may curse God every day of the year, and He won't punish you for that. But love Him, and He will come to you. He is working through love to draw you back to Him.

Though God has given us freedom, He also realizes that we are still very much hemmed in by our own self-imposed limitations. Therefore, He has given us intelligence through

---

* *Matthew* 22:39 (Bible).

which we can get out of this mess. We have no one to blame but ourselves if we don't use that intelligence rightly. Even God can't help us if we break His laws and bring suffering upon ourselves.

Some people go through life dull-minded—eating and sleeping, enjoying a few pleasures, very seldom thinking deeply. So many people don't really think. They have the consciousness that material life is everything. But this life is only a passing dream. So why should you live trying to please the world? Better to try to please God first, and then you will better be able to please all.

God will eventually give freedom to everyone, but it won't come to you until you have used rightly your free choice. Otherwise, there would be no point in His having given us free will. Animals have no freedom. God bound them by instinct. But in man He has implanted wisdom. Human beings have the free choice to go up or down, to become better or worse. And since He has given us this freedom, He remains silent; because He knows if He talked to us, we would be totally influenced by Him. He would be able instantly to convince us against doing wrong. And if He did that, He would indeed be a dictator. So even though He is almighty, He can't do anything for us that will interfere with our free choice. Do you not see that? Therefore, because He keeps Himself out of our decisions, remaining quiet, hiding His power, He is not a dictator. He knows we are in trouble, but there is no way He can redeem us unless we cooperate with Him through our own effort. By our own free choice we alone decide whether to accept Him or cast Him aside.

You Are Potentially Equal to God

Another thing, ordinary dictators never want anyone else to be like them. They are inimical to each other because they want to be unique and supreme. But God is not like that. He made you in His image; you are potentially equal to God since you are a part of Him. Each one of us has the ability to become godly, if he would cast off the eclipse of ignorance. You don't have to acquire anything; you have it already. The gold of the soul is right there within you, covered with the mud of delusion. All you have to do is scrape off that mud.

So you see, on the one side God is a dictator because He created us against our will. But He is surely trying to rectify that by being a spiritual dictator. He speaks only through His laws and draws only with His love. But because He doesn't manifest Himself on earth and demand to be elected as the almighty ruler, He is not a dictator. The Lord isn't campaigning for election, except in the individual election of your heart. When your heart will sparkle with the light of your soul's love for Spirit, when that love will destroy all the psychological prisons that have held captive your free choice, then He will come without your asking. He will say: "Your love is so dazzling, so enticing, that I would like to come to you, if you will let Me."

So God as a spiritual dictator will never use force, nor appear to the world and proclaim: "I am the Lord of the Universe." It is only when your soul will call to God and your heart will melt with love for Him that you will know Him.

Receiving God's Answers
to Your Prayers

This article is a composite of introductory material written by Paramahansa Yogananda for early editions of his book, *Whispers from Eternity*. When Paramahansaji revised *Whispers* for the then forthcoming eighth edition, he wrote a basically new Introduction.

While the instructions in this article refer specifically to the invocations in *Whispers from Eternity*, the principles expressed elucidate a science of prayer that is applicable to all who seek divine aid in changing their lives through the power of prayer.

God made man in His image. All those who know how to receive Him can realize the divinity sleeping within them by expanding the powers of the mind. Being children of God, we have potential dominion over all things in His universe, even as He has.

The question arises, Why is it that many of our wishes are not fulfilled, and that many of God's children suffer intensely? God, with His divine impartiality, could not make one child better than another. He originally made all souls alike, and in His image. They also received the greatest gifts of God: freedom of the will, and power to reason and to act accordingly.

Somewhere, sometime in the past, men have broken the various laws of God, and accordingly have brought about lawful results.

All men have been given absolute liberty to use human reason wrongly or rightly. Misuse of God-given reason leads to sin, which is the cause of suffering; the right use leads to virtue, the precursor of happiness. God, with His infinite nobility, would not punish us; we punish ourselves through our own unreasonable actions, and reward ourselves through our own good conduct. This alone explains why God's responsibility ended when He endowed man with reason and with free will.

Man has misused this God-given independence and thus has brought upon himself ignorance, physical suffering, premature death, and other ills. He reaps what he sows. The law of cause and effect applies to all lives. All the todays in one's life are determined by the actions of all the yesterdays, and all the tomorrows of one's life depend upon the way in which all the todays are handled and lived.

Thus it is that man, although created in the image of God and potentially endowed with His powers, loses his claim and birthright to dominion over his Father's universe, through his own faults and self-imposed limitations. The misuse of reason, and the identification of the soul with the transitory body, or with environmental or hereditary or world influences, are responsible for man's despairs and miseries.

How a Sleeping Son of God May Become an Awakened Son of God

Yet the fact remains that every human being, however wrong outwardly, is potentially a son of God. Even the greatest of sinners is but an unawakened son of God, a sleeping immortal, who refuses fully to receive His light by clarifying his consciousness. In John 1:12 we find written: "But as many as *received* Him, to them gave He power to become the sons of God, even to them that believe on His name."

The ocean cannot be received in a cup unless the cup is made as large as the ocean. Likewise, the cup of human concentration and human faculties must be enlarged in order to comprehend God. *Receiving* denotes capacity acquired by self-development; it is different from mere belief.

How the Belief of Being a Son of God Can Become a Realization

The purport of St. John's words is that those sleeping sons of God who awake, by following the law of spiritual discipline, receive or feel God by developed intuition and thus regain their latent powers as sons of God. It is ignorance that prompts man to imagine his littleness and limitations. *Ignorance is the sin of all sins.*

It is the man sleeping in delusion who acknowledges and emphasizes his dream of human weaknesses. It is wrong for a soul (in the garb of the ego) to believe itself limited by the body, instead of *knowing* itself as part of the unlimited Spirit. It is good and right to believe that one is a son of God, rather than the son of a mortal only, for it is metaphysically true that man is essentially made in the image of God. It is an error, therefore, for one to imagine that he is a perishable creature. Even by belief alone, one may gradually cultivate his intuitive knowing and some day realize his true soul nature as a son of God. Hence, a wayward child must start by believing this truth, as belief is the initial condition for testing and knowing a truth.

When in trouble, one automatically prays to an unknown God and expects relief. If freed from trouble, even incidentally, he believes his prayers were heard and responded to by God. But should his prayer request remain ungranted, he becomes confused and begins to lose faith in God.

Demand Versus Prayer

My purpose in presenting these sacred demands [in *Whispers from Eternity*],* received in the course of my various fruitful communions with our Father, is to enable my fellow beings to contact Him effectually. I prefer the word "demand" to "prayer," because the former is devoid of the primitive and medieval conception of a kingly tyrant-God whom we, as beggars, have to supplicate and flatter.

There is a great deal of beggary and ignorance in ordinary prayer. People pray haphazardly. Few know how to pray and touch God with their prayers; nor do they know whether their prayers are responded to or not, or whether things happened, unaffected by prayers. Nor do they distinguish between things that they need and things that they want. Sometimes it is very good that we do not receive what we think we want. A child may want to touch a flame, but to save it from harm the mother does not grant the child's wish.

God, though all-powerful, does not act unlawfully or arbitrarily merely because one prays. He has given independence

---

* Similar prayer-demands may be found in *Scientific Healing Affirmations* and *Metaphysical Meditations,* also by Paramahansa Yogananda (published by Yogoda Satsanga Society of India).

to man, who does with it what he pleases. To forgive human shortcomings so that man can continue his misbehavior without consequences would mean that God contradicts Himself—disregards the law of cause and effect as applied to the law of action—and handles human lives, not according to the laws created by Himself, but according to His whim. Nor can God be moved by flattery or by praise to change the course of His immutable laws. Must we then live without the intercession of the grace and mercy of God, and remain helpless victims of human frailties? Must we then inevitably face the fruits of our actions as if by preordination or so-called fate?

No! The Lord is both law *and* love. The devotee who with pure devotion and faith seeks the unconditional love of God, and who *also* brings his actions into harmony with divine law, will surely receive the purifying, mitigating touch of God. Any sin, and its consequence, can be forgiven the repentant devotee who loves God deeply enough, and thereby puts his life in tune with the all-compassionate Lord.

The best way lies neither in begging for favors or for amnesty from evil results, nor in being resigned and sitting idle, inviting the law of action to take its course. What is done by ourselves can be undone by ourselves. We must adopt the proper antidotes for our poisonous actions. For example, ill health can often be overcome by obeying laws of good health. But when chronic diseases and sufferings are beyond the control of human care; when the power of human methods fails to cure ills, physical or mental, revealing its limitations, then we must ask God to help—He who is unlimited in power. And we must lovingly demand as sons of God and not as beggars.

Every begging prayer, no matter how sincere, limits the soul. As sons of God, we must believe that we *have* everything the Father has. This is our birthright. Jesus realized the truth, "I and my Father are one." That is why he had dominion over everything, even as his Father had. Most of us beg and pray without first establishing, in our own minds, our divine birthright; that is why we are limited by the law of beggary. We do not have to beg, but to *reclaim* and *demand* from our Father that which we, through our human imagination, thought to be lost.

It becomes necessary at this stage to destroy the wrong thought of ages—that we are frail human beings. We must think, meditate, affirm, believe and realize daily that we are sons of God—and behave accordingly! This realization may take time, but we must begin with the right method, rather than gamble with the unscientific beggary of prayers and consequently be subject to disbelief, doubts, or the jugglery of superstition. It is only when the slumbering ego perceives itself not as a body, but as a free soul or son of God, residing in and working through the body, that it can rightfully and lawfully demand its divine rights.

Deep Attention and Devotion Are Necessary

These sacred demands reveal a few of the attitudes of the soul that have met with successful response from God. However, it is not enough merely to demand in another's language. One should not rely on a book on love when he meets his beloved, but should use the spontaneous language of his heart. If one uses another's language of love in demands addressed to God, he must make the words his own, by thoroughly understanding and dwelling upon their meaning, and applying to them the utmost concentration and love; even as it is not amiss when a lover addresses his beloved in the language of a great poet, and enlivens those words with his own love and feeling.

Blind repetition of demands or affirmations, without concomitant devotion or spontaneous love, makes one merely a "praying Victrola," which does not know what its prayer means. Grinding out prayers vocally and mechanically, while inwardly thinking of something else, does not bring response from God. A blind repetition, taking the name of God in vain, is fruitless. Repeating a demand or prayer over and over again, mentally or orally, and with deepening attention and devotion, spiritualizes the prayer, and changes conscious, believing repetition into superconscious experience.

The Divine Being cannot be deceived by a mockery of prayer, because He is the fountain of thoughts. He cannot be bribed at any time, yet it is easy to move Him with sincerity, persistency, concentration, devotion, determination, and faith.

Furthermore, repeating a long, intellectual prayer with the mind absent develops hypocrisy; and to pray or demand without understanding develops ignorance, fanaticism, and superstition. Repeating a demand with deepening concentration and faith is not mechanical repetition, but a changing, progressing power and mental preparation which, step by step, scientifically reaches God.

These sacred demands are logical, devotional, deep soul-outbursts. If one prepares the mind by concentration, and then deeply, with ever-increasing faith and devotion, mentally (or aloud, in congregations) affirms these scientific divine demands, one is bound to receive results. To reestablish your unity with the Divine Father as a son of God is your most important demand. Realize this truth, and you will have received everything.

Demand Unceasingly, and You Will Receive

After sowing the demand-seed in the soil of faith, do not dig it up now and then in order to examine it, or it will never germinate to fulfillment. Sow your demand-seed in faith, and water it by repeated daily practices in demanding rightly. Never be discouraged if results are not forthcoming immediately. Stand firm in your demands, and you will regain your lost divine heritage; and then, and then only, will the Great Satisfaction visit your heart. Demand until you establish your divine rights. Demand unceasingly that which belongs to you, and you will receive it.

In demanding rightly, there is no room for superstition, disappointment, or doubt. Once you learn to operate the right chain of causation that effectually moves God, you will know that He was not hiding from you, but that you were hiding from Him behind the shadow of self-created darkness. Once you feel, through intuitive *knowing*, that you are a son of God, then by the steady effort of mental discipline and devotional meditation you will have dominion over all things.

If your demand remains unfulfilled, unanswered, you can blame only yourself and your past actions. Do not become despondent. Do not say that you have resigned yourself to fate, or to the preordained commands of a whimsical God, but try, with increased effort after each failure, to get what you have not—what you did not receive because of your own fault, but what is yours already in Spirit. Demand with sacred devotion the recognition of your divine birthright as a son of God.

To know exactly how and when to pray, according to the nature of our needs, is what brings the desired results. When the right method is applied, it sets in motion the proper laws of God; the operation of these laws scientifically bears results.

Some Practical Hints

Select a demand from the contents according to your need. Sitting motionless on a straight chair, with spine erect, calm your mind. For as a wet match cannot be ignited, so a mind saturated with doubt and restlessness is unable to produce the fire of concentration, even when prodigious efforts are made to strike the cosmic spark.

The flame of inspiration is hidden within the lines of the prayer-demands in this book; but since they are presented through the mute medium of printer's ink, paper, and intellectual meanings, one must use his own intuition and devotion to bring forth their inner illumining flame. By the Christ-command of your deep intuitional perception, resurrect the inmost substance of words from the sepulcher of hollow, intellectual concepts.

Different minds reading the same prayer may interpret it differently. The vast ocean of truth can be measured and perceived only according to the capacity of one's own intelligence and perception. Similarly, the inspiration behind these prayer-demands will be felt according to the depths of one's own intuition and feeling.

In order to benefit fully from the God-warmth within these prayer-demands, one should take only a paragraph at a time from any demand, mentally picture the meaning, visualize the imagery of the figure of speech, and meditate deeply on it, until the fiery essence emerges, free from word limitations.

One may wish to read a complete prayer-demand to get a quick view of its entire meaning. But if he will then reread it, over and over again, many times, and then with closed eyes repeatedly try to *feel* the deep inspiration behind and within it, he will spiritualize that prayer—that is, rouse the inspiration slumbering beneath the thick silken quilt of words.

With eyes closed and lifted to the point of spiritual concentration between the eyebrows, meditate on the meaning of the demand you have selected, until it becomes a part of you. Saturate the demand with devotion as you meditate upon it. As your meditation becomes deeper, increase your devotion and mentally offer the demand as your own heart's outburst. Imbue yourself with faith that your heart's craving, expressed through this specific demand, is being felt by God.

Feel that just behind the screen of your devotional demand God is listening to the silent words of your soul. Feel this! Be *one* with your heart's demand—and be thoroughly convinced that He has listened to you. Then go about your duties, seeking not to know whether God will grant your demand. Believe absolutely that your demand has been heard, and that you will know that what is God's is yours also. Unceasingly meditate on God; and when you *feel* Him, you will acquire your rightful inheritance as His divine son.

Daily Blossoms From the Ever-living Plant of Prayer-Demands

These demands were given to me by the Universal Father; they are not mine. I only felt them and gave them expression through the avenue of words that I might share them with you. My blessing goes with them; and I pray that they may strike an answering note on the living harpstrings of your heart, so that you may feel them just as I have felt them.

Prayer-demands are like ever-living plants that ceaselessly put forth new blossoms. A prayer-plant retains the same branches of words, but daily yields fresh roses of God-feeling and inspiration, if one regularly waters the plant with meditation. The prayer-plant must also be protected from the ravages of doubt, distraction, mental idleness, leaving-meditation-until-tomorrow (the morrow that never comes), absentmindedness, and thinking-of-something-else while imagining that the mind is wholly on the soul force of a prayer.

Such parasites on the prayer-plants should be destroyed by faith, devotion to God, self-control, determination, and loyalty to a teaching. Roses of immortal inspiration may then be gathered daily from the plants of these prayer-demands.

O seeker after soul-awakening! be still, and let God answer you through your intuition-tuned soul. Learn to know Him by knowing your true Self.

The Wisdom Way
to Overcome Karma

Self-Realization Fellowship Temple, Hollywood, California,
June 6, 1943

Much has been written about the law of karma. But I am afraid that the karmic theory as sagely explained by the masters of India has been so distorted by nonunderstanding minds that the Western peoples have garnered a wrong idea about this great cosmic principle of cause and effect. You have relegated the word *karma* to a limited meaning, to refer only to the past. But this is erroneous. *Karma*, in general, means action, not merely the effects of past actions. It can refer to action performed in the past, or now, or that might be done in the future. When you say "water," you may be referring to water in general, or you may specifically mean fresh water, or salt water, or any other kind of water. So the real meaning of the word *karma* is any action you perform; and the sum total of all your actions, both good and bad, present and past. Actions that you are performing now are called *present* karma. Actions that have already been performed are called *past* karma. And when you refer to the *effects* of past actions you would say, "This is the result of my past karma." Even then you are not telling what kind of karma —beneficial or pain-producing.

Then comes the question, What are the springs of action? What influences you to act and behave in a certain way? Now we have launched into the heart of the matter.

You act in a certain way today, and you say, "I have been acting this way all of my life." We get into deeper water when I ask you to consider the influences on those actions. There are two ways you work: prompted by your own free choice and by influences. So many subtle influences are interwoven with your decisions that it is very difficult for you to judge which actions are performed according to your own free choice and which are performed under karmic compulsions of the past, or any other influences.

It is rare to see a truly "free" man. Most people think they are free, while their minds are utterly fettered by psychological chains. These are harder to get rid of than ordinary chains; for in their subtlety they are difficult even to recognize, not to speak of how to destroy them! It requires a great deal of knowledge to cut those psychological restraints.

There may be a million years of actions of past lives pursuing you. That is why an ordinary individual finds himself so helpless to destroy the binding effects of his karma. He feels hopelessly bound by those invisible chains—influences resulting from all the actions he chose to perform in past lives, through free will or through prevailing influences.

As tabloid tendencies, the actions you have performed in the past are present in the brain. Diagnosing those karmic influences is not a simple matter. But according to your salient features, inclinations, and moods you can detect what propensities have been trailing you and how strong an influence they are on your present life and your present actions.

The Influences on Man's Freedom of Action

Now, in addition to your karma from the past, what are the influences on your present life? World civilization is one of them. In whatever era a man is born, he is influenced by the civilization of that age. If one is born in the eighth century, he is influenced by that century. You are all dressing, for example, according to the present civilization. You have more materials to choose from than in past centuries. You are thinking more of comfort and style than of mere warmth and necessity. Similarly, you are all eating now according to the present civilization; for instance, there was no talk about vitamins in the sixth century. So your present consciousness and actions or behavior are influenced by this present-day society.

Then the next strong influence upon man is nationality. The soul identifies itself with the body and says, "I am American" or "I am a Hindu" and so on. It is not easy to get rid of that influence, of that identification. But why should you think that you are an American, or an Indian, or a Frenchman? And why did I used to think that I was a Hindu? You see, I say I *used* to think; because I am one with all mankind. I have trained myself that way—not to be prejudiced by nationality, race, or any other circumscription that limits the universality of the soul. I am subtly telling you how to overcome your karma too: Always remain universal in your attitude and habits of life. Then you become free.

The soul has worn many garbs: today you are an American and in the next life possibly Chinese, and so on. That is why it is unwise to hate any nationality, for hate attracts just as love attracts. Anything you hate, you attract to yourself that you may learn to overcome that prejudice. That is the law. For instance, those who hate a dark race will be born in that race—invariably. The greater the hatred, the stronger will be the karmic attraction to the object hated. The origin of the light and dark races was influenced by climatic conditions. Climate will so change that someday it will be natural to see the white races in the East and the dark races in the West. That will happen; but many years from now.

Then man is influenced by the community in which he lives. He is influenced by his neighbors: If he lives in an aristocratic neighborhood, he tends to behave in an aristocratic way; if he lives among businessmen, he behaves like them. Different kinds of people have different kinds of habits that influence you. Mix with artists and you will think that is the only way to be. (I am not condemning artists, but they need to be more practical-minded. You cannot live on beauty alone. "I slept, and dreamed that life was Beauty; I woke, and found that life was Duty."* You must see beauty in duty.) Remain in the company of spiritual persons and you will think spiritual thoughts. Environment is stronger than will power. If you want to be spiritual, seek good company and don't mix with those whose bad habits may wrongly influence you.

You are also strongly influenced by your family. You think that you belong to a particular group of people, the family unit. They have put a trademark on you, and their habits encumber you.

---

* From "Beauty and Duty," by Ellen Sturgis Hooper (1816–1841).

Lastly, everyone is drunk with some habits. Sometimes man is crazy about money, and sometimes he is crazy for love, and then for fame, and so on—all the time battered and bludgeoned by the influence of his own habitual past actions of this life and past lives. That is the hypnosis of karma.

Regaining Your God-given Freedom

Where is your freedom? How little freedom you have left! The freedom that God has given to you as His own, to touch the Milky Way and to feel your presence in the flowers and in the stars!—that freedom has gone completely because of the many influences upon you.

Most people are like psychological antiques, brittle with set ideas, with set influences. The minute you sit on them, they break! That is why our Indian astrologers say we are all puppets. I do not believe that. I believe you can destroy any karma you want to. If you close all the doors and windows in a room, darkness is there. But if you bring in the light, that darkness is gone instantly. Even the darkness that has permeated a cave for thousands of years is vanquished immediately when light is brought in. Will you reason that it will take light a hundred years to destroy those aeons of darkness? That is foolish.

So, we may have karma of past lives, under whatever civilization, nationality, community, and family we have lived; and of this life with the influences of this present civilization, nationality, community, and family; but if we *realize* we are gods, we will be free from that karma now. Every human being is made in the image of God. If you find that image within you, how can you have any karma? God as the Master of this universe has no karma; if you know that you are one with God, there can be no karma for you.

A venomous snake is not affected by the poison within it. It is also true that while delusion, or *maya*, is in the manifestation of God in creation, and that it affects us, it does not affect Him. That is not fair, is it? That is why He has to give us salvation; but it will not come unless we demand it.

Being made in God's image, we can be free from karma provided we claim our divine heritage from Him. You have been led to believe exactly the opposite. To believe in karma is to give strength to it. Why should you believe you are bound? You should think: "I am not a mortal being; I am a child of God." Then you cut at the root of karma: "Beyond the flights of fancy, formless am I, permeating all limbs of life. No freedom do I crave, nor bondage do I fear. For I am free—ever-conscious, ever-new Bliss. I am free. I am He, I am He, Blessed Spirit, I am He."* But as soon as you give in to the delusion that you are a human being, you have permitted all the karma of the past to envelop you.

This life is a den of thieves; its influences rob you of your divine inheritance. When you say, "I don't belong here," and you make the effort to get out, you will no longer be an unwilling captive.

Salvage Your Freedom With Wisdom and Discrimination

You must salvage your freedom. When you have made certain resolutions, have you been able to carry them out? If you have not, you are bound by karma. But if you have been able to do the things you wanted to do, guided by your discrimination— and not because of the influences of your past or present karma, or because of your national or social or family life—that is freedom. Judge everything from the standpoint of discrimination and wisdom. Let not your actions be governed by habits or blind obedience to social customs according to what other people think. Be free.

Once in a while you see a free man—one who doesn't walk in dead men's shoes, one who is free because his actions are not influenced by anything but wisdom. That is the mark of Mahatma Gandhi's greatness. When he went to England and visited the king and queen, he didn't put on a dress suit, as was the custom. He was received by them in his simple village loincloth and shawl. He enjoys great freedom because he lives his ideals and is not bound by social custom.

Whenever you do anything, ask yourself whether it is merely because of what other people may think about you, or whether you are following discriminative wisdom. That is the criterion by which I act. Even as freeborn Americans you do

---

* Paraphrase of a well-known Sanskrit chant by Adi Shankaracharya.

not know what real freedom is. Many people think that whatever comes into their brains they may do—and believe that to be freedom. But true freedom lies in doing what you should do when you ought to do it. Otherwise you are a slave. Be actuated by wisdom alone. If you are not able to do that, you are going to remain a slave for centuries of incarnations.

Now, to follow truth doesn't mean you have to bludgeon others with your convictions. Share truth only when it is welcomed or asked for. Otherwise, learn to be quiet; keep your own counsel. But when you feel you should speak, speak. Stand against the world if necessary. Galileo said that the earth goes round the sun; and he was crucified for that. Later it was found that he was right. But never do anything out of pride. To do so is to fall.

Learn to Act Wisely by Attunement With a True Guru

In every action, be guided by wisdom; never by a desire to hurt anybody. But if anyone is hurt because of your doing the right thing, you should not be afraid; you have to answer to yourself, not to anyone else. Even God is not your judge; you are your own judge. If you act wrongly, you are going to punish yourself. If you act rightly, you will free yourself. That is the justice of the law of karma. You are dictated to neither by God nor His angels, but by the law of action: What you sow, you reap. Whenever you meet with misfortune, do not put the blame for it on God. The blame rests with you alone—resulting from your past actions.

If you lack the wisdom to discern what is right, then tune yourself in with the wisdom of a wise man. Often what you think to be wisdom is not wisdom at all, but your own desires and karmic inclinations. That is why you should have a guru. Guru is one who is sent by God to free you. When you are in tune with his wisdom, you find freedom. Otherwise, you remain a slave to your whims. The way to freedom is to follow those who themselves are free. When I met my guru, Swami Sri Yukteswar, he told me to tune in my will with his will. He said that my will was strong, but governed by instincts; but when I tuned my will with his will, I found it governed by wisdom.

No one can incite me to do anything I know I should not do. I know what I am doing, guided by wisdom now. I am fully responsible for my actions, and I do not blame anybody else for the outcome of my actions. That freedom which Master gave to me I have never parted with.

"Understand this! By surrendering thyself (to the guru), by questioning (the guru and thine inner perception), and by service (to the guru), the sages who have realized truth will impart that wisdom to thee. Comprehending that wisdom from a guru, thou wilt not again fall into delusion."* It is so hard to progress on your own on the spiritual path, but it is the easiest thing if you have a true guru to whom you surrender yourself and whose interest is only in your spiritual welfare. I gave myself completely to my Master, and I found he gave his all to me. And through that surrender I found freedom. That freedom every soul craves. That is the way to overcome your karma.

A guru's only interest is to help you progress spiritually. If the teacher wants something from the disciple, he is not a master. The master's only desire is to give, not to take. But if the disciple has the wish to help the work of the master, that is to his credit—he is helped by giving to God's cause.

The masters create a few disciples who carry on their work. Masters are interested in souls rather than in crowds—souls that will follow and are really willing to discipline themselves. A true disciple is one who seeks liberation by accepting the guru's discipline, and who disciplines himself by the wisdom-guided instructions of the guru. But most disciples want to be gurus instead!

Here in the West the church members expect the minister to cater to them; he becomes their slave. I never ask for anything from you all for myself. I have suggested at times that you help the work, but I have kept myself free from enslavement to people. Even when sorely tried by financial problems of the work, I have not bowed down to anyone nor compromised my ideals. I have kept myself free. If Mt. Washington† is blown away from me, I shall not mind; and if it is left with me I shall joyously carry the burden of concern for it to my last

---

* Bhagavad Gita IV:34–35.

† Reference to the International Headquarters, the Mother Center, of Self-Realization Fellowship, atop Mt. Washington in Los Angeles.

day. Such is my principle. Wherever God keeps me, I shall carry on. For the will of the Father is my will.

How Guru's Discipline Frees One
From Imprisoning Whims and Habits

All your life you have been a slave, following your own whims. I remember in my youth I couldn't eat this or that food; but when I came under Master, he ironed out all those kinks of thought. First he found out what I didn't like to eat. He said, "So, you don't like this; you don't like that." After seven days he asked me how I liked the food I had been eating in the ashram. I said that it was marvelous. He told me then that I had been eating in the various preparations the very foods that I thought I couldn't eat! He helped me to conquer likes and dislikes by such discipline.

Most people of the West think only of comfort. Master never bothered about where I slept; and if I tried to be more comfortable in the human way, he criticized me. By such constructive criticism and training I found complete freedom from food consciousness, dress and social consciousness, and body consciousness. I was so happy, free from the prison of my own making. Master gave me that freedom by his guidance—freedom from habits and moods and limiting thoughts.

So, let not your will be the prisoner of your habits and whims. That doesn't mean you should not use your will. Learn to use it with discrimination, for then you are using the will of your Father.

Learn to compare your developing discrimination with the wisdom discrimination of the guru; for only then can you be sure when you are right. We are much too fond of our own thoughts. Whatever our notion, we want to drag out a whole body of scripture to support it. But when you compare your will with the master's will, and are guided by his will, then you know whether you are following wisdom or following instincts and your past karma.

The scriptures say you must have a visible master—that is, one who lived on earth. To follow the counsel of a true guru is the only way you can be sure your actions are leading you to freedom from karma. A wise man has no personal desire for you to obey him; but if you volunteer to be obedient to his guidance, he will certainly tell you the truth. He will tell you what is best for you; and no matter how many times you falter, or leave him, he will always speak the truth to you for your own good. He cannot be bribed in any way; such was my Master. He was the one among many who never hesitated to tell me my faults. He used to say, "There is the door; anytime you want to go, you are free to leave." Many fled; but I didn't leave. I knew he wanted nothing from me, but I wanted that Something which he had. Master told me his discipline would smart sometimes; but if I promised to be obedient, I must honor that promise. And I did. Here in America the teacher is made to feel he must deal with the church members with kid gloves. But Master's way was strong. He told me: "Your methods will be much milder than mine; but this is my way. Take it or leave it." I took it gladly! It made me a free person.

But no one can free you unless you make the effort to free yourself. God wants you to be free. He has given you free choice to follow the path of wisdom or to follow the path of karma. Try to do everything with wisdom; and at night examine yourself and see if you have succeeded. Be self-disciplined. If you can obey guru's guidance and remember to do what he says, and be ever watchful of yourself, you will suddenly see that you are free. Then every day you will feel freedom.

Wisdom Destroys the Roots of All Misery

Imagine what freedom you feel when you are free from the influences of this world, or your past, or your family, or neighbors, or your habits! You realize you are pure Spirit. You belong to no group, no nationality, no family, no habits. Karma belongs to the den of thieves where karmic people live. Always think, "I and my Father are one. I have no karma; I am free."

"O Arjuna, as enkindled flame converts firewood into ashes, so does the fire of wisdom consume to ashes all karma. Verily, nothing else in this world is as sanctifying as wisdom. In due course of time, the devotee who is successful in yoga will spontaneously realize this within his Self."* When you destroy the

---

* Bhagavad Gita IV:37–38.

causes of karma, you have destroyed the roots and future seeds of all suffering, all misery. You become the true sons of God; you have claimed your own true nature. It does not matter then what happens to the body. Those who are bathed in wisdom know that nothing can hurt them. Jesus knew he was going to be crucified, but he was not touched by this knowledge. By rebuilding his body-temple after death, he showed that he was free from karma.

To admit karma means to accept yourself as a mortal being. Do not admit you are a helpless mortal governed by karma. Affirm: "I am a child of God. I am His." That is the truth. Why shouldn't you proclaim the truth? As soon as you realize this truth, your status is changed. But when you admit you are a mortal, you bind yourself with the chains of the mortal being. You are the sons of God; you are gods. How could karma influence you? Refuse to be bound by karma; it is an old superstition of the ignorant to believe you cannot change your destiny.

Never say you are a sinner. How can you be a sinner? God is your Father. If He created this world with its potential for many evil ways, you would have to say that He too must be a sinner. That is the way I talk to God. It never hurts to speak truth to Him. If God can be away from the evil of His creation, so can we. As He is free, we can be free. Never again identify yourself with evil. You may have made a mistake, but it doesn't belong to you if you give it up. Destroy your karma by wisdom. Live in the consciousness of Spirit.

Today you say "I am Spirit" and tomorrow you do something wrong and want to give up. Don't accept your weaknesses. Jesus on the cross didn't give up! Even in the midst of the greatest torture or temptation, if you can hold on to your perception of wisdom, you will in the next minute be free. The wise retain that freedom even when facing death; but the ignorant fall back on their old mortal habits. If you give up and think that there is no chance for you, you have pronounced your own fatal judgment. You are the one who created your good and bad karma; and when you say there is no hope, you have failed. But when you think, "I am free, I am strong; even though bad karma strikes me, still I will not give up," then you will see your good karma coming forth. No matter how bad your karma is, try to diagnose your life and strive to do good, to do right, according to your wisdom. Your karma will change; you will see that your bad karma will change into good.

Every night keep a mental diary. See if your habits have crushed you. Whenever a person does wrong and says he can't help it, he is a slave. He should rather admit he did wrong and then try to do better. He may fall again; but he must say, "I will try harder!" That is the way to overcome. Do not give in. You are not a sinner; and anybody who calls you a sinner is himself a sinner.

The True Purpose of Religion

Do you see how much the church movement needs reformation? They expect people to follow religion by proxy. But truth has to be lived; it has to be realized as a part of one's own being. The church movement has done a lot of good, but it must really reform each individual. One moon gives more light in this world than all the stars—so is every truly reformed individual. To keep your minds on God, I seldom think of socials for our churches. I only discuss wisdom with you. I do not divert you from the real purpose of religion: to know God.

That is why Self-Realization Fellowship is creating churches of all religions,* that all people can feel the spiritual barriers gone

---

* Paramahansaji envisioned Self-Realization Fellowship temples as sanctuaries for the perpetuation of the ideals of actual God-communion and a common spiritual brotherhood. "Self-Realization Fellowship," the Guru explained, "signifies fellowship with God through Self-realization, and friendship with all Truth-seeking souls." He included in his prayer invocations not only God and the Gurus of the YSS/SRF path, but also "saints of all religions." In this same spirit, when founding his Self-Realization temples in Hollywood and San Diego in the early 1940s, he referred to each of them as a "Church of All Religions."

In using such terms as the "unity of all religions" and "uniting all religions," he explained that he was not suggesting the merging of various beliefs and practices from different religions into one homogenous hybrid, which would be highly illogical and unnecessary considering the vast cultural and psychological diversity of the human race. Indeed, each expression has its place, even as he defined his work of Yogoda Satsanga Society of India/Self-Realization Fellowship as a "special dispensation." In his book *The Science of Religion* (published by Yogoda Satsanga Society of India), he speaks of the true basis of religious unity:

"If religion means *primarily* God-consciousness, or the realization of

and come together to really seek God. Jesus said: "For where two
or three are gathered together in my name, there am I in the
midst of them."* The primary goal of the church should not be
to build more churches and gather in more converts, but to give
God-realization. Hives without the honey of God-communion are
nothing. Jesus warned that the "blind cannot lead the blind." If
you have not God, you cannot give God to others. I told Master I
would never stand before a congregation and talk about God unless he gave me the experience of God. That is the important
thing, to have that divine experience of God.

God has given us the methods to destroy karma: Guide
your actions by wisdom, not influences; be self-disciplined and
follow the wisdom-guidance of a true guru; believe in your divine inheritance as a child of God made in His image; associate with good company, such as coming here to church regularly; and practice the techniques that will give you actual
personal experience of God. "Hear about the wisdom of Yoga,
equipped with which, O Arjuna, thou shalt shatter the bonds
of karma."†

Here we teach you what to do in the silence of meditation,
especially the practice of *Kriya Yoga,* so that you truly experience God-communion. That is why Self-Realization Fellowship [Yogoda Satsanga Society of India] is reaching all over the
world. This path is sent by some of India's greatest masters to
Christ-ianize the churches and to show that the real meaning
of religion is to realize God. Each of you by the example of your
life must be a messenger of this light.

God both within and without, and *secondarily* a body of beliefs, tenets, and
dogmas, then, strictly speaking, there is but one religion in the world, for
there is but one God....If religion is understood in this way, then and then only
may its universality be maintained; for we cannot possibly universalize particular customs and conventions."
* *Matthew* 18:20 (Bible).   † Bhagavad Gita II:39.

Realize Your Christ-Immortality!

Mid-1930s

On the screen of time, a drama of life is being enacted in the mundane movie-mansion. The Cosmic Motion-Picture Director has been projecting on the screen the many and varied pictures of ancient, medieval, and modern times. He films pictures of war, famine, poverty, tragedy, comedy—good and evil—to keep the audience entertained throughout eternity. The appetite of entertainment-loving minds being enormous, the Cosmic Movie Director is trying to film and play an omnibus of pictures.

This earth is meant to be a place of mirth, a temporary pleasure-house for immortals. Because we forget this and become identified with the earthly drama, we suffer. We must remember that our real home is in the mansion of changeless, ever new, blissful, omnipresent Immortality.

Unwise souls who play truant and get intoxicated with mundane desires and delusions want to dally in the earthly moviehouse, experiencing the excitement of pleasure and pain, health and disease, life and death.

Creation came into being through a desireless desire of Spirit. The Lord was one and alone with no one to enjoy His joy. So He wished to express His bliss through many. He sent on earth immortals, individualized images of Himself, to watch the short ever-changing dramas of life and death. Contrarily, while the immortals were enjoying their individuality, they fell into the trap of duality. Through identification with the characters in this earthly movie, the godly immortal souls succumbed to the disease of delusion: the mortal consciousness of change.*

---

* Reference to the Hindu concept of *maya*, cosmic delusion; and *avidya*, ignorance. In *Autobiography of a Yogi* Paramahansa Yogananda wrote: "Those

As one wealthy prince thought himself a poor miserable beggar when he was drunk in the slums, so immortals imagine themselves to be sick or well, alive or dead, happy or miserable when intoxicated with the delusion of change in the mortal show of this earth. I would prefer even to be bored with my immortality rather than undergo the nightmare of earthly dream-death from a malignant disease.

Unwise immortals, while playing in a tragedy on earth, identify themselves with that temporary role. Taking it too seriously, they begin to moan if they have to play that they are dying in poverty. If an immortal faints, thinking he is dying from a gunshot wound that was only a dream injury in a dream play, then he is foolish. Befuddled immortals inflict on themselves so many ridiculous mental tortures.

Some rich men, dying with nervous-breakdown dreams, say: "If only I could live on this earth with a healthy body, I would be glad to live without a penny." So they reincarnate as healthy men but without money. Then they struggle and struggle for money, and when they are dying of starvation they say: "If only I had health and money, how happy I would be." So they reincarnate with plenty of money and health, but without happiness. On their deathbed they think: "If only I could have happiness, I would forgo health and riches." The next time they come back to earth very happy but without health or riches, for which they soon realize a need—and so the cycle continues.

In this way immortal souls repeatedly punish themselves, because they never can find on this earth complete satisfaction.

---

who cling to the cosmic illusion must accept its essential law of polarity: flow and ebb, rise and fall, day and night, pleasure and pain, good and evil, birth and death....The world illusion, *maya*, manifests in men as *avidya*, literally, 'not-knowledge,' ignorance, delusion. *Maya* or *avidya* can never be destroyed through intellectual conviction or analysis, but solely through attaining [by yoga meditation] the interior state of *nirbikalpa samadhi*."

"The soul has descended from the universality of Spirit," he said on another occasion, "and become identified with the limitations of the body and its sense-consciousness....The soul remains essentially untouched and unchanged by its confinement in the body. But, through *maya* or delusion, it becomes subjectively identified with change and mortality, until the consciousness evolves and, through Self-realization, reawakens to its immortal state." (See *maya* in glossary.)

To die of a broken heart and enter the grave with desires that were unfulfilled by seeing or playing in this earthly movie-house is extremely foolish, for this earthly drama could never afford the perfect happiness of Spirit.

Some people die longing for perfect human love. Others die dreaming of perfect happiness through the attainment of wealth and fame; but they are all deceived, for to own this whole earth and be adored by all its people is very little compared to what is lost by remaining a prodigal mortal. To contact Omnipresence is to own the whole cosmos with all its entertainment and ever new immortality. In comparison, to own this earth is nothing; it would be fraught with sorrows, and at the time of death the delusion of its being wrested away from you would torture the soul.

Material things cannot be owned by anybody, for at death they must be left behind and given to others. We are only allowed to use the objects of this world. So it is foolish to be possessed by material possessions. Just pray to be given the use of what you need, and the power to create those things at will.

Since death compels us to give up everything, even a millionaire dies poor. Rather be like Jesus: he was materially poor, but rich with God; he had nothing material in life, yet having God he had all, even after death. Worldly-minded rich people have everything in this life and nothing hereafter.

Remember, no matter who you are or what your condition is, do not think your trouble is the worst in the world. Even if you are playing a part fraught with poverty or disease, there are others who are enacting a part worse than yours. In this earth life, to be a millionaire or a poor man is the same *if you but understand*. If you see yourself as an actor in this earthly movie-house, all you have to remember is to play your role, small or big, cheerfully and well. That is all.

During the playing of your part, agreeable or otherwise, do not wish to play somebody else's role. Complete your own assignment, or you will have to spend aeons of time in the enactment of imperfect human parts, changing from one to another according to the change of your desires. Get away from this entrapment. The only way to foil disappointments of will-o'-the-wisp prosperity, fame, and earthly happiness is not to feel sorry when you are denied what you think you want. Of course, you will say: "Our desires are conditioned by our needs. We want food because hunger was given to us." I admit that; but I am talking of a greater freedom in mind and soul. When you attain that, not even tattered robes or death by starvation can produce inwardly an iota of unhappiness.

When you possess the all-in-all God-consciousness, even if you have nothing of material possessions, yet you have all. People who really contact God can never feel poor or left out; nor can they consider the rich as more fortunate than themselves. Instead, the man who is intoxicated with God-happiness pities everybody else.

When Jesus said, "Foxes have holes, and birds of the air have nests; but the Son of man hath not where to lay his head,"* he was not bemoaning his poverty. Rather, he was signifying that he was the owner of the cosmos; one with Omnipresence; thus he could not remain caged in a small place as earthly creatures do.

Jesus had no bank account; nor did he exhort people to demonstrate prosperity first, as some modern religious organizations do—teaching their members to pray to God or to go into the silence with both eyes fixed on the granting of material desires. Jesus warned: "Bread, the men of the world (matter-loving, shortsighted people) seek after; but seek ye first the kingdom of God and all these things (prosperity, wisdom, happiness, riches) shall be added unto you"—without your having to pray for them.

The person who finds God owns the cosmos; and owning the cosmos he owns everything in it. Jesus had full realization of his oneness with the Father. That is why he could do many things that deluded mortals could not do. He raised the dead. He rebuilt his mutilated body. Compare a millionaire on his deathbed, forced away from his home and fortune without a penny, with Jesus Christ after death, who owned the Kingdom of Omnipresence. So, do not desire to be a millionaire; it is a waste of time to delude yourself with material desires. Rather wish and strive to be a Christ. Invest your time in daily meditation, ever longer and deeper; this is the quickest way to become a Christ.

---

* *Luke* 9:58 (Bible).

What of it, even if you became a millionaire? You would then want still more; and would perhaps die of heart failure, working for another million. To strive for God-contact in meditation is pure joy. You will be happy when you meditate; and you will be happier still when you arrive at the end of the trail of meditation and meet God, the King of ever new joy.

During your sojourn on earth, remember that you are only a movie actor. You may be called upon to enact any part, tragedy or comedy; you must play it well, and as you watch your tragic portrayals say: "That was a fine, sad picture and I played my part well." Likewise, if you can say: "Lord, I played the parts of birth and death well; I played the sad and joyous parts well, and my roles brought me great satisfaction and joy; and, Lord, I was highly entertained with Your marvelous earthly movies, but I did not create any new desires to play new parts," then perhaps He will say: "All right, you need not stay in the movie colony of the earth any longer. Come back to My Home of Eternity, My Home of Ever New Joy."

To each prodigal immortal, God says: "Son, know this: you are eternally My child, naughty or good, whether on earth or in heaven. But when you forget that your Home is in My Kingdom and get mixed up with My earthly shows, you make yourself miserable. When you will realize you are an immortal, made in My blissful image, you can remain on the earth enjoying earthly dramas with an immortal's attitude; or you can come Home and rejoice in the ever-entertaining, ever-new, joyous entertainment of My unending Blissful Nature."

Wash your hands of all desires now, yet perform your earthly duties with an increasing ambition to please God and to make others happy; then when the door of death is opened, your spirit will laugh and dance and shout: "Now through this opening I shall dash to my Home of Immortal Bliss." Disappoint all the adversities of earth-binding attachments so that they will not bring you here on earth anymore; being unshackled, race straight to your home in God.

You will tire of all things quickly once you have them. You will tire the quickest if you win every material thing you desire; but there is one thing you will never be tired of, either now or throughout eternity, and that is the ever new Joy realized in God-contact. Joy that is always the same may cause boredom, but Joy of God, which is ever new and continuous, will entertain you forever. Such Joy can be found only in deep meditation.

Deluded immortals travel through many corridors of incarnations—rising, falling, hoping, rejoicing, weeping. Nature keeps excitement-loving individuals entertained with variety, a mixture of sorrow and pleasure. Christlike souls are busy with the ever new, continuous, changeless Joy in everything—in God.

Christ, one with God's omnipresent consciousness, is blowing with the wind, laughing in the brooks, twinkling in the stars, blushing in the sunset, and gently smiling in the blossoms with his fragrant presence. Christ is dancing on the sea of human emotions and thoughts. Christ is joy in all hearts and in all things. Those who have their eyes of wisdom closed perceive the dark qualities of suffering, death, disease, sorrow, and fleeting pleasure. With open eyes, Christ sees naught but light, laughter, and beauty, which he prays will become manifest to earthly souls, when with devotion they too have opened their all-seeing wisdom-eyes and reawakened to their blissful immortality.

Increasing Your Magnetism

*First Self-Realization Fellowship Temple
at Encinitas, California, July 28, 1940*

Thought is infinite. Whatever your branch of study, once you have put your mind on a particular subject, your thought can go on indefinitely in that direction. There is no end to the wisdom or information you can draw upon. Do you know that each one of you is interpreting what I am saying in a slightly different way? Each person experiences a mental process that differs from everyone else's. What is that mental process?

Suppose someone pinches you. First you feel a physical sensation. From the stimuli of the sensation comes perception. Then, having perceived the sensation, your mind forms the thought, "I have been pinched." That is conception. The process from sensation to perception to conception is an individualized response. Because the inner being and working of each person is unique, the sum total of his reactions to any given experience will be different from that of any other person's. This totality of what you are inside—your thoughts, feelings, responses, motivations—determines the quality of your magnetism, your power of attraction.

Magnetism is the greatest force through which you can draw unto yourself friends and goodwill. We all like to be noticed; no one wants to feel ignored or forgotten. Even a child will deliberately act up to get attention. We also like to be thought well of; we want others to like us. But how many of us give to others the understanding and consideration we think we merit from them? We express the greatest compassion and forgiveness toward our own weaknesses, while all too readily we criticize and condemn others for their faults. Can we as easily stand up before others and tell all our own faults since childhood? No. But unless we learn to behave, we can't show others how to behave, and have no right to be intolerant of their shortcomings. The world is full of those who want to reform others, but not themselves. Unless we develop a constructive critical estimate of ourselves, we will go on year after year unchanged. What is important is self-reform: for if we ourselves have reformed, we shall reform thousands by our example. Example does speak louder than words.

Begin by Being Kind to All

How to become a king of hearts, loved by all? Become more saintly, so that like a true king you sit on the throne of love in the hearts of others. Begin by being kind to all. Unkindness is a spiritual disease. If you indulge in unkind acts and feelings, you make yourself miserable and damage your nervous system. When you see others behaving unkindly, it should give you greater determination to be kind. I practice this all the time. No matter how hurtfully others behave, they cannot make me react with meanness. The more unkindness people show to me, the more understanding I give to them. Sometimes, in order to stress an important lesson, I speak very strongly to those who have come to me for training. But I am never angry or unkind. Those who receive such discipline have seen that at the height of the scolding, when I seem to be most displeased, I can shut off fiery speech and use the gentlest of words. That self-control has tremendous power. Never allow your voice to be harsh out of anger or vengefulness. Like a flower, shed petals of kindness when you are aggravated by others or attacked by the evil in them. By self-control and right behavior you will ultimately realize that you are a part of the Eternal Good; you do not belong anymore to the wrong ways of this world.

The Inner Self Must Be Cultivated

To be truly attractive, you must be attractive mentally and spiritually as well as physically. The present generation links attractiveness to the style shops and beauty parlors. But beauty has to be more than external. You can be looking at the most handsome man and the most beautiful woman in the world; yet right beneath their pleasing appearance you may discover much hidden ugliness. They are like the magnificent sarcophagi from the tombs of ancient Egypt: How beautiful, how perfect the carved images look! But when you lift the cover, you find nothing beautiful in the dead form within. If the spiritual qualities of our true soul-nature are dead, an attractive physical body is little more than a casket to hold the inner withered consciousness.

It is fortunate, of course, that some physical attractiveness covers the ugliness of our bones, sinews, and internal organs. But why be so preoccupied year after year in adorning only the outer form? America seems very much a place where people concentrate on keeping up their outer image in order to hide their age. I have seen many people looking forty who were really sixty. And that is good. Why shouldn't you keep the body fit and attractive? You can make your body whatever you want it to be. Why be careless and let it "go to pot," as they say? Watch your weight. If your form is disproportionate, it is most likely because of laziness or overeating. Some people diet or fast one day, and then more than make up for it the next day. Get plenty of exercise and learn to be more careful about what you eat.

But such are the infinite potentials of life—so much to learn and to do—that if you are primarily intent on enhancing your physical being, you won't have time to do anything to improve yourself inwardly. Beautifying oneself before the mirror—painting the face, coloring the hair—may help one to be noticed in the business or social world, and there is nothing wrong with that; but it will not improve the inner personality, the inner self. My point is that you have to give some time to the inner self also.

In the East, the concentration is mostly upon inner attractiveness; and in the West, more emphasis is placed on physical attractiveness. What is necessary is a combination of both. I would rather be mentally attractive than physically attractive. But if I can be both, that is even better. We must learn to simplify the externals of our life and take time to beautify our inner self. That is the way to develop true magnetism.

You might be quite conscious of someone's homeliness, at first meeting, and then realize that his inner personality is very attractive and magnetic. Socrates was like that. So was Lincoln. They had a magnetism born of beautiful inner qualities that drew others to them. When you have that kind of divine attractiveness, the physical features are of less importance.

Your physical appearance, especially the eyes, shows more or less what you were like in previous lives, so deeply does the inner being impinge on the outer form. The eyes are one's most significant physical feature. You should learn to make your eyes beautiful. How? The eyes clearly reflect what you are within. So there is but one method that can beautify the life and expression in the eyes: the inner cultivation of beautiful thoughts and feelings.

Some eyes are very cruel; others are mean, or selfish. No matter how sweet such a person's words or actions are, you can see what he is really like through the expression of the eyes. He cannot hide himself behind those open windows. So think wholesome thoughts, constructive thoughts. As a being privileged to be made in God's image, you have no right to disfigure your inner life.

Develop peaceful eyes, calm eyes, strong eyes, divinely loving eyes, by cultivating these qualities within. By this method alone you can develop an inner attractiveness that completely transcends the limitations of physical appearance.

Turn Your Trials Into Triumphs

It is never too late to improve oneself. Watch your thoughts, feelings, and actions, and guide them rightly. At the end of each day, analyze yourself: How have you lived this day? To be really living is to strive constantly to improve oneself; physically, mentally, morally, spiritually. A person who has not become stationary, but continues to change for the better—day after day, year after year—develops magnetism.

Use every trial that comes to you as an opportunity to improve yourself. When you are passing through the difficulties and tests of life, you usually become rebellious: "Why should this happen to me?" Instead, you should think of every trial as a pickax with which to dig into the soil of your consciousness and release the fountain of spiritual strength that lies within. Each test should bring out the hidden power that is within you as a child of God, made in His image. Our tests are not meant to destroy us. Only those who are cowards, and who don't acknowledge the all-perfect image of God within, become rebellious and surrender to their trials as though those tests were unconquerable destructive forces. It is an injustice to your potential as a human being to so regard your tests. The right attitude is to use each trial as a stimulus to strengthen your inner self. If the wrestler doesn't fight with stronger opponents, he will not become stronger himself. So when you face all your difficulties bravely, with spiritual strength, you become even stronger and more powerful. By conquering when you are tested, you will revive the forgotten image of God within you, and become consciously one with the Father again. So we must remember to use our God-given strength to overcome our trials, and thereby strengthen our inner lives. That divine inner strength is the source of our magnetism.

The Power of Good Company and Deep Attention

Another help toward developing your magnetism is deep attention: by this power you can draw on others' magnetism. Learn to put your full attention on everything you do. Whenever you are with someone, be a good listener. By attentiveness, tune in with people who have those attractive qualities you wish to develop. If you want strength, mix with those who are strong. If you want to develop your business sense, be with businessmen. If you want to develop all-powerful divine magnetism, mix with those who love God. You will develop much faster this way than if you merely read books on these subjects.

Saints and others who have accomplished much in this world have had great magnetism. By thinking deeply of great men you can receive their vibrations. Ordinarily, we receive knowledge through the senses of sight and hearing: by reading books or listening to discourses. But greater than these is direct contact with a man of wisdom. You gain knowledge much quicker through such association. Even if that great soul lives ten thousand miles away from you, if you think of him and concentrate on him with deep attention, you can receive his vibrations. You will begin to get something that is beyond mere words: you can receive another's magnetism through the mental channel of thought.

Krishna, Buddha, Jesus—these great ones manifested the highest quality of magnetism. Every time I see an image of one of the great ones, or think of them, I get their vibrations. When I contact Jesus I feel the consciousness of God as the Father. When I think of Ramprasad,* I feel the vibration of God as the Mother. This attunement with divine ones does not come about merely by thinking of them for a few moments. It is only by meditating day after day on a great saint that you will begin to receive the spiritual vibrations of that saint.

There is also great value in visiting places where saints have lived. Assisi, the abode of St. Francis; Bodh Gaya, where Buddha attained enlightenment; Jerusalem, where Jesus preached—such places are forever permeated with the vibrations left there by the divine souls who walked those grounds. Their vibrations will remain until this earth is dissolved. Where souls have communed with God, there you will find greater communion and response from God. Often such pilgrimages completely change one's life for the better.

Direct association with a God-realized man of wisdom may be through personal contact or deep meditation. The important point is to attune your consciousness with his. When you are in tune with a great soul who loves God, that attunement gradually changes your life in a most wonderful way. Your will does not become enslaved; it becomes expanded. This is the difference between attunement to an ego-centered person and being in tune with a true guru. The magnetism of a God-realized soul will put you in tune with the magnetism of God.

God Is the Supreme Magnetic Force

Jesus said: "Seek ye first the kingdom of God...and all things will be added unto you." God is the Supreme Power behind all powers; the Supreme Love behind all loves; the Supreme Artist behind all art. When you put your mind on God, the Supreme Magnetic Force, you surcharge yourself with divine magnetism; and you can attract unto yourself all things. If you think of God in deepest meditation, if you love Him with all your heart, and feel completely at peace in His presence, without wishing for anything else, the divine magnetism of God will attract unto you

---

* A Bengali saint, Ramprasad (1718–1775) composed many songs in praise of Kali, one of the aspects of the Divine Mother.

everything you ever dreamed about, and much more. In every department of my life I have demonstrated this truth: If you love God for His own Self, not because of what He can give you; and if you are completely attracted by His divine magnetism, that power from Him goes out of your own heart and mind, and by your slightest little wish, you will attract unto yourself the fulfillment of that desire. If you have unconditional love for God, He drops thoughts in others' brains, and they become instruments to fulfill even your unspoken desires.

So divine magnetism, by which you can attract anything unto yourself, is the kind of attractiveness you want to develop. Always desire that which is good, that which is noble, that which is pure. Then, as a divine man, filled with the magnetism of God, you can never fail to attract anything you want.

Meditate deeply, and send forth the call of your soul to God: "Lord, Thou must come into my body temple. Whether it is broken by disease, old age, or other imperfection doesn't matter. Whatever the condition of my temple, I know Thou wilt enter it as soon as Thou knowest I truly love Thee and I know that Thou dost love me."

When this realization comes, the body that was so dear to you does not mean that much to you anymore—you want to give more importance to your inner life than to vain material pursuits. The divine man who loves God more than self finds that the attractiveness within himself is God; he then loses his attachment to the gross body: "O Lord, whether my body walks the pathways of earth singing Thy name, or falls asleep in the ocean of death, I am ever with Thee. Life and death may sing their songs, but I am one with the Song of Eternity. I cannot die, for I am the Breath of Eternal Life."

Now, please pray with me: "Father, I have thrown off all negative thoughts. I was bound by the iron chains of materialism, but Thy magnetic presence is changing me; I realize I am made in Thine image. I am a divine magnet. Thy magnetic current flows through my hands; the magnetism of Thy wisdom flows through my brain, the magnetism of Thy love through my heart, the magnetism of Thy joy through my soul. *Aum,* Peace, Amen."

Preparing for Your Next Incarnation

Self-Realization Fellowship Temple,
San Diego, California, June 11, 1944

Our subject today is to help you understand why you are here on earth, so that you can free yourself from compulsory future incarnations. Reincarnation is not compulsory unless you make it so.

Life is a vast school. There is a lesson to be learned in everything. But just as naughty boys in school engage in mischief, try to distract the other children, pay no attention to the teacher, and then fail to graduate and have to take the same class again, so it is with most people. They are "bad boys" in the school of life, always getting into trouble because they don't listen to the teacher. Life is teaching you all the time; you are a bad student if you don't pay attention. Think about that; it is the sum of what I want to tell you.

"Bad boys" who fail their exams have to return again and again in shame to confront the same lessons. Good students, however, develop into wise men. Christ, Krishna, Buddha, and all the enlightened ones finished their training, graduated with honors, and went back to God. They don't have to come to this school of life anymore, unless of their own free will they return again as teachers, "saviors," to help others.

Reincarnation means that you did not finish your schooling; you have yet to pass in all the grades of physical, mental, and spiritual unfoldment, which will earn for you a diploma of perfection and freedom. What is the cause of failure?

Understanding Why We Are Here

Primarily, we do not understand why we are here. Most people think life is just for acquiring necessities and wants, seeking pleasure and human love, and surrendering at last to the grave. Human beings start life programmed with set tendencies and unfulfilled desires from the past. Then, with their little remaining free will, they imitate each other's desires and actions. If they associate with businessmen they want to be like them; if they are with artists, art becomes everything. God meant us to be practical in this world—He has given us hunger that has to be satisfied—but to go after only food and shelter, money and possessions, is to forget the true Source of happiness. Satisfy your needs, pursue your worthwhile goals in life, but give yourself to God first. Your schooling will then come under His wise and loving tutelage. He knows all your stored-up karma and what is best for you. Don't resist Him.

Unfulfilled desires are the root cause of reincarnation. You don't have to be a king in order to have complete fulfillment. Nor do you end desires by giving up everything and becoming a poor man. You have your own self-created destiny with its lessons to be learned, and you must play well that part for which you were sent here. If everybody on the stage wants to be a king or queen, there will be no play. An actor with even a minor part can ruin the entire production by a poor performance. Every role is important; everyone should interact harmoniously for the success of the play. The Lord has been trying to make a good drama out of His creation, but I am afraid that most actors have bungled it.

The ideal is to do your best, but be objective, nonattached. Pay attention to the studies life places before you. They contain the lessons you must learn. Don't play at random and create new desires, endless desires. The Hindu scriptures say that it takes about eight million incarnations (progressing upward on the scale of evolution) before one becomes a human being. And now, after gaining a human form, how can you waste so much time on things that are fruitless? Time is so precious. At long last, your soul has a vehicle capable of the full expression of divinity, of manifesting "the image of God" in which you are made.

Every morning ask yourself, "What do I want?" "Nothing, nothing but You, Lord. If You want to take me from this world now, I am ready to go." That is the right attitude. But it is not easy to hold on to it, because a thousand temptations will come in your path to see if you have finished your desires.

Once when talking to Amelita Galli-Curci, the famous operatic prima donna who had such an angelic voice, I asked her, "Have you finished your desires?"

She replied, "Of course."

I continued about other things, and then suddenly asked her, "What are your feelings about music?"

"I love it," she said; "I want to sing in heaven!"

"Then you will have to come back to earth again," I replied. "That desire is not finished." Then she understood.

When I started on the path to God, my family tried to interest me in other things. An important position was offered to me, and I prayed to God for guidance. He said, "What do you want with it? Go after supreme happiness first." My cousin [Prabhas Chandra Ghosh] got my job and also my wife-to-be. Through God's grace I was free!

If You Keep Your Mind With God, You Will Be Free

When desires come, be guided by wisdom, not by whim or stubbornness. If you can control your senses and keep your mind with God, you will be free. But if, on the last day, when the time comes to go to the Heavenly Father, the angels say, "Do you like strawberry shortcake?" and you answer, "Oh, yum, yum!" they will tell you, "Then you have to go back to America." Or they may ask, "Do you like curry?" "Yes, Lord!" "Then go back to India. You can't stay with the Father because your earthly desires are not finished."

The divine man enjoys everything, but is not bound by anything. He appreciates the use of the objects in God's creation, but when he is through with them, he is through. Do not harbor traces of desires. Live in this world working only to fulfill God's will. Tell Him, "I did not ask for this body; but You gave it to me, so I will look after it and see to its needs, and use it as an instrument to serve Your will on earth." When you are impersonal with the body in this way, you become personal with God. I want you all to get to that state. But it will not come by reading books, nor if you fritter away your time in diversions. Meditate. Be steeped in meditation. This morning I hardly remembered sleeping last night; and when

I lifted my eyes upward, they became fixed in the state of *samadhi*. The world, like an ocean, was moving in me. I felt the whole universe throbbing within myself.

Learn the lesson that you are not a man nor a woman, but a soul made in the image of God. Otherwise, God will have to send you here again and again until you outgrow your ignorance and realize your true Self. Become so conscious of God that you know He is the only Reality. The more you meditate, the more that thought will be paramount. Try as it may, the world will not be able to take that consciousness away from you.

When I started my search for God, I shunned everything that took my mind from Him, as though it were poison to me. I even avoided too much contact with people who were not of like mind, because I did not want to be influenced by them. Milk will not float on water; it will mix, and become diluted. But when milk is churned into butter, the butter can float on water. Similarly, as a serious seeker, make firm your consciousness in God. Free yourself first. Then no one will be able to exert any wrong influence on you; you will change them. Otherwise, if your will is weak and somebody suggests some nice temptation to you, you will run after it. But when you are convinced that true happiness is within yourself in your relationship with God, then nobody can pull you away from that; others will instead follow your example.

God is for all who will seek Him. Give your nights to Him. The days belong to the Devil, because he keeps us busy and embroiled in the relativities and delusion of this existence. But if you give your nights to God, and strive in the daytime to remember Him in the midst of your activities, you will be drunk with Him all the time. The divine man is always intoxicated with the Lord. Work doesn't take my consciousness away from Him; it is the greatest pleasure. I have hardly even been sleeping these days. I feel the greatest joy, the greatest blessing of God I ever had. That is what I live for. To be with Him and to work out His wishes; on these two things my life revolves.

Fulfilling Your Duties to God and Man

Even a materialistic man who is constructively busy is better than an idle "spiritual" man. To be lazy and give no earthly service is to be forsaken by God and man. But those who fulfill their duty to man but not to God are like the mule that carries a bag of gold on its back, knowing only its weight and not its worth. Actions without the thought of God are both burdensome and binding; actions performed with the consciousness of God are freeing. Renunciation of material duties to serve only God is all right, because it is to Him we owe our first allegiance; no duty could be performed without the power borrowed from Him. The Lord forgives whatever sins accrue from the nonperformance of lesser duties by those who forsake all else for Him.* Renunciation means to put God first, whether one follows the path of the world or the path of monasticism.

My brother said to me, "Money first; God later." He died before he had a chance to find God or to use his money. Remember the words of Christ, "But seek ye first the kingdom of God, and His righteousness; and all these things shall be added unto you."† When you find God, everything comes to you. When He takes hold of you, you can never fall. Your mistakes will be righted; your errors will be transformed into wisdom. That is what I have found.

The Right Attitude Toward Suffering

There are two kinds of seekers: those who are like the baby monkey and those who are like the kitten. The baby monkey clings to the mother; but when she jumps, it may fall off. The little kitten is carried about by the mother cat, content wherever she places it. The kitten has complete trust in its mother. I am more like that; I give all responsibility to the Divine Mother. But to maintain that attitude takes great will. Under all circumstances—health or sickness, riches or poverty, sunshine or gray clouds—your feeling must remain unruffled. Even when you are in the coal bin of suffering you don't wonder why the Mother placed you there. You have faith that She knows best. Sometimes an apparent disaster turns into a blessing for you.

---

* "Forsaking all other *dharmas* (duties), remember Me alone; I will free thee from all sins (accruing from nonperformance of those lesser duties)" (Bhagavad Gita XVIII:66).

† *Matthew* 6:33 (Bible).

When the Golden Lotus Temple went,* I at first thought it was a terrible catastrophe; but it turned out otherwise, because it made me go on to found other temples and ashram centers.

Gloom is but the shade of Divine Mother's hand outstretched caressingly. Don't forget that. Sometimes, when the Mother is going to caress you, a shadow is caused by Her hand before it touches you. So when trouble comes, don't think that She is punishing you; Her hand overshadowing you holds some blessing as it reaches out to bring you nearer to Her.

Suffering is a good teacher to those who are quick and willing to learn from it. But it becomes a tyrant to those who resist and resent. Suffering can teach us almost everything. Its lessons urge us to develop discrimination, self-control, nonattachment, morality, and transcendent spiritual consciousness. For example, a stomachache tells us not to eat too much and to watch what we eat. The pain from loss of possessions or loved ones reminds us of the temporal nature of all things in this world of delusion. The consequences of wrong actions impel us to exercise discrimination. Why not learn through wisdom? Then you won't subject yourself to unnecessary painful discipline from the hard taskmaster of suffering.

Finding the Divine Love Behind Human Love

There is suffering inherent even in the satisfaction derived from human love. Devoid of the quality of divine love, human affection is a blind alley that entangles and limits us. I realized this when my mother was taken away by death. How disillusioned millions of people have been who thought human love was the only thing to live for. They were fooled, and thereby did themselves a great injustice. Where are all those they loved and lost? What is the lesson to be learned? It is to love the Love behind human love.

Who is your father or mother but the Divine Father-Mother who has taken human form to love and care for you?

---

* The first Self-Realization Fellowship Temple, dedicated in 1938 on the grounds of the SRF Hermitage in Encinitas, was on a bluff overlooking the Pacific Ocean. This temple was lost to the gradual erosion of the shoreline; it was later replaced by another SRF temple in Encinitas.

Why doesn't someone else's father feel for you in the same way as your own? Because the Divine took a personal interest in you and planted that paternal feeling in a particular being to whom you were karmically attracted. God also became the mother to love you unconditionally; hers is a blind love unless it is imbued with divine consciousness. The father's love is more tempered with reason and law.

The Bible teaches: "Honor thy father and thy mother...." * But it further commands: "Thou shalt love the Lord thy God with all thine heart, and with all thy soul, and with all thy might."† When I say father or mother these words have an absolutely different meaning for me now. I have realized the Father-Mother behind my parents, the Someone Else who was loving me through their parental love.

If you remembered all the mothers and fathers you have had through incarnations, you would not know which ones to love as your own. You think of your present home as where you belong. But if you were to die and be born next door to your former parents they would not love you in the same way as they did before. Who loves you but God? It is He whom you must seek. I once had a vision in which I realized it was the Mother Divine who had taken the forms of my mothers in many lifetimes to love and guide me. Now in every woman I behold the motherly quality of the Divine Mother. Thus should we learn to see the Mother behind all mothers, the Father behind all fathers, and the Friend behind all friends.

Friendship—The Purest Form of Love

Friendship is the purest form of God's love because it is born of the heart's free choice and is not imposed upon us by familial instinct. Ideal friends never part; nothing can sever their fraternal relationship. I have never lost a true friend. Even though two to whom I gave sincere love became inimical, I am still a friend to them. To be a true, unconditional friend, your love must be anchored in God's love. Your life with God is the inspiration behind true divine friendship with all. True

---

* *Exodus* 20:12 (Bible).   † *Deuteronomy* 6:5 (Bible).

friends bring mutual progress to one another.

The guru-disciple relationship is the highest expression of friendship, for it is based on unconditional divine love and wisdom. It is the loftiest and most sacred of all relationships. Christ and his disciples were all one in spirit, as are my Master [Swami Sri Yukteswar] and I and those who are in tune with me, because of the common bond of God's divine love. Drinking His love together from the chalice of sincere hearts is the unifying sacrament of this relationship.

In human friendship familiarity should be avoided, or after a little while friends may take advantage of each other. But in divine friendship there is ever-increasing respect; each one thinks only of the highest welfare of the other. That is the nature of the divine friendship between guru and disciple. One who partakes of this relationship is on the way to wisdom and freedom.

Whenever I speak to others, as in these services, one form appears before me: my Guru. His influence is paramount in my life. Even now, though he is no longer on this earth plane, he is always with me.

Spiritual Ideals for a Fulfilling Marriage

If you seek the One Friend behind all friends, true friendship can be established in all of your relationships—familial, fraternal, marital, and spiritual.

Friendship is vital in a marital relationship. Sex alone will not bring a couple closer together; in fact it will all too soon throw them apart if the higher instinct of true love and friendship is not predominant. When sex is made the most important part of a marriage, the couple lose interest in one another when the initial blush of sensual gratification pales. Those who do not discriminate between true love and sense attraction are disillusioned again and again.

People who want to marry should first have to learn to control their emotions. Two people placed together in the arena of marriage without this training battle worse than opponents in a World War! Wars, at least, come to an end after a time; but some marital partners engage in combat throughout life. You would think that in a civilized society people should know how to get along, but few have learned this art. A marriage should be nurtured on high ideals and the wine of God's inspiration; then it will be a happy and mutually beneficial union.

Once in Boston I was invited to speak at the silver wedding anniversary celebration of a supposedly ideally happy couple. The moment I entered their home I felt something was wrong. I asked two trusted students to quietly observe the couple throughout the evening. They told me that when the husband and wife came before others they smiled and addressed each other sweetly, "Yes, my dear," "Of course, my dear"; but when they thought they were alone in the kitchen or pantry, they fought like anything.

So I talked with them: "Why do you behave like this? I feel great inharmony in this home. There is a lot of iron in this silver wedding." At first they were offended. But I pursued the matter. "What do you gain by fighting all the time?" I gave them a good talking to. They approached me later and asked my forgiveness. I told them, "You stay together just because of your reputation as an ideal couple, but I want you to truly live that way, for your own happiness."

One's ideals should be lived in behavior, thought, and speech. If two people come together and their moods are wrong, they become insincere with each other. When deception creeps in, the marriage is "on the rocks." Why this hypocrisy? Such mistakes should be prevented from the very beginning.

Balancing Feminine and Masculine Qualities

It seems there has always been a rivalry between man and woman. But they are equals; neither one is superior. Be proud of what you are in this life. You are a soul that has been in both male and female bodies in different past incarnations. If you are a woman now and you envy men, you will have to reincarnate as a man. And take heed: if you are a man now and feel superior to women, you may have to be born as a woman. Man argues that woman is emotional and cannot reason; and woman complains that man cannot feel. Both are incorrect. Woman can reason, but feeling is uppermost in her nature; and man can feel, but in him reason is predominant. The ideal is to balance reason and feeling in one's nature. Those who are too womanish do not find soul freedom, and neither do those who are too mannish. Each sex should strive toward a balance by learning from one another through friendship and understanding. In the great saints we see combined the ideal masculine and feminine qualities. Jesus was like that; so were all the masters. When you have attained that perfect reason-feeling equilibrium, you will have learned one of the major lessons for which you were sent here.

Life is meant for God-realization. Don't live in a one-sided materialistic way. Have self-control, master all of your senses, act with wisdom, conquer life, and find freedom. The average life span is seventy years of schooling. When death comes you will not have finished your education and will have to come back to this school again, unless you have found God, and acquired all His wisdom, and expressed all His blessings in your life.

Start in earnest on this path of learning. From the beginning saturate yourself with God. Love Him more than His gifts. He has everything except your love. He created us, that perchance we would use His gift of free will to seek Him. The only reason we are here is to find God and go back to Him. Love God first and make your body a temple of God. Do everything with the thought of Him. Go after the Supreme Happiness, and share Him with others. Perfect your love in God's love, and include all humanity in your love.

If you have children, train them in the right ideals to help bring them back to God. Every one of you has a tremendous work to do: Convert others to God by your spiritual example. To help others find God is the highest gift you can give.

So remember, God first! Start today, not tomorrow. "If thy hand offend thee, cut it off."* You need will power and right guidance to succeed. Exercise your will guided by your guru's wisdom, and you will overcome all impediments in your path.

Free Yourself From the School of Troubles

Don't expect perfection or permanent happiness here; you will not find it. This world will always be full of troubles. Why

---

* *Mark* 9:43 (Bible).

be interested in this school of discipline? Finish your lessons for good, that you may not be sent here again and again against your will. Free yourself from this school. Conquer all. Live for God, work for Him, think and will for Him. Body, mind, soul, will, senses—everything must be with God. Then you will be free and ready for the journey Home. And you won't have to come back to the troubles and difficulties and wars of this world.

When your schooling is done, and the end comes, and people are crying at your passing, you can rejoice and say, "Beloved One, Master Death is opening for me the gate to freedom. I have had enough schooling now. I shall be a pillar in Thy temple, and shall go no more out,* unless You will me to do so. If You wish it, I will come again and again to help free others."

My incarnation is voluntary. I have finished my schooling, but I don't want to go back to God until others have been freed. As long as there will be a brother weeping by the wayside I shall come to wipe away his tears and take him with me to God.

Many people hurt and destroy themselves through ignorance and wrong desires. I have come to help them, to teach them and take them with me to that Infinite Shore from which there is no compulsory returning. It is wonderful to learn all of life's lessons and then teach others how to finish theirs. Then, when the last day comes, there is no fear or regret. As the dying divine youth said, "Don't cry for me, ye who are left on this desolate shore, still to mourn and deplore; it is I who pity you. My Beloved comes in the dazzling chariot of death to take me away to the Kingdom of Deathlessness, to the Palace of Bliss-Dreams. Oh, dear ones, rejoice in my joy!"†

---

* *Revelation* 3:12 (Bible).

† From "The Dying Youth's Divine Reply" in *Songs of the Soul* by Parama-hansa Yogananda (published by Self-Realization Fellowship).

The True Signs of Progress
in Meditation

Circa 1930

As the journey of one's existence progresses, one finds by deeper insight into the soul that the quest of life is "Who am I; why am I here?" The animal has no power to analyze its condition and its environment; only man has that rational capacity. As such, man is meant to use that power to improve himself and to get the most out of life. Superior intelligence was not given to the human being merely to be used to eat breakfast, lunch, and dinner; marry and beget children. It was given that man might understand the meaning of life and find soul freedom.

Beyond all the books that are written, it is God's Book of Nature that remains the most difficult to understand. But the whole of creation, including the chapter of human existence, can be read when God becomes your teacher. India has shown the way to divine communion with Him through the right methods of meditation. God-contact becomes possible when by meditation one has attained mastery over the restlessness of the mind. One cannot meditate with uncontrolled thoughts running in every direction. A mind that does not belong to you, a mind that is wholly occupied by the senses, can neither be offered to God nor received by Him. Wherever your heart is, there will your mind be also. If you can control your feelings and sensations, then you can put your mind on God.* Having God, you shall have everything else. That is why Jesus said, "Seek ye first the kingdom of God, and His righteousness; and

---

* The path of *Kriya Yoga* as taught in Paramahansa Yogananda's *Yogoda Satsanga Lessons* includes scientific techniques of interiorizing the consciousness and freeing the mind from sensory distractions, so that one is able to become wholly absorbed in divine inner communion.

all these things shall be added unto you."*

As you commune with God through meditation, you will find yourself resurrected in His Being. His spirit alone can right all evils in the world and in oneself. But man must make the effort to realize that Divine Consciousness and to manifest the Lord's infinite goodness within himself. The earnestly striving devotee knows that virtue is more charming than vice; and that acting under the influence of good habits is more pleasant than acting under the deceptively benign influence of bad habits. Good habits bring joy; bad habits bring sorrow. Habits of yielding to passions result in suffering. Habits of yielding to the mechanical routine of worldly life beget monotony, indifference, vexation, worry, fear, disgust, disillusionment.

Habits of attending church and sacred lectures produce fitful inspiration and momentary desire for God. But habits of devotional meditation and concentration produce realization.

Meditation may seem to be one of the most difficult habits to form, for the beginner is subject to many delusive thoughts about getting speedy results. The results of meditation come slow, but sure. Many novices desire some form of spiritual "entertainment." Others expect their efforts to be rewarded right away with the manifestation of heavenly lights, saints, and deities; but this expectation is premature. Real visions come by prolonged and steady spiritual advancement. Premature experiences of phenomena are generally hallucinations. To avoid the intrusion of such false imagery from the subconscious mind, it is helpful during meditation to keep the eyes half-open and fixed firmly at the point between the eyebrows— the seat of concentration and superconscious perception. Above all, do not love or desire visions more than God.

The true signs of progress in meditation are the following:

- An increasing peacefulness during meditation.

- A conscious inner experience of calmness in meditation metamorphosing into increasing bliss.

---

* *Matthew* 6:33 (Bible).

- A deepening of one's understanding, and finding answers to one's questions through the calm intuitive state of inner perception.

- An increasing mental and physical efficiency in one's daily life.

- Love for meditation and the desire to hold on to the peace and joy of the meditative state in preference to attraction to anything in the world.

- An expanding consciousness of loving all with the unconditional love that one feels toward his own dearest loved ones.

- Actual contact with God, and worshiping Him as ever new Bliss felt in meditation and in His omnipresent manifestations within and beyond all creation.

Focusing the Power of Attention for Success

Self-Realization Fellowship International Headquarters,
Los Angeles, July 11, 1940

Success has a relation to the satisfaction of the soul in the context of the environment in which one lives; it is a result of actions based on the ideals of truth, and includes the happiness and well-being of others as a part of one's own fulfillment. Apply this law to your material, mental, moral, and spiritual life and you will find it a complete, comprehensive definition of success.

People think of success in different ways, depending on their aim in life. You even hear of it in connection with stealing: "He was a successful thief"! This shows that not all kinds of success are desirable. Our success must not hurt others. Another qualification of success is that we not only bring harmonious and beneficial results to ourselves, but also share those benefits with others. Suppose a wife engages in the spiritual practice of prolonged periods of silence, and at such times refuses to talk even to her husband and children. Though she may succeed in keeping silent, and thereby gain some degree of personal inner peace, her behavior is selfish and detrimental to her family's happiness. She is not truly successful unless the accomplishment of her good intention also benefits those to whom she has a responsibility.

Likewise, the attainment of material success means more than that we are individually entitled to enjoy our prosperity; it means that we are morally obligated to help others to create a better life as well. Anyone who has the brains can make money. But if he has love in his heart, he will never be able to use that money selfishly; he will always share with others. Money becomes a curse to the miserly, but to those who have heart it is a blessing.

Henry Ford, for example, makes a lot of money, but at the

same time he doesn't believe in charity that simply encourages people to be lazy. Rather, he provides work and a livelihood for many. If Henry Ford makes money by giving others prosperity too, he is successful in the right way. He has greatly helped the masses; American civilization owes much to him.

Even the greatest of saints are not fully redeemed until they have shared their success, their ultimate experiences of God-realization, by helping others toward divine realization. This is why those who have that attainment are dedicated to giving understanding to those who don't understand.

Thus, if you find joy and pleasure in the culture of your mind to achieve true success, not only do you insure your own happiness, but that of others as well.

A Different Standard of Success in East and West

There is a different standard of success in the East and in the West. But the East is fast imitating the worst of what it sees in movies from the West. The storybook ideal of happiness that the movies depict brings some solace to your heart; but when you look at real life, you see that success is not so simple. Life can often be cruel. You have to fight even to live. Think of all you have to do just to feed the body and keep it strong and free from disease. Even if you succeed, that success is only temporary, because eventually the body has to be dumped into the earth again. To have a successful existence you have to fight so many forces, within and without, that would rob you of worthwhile achievement.

The West concentrates on the partial or temporary success that belongs to this present life. The East concentrates on the complete success that belongs to eternity. Those who have attained eternal success we call *siddhas,* * which means those who have been judged successful by the Master of the Universe. Such a one is completely happy in body, mind, and spirit. He may have few or no possessions, yet he has great wealth—mental contentment, and spiritual understanding of the correlation of the soul and Spirit, and of the body and its essential relation-

---

* Sanskrit, "one who is successful"; i.e., one who has attained Self-realization, union with God.

ship with the Cosmic Life. That is true success. In the East, they nurture in the child's mind the desire for this kind of success. In the West, you give your child a little bank and teach him to look to money for fulfillment. To strive for sufficient material means is good, but children should also be taught the value of success that will never fade. Soul wealth lasts forever in the bank of eternity, and you can draw happiness from it any time.

But even spiritual success can be one-sided, if you have material responsibilities and are unable to meet them. Only a great yogi who has freed himself from the laws of nature can completely ignore all material concerns. In the East, the doctrine of spiritual happiness was nurtured and material sufficiency was more or less neglected. In the West, you have some physical comforts, but very little mental happiness. What is needed is balance between the two. If you only go after one thing in life, no matter what it is, you will become one-sided. For example, an artist may concentrate on his art to the exclusion of other important considerations. The result of this imbalance is that he becomes nervous and unhappy. But art and God together are a marvelous combination! Business and God, science and God, service and God—such combinations make for all-round success and happiness.

Wealth on the one hand, and disease and trouble on the other, have numerous aspects. The beauty of the West is your cleanliness. Here the mosquitoes and bedbugs haven't much chance to survive, whereas in the East they are plentiful. But don't congratulate yourselves too much about that; for here you have worse things—such as unpaid bills and financial worries from living on the installment plan—that bite your peace.

There Is More to Life Than Mere Existence

God didn't create this earth as a place for us to just eat, sleep, and die; but to find out His purpose. A few wise ones have beheld the divine schema, but so many others are blind and don't see it. The earth becomes a torture chamber to those who live in ignorance of God's plan. But when you use life's experiences as your teacher, and learn from them the true nature of the world and your part in it, those experiences become valuable guides to eternal fulfillment and happiness.

The Lord has made delusion so strong! We are living in a bedlam. You think money means happiness, but when you get it you find you are still not happy. You may have money and lose your health; or have good health and lose your money; or you may have money and health, and lots of troubles with people. You do good to others, and they give you hatred in return. Without God, nothing in this world will satisfy you. And it is significant that God tries to tempt us away from Him with material lures; He wants to know whether we want the Giver, or only His gifts.

If God had wanted us to live only in worldly consciousness, we would be wholly content with the things of the world, with following the ways of the world. Have you ever watched a flock of sheep? One jumps and all the others jump after him. Most people are like that. Somebody starts a fad or sets a pattern of action, and everybody else follows. Through the ages it has been like that. Each nation has its own customs; and we can't say they are all perfect. But who is to say whether a particular kind of life or custom is ridiculous? One way to judge is to remember that, in the beginning, all customs had a reason behind them. If we find that reason still applicable, the custom has a useful purpose; but it is foolish to follow custom blindly. We have to find out what is truth and what gives real happiness, and follow that.

Life Should Be Simplified

If you analyzed objectively the idiosyncrasies of human behavior, you would see how humorous some of our habits and customs are. Here in America you follow so many rules! You dress just so: dinner jackets for dining, evening jackets for going out, sport jackets for leisure—I even saw an advertisement for smoking jackets! And wives wonder why men like to get out into the country for a holiday where they don't have to wear socks and neckties. Once in a while it is good to get away from conformity to a monotonous schedule. To be methodical and efficient is commendable, but to become overly organized is a detriment to happiness.

In India, homes are simple, dress is simple. Here, life is so complicated that happiness flies away while you are trying to do things in a certain way. Why complicate life by insisting that the table must be just so, the house must be just so? When we invite people to our homes in India, everyone dances with joy. They look forward to it. In America, you invite guests and then spend frantic hours in preparation to be sure everything is exactly right. By the time your guests come, you can hardly wait for them to depart!

Living should be simple; dress should be simple; eating should be simple. I used to think it was not economical to eat in a restaurant, but once in a while it is. You can't afford to spend so much time in the kitchen that you haven't time for other more important things. When I was traveling and teaching, I used to simplify my diet, and just kept a bottle of milk and some lettuce and cheese on the windowsill. It was all so easy!

Heaven Is Within, Not in Things

Our training in the ashram in India was severe. We learned to curb our desires, and not to cater to our likes and dislikes, nor to have preferences. We were grateful for everything that came to us. With all that you have here, many of you are just as miserable with your possessions as you would be without them. Your wants are endless. In the morning, after the husband shaves and dresses, the first thing he wants is breakfast. At the table, he wishes his wife had fixed something different, and she wishes she had better dishes and silverware. Day after day, they go on wanting this and that, until nothing satisfies them—not even each other, nor their children! They are not happy at all. And because they are discontented, they turn on those closest to them. The wife nags the husband, the husband shouts at the children, and the children rebel and get into trouble with wrong friends. The thing is this: it is not wrong to have possessions, but it is wrong to be possessed by possessions. You must be free from attachment.

My heaven is within me; so when I am enjoying our beautiful place in Encinitas, my inner heaven makes it even more heavenly. Without that inner contentment, even a paradise on earth can become a hades.* I see that if it were not for my

---

* "To the disunited (one not established in the Self) does not belong wisdom, nor has he meditation. To the unmeditative there is no tranquility. To the peaceless how comes happiness?" (Bhagavad Gita II:66).

inner joy, the problems of the heavy responsibilities I have undertaken here could make me so unhappy, I would like to run away. The greatest enemy of happiness in this country is the bills! There is much I like about America—I especially love the people—but your idea that you have to have certain things in order to be happy is a delusion. Even after you get them, you still are not happy! What is the sense in following the will-o'-the-wisp of material happiness? Live simply. Don't have so many things to take care of. It seems so wonderful when you buy something new. But after a while the newness wears off and you have no time for it, or you forget about it and want something else. But the bills don't forget you!

Control your life; make it as simple as you can. Have money in the bank for needs and emergencies. Save more than you spend on unnecessary "necessities." And always include someone else in your happiness. When you do for others, you yourself will never be left wanting. I know that if I walked away from this place right now, I would never miss it. And I would never go hungry; everything I need would be given to me. This is not a boast; I have seen that force working in my life. Whether I am floating on the surface of life or drowned in the depths of the sea, I know that I am with God and nothing can touch me. That realization has given me supreme happiness. Without the understanding and experience I received from this teaching of India, I would have been the most miserable person in the world. Though I have earned a lot of money, I refused to let it make a slave of me. I have never let money touch me. I gave it all away to God's work to help others. My inner happiness is my greatest possession; it is wealth beyond the dream of kings.

Your Success Is What You Have Attained Within

When you see the masses who have no real happiness or success, don't think that life is meant to be this way. You can make of yourself whatever you want to be. It is what you have attained within that determines your success. If you have nothing within, you have no happiness. And if you have nothing outside, but are happy within, you have all success. So you cannot judge people by their outer circumstances. Right amongst you in the crowd there may be one of exalted spiritual stature who has attained real soul peace and happiness within.

This is why moral success—freedom from the dictates of wrong habits and impulses—gives more happiness than material success. In moral success there is a psychological happiness that cannot be taken away by any physical condition. You can spend all your time making money, but it won't produce the lasting comfort and security you are looking for. In fact, it will bring more misery, because peace and happiness are in the mind, not in things. If you do not also devote time to the discipline of your mind, no amount of material prosperity will satisfy you. This discipline is not a process of torture, but the training of the consciousness to adopt those thoughts and actions that lead to happiness.

Your happiness is your success, so let no one take your happiness away from you. Protect yourself from those who try to make you unhappy. When I was young, I used to feel very impatient when someone told an untruth about me; but then I found it is much better to have the satisfaction of my conscience than the approbation of people. Conscience is intuitive reasoning, reporting the truth about yourself and your motives. When your conscience is clear, when you know you are doing right, you are not afraid of anything. A clear conscience mirrors a certificate of merit from God. Be immaculate before the tribunal of your conscience and you shall be happy and have the blessing of God.

If you don't make money, it is because you don't really concentrate on it; similarly, if you aren't happy, it is because you don't concentrate on being happy. The mule that carries a bag of gold on its back doesn't know the value of that load. Likewise, man is so absorbed in toting the burden of life, hoping for some happiness at the end of the trail, that he does not realize he carries within him the supreme and everlasting bliss of the soul. Because he looks for happiness in "things," he doesn't know he already possesses a wealth of happiness within himself.

Put Your Duties in Proper Perspective

The teaching of Yoga does not advise you to fly away from your duties in the world. It tells you to saturate yourself with the thought of God while you do your part in this world where He has placed you. If you desire a life of seclusion in the forest or in the mountains, thinking that in the freedom from duties there you will find God, you must have the will to sit all day, day after day, in meditation. Certainly that effort is commendable. But it is much greater to be able to be in the world but not of it—to perform your true duties for the benefit of others while keeping your mind on God. "By forsaking work no one reaches to perfection....O Arjuna, remaining immersed in yoga, perform all actions, forsaking attachment (to their fruits)."*

You must think of greater and lesser duties in proper perspective. And don't let one duty contradict another. In the Sanskrit scriptures there is a divine law, one of the most beautiful laws ever given to the world: "If one duty contradicts another duty, it is not a true duty." If you seek financial success at the cost of health, you are not fulfilling your duty to the body. If you are so crazy about religion that you neglect your material responsibilities, you are not balanced; you have allowed one duty to contradict your obligations to your body and family. If you lose sight of your duty toward God because you give all your attention to fussing about your family, that is not duty.

Many ask, "Shall we first acquire material success to fulfill our worldly obligations, and then seek God? Or should we have God first and then go after success?" By all means, God first. Never begin or end your day without communion with Him in deep meditation. We should remember that we could not perform any duties without the power borrowed from God. So it is to Him we owe our first allegiance. If you do your other duties but forget God, He doesn't like that at all. The ideal is to perform all duties with the sole desire to please God.

To speak of seeking God and material fulfillment together sounds good; but unless you meditate deeply and regularly so that you anchor your consciousness in God *first,* the world will claim all your attention and you will have no time for Him. Without the consciousness that God is with you, your material duties usually turn into methods of torture. But if you have God with you all the time, and do your duties with the consciousness of God, you can be the happiest person. "Their thoughts fully on Me, their beings surrendered to Me, enlight-

---

* Bhagavad Gita III:4 and II:48.

ening one another, proclaiming Me always, My devotees are contented and joyful."* If I had not had the training of my guru, Swami Sri Yukteswar, which gave me that divine consciousness, I would have lost heart long ago, trying to help people and to build this work, and sometimes getting slaps instead of cooperation.

I used to argue with Guruji that organizations are hornets' nests. Everyone expects you to please *him*. But I have found that if God comes first, spiritual organization is a hive and God is the honey that nurtures others with divine love and peace. If you rule others with the attitude, "I am king," they will soon dethrone you. But if you guide others with sincere love, you can be a king of hearts. Of course, your love is reflected more in true hearts; and when you love all impartially, you can recognize those who respond to that love. Jesus alluded to this, when he upheld the devotion of the woman who anointed his head with costly ointment,† and the "good part" that Mary had chosen as she sat absorbed at his feet instead of helping her sister Martha with serving the other guests.‡

Divine Love Is Unsurpassable

If you could but realize the romance that some devotees have with God! No other experiences can equal that joy. I knew a saint who was so engrossed in God, his face was aglow with the Divine. I asked him about his family life. He said, "That is past and gone. I know no other life now than that which I have in God."

I told him about my father and how much he had done for me. He said, "You are ungrateful; you have forgotten that the Heavenly Father gave you your good earthly father. When I felt the call of God I reasoned, 'Suppose I died; who then would look after my family? The One who has given me life will look after them.' I *knew* that He would." And God did help him because he sincerely gave his life to God alone.§

"He who watcheth Me always, him do I watch; he never

---

* Bhagavad Gita X:9.   †*Matthew* 26:7–13 (Bible).   ‡ *Luke* 10:39–42 (Bible).

§ To the devotee who has freed his soul from all earthly desires and attachments, and is anchored in supreme love for God, the Lord says: "Forsaking all

loses sight of Me, nor do I lose sight of him."* In every nook of
nature, hidden in the flowers and peeking through the sparkling
window of the moon, my Beloved plays hide-and-seek with me.
He watches me always through the screen of nature, the veil of
delusion.

Never ignore the Lover behind all lovers. Let not your heart
beat with the emotion of the world, but with the thrill of divine
love. That love is unsurpassable. The moment divine love possesses your heart, your entire body becomes blissfully still:
"When the Master of the Universe came into my body temple,
my heart forgot to beat, and all the cells of my body forgot
their duties. They were transfixed, listening to the voice of Life
Immortal—the Lover of all life, the Life of all lives. My heart,
my brain, all the cells of my being were electrified, immortal-
ized with His Presence." Such is the love of the Lord.

The sorrow produced by hatred and war proves that spirituality and kindness are superior forces. Hate is destructive; love
is the greatest constructive force. So, dear friends, from the stu-
pidity of hatred and the madness of war, learn to love God. His
love bestows an all-fulfilling success that nothing else can give.
Love alone will bring fulfillment to the world. If all nations
loved each other, and were anxious to help each other—not by
force and wrong methods, but by love and kindness—there
would come true and lasting worldwide success.

Think of the billions spent on killing one another in war!
Shame on humanity! Where will it all end but in suffering and
destruction? The only way to bring this misery to an end is by
love. As long as one nation builds bigger weapons for defense,
other nations will try to find even better methods to defend
themselves, and people will live in constant terror. Why don't
all nations cultivate love and understanding instead of hatred
and war?

A universal religion of love is the real answer. Love makes

---

other *dharmas* (duties), remember Me alone; I will free thee from all sins (accruing from nonperformance of those lesser duties)" (Bhagavad Gita XVIII:66).

* Bhagavad Gita VI:30, as frequently paraphrased by Paramahansaji, who has
given this literal translation: "He who perceives Me everywhere and beholds
everything in Me never loses sight of Me, nor do I ever lose sight of him."

you victorious; it makes you a conqueror. Jesus was one of the greatest conquerors of all, wasn't he? A conqueror of hearts.

The Power Behind All Power

First and foremost, be successful with the Master of the Universe. You become so engrossed in material duties, you say you have no time for God. But suppose God says He has no time to beat in your heart, to think in your brain. Where will you be? He is the Love behind all loves. He is the Reason behind all reason. He is the Will behind all wills, the Success behind all success, the Power behind all powers; the blood in your veins; the breath behind your words. If he takes His power away, my voice will be silent and I shall speak no more. If His power doesn't express through our hearts and brains, we will lie dumb forever. So remember, your most important duty in life is your duty to God.

The Practicality of Seeking God First

All scriptures teach: "Seek ye first the kingdom of God."* But see how people separate from their daily lives the spiritual doctrines they read or hear about in church. When you practice and apply principles of truth, you will realize the practicality of all spiritual, mental, and physical laws. When you read scriptures superficially, you don't get anything from them. But if you read truth with concentration, and really believe what you read, those truths will work for you. You may want to believe; you may even think you believe; but if you really believe, the result will be instantaneous.

There are various degrees of belief. Some people don't believe at all. Some want to believe, others believe a little bit, and some believe until their belief is tested. We are so certain of our convictions, until they are contradicted; then we become confused and insecure. Faith is intuitive conviction, a knowing from the soul, that cannot be shaken even by contradictions.

The practical purpose behind the scriptural injunction to seek God first is that once you have found Him, you can use His power to acquire the things your common sense tells you are right for you to have. Have faith in this law. In attunement with

* *Matthew* 6:33 (Bible).

God you will find the way to true success, which is a balance of spiritual, mental, moral, and material attainment.

Nurture the thought: I must find God. Let that thought predominate throughout the day, especially in the gaps of time between your other duties. Transfer your attention to the more important concerns in life. Too much time is wasted in superficial interests. When students are with me, I always turn their attention toward God. They may say, "The ocean is lovely," or "The grounds are beautiful."* I say to them, "Remain quiet. Don't feel you have to talk all the time. Go within and you will see the Loveliness behind all beauty."

Most people are like butterflies, flitting aimlessly. They never seem to really get anywhere or to stop for more than a moment before they are attracted by some new diversion. The bee works and prepares for hard times. But the butterfly lives only for today. When winter comes, the butterfly is gone, while the bee has stored-up food to live on. We must learn to gather and store the honey of God's peace and power.

Restless butterfly types are concentrated on movies and useless activities. If you have God first, it is all right to go to movies once in a while, but mostly they are a waste of time. In the early stages on the spiritual path, you must seek quiet places where you can regularly get away by yourself and be free to think of God. When you are with people, be with them wholeheartedly; give them your love and attention. But also take time to be alone with God. I seldom see anyone in the mornings; that is my time of seclusion. And don't mix too much with the "social set." There is no happiness in it. Be selective about your company. Choose a wise man or some good friends who will instill spiritual thoughts in you; and get busy with God.

Meditation Removes Mental Limitations

Reading worthwhile books is much better than spending time on foolishness. But better than reading books is meditation. Focus your attention within. You will feel a new power,

---

* The Self-Realization Fellowship Ashram Center in Encinitas, California, overlooks the Pacific Ocean. The grounds there and at the Mother Center in Los Angeles are beautifully maintained to express the reflection of God in nature.

a new strength, a new peace—in body, mind, and spirit. Your trouble in meditation is that you don't persevere long enough to get results. That is why you never know the power of a focused mind. If you let muddy water stand still for a long time, the mud will settle at the bottom and the water will become clear. In meditation, when the mud of your restless thoughts begins to settle, the power of God begins to reflect in the clear waters of your consciousness.

Do you know why some people are never able to acquire health or make money, no matter how hard they seem to try? First of all, most people do everything half-heartedly. They use only about one-tenth of their attention. That is why they haven't the power to succeed. In addition, it may be their karma, the effects of their past wrong actions, that has created in them a chronic condition of failure. Never accept karmic limitations. Don't believe you are incapable of doing anything. Often when you can't succeed at something it is because you have made up your mind that you cannot do it. But when you convince your mind of its accomplishing power, you can do anything! By communing with God you change your status from a mortal being to an immortal being. When you do this, all bonds that limit you will be broken. This is a very great law to remember. As soon as your attention is focused, the Power of all powers will come, and with that you can achieve spiritual, mental, and material success. I have again and again used that power in my life; and you can do so too. I know that power of God can never fail. Though every other power you acquire will bring bits of success, that success will not last. But when your attention becomes divinely centralized, it will burn always as a great light that will reveal God.

When a problem thwarts you—when you find no solution and no one to help you—go into meditation. Meditate until you find the solution. It will come. I have tested this hundreds of times, and I know the focusing power of attention never fails. It is the secret of success. Concentrate, and don't stop until your concentration is perfect. Then go after what you want. As a mortal being you are limited, but as a child of God you are unlimited. Connect your concentration with God. Concentration is everything. First go within; learn to focus your mind and to feel the power of God. Then go after material success. If you want health, first go to God and connect yourself with the Life behind all life; then apply laws of health. You will see that this is much more effective than relying solely on doctors. Commune with God and then go after health or money or seeking a partner in life.

To get response from God, you must meditate deeply. Each day's meditation must be deeper than the previous day's. Then you will find that as soon as your attention becomes focused, it burns out all deficiency from your mind, and you feel the power of God come over you. That power can destroy all seeds of failure.

Keep Your Attention Concentrated

When I first started on this path, I was very restless in meditation; but the time came when I sat for forty-eight hours, completely absorbed in the ecstasy of God. Think of that power! Concentrate on that power.

Watch your time. Don't waste it. You decide to make a quick trip to town to get something you need, but how easily other things distract you. Before you know it you have been gone for hours. At the end of the day, you see how your attention was scattered. It lost all its accomplishing power. The mind is like a bag of mustard seed. If you spill those seeds on the floor it is hard to pick them up again. Your concentration must be like a vacuum cleaner, drawing those scattered seed-thoughts together again.

When you have finished your duties at the end of the day, sit quietly alone. Take a good book and read it with attention. Then meditate long and deeply. You will find much more peace and happiness in this than in restless activities in which your mind runs riot in all directions. If you think you are meditating, when all the while your mind is scattered, you delude yourself. But once you learn to concentrate on God, there is nothing like it. Test yourself. Go on a picnic, go into town, socialize with friends; at the end of the day you will be nervous and restless. But if you cultivate the habit of spending time alone at home in meditation, a great power and peace will come over you. And it will remain with you in your activities as well as in meditation. Seclusion is the price of greatness.

Focusing the Attention on God's Power
Assures Success in Any Endeavor

The great man always does everything with the power of attention. The full force of that power can be attained through meditation. When you use that focusing power of God, you can place it on anything and be a success. Use it to develop body, mind, and soul.

Therefore, friends, my last word is this: Focus your attention on God and you shall have all the power you want, to use in any direction. And if you faithfully follow the scientific Self-Realization methods of concentration and meditation, you will see that there is no quicker or surer way to unite yourself with God.

Quickening Human Evolution

Buffalo, New York, May 29, 1927*

Do you realize how you spend your life? Very few of us are aware of how much we can put into and get out of life if we use it properly, wisely, and economically. First, let us economize our time—lifetimes ebb away before we wake up, and that is why we do not realize the immortal value of the time God has given us. Too much time is spent in rushing, in getting nowhere. We should stop, think, and try to learn what life can give to us. Most people do not think deeply at all—they just eat, sleep, work, and die.

Sixty years is the average lifespan, but do you know how many years you actually live? Most people sleep from six to ten hours a day—one-third of their life, twenty to twenty-five years, is gone, spent in unconsciousness. Thus only forty or thirty-five years are left. About five or ten years are spent in gossip or talking about nothing, and amusements. That brings it down to thirty—and out of those thirty years, what else do you do? Eat and do nothing, and of course attend to business. Business is necessary for the purpose of maintaining the bodily animal, which takes most of your time. Actually scrutinize your life—you have left hardly ten years!

In the morning, most of you wake with the consciousness of coffee and toast—you toast yourself with breakfast consciousness; no thought of God to refresh your spirit—then rush to business. The day passes—hurry, worry, and at noontime, coffee and doughnuts; you don't even eat right! Evening comes—

---

* From notes printed in an early issue of *Self-Realization* magazine. Excerpts were subsequently revised under Paramahansaji's direction and republished in various YSS/SRF publications, including later issues of the magazine and *Yogoda Satsanga Lessons*. The talk is herewith reconstituted and published in its entirety.

movies and dancing. You come back late at night, go to bed, get up in the morning, and start in again with the breakfast consciousness. This is the way you spend your life.

Life's Purpose Is to Grow in Knowledge and Wisdom

In your sixty years of life, many things are necessary just to keep the body vehicle all right; but that is not the sole purpose of life. Do not think that in order to be well-clothed and fed you have to have millions—you don't have to lead a sophisticated life in order merely to feed and care for the bodily animal. Life's goal is much more than that. This world is a vast school in which we ought constantly to strive for greater knowledge and wisdom.

Ask yourself now this question: How many good books have I read in this life? Every day about two dozen new books are being printed in America on ethics, music, literature, botany, logic, science, the scriptures, immortal truths—how are you going to pack all this knowledge into your ten years of life? Then again, sixty years is not the life of everyone; just the lucky ones have even that. What assurance have you got that sickness will not come and shorten your life? And yet you are idling and having bridge parties! I have no objection if you have a good purpose for doing so. But are you going to fritter away your time standing on the sidewalk, watching the crowds pass by or looking through the windows at many things you don't need and want to buy? Are you going to waste your time by the wayside?

How are you going to learn all the things you want to learn? Doesn't your heart throb to learn everything worthwhile that is going on in the world? How is it possible for the average human being to attain all wisdom? How are you going to find time to read of Jesus, of Aristotle, of all the great poets? Life seems hopelessly short when you think of that. You read a few books, and think you know it all. In the cities you have wonderful libraries, but few people go there. Think of all the knowledge and wisdom that human beings have gathered from the school of life; how, in these few years, are you going to pack it in your brain? Is it possible? As long as you live on this earth, as long as the power in the eye enables you to see the stars, as long as you enjoy God's sunshine and breathe His air, so long will you yearn for knowledge.

Most human beings walk through life with an empty skull. They think there is a brain there—they *think* it, that is all; they walk in emptiness. "Oh, yes, I have a wonderful library at home. Come on, I will show it to you." Beautiful but untouched! Music, poetry, science, everything is there. With all the things you want to learn, you don't want to waste your time. You are filled with unhappiness most of the time because you do not keep the mind worthily engaged. Think of Plato, Shakespeare, Maeterlinck, Lord Shankara, and their works. Think of the privilege you have. You can converse with all of them at will through their wonderful books. Instead of that you are wondering all the time what show you are going to see next!*

It is good once in a while to be entertained; but if you spend your life in useless pastimes, and in gossiping about others—being interested in others' faults rather than recognizing your own—the loss is yours. You have lots of housecleaning to do yourself.

You create such a limited sphere of interest around yourself. A tailor died one night and went to heaven. In the morning he began looking around for a Singer sewing machine. His narrow habit was still with him, even though in heaven he had no need for clothing; he was clad in garments of light. You, too, are wasting priceless time on nonessentials when the treasures of God are around you, ready to be received.

Wisdom comes, knocks at your gate, gently asking, "Let me in," but there is no answer, no thought, no response there. Cheap, sensational novels call you hoarsely with their grossness, and your thoughts rush out to receive them with open hearts. You develop a taste for inferior things thus. If you cultivate a liking for rotten cheese, you lose your taste for good, fresh cheese. As you develop a taste for inferior things you lose the taste for better offerings, and you think yourself unable to be otherwise, because of the compelling power of bad habits. Cultivate the good habit of using this life for pursuing interests that are more worthwhile.

---

* In his talks in later years, when television entertainment was making its debut, Paramahansaji decried the potential of this medium to usurp the time and mind of viewers.

Schedule your life. Read the world's best books; don't waste time reading this and that indiscriminately. Read of medicine, astronomy, science, the scriptures. But one field needs to be your first concern: You must find your vocation. By contact with the Cosmic Vibration in meditation* you will be led to the goal that is right for you; you will be led to the work you ought to do. Concentrate upon making yourself proficient in that. Many try ten kinds of endeavor without getting really acquainted with any. As a beginner in self-development, you cannot absorb everything about many things; learn a little about everything and everything about one thing.

Evolution Can Be Accelerated

Still, knowledge is so vast, spiritual wisdom is so vast. And though the earth is but a speck in the universe, it is immense to us. Yet with the march of human progress, our world is becoming small—every day it is growing smaller, due to modern transportation facilities. Soon we will have to take a trip to other planets to have adventure in travels! Electricity goes anywhere in a second—why can't we, whose bodies are essentially electromagnetic waves? But we are progressing in numerous ways, doing ordinary things more quickly. The adoption of better methods in business and transportation, mass production by huge machinery, have quickened evolution. Think of the time of life used up just in weaving of cloth by hand in the past! That time has been saved by modern machinery. So the evolution of society has been quickened by the adoption of increasingly better methods. Why can't we accelerate human evolution as well—to learn how to weave lives more quickly into all-round success? How is the human brain going to acquire in a lifetime all knowledge and wisdom? That is my question.

When I met Luther Burbank, he showed me a walnut tree and said, "I took off more than one hundred years from its

---

* Reference to the Yogoda Satsanga Society technique of meditation on God as *Aum* (see glossary). Immanent in the *Aum* vibration is the Christ Consciousness *[Kutastha Chaitanya]* or Universal Intelligence; communion with *Aum* therefore brings the meditator into contact with the Infinite Source of divine guidance and wisdom.

usual period of growth. I grew that tree in twelve years." And you could see that the tree was already bearing walnuts!

If the walnut tree can be made to mature in twelve years instead of one hundred and fifty years, there is a chance for human beings also. In sixty years of existence, it is possible for a human being to develop so that he can be a center of all knowledge. That is the point I want to drive home in your mind. I have cited how machinery hastened world evolution. Where did machinery come from?—from the factory of human minds. As man quickened evolution in society and business, so he can quicken his evolution in all branches of his life, including the faculties of his inner life.

Burbank also made almonds have soft shells, made over the tomato, and created the Shasta daisy from bulbs and the cactus without thorns. In primitive times the different animals used to eat the cactus, so the cactus developed protective thorns. When one life begins to hurt another life, that life develops weapons of defense. Burbank told me that during his experiments in developing the spineless cactus, every day he went into the garden and talked to the barbed plants: "Please, beloved cactus, I am Luther Burbank, your friend. I am not going to hurt you at all, so why develop thorns?" And so the thornless cactus was developed. By talking, by attention, by thought-force and knowledge of nature's laws, you can impress certain vibrations on protoplasm, and thus consciously guide and hasten the process of evolution.

Increasing the Receptivity of the Brain

Professor James of Harvard said that most of our habits come through heredity. Feeblemindedness in people, science says, cannot be helped. Scientists take measurements and believe too much in the stamp of heredity. They have yet to learn how by awakening the brain cells man can quicken his evolution. The power of receptivity of the brain cells can become so heightened that a man can receive, in a single lifetime, all the knowledge he wants to absorb within himself.

In education there is a vast difference between the methods applied by teachers in India and in the West. In the West they pump ideas into the brains of children. "How many books have

you read; how many teachers have you had?" A man returned
from college with a Ph.D. in making sugar from different fruits.
He was asked if sugar could be made from the guava fruit. After
some deep thought he said, "I did not study that. It was not in
my curriculum." Using common sense was beyond him.

It is not a pumping-in from the outside that gives wisdom; it is the power and extent of your inner receptivity that
determines how much you can attain of true knowledge, and
how rapidly. The man who has the power of receptivity quickly
grasps everything. People with no receptivity may be exposed
to the same experiences or information, yet not really see nor
fully comprehend what is there. An intelligent man lives far
ahead of the idiot. Your experiences bring wisdom according
to the measure of the cup of your receptivity.

Focused Concentration Makes You Keenly Receptive
to Wisdom

How can you increase your receptivity, and thus quicken
your evolution? By consciously condensing all your experiences
through the power of concentration. Concentration means to
gather in your attention, focusing it to one point; condensation means to use that concentrated attention to do something
quickly that ordinarily would take a long time. By concentration you can condense each experience and garner whatever
wisdom is to be learned from it. By condensation of individual
experiences you can compress all your experiences, and the wisdom they contain, into a shorter length of time and thus gain
much more than if you go through life haphazardly.

I will tell you of such an experience. A friend of mine said
I was all right as a spiritual man, but that I could not succeed
in business. I replied, "I am going to make five thousand dollars in business for you, within two weeks." He said, "You will
have to show me. I am 'from Missouri.'"

I did not rush to invest money on unwise things. I used
concentration, disengaged my mind from all disturbances, and
focused my attention one-pointedly within. Most of you have
the searchlight of your attention turned outside all the time instead of inside; you should turn the searchlight of the mind
within, to reveal the Divine Source. (We are living on the outer

side of the universe; the inner side is more tangible and real, for there the subtle laws operating behind all outer phenomena can be perceived. Every change in business, every change in the planetary system, in our physical bodies—everything is recorded there.) Ordinarily, men do not concentrate—the mind is restless, and the restless mind jumps at conclusions and races for something that does not rightfully belong to one. You must obey divine law. Remember: Concentrate, and then ask Divine Power to help you.

So I touched that Source; and as soon as I had made that contact there were shown to me lots of houses. But I did not sit quietly in my room and say, "The Heavenly Father will open the ceiling and drop five thousand dollars in my lap" because I had favored Him with a fervent prayer. I bought the Sunday papers and looked at real estate advertisements. I picked out a few houses, and told my friend to invest his money in them.

He said: "Everything seems pretty shaky," and I said, "Never mind, doubting Thomas, don't spoil success by your doubts."

In two weeks there was a real estate boom and prices of houses went way up high. He sold the houses and had a clear profit of five thousand dollars. I showed him that the power of God works through the mind wherever we apply it with faith.

Concentration, when directed by Divine Power, does not allow you to ramble through wrong investments; you go straight to success. If that mind power can be applied in business it can be applied in other things—in music and writing, for example. I always start from within to bring knowledge out, and not from without to pump knowledge in. All the musical instruments I play I learned that way. Perhaps I was too proud to think about going to a teacher; I thought, "Well, the first man who started to make music did not learn from anybody; why can't I do the same?" (It is all right to say that, but if you stand and wait while you reinvent the trolley car, you will be a long time getting to your destination!)

All questions I have had have been answered; as fast as God can respond, I receive direct replies from Him. Start from within, not from without. That is how anyone can get the experience of many years within a short time. You have not

to read all the books in the library. You have not to learn everything from schools or teachers. Poetry, music, all knowledge,
come without limitation from the inner source, from the soul.
In one short span of human life, how else are you going to find
out answers to all the mysteries of the body, and the mysteries of an infinitude of divine wisdom, if you do not tap your
inner source, which is omniscient?

How an Ignorant Devotee Found That the Divine
Must Be Sought Within

There was a Hindu devotee who was puzzled trying to decide what scriptures he should read, and what idol he should
worship. (Idols are used in India to help fix the mind in concentration on a particular aspect of the one formless Spirit, and
are respectfully kept covered in a temple so that the birds and
weather will not destroy them.) So this devotee said, "Which
god shall I worship?" He would buy one idol, and then he
would be afraid the others would get angry. So he would buy
another. He had two big trunks in which he carried all his
holy books and images, suspended from his shoulders on a
pole. Every day somebody would tell him he had better worship this god or that god, and read this or that holy book—so
heavier and heavier the trunks grew. He saw he would have to
buy a third trunk! But he thought, "It is not possible to carry
three trunks." He sat by the side of a pond and began to weep:
"Infinite Spirit, tell me which book to read, and which idol to
worship. As soon as I worship one god I think the others are
getting angry."

It so happened that a saint passed by that way, and seeing
the crying man, said: "Son, why are you weeping? What is the
matter?"

"Saint, I don't know which book to read; and look at
these hundreds of idols! I don't know which one to please."

The saint said, "Close your eyes and pick up any book
and follow that book throughout life; and drop the idols on a
rock and break them one by one. The one that does not break,
worship that one."

So he picked up one book. Most of the idols were made of
clay, and all broke except one that was made of solid stone.

Then the saint suddenly came back and said, "I forgot to tell you something. Now that you have found your god, go back home. But if you find a more powerful god than this one, worship him. Always worship the more powerful god."

So the man went home, and on his little altar he put the stone idol, worshiping and offering fruits. Every day he discovered the fruit was gone, so he thought, "The saint certainly told me of the right idol. Since he has eaten the fruits he must be a living god."

One day, overcome by curiosity, he thought he would watch how a god eats. He opened his eyes just a little, and while he was praying he saw a huge mouse come and eat the fruit. Then he said, "Look at that stone idol. It cannot eat the fruit, but the mouse can, so it is a more powerful god." He caught the mouse by the tail and tied it on the altar.

His wife said, "You have gone crazy."

"No, I have not gone crazy. I am just following the instructions of the saint to worship whatever form of God is the most powerful." So he put the stone aside and began to worship the mouse instead.

One day he was meditating when suddenly he heard a great noise. Opening his eyes he saw a pussycat eating the mouse. He thought, "That is interesting. The pussycat is more powerful than the mouse. So I must worship the cat." He got hold of the cat and made a place for it on the altar. The cat did not have to catch mice anymore, receiving an offering of milk every day without any labor on its part. Day after day the man's meditation grew deeper and the cat got fatter.

After each meditation the man used to drink a bowl of milk placed before him by his wife. The pussycat was not satisfied with what she got, so she concentrated on the man's bowl of milk. One day she drank it up and went back and sat on the altar. The wife came in, saw the milk gone, looked at the cat sitting on the altar feigning innocence, and went and got the broom. Her husband's meditation was broken by the noise of the broomstick falling on the yowling cat. He looked at his wife chastising the cat, and he thought, "That is interesting. My wife is more powerful than the pussycat, so she is a better god than the cat." Then he demanded that his wife sit on the altar. So she sat, and every day he meditated on her.

Of course, the wife still cooked food for her husband, and after he finished worshiping her he would eat his meal. It so happened that one day he bit down hard on a piece of charcoal in the rice. "Why did you put charcoal in the rice? Why did you do that?" the man shouted at his wife.

To which the wife apologetically replied, "Master, I did not deliberately put charcoal in the rice. Forgive me; I am thy servant."

Then he said, "Ah, that's interesting. So you are my servant; you like to serve me. Then I am more powerful than you are. Then I am the most powerful god. God is in me! I have found Him now, within myself."

You won't find God anywhere unless you find Him within. Find Him within, and you shall find Him without, everywhere. If you find Him in the temple of your soul, you find Him enshrined in all temples and churches, and in all souls.

Kriya Yoga: Scientific Method
of Accelerating Human Evolution

It is impossible in this life to read all the Vedas and bibles, and to follow all the systems given to be godlike. How then are you going to achieve the goal of your evolution? You must search within, just as the devotee in the above story found out.

You cannot possess all wisdom unless your brain is evolved accordingly. Everything depends upon the receptivity of your mind, brain cells, and the subtle astral centers of life and consciousness in the spinal column. This body changes every twelve years; that is why at twelve, twenty-four, and thirty-six years we find distinct changes occurring. If there were no obstruction of disease and other karmic consequences of breaking natural laws, with the change of years and change of body the mind would change correspondingly. Disease and wrong living retard that evolution, but normally in twelve years your brain develops in such a way that it displays a slight refinement of mentality.

If natural evolution takes twelve years of growth and change of tissues to manifest improved patterns of thoughts, then to make the brain receptive to all wisdom would seem to require that you wait almost indefinitely. To accelerate this process of evolution, there is a method that the masterminds of India have taught of revolving specific vital currents around the spine and brain. By practicing this method—revolving the current around the six (twelve by polarity) astral cerebrospinal centers—you can gain the result of one year's ordinary physical evolution. That is how many saints quickly acquire spiritual knowledge, far beyond that of theoretical theologians. Things which they perceive instantly would require years of ordinary study and experience. Revolving this current around the centers of divine life and consciousness in the spine and brain develops their receptivity. In a year of such practice—even twenty minutes a day—you can get the result of many years of natural evolution. Jesus Christ did not go to college, yet not one among the world's great scientists knows of God and nature's laws as he knew.*

Experiential knowledge ordinarily comes through the channel of the senses; but the senses do not give you more than the knowledge of phenomena—the superficial appearances of the real substance. When by concentration and practice of the above-mentioned method all the fine spinal and brain cells are tuned to the cosmic source, they become highly magnetized,

---

* The practice referred to is *Kriya Yoga*. In *Autobiography of a Yogi* Paramahansaji recorded that *Kriya* is "the same science that Krishna gave millenniums ago to Arjuna; and that was later known to Patanjali and Christ, and to St. John, St. Paul, and other disciples."

"The ancient rishis discovered that man's earthly and heavenly environment, in a series of twelve-year cycles, push him forward on his natural path. The scriptures aver that man requires a million years of normal, diseaseless evolution to perfect his human brain and attain cosmic consciousness....Through proper food, sunlight, and harmonious thoughts, men who are led only by Nature and her divine plan will achieve Self-realization in a million years. Twelve years of normal healthful living are required to effect even slight refinements in brain structure; a million solar returns are exacted to purify the cerebral tenement sufficiently for manifestation of cosmic consciousness....

"The *Kriya Yogi* mentally directs his life energy to revolve, upward and downward, around the six spinal centers (medullary, cervical, dorsal, lumbar, sacral, and coccygeal plexuses), which correspond to the twelve astral signs of the zodiac, the symbolic Cosmic Man. One-half minute of revolution of energy around the sensitive spinal cord of man effects subtle progress in his evolution; that half-minute of *Kriya* equals one year of natural spiritual unfoldment."

charged with divine intelligent power.

Some say that our brain cells at birth have come already patterned with fixed traits and, therefore, cannot be remolded. This is false. Since God made us in His image we cannot have limitation. If we probe deeply enough within ourselves we will know that this is so. Even in the feebleminded, God's power is present as much as in the greatest man. The sun shines equally on the charcoal and the diamond; it is the charcoal that is responsible for not reflecting the sunlight as does the diamond. All congenital limitations come through man's own transgression of a law sometime in a past incarnation. But what has been done can be undone. If the brain cells of a feebleminded person are awakened with the searchlight of concentration focused within by the above method, he will display the previously eclipsed intelligence the same as the intelligent man.

Your body is made up of 27,000,000,000,000 cells. Every cell is like an intelligent being.* You have to educate the dormant intelligence in each cell in order to know all there is to know in this world. But you have never trained those cells. That is why you are all the time full of melancholia and passing fancies, and suffering from lack of understanding.

The great scientific method of mental and spiritual progress is to magnetize the cells by sending life current around the brain and spine, thereby securing the evolutionary advancement of one year's healthful, harmonious living. Twenty minutes of this practice daily will greatly refine your mentality. When you have revitalized the brain cells, when the divine magnetism touches them, every cerebral cell becomes a vibrant brain; and you will find within yourself myriads of awakened brains ready to grasp every vestige of knowledge. With these awakened brains, the multitude of cellular mentalities in the body will awake and all things will be apprehended by you. You will study the vast book of Nature and Truth with twenty-seven thousand billion awakened and spiritualized

---

* Decades after Paramahansa Yogananda gave this lecture, biologists identified the DNA molecule that exists in the nucleus of each cell. Experimentation has proved that present in the DNA of every individual cell is the information and intelligence to grow an entire new body and brain.

microscopic brains and mentalities. Why be satisfied in half-educating a small part of your brain only?

All Knowledge, All Success, Are Achievable in This Life

Whenever you want to know something, don't start with data—retire within and concentrate. Seek guidance from within. When the mind is receptive, then bring the data; start working out the business or mental solution. Do not be filled with discouragement and say it cannot be done.

Every human being is a representative of the Infinite Power. You should manifest that Power in everything you do. Whenever you want to produce something, do not depend only upon the outside source; go deep within and seek the Infinite Source. All methods of business success, all inventions, all vibrations of music, all inspirational thoughts and writings, are recorded in the annals of God.

First, determine what your goal is; ask divine aid to direct you to the right action whereby your objective will be fulfilled; then meditate. Afterward, act according to the inner direction that you receive; then you will attain what you want. When the mind is calm, how quickly, how smoothly, how beautifully you will perceive everything! Success in everything will come to pass in a short time, for Cosmic Power can be proved by the application of the right law.

The scientific man or the businessman or anyone seeking success would accomplish more if he concentrated upon increasing the receptive quality of his brain cells, instead of depending just on books and college work for his progress. The world starts with books and outside methods, but you should start by increasing the receptivity of your intuition. In you lies the infinite seat of all knowledge. Calmness, concentration, and condensation of experiences by intuitional perception will make you master of all knowledge. Do everything with full attention, never in a haphazard way. Do not try to do too many things at a time; perform the most important duties of life first, with heartfelt enthusiasm and closest attention. Do not indiscriminately swallow useless ideas. Why should you walk in dead men's shoes? Don't let yourself act like an intellectual Victrola, content to parrot the untested opinions of others.

Where are you seeking, my friends? Prayers have been asked, but God has not answered. But with the awakened brain cells—intelligent beings whom you have kept uneducated—made vibrant with the joy of God, all knowledge can be had in this life, Eternity realized now. Awake!

Proof of God's Existence

Written circa 1940

Someone once asked me, "Can you give me an explanation that will help me to believe in the existence of God?"

"Yes," I replied. "How else can you account for the obvious intelligence that underlies all creation, from the single atom to complex man?" Then I further explained to him in this way:

Here is a table; on it is a pitcher of water; throughout this room there is air to breathe; outside there is a tree, the sky, the warm sun. Each of these things is disparate in appearance. But they are all the result of a differentiation of one universal vibration.

How is it that this one vibratory cosmic energy becomes solids, or liquids, or gases? By what mysterious process are these varying rates of vibration so coordinated as to make human life possible? Behind all manifestation there must be a guiding Intelligent Force that is the prime cause of all creation. For instance, we are here on our little earth, somewhere in space, orbiting the far distant sun of our universe. Without the cooperation of the sun's light and warmth, life on earth could not exist. We have the sensation of hunger, and Nature supplies our need for food; when ingested, some unknown Power transforms that food into energy and tissues for the body. All the miracles of life that we take for granted are proof of the existence of an omnipresent divine Intelligence behind the processes of nature.

Beholding the blossoms of the earth and the starry flowers in the infinite fields of the sky, how can one not wonder, "Is there a hidden Beauty behind these finite patterns? Is there an Intelligence behind man's intellect?" The blossoms of life in the garden of earthly existence are enchanting to behold. But somewhere there is a fount of Beauty and Intelligence, even more enthralling, from which we have come and into which we shall merge again.

Everything in the universe is related. And through the right use of our God-given human intelligence we begin to see that all life is linked to one Supreme Intelligence. We may sometimes think we are puppets of destiny; but when we project our intelligence beyond limited delusive forms and examine the extent of our consciousness and mental perception, we realize that within us there is a spark of the divine Power, That which is creating and sustaining all life, just waiting to be kindled.

In the scriptures of every true religion we read that God is all-powerful, infinite, and eternal. Through the windows of the scriptures we glimpse the divine Power in which all things are rooted. But our minds with their finite understanding, conditioned by the laws of causation, cannot encompass eternity; so we live within the limited circle of our mental capacity. Almighty God is both within and beyond that circle.

In the Bhagavad Gita it is said, "Some behold the soul in amazement. Similarly, others describe it as marvelous. Still others listen about the soul as wondrous. And there are others who, even after hearing all about the soul, do not comprehend it at all."*

In countless ways, human reasoning shows us that God is the cause of all things. But proof of the existence of God cannot be had by intellectual deduction alone. If we are to realize God, which is the sole purpose of our existence, we must learn to go beyond ordinary thought processes, for He is beyond the measure of human reason. He cannot be fully grasped by a mind always occupied with objects of desire and with emotional disturbances of pleasure and pain.

To attain a higher state of consciousness and divine perception, it is necessary through meditation to withdraw the mind from its continual restless activity. In that interiorized state, spiritual sensitivity, or intuition, awakens. Intuition is that power of Spirit inherited by the soul by which truth is perceived directly, without the medium of any other faculty. As the vastness

---

* II:29. The Self is Spirit manifested in man as the immortal individualized soul, a perfect reflection of God. Realization of the Self that dwells within is the first introduction to Spirit, the Lord who is both immanent (omnipresent in all creation) and transcendent (the Blissful Absolute).

of the ocean cannot be contained in a small cup, so it is impossible to receive infinite wisdom in the finite cup of human intelligence. Man's consciousness must be expanded if it is to hold the illimitable ocean of truth.

Proof of God's Existence Is Felt in Meditation

As confined water rushes out in all directions when the walls that hold it are broken, so also the consciousness of man is freed when the embankments of bigotry, egocentricity, and restlessness are broken. By the practice of meditation, the consciousness expands and merges with the blissful, omnipresent consciousness of Spirit.

The purpose of meditation is to calm the mind, that without distortion it may mirror Omnipresence. Calmness in meditation is the primary positive state of mental expansion; the bliss of divine union with God is the final state.

The ultimate proof of God's existence will come through your own experience in meditation. Once you have found Him in the cathedral of silent meditation in the depths of your soul, you will find Him everywhere.

Doubt, Belief, and Faith

Circa early 1930s

Everything in the Lord's creation has some specific utility. All matter, however insignificant, has a particular purpose and effect. This is true also in regard to the thoughts or sentiments that present themselves to our consciousness and then pass away. We little know what effect such notions produce in us, or in what lies their utility for which reason they were created within us. If you think of a piece of copper, you know its usefulness. But when you consider a single thought, what is its utility? Analyze that query. As the world is composed of atoms and molecules, so the inner being, the nature or character of a person, is composed of "atoms and molecules" of thoughts. If you wish to understand the quality of your inner light, trace the growth of every thought and in the balance of your judgment weigh its relative utility.

Today we shall weigh the sentiments of doubt, belief, and faith. These are the crux of controversy in religion. Great teachers exhort people to believe and have faith in God and scripture, and warn against the potential devastation of doubt. But without discrimination the utility of this counsel may not be understood.

Since nothing has been created without having some use, I cannot agree with scriptural moralists who at the very mention of doubt turn up their noses at an angle of 120 degrees. Instead let us judge why the principle of doubt has come into the world at all. Wherein is doubt bad—or good!—for human beings? Unless we analyze the psychology of doubt, and of belief and faith, we cannot reasonably adopt or reject these sentiments on the basis of their being beneficial or destructive.

By analysis, we find in the concept of doubt a constructive as well as a destructive element, according to its application. I need not discuss at length the destructive element, for its adverse effects are commonly acknowledged. Because of its potential harm, some religionists, particularly those who hold blindly to dogmatic beliefs, advocate the eschewal of all doubt in favor of unquestioning acceptance. But to avoid doubt is to choose not to think.

Destructive doubt is paralyzing. It inhibits constructive thought and the power of will. It blocks receptivity to the beneficent workings of higher forces and laws in the universe, and to the ever-ready-to-help grace of God. It produces an inner disquietude and sense of hopelessness. It resists progress and rejects ideas on the whims of ignorance, prejudice, or emotion.

But let us consider the constructive element of doubt.

If Man Could Not Doubt, He Could Not Progress

The predominance of matter before our eyes in the form of objects and beings prevents our perception of the whole of truth. It is by doubting the preeminence of matter that the existence of God is established. If matter, a conglomeration of atoms, is all there is, then how do these invisible particles hold a parliament and bring forth and govern such an organized universe? It is impossible that inanimate atoms could put themselves together and produce intelligent beings. So the acceptance of God, an Intelligent Consciousness as the creator of this world, was established from materialism by applying the constructive, progressive element of doubt. This constructive element is the scientific current of thought by which we question in order to know what is true. Without this, if we merely accepted things as they appear to be, man would become as animals. Some ancient civilizations held the view that the sun, moon, and stars were deities governing their lives. Man outgrew that concept by the process of doubt. Through constructive questioning, such belief was found to be wanting. If man could not doubt, he could not progress; the world would be mired in ignorance. We would not be able to differentiate theory or fallacious arguments from the truth if we did not question. It is therefore right to apply the laws of reason.

Doubt decides a hypothesis. Scientists take such a theorem and investigate it along with their ever present examiner, Mr. Doubt. Nothing is taken for granted. The proposition is carried to a conclusion to see whether it works or not. If it doesn't, it is set aside or restructured. If scientists remained satisfied with the status quo of knowledge, there would be no furtherance of civilization. There is a great lesson therein.

In regard to religion, scientists should employ the same openness of the constructive element of doubt with which they approach their research in science. For far too long science has been locked into the destructive element of doubt in dismissing religion offhand as superstitious dogma. If it were the aim of the consortium of construction workers only to demolish all defective buildings rather than reconstructing them, or without replacing them with improved structures, that would be disastrous. It is the same with those who would do away with morality and religion, leaving behind no structure for the housing of divine principles that can be proven essential to the welfare and happiness of human existence. Of course, even the destructive element of doubt may be necessary to rid us of long-held errors; but if that process obliterates truth as well, then it is harmful to humanity.

Constructive Doubt Moves Us Toward Truth

Doubt is dynamic energy that should be properly harnessed to move us to progressive actions. If by constructive doubt we destroy some of our cherished theories, even that is better than just blindly and dumbly following others—"the blind leading the blind." Constructive doubt in regard to divine matters will move us toward truth more quickly than will dogmatic belief. The latter makes us lack the clarity of mind necessary to perceive correctly the truth already given to us by God. Dogmatism confounds the ability to fathom the depth of the verities preached by the great ones, such as Jesus in the New Testament and Lord Krishna in the Bhagavad Gita. Religion, like science, should be given a proper test. That is how the God-knowing *rishis* of old attained their realization: they investigated, found, and proved for themselves those invariable principles that demonstrate and make manifest the Eternal Reality.

The great masters ask us to believe, but they do not say we should not use constructive doubt to question. Suppose some error is printed in scripture; instead of "Do not steal," the word *not* is left out so that it reads "Do steal." To accept blindly is to accept errors that creep in—the slip of the pen of the writer, the error of the printer.

Apply the test of reason. If you can analyze ideas with unprejudiced respect and discrimination, you will more readily apprehend truth and discern what is untruth. You are endowed by God with the power to understand if you but use your instruments of intelligence according to the laws He has given. Treat religion with the same spirit applied to the sciences. Without doubt and investigation, many will not reach truth. Reasonable questioning will destroy the shaky supports of dogmatic fanaticism and help to build instead a strong foundation of beliefs whereon the superstructure of faith might rest.

Faith Begins With Constructive Belief

Belief and faith are often used synonymously, and thus not always correctly. Faith is something much more than mere belief, as will be shown. In belief, as in doubt, there is a constructive and a destructive element. Applied constructively, adherence to valid beliefs leads to realization. Noumenal truths cannot be understood by the sensory mind. Phenomena can be interpreted by the intellect from sensory experience, but not the substance, or noumena, underlying it. This requires inner enlightenment. Thus does the teacher who has attained realization say to the undeveloped disciple, "Until you are able to understand, believe and follow me." That does not mean blind acceptance. Constructive belief has reason within it. Reason and feeling confirm that there is some truth behind every valid belief. If one can gain access to his inherent discriminative intelligence, he can arrive at that truth—the inner comprehension of truth that is attainable only by the spiritual development of the soul's intuitive powers of perception. Until then, there might be contradiction between the devotee's reason and the master's realization. So true masters must ask their disciples to believe, to take for granted certain concepts on their authority, knowing that in time they can realize those truths for themselves. Such is the principle of any investigation.

If a mathematics professor explains calculus to you, but you close your mind and say you do not believe him, because at the moment you do not understand, then he cannot teach you. First you have to take pencil and paper and obey his instruction. Then if you do not get the promised results you will be justified in doubting. But you must be careful before you pronounce judgment; be sure you do not commit any error in solving the problem. So you see, you must begin with belief.

The Fundamentals of Belief

Belief is a state or habit of mind in which trust, confidence, is placed in some person, thing, or doctrine; such as a persuasion of the truths in religion. Belief is a conviction or feeling of the truth or reality of that which is believed.

The elements of belief are assent, credence, assurance, reliance, persuasion, conviction, faith.

Belief, faith, persuasion, conviction, are present singularly or in combination in the idea of assent. Belief and faith differ chiefly in that belief as a rule suggests little more than intellectual assent, while faith implies total trust or confidence— as in one whose persuasion or belief has ripened into faith.

A persuasion is an assured opinion, an idea of which one has convinced himself, as "It is my persuasion that he is a dishonest person." It implies that this assurance is induced by one's feelings or wishes, rather than by argument or evidence.

Conviction stands for a fixed and settled belief, as "His persuasion has been forged into a feeling of certainty."

Credence gives substance to belief; something must be considered believable to be held as true.

Belief depends also on reliance, which is confidence in the thing believed arising from supportive evidence.

Implicit in belief are the elements of will and imagination. Without willingness one cannot believe. And since belief is an uncertain waiting in the hope of obtaining a result, it involves also imagination. John imagines that he will be successful in the jute business. Hence, he is said to believe in his business venture. The elements of will and imagination in belief make it a powerful force for good or ill.

Injudicious Beliefs Seem a Wastage of Good Energy

Belief in a deceitful person, a failing business, or a false doctrine seems to be a sheer wastage of man's good energy through its wrong direction. Such injudicious beliefs achieve little more than bitter experiences. A hypocritical friend may long command our belief in him, a doomed business may similarly persist in our minds as worthy of support, but sooner or later they are sure to lose our belief through the revelation of facts. Hence, in material things wrong beliefs are liable to be less wasteful, since our minds are bent toward tangible results.

In contrast, concerning spiritual matters, our mental attitude often remains vague and visionary. Teachers or doctrines exhort us to believe and have faith, while offering very little explanation or understanding as to the nature of this virtue and how to possess it. Blind acceptance is the general rule and the only recourse for most adherents. Hence, belief and faith in connection with religious life are least understood. Their dynamic power, for the majority of religionists, remains something nebulous, indefinite, unculturable—the possession of a gifted few on whom God has bestowed His grace. For the many others, belief in spiritual matters is employed blindly, because things of the Spirit are deemed mystical and beyond human ken.

An erroneous belief, if held to without scrutiny, develops into tenacious dogmatism. A belief that is disproved changes from dogmatism to unbelief. On the other hand, if one believes in a true doctrine and follows it persistently, that belief gradually crystallizes into conviction and faith. So we see that a belief, whether false or true, is provisional. It can only be temporary, for it is subsequently metamorphosed either into dogmatism or unbelief, or into faith.

Rudimentary or immature belief not secured in truth is of three kinds: (a) blind, (b) steady and strong, (c) curiosity-awakened.

(a) Belief born of emotion or sentiment begins with high-sounding "faith," as "I will follow you unto death." But it ends in violent denunciation when tested with criticism or contradiction.

(b) The followers of the second group add tenacity to blind belief. They live and die in the same emotional convictions, even if wholly erroneous. This is little more than the savage state of existence, which is controlled by superstition.

(c) Persons are a bit safer with beliefs that begin and end

in curiosity. When they find out that their inquisitiveness has led them down a wrong path, they quickly give up that pursuit and are delighted to seek after something new.

Beyond these three is investigative belief. This is based on logical acceptance. It always keeps its eyes and ears open, ever ready to inquire about anything to which it has been attracted by persuasion or interest. This form of belief, however, can easily develop into a habit of fickleness; it may capriciously give up not only that which is erroneous, but also that which is true.

The Genesis of Faith

What is needed is investigative belief with sincerity and reverence, followed up with persistence in true beliefs, or at least in those beliefs that constantly manifest convincing results. Through the aperture of patience, drop by drop, the chemical of truth enters and crystallizes such belief into solid faith. But unless belief is founded on truth, it will not sustain the conviction that produces progress toward faith.

Faith may manifest itself in many areas of belief if there is truth inherent in one's sincere convictions:

- Firm belief or trust (as in a person, thing, doctrine, or idea), such as faith in God, faith in medicine.
- Recognition of spiritual realities and moral principles as supreme.
- Historical faith, as in the truthfulness and authority of scriptural narrative and teachings. Or practical faith—through the acceptance by the intellect, affection, and will—in God's favor extended to man through His divine emissaries.
- The aggregate of that which is believed: a system of religious beliefs, as the Christian faith or Vedic authority.

The result of faith is the stable quality or state of faithfulness, fidelity, loyalty.

Have Intrepid Faith Despite Life's Enigmas

Life, its substance and purpose, is an enigma, difficult yet not unknowable. With our progressive thinking, we are daily solving some of its secrets. The minutely and scientifically calculated devices of this modern age are certainly remarkable.

The proliferating discoveries of physical science are creditably giving us a clearer vision of the ways by which life can be improved. But in spite of all our devices and strategies and inventions, it seems we are still playthings in the hands of destiny, and have a long way to go before we can be independent of nature's domination.

To be constantly at the mercies of nature—surely that is not freedom. Our enthusiastic minds are rudely seized by a sense of helplessness when we are victimized by floods, tornadoes, or earthquakes; or when, apparently without rhyme or reason, illness or accident snatches our dear ones from our bosom. It is then that we know we really haven't conquered much. In spite of all our efforts to make life what we want it to be, there will always remain certain conditions introduced on this planet—infinite and guided by an unknown Intelligence, operating without our initiative—which preclude our control. At best, we can only work and make some improvements. We sow the wheat and make the flour, but who made the original seed? We eat the bread made from the flour, but who made it possible for us to digest and assimilate it?

In every department of life there seems to be, in spite of our instrumentality, an inevitable Divine dependence without which we cannot get along. With all our certainties, we still have to abide an uncertain existence. We do not know when the heart is going to fail. Hence comes the necessity of a fearless reliance on our true immortal Self and on the Supreme Deity in whose image that Self is made—a faith that acts without egoism, and plods on merrily, knowing no trepidation or constraint.

Exercise absolute fearless surrender to that Higher Power. Never mind that today you make the resolution that you are free and undaunted, and then tomorrow you catch the flu and become miserably sick. Don't weaken! Command your consciousness to remain steadfast in its faith. The Self cannot be contaminated by sickness. Maladies of the body come to you through the law of self-created habits of ill health lodged in your subconscious mind. Such karmic manifestations do not disprove the efficacy, the dynamic power, of faith.

Hold to the helm of faith, and mind not the buffeting of untoward circumstances. Be more furious than the fury of misfortune, more audacious than your dangers. The more this newfound faith will work its dynamic influence on you, the more your slavery to weakness will wane proportionately.

Not a corpuscle of blood can move, nor a puff of breath enter your nostrils, without the commandment of the Lord. Hence, absolute surrender to God is the criterion of faith. This surrender is not laziness, expecting God to do everything for you—your utmost effort to bring about the desired result is also necessary—rather, it is a surrender through love for God and veneration of His supremacy. No matter what the obstacles, I would work to the last breath in me in complete surrender to God, but I would never surrender through cowardice or fear of failure.

Faith Is Ever Secure—Direct Perception of Truth

Faith not only produces results in healing or in other successes, it is also the power that reveals the outworking of spiritual laws that underlie all so-called miracles.

"Faith is the substance of things hoped for, the evidence of things not seen."* Hoped-for "impossibilities" will be realized through the power of this faith—which believes without seeing, which believes even in the face of all odds.

Faith is realization itself. It harbors no destructive element, as does belief. Belief can be swayed or destroyed by contrary evidence and doubt; but faith is ever secure, because it is direct perception of truth. Once the world was believed to be flat, but with the progress of science it was found to be round; so that was only a belief, which had to be given up. But faith cannot be contradicted, for it is the developed expression of the unerring intuition within us, which brings us face to face with theretofore unseen realities. One may thus rightly refer to blind belief, but not blind faith.

The soul's realization of truth expresses itself to us through intuition, and the resultant *knowing* is faith. Intuition is that point wherein a conviction suddenly changes into the direct perception of the truth of that belief. It requires no intermediary, no proof from the testimony of the senses or reason.

---

* *Hebrews* 11:1 (Bible).

For example, how do you know you exist? You know because you know. There is no doubt. Nothing in this world would make you believe otherwise. Even if you were paralyzed and could not see yourself, still you would feel or *experience* your existence through the perception of the soul.

Faith is the A,B,C,D of intuition. It is a deep feeling of *knowing* within you. Most everyone has experienced a hunch that has come true. That is a manifestation of developing or uncontrolled intuition. Intelligence directed to the outward world interprets phenomena; faith turned inwardly interprets by its contact with noumena the intuitions of the soul. All things can be brought to light by the power of faith.

In Calmness, Intuition Gives Birth to Faith

The Sanskrit word for faith is wonderfully expressive. It is *visvas*. The common literal rendering, "to breathe easy; have trust; be free from fear," does not convey the full meaning. Sanskrit *svas* refers to the motions of breath, implying thereby life and feeling. *Vi* conveys the meaning of "opposite; without." That is, he whose breath, life, and feeling are calm, he can have faith born of intuition; it cannot be possessed by persons who are emotionally restless. The cultivation of intuitive calmness requires unfoldment of the inner life. When developed sufficiently, intuition brings immediate comprehension of truth. You can have this marvelous realization. Meditation is the way.

Meditate with patience and persistence. In the gathering calmness, you will enter the realm of soul intuition. Throughout the ages, those beings who attained enlightenment were those who had recourse to this inner world of God-communion. Jesus said: "When thou prayest, enter into thy closet, and when thou hast shut thy door, pray to thy Father which is in secret; and thy Father which seeth in secret shall reward thee openly."* Go within the Self, closing the door of the senses and their involvement with the restless world, and God will reveal to you all His wonders.

In the inner communion of the soul with God, intuition begins to unfold naturally. Initially, a sort of provisional trust

---

* *Matthew* 6:6 (Bible).

is necessary. Know that God is with you and that you are His child, made in His image. Surrender to Him through love. That conviction will gradually transform itself into faith through intuition. Beyond the senses and intellect, intuition manifests in the calm consciousness as feeling, perceived mostly through the heart. When such feeling comes in meditation, you receive through it a definite sense of right direction and unshakable conviction. Increasingly you will be able to recognize and follow this intuition. That doesn't mean you give up reason. Calm impartial reason can also lead to intuition. Use common sense. But remember that arrogant or emotional reasoning leads to misconceptions and mistakes.

Reject the destructive element in doubt and belief, and apply the constructive element. March on to the kingdom of faith. This is the way of development. In the calmness of meditation your consciousness will be able to focus on truth and understand. In that state faith develops; through unfolding intuition you receive "the evidence of things not seen."

Visions of India:
Evolving the Higher Self

Uniting East and West culturally and spiritually by an "exchange of their finest distinctive features" is an ideal for which Paramahansa Yogananda was noted throughout his life's work. The following article is one of his early commendations of his spiritual motherland, and what India had to offer to and receive from the West. Though the passage of many decades has wrought changes in circumstances and conditions in India and throughout the world, the underlying premise of this "vision of India" in the 1920s remains both valid and valuable as an overview of East-West unity. The central theme of India's spiritual message to the world is the importance of the unfoldment of the higher Self, which inspired Paramahansaji's words in the second half of this article.

India is an epitome of the world—a land of diverse climates, religions, commerce, arts, peoples, scenery, stages of civilization, languages.

Her civilization dates back many thousands of years. Her great seers, prophets, and rulers left records behind them that prove the great antiquity of the Aryan civilization in India. *

Many Western travelers visit India, see a few of the street magicians, sword-swallowers, or snake-charmers, and think

---

* The ancient name for India is *Aryavarta*, literally, "abode of the Aryans." The Sanskrit root of *arya* is "worthy, holy, noble." The later use of *Aryan* to signify not spiritual, but physical, characteristics, is considered by some ethnologists, including the renowned Indologist Max Müller, to be a misinterpretation of the original meaning.

In *Autobiography of a Yogi*, Paramahansa Yogananda wrote: "Nothing in Hindu literature or tradition tends to substantiate the current Western historical theory that the early Aryans 'invaded' India from some other part of Asia or from Europe. The scholars are understandably unable to fix the starting point of this imaginary journey. The internal evidence in the Vedas, pointing

that is what India has to offer. But these men do not represent
the true India. The real life and secret of India's vitality is her
spiritual culture, from time immemorial, which has made her
the motherland of religions. Although the West can teach India
much about methods of sanitation, business, and development
of resources—and although India needs "business missionaries"
like Henry Ford and Thomas Edison—yet the Western lands too
are thirsty, consciously or unconsciously, for the practical spiritual lessons in which India has specialized for centuries.

In Western cities, science has progressed so far that the
physical man is usually well taken care of, fed and clothed and
sheltered. Yet physical and material comfort without mental
and spiritual peace and solace is not enough. As the spiritual
model of all religions, India has been the unproclaimed
reformer, the grand inspirer of human minds and souls. Her
greatest and richest legacy to mankind has been the techniques
for the scientific spiritual culture of man, discovered and handed
down through the centuries by her saints and seers.

India is a land of mystery, but of mystery that reveals itself
to the sympathetic inquirer and seeker. India has the grandest
and highest mountains in the world—the Himalayas. Darjeeling,
in the north, is the Switzerland of India. The unique ruins of
ancient castles and spacious palaces of princes in Delhi; the
vast extent of the Ganges, made sacred through the centuries
by the meditation near its banks of many God-realized saints;
the sun-gilded teeth of the Himalayan mountain-ridges; the
ancient places of pilgrimage and the caves of meditation where
yogis and swamis saw the faggots of ignorance set ablaze with
the wisdom of God; the Taj Mahal at Agra, the finest dream of
architecture ever materialized in marble to symbolize the ideal
of human love; the dark forests and jungles where the lordly
tigers roam; the blueness of the Indian skies and the bright sunshine; the sumptuous varieties of Oriental fruits and vegetables; the multifarious types of people—all tend to make India different, fascinating, romantic, never-to-be-forgotten.

---

to India as the immemorial home of the Hindus, has been presented in an
unusual and very readable volume, *Rig-Vedic India,* by Abinas Chandra Das,
published in 1921 by Calcutta University."

A Land of Great Contrasts

India is a land of great contrasts—untold riches and utmost poverty; the highest mental purity and coarse, plain living; Rolls Royces and bullock carts; gaily caparisoned elephants and quaint horse-wagons.

In the north, we find blue-eyed and blonde-haired Hindus, and in the hotter south, the dark sun-kissed skins of the tropics. From start to finish, India is a land of surprises, of contrasts and extremes. Life becomes prosaic with too much business, too many dull certainties; so in India one feels that life is a great adventure, an experience of mystery and surprise.

India may not have material skyscrapers and all the sometimes spiritually enervating comforts of modern life—she has her faults, as all nations have—but India shelters many unassuming, Christlike spiritual "skyscrapers" who could teach the Western brothers and sisters how to glean the fullest spiritual joy out of any condition of life. Those scientific mystics and seers—who have known Truth by their own effort and experience rather than remaining satisfied with ordinary, personally unverified beliefs—can show others how to develop their intuition and bring forth the fountain of peace and satisfaction from beneath the soil of mysteries. Though I have had the advantage of some Western education, yet I feel that in India alone I found the true solution to the mysteries of life.

Visions of India's Life-giving Philosophy

From time immemorial, India's greatest minds have specialized in discovering and understanding the philosophy and meaning of life. One of the oft-disputed philosophical questions is whether the goal of human life is service or selfishness. Once I had a big controversy with a European who repeatedly and blindly affirmed that the goal of life was service, while I maintained that it was higher selfishness. I asked him again and again for his reasons in believing in "service"; but instead of satisfying my discrimination, he kept on reiterating, "Service is the goal of life. It is blasphemous to doubt that."

Finding him so dogmatic, I asked him, "Is service the goal of life because the Scriptures have declared it?"

"Yes," he vehemently replied.

"Do you believe everything literally in Scripture?" I questioned him. "Do you think Jonah was swallowed by a whale and came out alive after a few days? How do you account for it?"

"No, I do not understand how he could do that," my friend said.

That was just the point. In order really to know the truth contained in scriptural stories—and in order to understand what is erroneous or right, literal or metaphorical, in scriptural writings—one must use reason, discrimination, and the power of intuitional verification developed through meditation.

Many people think that whatever is in print must be correct. In particular, most religionists believe that anything wearing the robe of scriptural authority is absolutely beyond question. But putting on an outward garb cannot make one infallible. Writers of scriptures can also make mistakes; or more traditionally, hide truths in the veils of allegories, metaphors, and parables. In order to know the truth of a given doctrine, we must live it and find out if it works or not—give it the acid test of experience. Let us get out into the world beyond dogmatism and compare our religious beliefs with the religious experience and realization of true teachers. Let us be iconoclastic of errors within us that need to be abolished. We should not harbor an undigested mass of theology and thus suffer from chronic theological indigestion.

The Ideal of Service as Explained by India's Sages

The law of service to others is secondary and corollary to the law of self-interest or self-preservation, which may be termed "selfishness." No sane man ever does anything without a reason. Religious doctrines and instructions may be based either on blind superstition or on real religious experience. The real reason behind the scriptural injunctions to "Serve thy fellowmen," and "Love thy neighbor as thyself" is that the law of service to others is to be obeyed by all devotees who would expand the limits of their own self.

No action is performed without reference to a direct or indirect thought that is selfish; the very giving of service is indispensable to receiving service. To serve others by giving financial, mental, or moral help is to find self-satisfaction. If anyone knew beyond doubt that by service to others his own soul would be lost, would he serve? If Jesus had felt that by sacrificing his life on the altar of man's ignorance he would displease God, would he have acted as he did? No! He knew that although he had to lose the body he was gaining his Father's favor and the emancipated rejoicing of his own soul. Such immortal sons of God, and all martyrs and saints, make a good investment—they spend the little mortal body to gain immortal life. Nothing worthwhile is gained without paying a price.

Thus not even the most self-sacrificing act of service to others can be shown to be done without any thought of self. It is logical, therefore, to say that higher selfishness, or acting for the good of the higher Self—rather than service to others without thought of self—is the motive of life.

Man knows that he must give service to others, or otherwise he cannot rightly receive service from them. All beings are to some degree interdependent. If farmers gave up agricultural work, and businessmen gave up their service of transportation and distribution, not even the renunciant could maintain himself. Nowadays, with increased population and wealth, even forests are divided off and owned by big landowners who placard the trees with signs warning the trespasser that he will be prosecuted for coming onto another man's property. So the renunciant cannot logically say, "I will not work or earn my living—I will subsist on the wild fruits of the forest." He must contribute some service for which, in return, he is entitled to receive material sustenance. Hence, service given and received—whether by the businessman who serves in a material way or by the spiritual renunciant who serves in a divine way*—has reference to the goal of a lower or higher selfishness.

Three Kinds of Selfishness—Evil, Good, and Sacred

We should, however, clearly distinguish the three kinds of

---

* "Solitude is necessary to become established in the Self, but masters then return to the world to serve it. Even saints who engage in no outward work bestow, through their thoughts and holy vibrations, more precious benefits on the world than can be given by the most strenuous humanitarian activities of unenlightened men."—Paramahansa Yogananda, in *Autobiography of a Yogi*.

selfishness: evil, good, and sacred. Evil selfishness is that which actuates a man to seek his own comfort by destroying the comforts of others. To be rich at the cost of others' loss is sin, and is against the interests of the higher individual Self of the person who engages in such selfishness. To delight in hurting others' feelings by carping criticism is also evil selfishness; this malignant pleasure is not conducive to any lasting good. True and good selfishness motivates a man to seek his own comfort, prosperity, and happiness by also making others more prosperous and happy. Evil selfishness hides its many destructive teeth of inevitable suffering beneath the apparently innocent looks of temporary comfort-assurances. Evil selfishness encloses one in a small circle and shuts out the rest of humanity. Good selfishness takes everybody along with one's own self into the circle of brotherhood. Good selfishness brings many harvests—return services from others, self-expansion, divine sympathy, lasting happiness, and Self-realization.

Good selfishness should be practiced by the businessman, who, by sincere, honest, wholesome, constructive actions and labors, enables himself to look after his own and his family's needs and provides a useful service to others. Such a businessman is far superior to one who thinks and acts only for himself, with no regard for those he serves or those dependent on him for support. The latter is acting against his own best selfish interests; for according to the law of cause and effect, he himself will in time attract suffering. The wealth of many misers is left to relatives, who often squander it on wrong self-indulgences. Such selfishness, in the end, helps neither the giver nor the receiver.

To avoid the pitfalls of evil selfishness, one should first follow and establish himself in the pattern of good selfishness, wherein one thinks of his family and those whom he serves as part of himself. From that attainment, one can then advance to a practice of sacred selfishness (or unselfishness, as ordinary understanding would term it) in which one sees all the universe as himself.

Being Sacredly Selfish

Feeling the sorrows of others and reaching out in order to make them free from further suffering, seeking happiness in the joy of others, constantly trying to remove the wants of increasingly larger numbers of people—this is being sacredly selfish. The man of sacred selfishness counts all his consequent earthly losses as sacrifices deliberately and willingly brought about by himself for others' good, and for his own great and ultimate gain. He lives to love his brethren, for he knows they are all children of the one God. His entire selfishness is sacred, for whenever he thinks of himself, he thinks not of the small body and mind of ordinary understanding, but of the needs of all bodies and minds within the range of his acquaintance or influence. His "self" becomes the Self of all. He becomes the mind and feeling of all creatures. So when he does anything for himself, he can only do that which is good for all. He who considers himself as one whose body and limbs consist of all humanity and all creatures certainly finds the Universal All-Pervading Spirit as himself.*

He does not act with any expectation; but, with his best judgment and intuition, goes on helping himself as the many, with health, food, work, success, and spiritual emancipation.

Working with good selfishness and sacred selfishness brings one in touch with God, who rests on the altar of all-expanding goodness. One who realizes this works conscientiously, only to please the ever-directing God of Peace within.

---

* "He sees truly who perceives the Supreme Lord present equally in all creatures, the Imperishable amidst the perishing....When a man beholds all separate beings as existent in the One that has expanded Itself into the many, he then merges with Brahma" (Bhagavad Gita XIII:27, 30).

Miracles of Raja Yoga

Compilation of a lecture and article of the same title,
circa 1926–27; with quotations from Autobiography of a Yogi

> *A "miracle" is commonly considered to be an effect or event*
> *without law, or beyond law. But all events in our precisely*
> *adjusted universe are lawfully wrought and lawfully explica-*
> *ble. The so-called miraculous powers of a great master are a*
> *natural accompaniment to his exact understanding of subtle*
> *laws that operate in the inner cosmos of consciousness.*
>
> *Nothing may truly be said to be a "miracle" except in*
> *the profound sense that everything is a miracle. That each*
> *of us is encased in an intricately organized body, and is set*
> *upon an earth whirling through space among the stars—is*
> *anything more commonplace? or more miraculous?*
>
> *—Autobiography of a Yogi*

Raja Yoga, the "Royal Yoga," is the science of God-realization, a step-by-step means of reuniting the soul with Spirit—
man with his Creator—developed by the *rishis* of ancient
India, with proven and uniform results. *Raja Yoga* was master-
fully systematized by the great sage Patanjali in his *Yoga Sutras.*
It combines the highest from all other yoga disciplines: devotion, right action, physical and mental self-control, and divine
communion through scientific techniques of concentration
and meditation. The fulfillment of the path, God-realization,
"makes all things possible" for it teaches how to make the mortal immortal.

The West excels in the physical sciences, which give us material knowledge and inventions. The East excels in spiritual science, which tunes the soul to the Infinite. I find that the people
in America, however, are yet very uneducated in the spiritual science and real truths of the East. There are many misconceptions.

The Real Spiritual Savant Is Not a Magician
or Fortune-Teller

While I was in Seattle, I went to the immigration agency to apply for a visa to go to Vancouver, British Columbia. It was on that occasion that an immigration official became sarcastically fascinated with my ochre turban.

I had waited in the office for some time, but the man at the desk made no attempt to attend to my wants, or even to acknowledge my presence. So I tapped on the counter to attract his attention. This finally succeeded in getting him to arise reluctantly from his desk and inquire as to my business there. The officer looked at me with scorn, his eyes fixed on my turban, and said, "Do you gaze at crystals, tell fortunes, swallow swords? Are you a snake charmer?"

I assured him that it was not my purpose in America to tell fortunes or charm snakes. I was not a fakir; I had come to ask for a passport to Vancouver. I was told to come back the next day.

The following day I returned with a book I had written and copies of some of my poems. I said nothing, but presented these to him. He was surprised. When he had obligingly read a few lines and had a look of apology in his eye for his rash inference, I looked at him smilingly and said, "Dear officer, did you know that the Hindus never had any factory where they knew the art of making crystal balls? Crystals are of western origin. Hence it is news to me that the Hindus gaze at crystals.

"As regards fortune-tellers, there are quite a number right here in America as well as in India. But whenever you meet an American gentleman do you ask him, 'Are you a fortune-teller?'"

Every Hindu is not a fortune-teller. They don't believe in flattering an unmarried woman by telling her fortune, saying that she is going to have a good wealthy husband, and then relieve her of three or four dollars for this contrived forecast. Wise Hindus can teach you how to solve the problems of life and change your "fortune." Your present poverty or opulence, disease or health, is brought about by your own past actions; and your present life and actions will determine your future. Spiritual savants can diagnose scientifically how the law of cause and effect applies to human actions and lives. They do not believe in fate, a predestined happening without a cause. They do not fool people by predictions conjured through the trickery of imagination, equivocal words, or fraud. The real Hindu astrologers make a scientific study of the law of causation governing human actions. And they do not merely tell you your past or predict your future, but rather teach you the art of averting an unwelcome event or stimulating the fruition of a desirable event coming to you as a result of your past evil or good actions. Good astrologers tell their students only what will benefit them, not what will merely satisfy idle curiosity. They say there is no use in telling you what is coming to you anyway unless there is a way to control or regulate that self-created destiny. Sometimes ignorance is bliss.

I said to the immigration officer, "Sir, I haven't had the singular, dangerous experience of swallowing swords or taming cobras, which our masterful street magicians often do in open daylight before the scrutinizing gaze of people. Though some may possess unusual powers, they are at the same time skilled in sleight-of-hand tricks. They perform magic by producing optical illusions. Therein the Eastern magician is superior to his Western counterpart."

Then, in a light mood, I challenged the officer: "I have seen some hypocritical Western people wearing hats and dress suits, but I never connected hypocrisy with the wearing of hats. How did you happen to connect snake-charming with my turban?"

By this time the prejudicial wrinkles in the officer were smoothed out. In a very friendly tone he said, "I am sorry. No doubt many good turbaned Hindus have to suffer the persecution of public opinion because some turbaned Indians have produced a wrong impression on our people."

I responded, "You cannot expect all Hindus to forsake turbans because some Hindus are far from exemplary, just as I do not expect all Western brothers to forsake their hats because some have practiced hypocrisy while wearing hats. Western tourists go to India and see our poorly dressed coolie laborers, and watch the performances of the street magicians or fakirs, and they think the Indian needs to wear swallow-tail coats and neckties to be civilized. Customs and mannerisms are nonessentials resulting from certain climatic influences. The real development of man consists of the development of his mind power."

So the American tourist visiting India must take care not to misconceive the real yogis of India. The real yogis are distinctly different from the magicians, sword-swallowers, instantaneous mango tree growers. The latter are mere entertainers. The former are great souls, very difficult to recognize because of their quiet, unassuming ways and simplicity, yet possessing divine knowledge and miraculous powers like those demonstrated by Christ. As Jesus said, "Except ye be converted, and become as little children, ye shall not enter into the kingdom of heaven. Whosoever therefore shall humble himself...the same is greatest in the kingdom of heaven."* It is through divine simplicity and humility that one can attain great breadth of power and vast wisdom.

Physical and Mental Miracles—The Need for *Raja Yoga*

"All creation is governed by law. The principles that operate in the outer universe, discoverable by scientists, are called natural laws. But there are subtler laws that rule the hidden spiritual planes and the inner realm of consciousness; these principles are knowable through the science of yoga. It is not the physicist but the Self-realized master who comprehends the true nature of matter. By such knowledge Christ was able to restore the servant's ear after it had been severed by one of the disciples."†
    —*Swami Sri Yukteswar, in* Autobiography of a Yogi

There is no difference between physical laws and super-laws or miracles worked by the knowledge of the mechanism of the human mind. The Americans work miracles through use of physical laws; advanced yogis work mental miracles. The operation of radio and telephoto cameras are still miracles to many Hindus, and the workable miracles of the mind so often displayed by the yogis of India are unknown to the Americans. In these days of marvels of constant inventions it would be wise for

---

* *Matthew* 18:3–4 (Bible).

† "And one of them smote the servant of the high priest, and cut off his right ear. And Jesus answered and said, Suffer ye thus far. And he touched his ear, and healed him" (*Luke* 22:50–51, Bible).

the Americans to at least investigate thoroughly the discovery of spiritual miracles by their Hindu brothers. Miracles are nothing but the operation of supermental and cosmic laws. Jesus and the masterminds of India know how to operate them. To ordinary people such works appear as miracles, but they are really the result of natural operation of certain higher, hidden laws.

Yoga unites mind power with cosmic power. The *Raja Yoga* principles of concentration were easily practiced even by the rajas or royalty of India who were engrossed with the multifarious duties of their states. These methods, which bring power over one's own destiny and which can turn failure— material, moral, social, or spiritual—into success, can fit in equally well with the busy and worried life of the Western rajas and maharajas, the American millionaires and billionaires.

Human nature is everywhere the same. The American needs poise and spiritual strength just as much as the Hindu does. The American makes the machine work hard for him, while the Indian has to make his living by doing his work manually. Theoretically, therefore, the American businessman has more time than the proverbially spiritual Hindu to devote to developing mental miracles.

The superiority of acquiring "miraculous" mental powers over the acquirement of business skill is that the former has no limitations as does the latter. The ordinary intelligent businessman may be broken down by hard competition. When his business intelligence is exhausted, he utterly fails. But the Hindu savant says that when the intellectual resources give out one does not need to give up. He can use his unlimited superpowers for the materialization of a desire. As God is all-powerful, so also, by *Raja Yoga,* uniting with Him consciously, man likewise becomes powerful.

In trying to cure chronic disease, acquire success, or attain peace of mind through physical means, there are limitations. Everything is governed by the law of cause and effect. If you try and have tried repeatedly and still do not succeed in curing your physical and mental ills, you must find wherein lie your limitations. Why hope and expect success to result from the use of a limited force? You need to open the door within to learn super-miracle powers by which life can be fully developed. Otherwise, you live in a state of gambling with your self-created destiny.

See the state of mind of so many people. They think they are so wise—all rushing for money to satisfy their desires for security and pleasure. They use their life like a train speeding to one goal—money, money. Failing to use reason to see where this course will take them, they play with material ambitions until they are spirited away from this earth empty-handed. Life in such an existence is tasteless, meaningless. What is the purpose of our life here and beyond? The masters teach the method by which everyone, even the most materially successful with all their diversions and comforts and wealth, can make life complete—physically, mentally, and spiritually.

Behave as master of yourself, guided not by habits, but by free will and the wisdom of God-realization. You have the privilege and choice to make your own heaven right here; you have all the means to do so. God has given you the power to know Him. In *Raja Yoga* He has given you the science of how to direct your mind to Him—the real science of prayer by which you can contact God and commune with Him.

Miracles Historically Recorded

I will relate a few authentic, historically true, miraculous achievements of the yogis of India, showing that they lived far ahead of the modern times and performed miracles still far remote from the comprehension of modern material science.

About seventy years ago, the holy city of Banaras was agog with the miracles of Trailanga Swami.* He was two hundred and fifty years old, and it is said he used to remain below or floating on the surface of the Ganges two or three days at a time; he read people's minds like books; he drank poisonous liquids by bowlfuls without dying, and seemingly had done all kinds of miracles, as did Jesus Christ. The story goes that once, for disregarding the laws of the city, he was put in jail. He was seen the next minute walking on the roof. He had many wonderful powers. Can science tell us of anyone else who has lived for two hundred and fifty years?

---

* See *Autobiography of a Yogi,* chapter 31.

Another miracle of *Raja Yoga* was demonstrated when Sadhu Haridas permitted himself to be buried alive underground for six weeks. In the nineteenth century, in the court of Prince Ranjit Singh—emperor of the Punjab—and under the seal of French and other European doctors, the miraculous performance of Sadhu Haridas was historically recorded. After Haridas's body was waxed all over, sewn securely in a sack, and then sealed in a stone chest, the emperor buried the *sadhu* several feet below the earth in the royal courtyard. Careful watch was maintained over the site for six weeks. Millions of people waited for the news about the *sadhu's* disinterment after the six weeks had passed. The stone chest was opened, the cloth and wax were removed, and the body was examined by French and English doctors and pronounced dead. Yet in a few minutes Sadhu Haridas blinked his eyes and came back to life. Boom! went the cannon from the ramparts of the emperor's fort at Lahore (Punjab, India), heralding and declaring that Saint Haridas was alive. In any comprehensive historical book on India this occurrence will be found recorded.

Even to this day there are saints who once in a while publicly demonstrate miraculous powers. My teacher's teacher, Lahiri Mahasaya, was seen by my mother in an ecstatic state in which for a prolonged time he suspended all life processes.* But it is considered a spiritual degradation and blasphemy against God's laws for great yogis to demonstrate their powers merely to satisfy the idle cravings of curiosity-seekers. It took me a long time to recognize the miraculous power of my master, Swami Sri Yukteswarji, though I had close contact with him.

My Master Showed Me the Unfailing Power of God

Sri Yukteswar was reserved and matter-of-fact in demeanor.
There was naught of the vague or daft visionary about him.
His feet were firm on the earth, his head in the haven of

---

* "To the awe of all beholders, Lahiri Mahasaya's habitual physiological state exhibited the superhuman features of breathlessness, sleeplessness, cessation of pulse and heartbeat, calm eyes unblinking for hours, and a profound aura of peace. No visitors departed without upliftment of spirit; all knew they had received the silent blessing of a true man of God."—*Autobiography of a Yogi*

heaven....My guru was reluctant to discuss the superphysical
realms. His only "marvelous" aura was that of perfect
simplicity. In conversation he avoided startling references;
in action he was freely expressive. Many teachers talked of
miracles but could manifest nothing; Sri Yukteswar seldom
mentioned the subtle laws but secretly operated them at
will.

"A man of realization does not perform any miracle
until he receives an inward sanction," Master explained.
"God does not wish the secrets of His creation revealed
promiscuously. Also, every individual in the world has an
inalienable right to his free will. A saint will not encroach
on that independence."

—Autobiography of a Yogi

I have seen many miracles performed by my Guru; and of
all the wonderful things witnessed, I shall declare to the world
that I secured my A.B. degree through his miraculous power.
During my college days, I used to visit and stay with him in his
ashram almost every day, absorbed in the wisdom of his presence and in the practice of meditation. My studies were so much
neglected that I hardly knew where my college books were.
Five days before the university examination, I told Master I
wasn't going to appear at the examination. His warm countenance changed suddenly, and he said, "Then all my relations
with you cease this instant." He insisted and said, "All I ask of
you is to *appear* at the examination." He declared I would pass
even though I had not studied. I agreed reluctantly, thinking
just literally to carry out his behest "to appear," and that I would
fill up the answer pages with his teachings.

Next he asked me, at first gently, then vehemently, to seek
the help of a certain friend of mine, Romesh Chandra Dutt, an
honor student. Every morning of all those days that my A.B.
examination lasted, I was to ask Romesh whatever questions
came to my mind, and to remember his answers. Romesh tu-
tored me in my various subjects and answered all my queries.
This Calcutta University A.B. degree, in some respects, is more
difficult to obtain than even a Harvard A.B. degree. There is
so much injustice and difficulty set in the path of those being
examined. I did as Master told me; and strange to say, I found

in my examinations the very questions Romesh had been unconsciously guided to tell me to prepare for, or for which he had provided answers in the hours of his tutoring. After the first day I confidently declared to the world that I was going to pass; and when indeed I received the A.B. degree, my father and friends, who had given up all hopes about the success of my college life, told me I had performed a miracle. That is why I am fond of putting the A.B. after my name in all my books and articles; the title reminds me of this singular experience and blessing bestowed by my Guru's divine power.* When I had questioned Master as to how this had become possible, he just replied that faith, works, and knowledge of supermental law can work miracles, where physical efforts of man fail.

I remember that a friend of mine, seeing me a devout follower of Master and negligent of my studies, had once ridiculed me and said, "I am sorry to tell you that your Guru and God won't make you pass your examinations." And half in faith and half for the sake of argument, I replied, "Why not?" Little did I dream at that moment that I would see such a dramatic fulfillment of my declaration.

My Master is still living in flesh and blood in India, and I dare not tell all the wonderful things I have seen.† This much I can say: Throughout the whole western world I have not found a single one like him. I would accept all the poverty, famine, inconveniences of life in India in preference to the comfortable American life, to sit at the feet of one like my Master. By the mere touch of the hand or feet of a God-realized master, a receptive disciple becomes entranced in the great spirit of God.

---

* Shortly after this talk, Paramahansaji gradually dropped the use of his university title, feeling that it had served the purpose for which Sri Yukteswar had helped him to secure it—to introduce him to a skeptical Western audience: "Someday you will go to the West," Sri Yukteswar had said. "Its people will be more receptive to India's ancient wisdom if the strange Hindu teacher has a university degree."

† Swami Sri Yukteswar entered *mahasamadhi,* a yogi's final conscious exit from the body, on March 9, 1936. (See *mahasamadhi* in glossary.)

The West in 1927 was not prepared for the inspirational revelations abounding in the lives of divine yogi-Christs of India that were forthcoming twenty years later with the publication of Paramahansa Yogananda's *Autobiography of a Yogi.*

Direct Knowledge of Laws of Truth

"Spiritual advancement is not to be measured by one's displays of outward powers, but solely by the depth of his bliss in meditation....

"How quickly we weary of earthly pleasures! Desire for material things is endless; man is never satisfied completely, and pursues one goal after another. The 'something else' he seeks is the Lord, who alone can grant lasting joy....

"After the mind has been cleared by Kriya Yoga of sensory obstacles, meditation furnishes a twofold proof of God. Ever new joy is evidence of His existence, convincing to our very atoms. Also, in meditation one finds His instant guidance, His adequate response to every difficulty."

—Swami Sri Yukteswar, in Autobiography of a Yogi

Americans who are good listeners and love real progress now ought to go deeper than mere listening to the philosophical message of India's spiritual science. They should learn the technique by which the super-miracles of the mind can be understood and the higher laws applied to make life not only financially successful, but blissful in every way.

Thinking and knowing are two different things. If you follow the lessons of this *Raja Yoga* teaching of Yogoda,* you will have something you never had before in your life—direct perception of truth. I know I can follow what my Guru and *Paramguru*† taught and have realization, rather than suffer "spiritual indigestion" from swallowing beliefs blindly or trying to assimilate them intellectually. Belief founded on dogma or mere intellectual knowledge cannot support you for long when the evidence of the world goes against it. You must have the strength of conviction born of realization; then even mountains of obstacles cannot stand in your way. You can demonstrate the truth Christ and the Great Masters preached.‡ It is your own

---

* Yogoda Satsanga Society (see glossary) is the name by which Paramahansaji's society is known in India. He also used the term *Yogoda* in connection with his work in America in the early years.

† *Paramguru* means the guru of one's guru. (See glossary.)

‡ "If ye have faith, and doubt not...if ye shall say unto this mountain, Be thou removed, and be thou cast into the sea; it shall be done" (*Matthew* 21:21, Bible).

fault if you let yourself be deceived. Seek wisdom!

You cannot remain without doing something; be busy doing something worthwhile. That is what my Master taught me. His whole interest was to bring us in contact with God. People barter their happiness to acquire little things. God is the storekeeper of the universe; seek Him, and the whole store will be open to you. It is your actual experience of God and truth-realization that will bring you there.

The Inner Door to Divine Power and Bliss

How did Christ resurrect his crucified body? How did Lahiri Mahasaya and Sri Yukteswar perform their miracles? Modern science has, as yet, no answer; though with the advent of the Atomic Age the scope of the world-mind has been abruptly enlarged. The word "impossible" is becoming less prominent in man's vocabulary.

—Autobiography of a Yogi

Success, wealth, cure of chronic disease, control over habits —all can be attained. If you exhaust all material methods and efforts, do not continue helplessly to solicit these impotent past resources. Open the inner door and vitalizing spiritual power flows in—all weakness and failure vanish. Why not awake to God's help? Have calmness born of concentration on Spirit; meditative calmness is a boundless reservoir of divine power.

God is not partial. If you follow the law, you will find Him. When I found Him within, I found Him in everything. Even as a little boy I yearned for God. I once wrote a letter to Him. Yes, I really did; and I posted it addressed to "God in Heaven." Certainly when we write to someone, we expect an answer. When no reply came, my waiting and expecting brought floods of tears. The answer came at last—not so many words printed on paper, but in a great vision of light. How wonderful! You *can* receive God's response if you will try, and do not give up. Put your questions seriously and feelingly from within, send them to God in your deep meditations, and, most truly, you will receive your answer.

The Lord can be coaxed nearer to us only by the law and by love, by real communion from within, with unceasing yearning until there is response from Him. If once the outer wall of ignorance is broken by scientific meditation, He will show the door to His presence. Knock hard and keep it up, persistently. It will open, and the infinite powers and bliss of God will be at your command.

Affirm with me: "I and my Father are One; He in me, and I in Him. Peace, bliss, omnipotence, reign in me—in the God in me."

Resurrection: Renewing and Transforming Your Body, Mind, and Spirit

A lecture delivered by Paramahansaji before students of his Washington, D.C., Center, April 7, 1929*

Thought is infinite! Each word represents an ideal conception of the Infinite, because behind each word and thought is a manifestation of Spirit. Many waves of thought are dancing in the waves of consciousness; but behind that, there is the great unceasing Ocean of Truth. Our thought expressions are waves of this ocean of understanding.

What is the meaning of resurrection? To live again! To rise to renewed life! What rises again—and how? We must understand in what way resurrection means to live again. Everything is undergoing a process of change. These changes are either detrimental or beneficial to the object that changes. For example, if I take a dirty glass and strike it on the floor, it will be changed, will it not? But this change will not be beneficial; it will be harmful to the object. However, if I wash the glass and make it shine, that change is beneficial. *Resurrection means any beneficial change to an object or to a human being.*

You can resurrect your old furniture in the carpenter's or upholsterer's shop. You can resurrect your house through the help of architects. But we are talking of resurrecting the human body. In this context, resurrection means any uplifting change. You cannot remain at a standstill. You must either go forward or backward. That is a great and inspiring truth, that in life you cannot remain stationary. Either you must accept changes that are harmful to you or those that are beneficial to you.

---

* Under the direction of Paramahansa Yogananda, portions of this talk, as well as of other early talks and articles, were incorporated into the compilation of the *Yogoda Satsanga Lessons.*

Every human being is an expression of the vast, immeasurable Spirit. Isn't it marvelous, when we see how human beings, without any motors, without any wires, without any visible source of power, run smoothly? The human machine wakes up in the morning, eats breakfast, goes to work, goes to lunch, goes back to the office, has dinner, goes to the movies (or perhaps enjoys some hobby at home); then it goes to sleep, to wake up and do the same things all over again, day in and day out. As mortal beings, we are controlled by something that operates like radio—the intelligent active and vital energy let loose by God in the creative laws of Nature.* Ships can be moved by radio; similarly, we are controlled by the "broadcasts" of natural laws of the infinite omnipresent Spirit.

But the point is, we are not automatons. Our soul is a reflection of Spirit. Just as the sunlight falling on a body of moving water becomes broken up into myriad scintillations, so Spirit, shining on vibratory creation, has become reflected therein as individualized Spirit, or the soul, in each human body and mind. Now, although this soul is a reflection of Spirit, it has become identified with the body, and has put on all the limitations of the body and of the mind. Yet it is trying very hard through processes of evolution to resurrect itself from the distortions caused by thralldom to the body and mind. But it is easier said than done, isn't it? Resurrecting the reflected soul-image signifies taking it away from the distorting restlessness of body consciousness and reuniting it with the original all-pervading undistorted Light of Spirit.

Theory and Practice

There is a story that when a certain charismatic preacher† met God in Heaven, he said to Him, "Don't You remember me? I introduced You to crowds in big halls and sent them up to Heaven by the carloads." Then God said, "You sent them all right, but none arrived." Sometimes we pray theoretically; and we think we are resurrected from our blemishes, but it is

---

* *Prakriti:* the active expression of Spirit as Creator.

† Evangelist Billy Sunday (William Ashley Sunday, 1862–1935), as told in the humorous satire, *Heavenly Discourse,* by Charles Erskine Scott Wood.

only imagination. The facts of our words and actions prove something different. Resurrect your Self. Resurrection must take place not only theoretically; it must occur practically. Even theoretical prayer is better than nothing at all, but sometimes it is a detriment to practical understanding.

Let us study first about mental resurrection. In the beginning of life, the soul plays with the body instrument; gradually it becomes the slave of the body. Hence we must learn to live a life above the physical plane. Mental development is a product of physical development, or evolution. We find, according to natural evolution, that the soul resurrects itself to the plane of intellect or the plane of prosperity—manifesting the unique endowments of human beings—and then rises to the plane of spiritual realization, which gives a meaning to all prosperous development and intellectual attainment. Intellectual attainments are undoubtedly helpful—all good things help. Gradually, we understand the way to resurrect the body into the Spirit, by spiritualizing the body and mind to become fit instruments for the expression of Spirit.

Resurrection means to free the soul from the cage of ignorance; to uplift and release the soul from the bondage of mortal consciousness. Human life is sometimes very beautiful, but one who is attached to it is like a bird of paradise in a cage. You open the bird's cage, but because of attachment and habit, it may not want to fly away. Isn't it a pity that the bird does not want to go out into the boundless freedom whence it came? Yet it is afraid. We also, feeling ourselves slipping out of body consciousness in deep meditation, may think: "Will I slide into the Infinite and never come back?" We are afraid to try the skies of limitless consciousness. We have lived too long identified with the body; and now we shrink from entering our infinite omnipresence, frightened to resurrect the omnipotence and omniscience of our soul. To resurrect our innate wisdom from the bondage of the body is spiritual resurrection.

Bodily Freedom Is Not Real Freedom

I will talk of body resurrection now, of promoting those uplifting changes in the body that are beneficial to you. What I have to say first is about living-dead people walking on the streets.

Many people think that they are free because they can think and speak, move their hands and feet, and walk freely on the city streets. But they are not free. They are in bondage, chained by Nature and their subconscious habits, like men walking in their sleep. There are many forms of physical bondage. If you have not been able to resurrect yourself from the bondage of sickness, for example, then you are still imprisoned behind the bars of matter. To resurrect yourself from disease by right living is extremely necessary. After many years of deep study, I found "in a nutshell" how to express health—by contacting Cosmic Energy.*

We must also understand about food values. Meat is detrimental to your system; but so is an improperly cooked vegetable dinner of killed vitamins. Resurrect your mind from the bad habits of wrong eating.

Vitamins are absolutely necessary to the system for the harmonious development of physical strength. Vitamins are the brains of the food. Vitamins are rearranged in the system to give vitality to the body. They are sparks that set the gunpowder of chemicals in motion.

Unsulphured figs and raisins are nature's candies. The ordinary figs and raisins are mummies. They are so treated that they do not decay; but they have no life. You can write these figs and raisins into your will and leave them to future generations as heirlooms! Sun-dried figs live only three months. In the mummy kind, the sulphur fumes passed through them kill all the vitamins. Isn't it too bad to preserve things by killing the good part?

It is good to boil eggs hard because they may contain germs from sick hens.

If you remember the basic rules—an abundance of fresh fruits and vegetables, not denatured by improper cooking or storage, and nuts, whole grains, and some dairy products—you will not be making any transgression on nature.† Only after

---

* *Prana,* the intelligent, finer-than-atomic energy that constitutes the life-principle of the physical cosmos. Practice of Self-Realization Fellowship [Yogoda Satsanga Society] techniques, particularly the Energization Exercises, enables one to recharge the body with this cosmic energy, or universal *prana* (see glossary).

† Though Paramahansa Yogananda recommended that one's daily diet include

years of experiment I have found the effectiveness of all this. I shall broadcast this information. Nature will not listen to excuses of your years of transgression against her health rules. If you eat sensibly, then if you are in the habit of breaking some laws occasionally, it will not so much hurt you.

I have never felt better in my life. Though sometimes I was sickly in my youth, I have very strong muscles now. Of course Yogoda [Self-Realization Fellowship techniques], and not only food, helps that.

Right Food Must Be Taken

I recently met a man called Uncle Billy Ries—seventy-nine years old. He has grown a full shock of hair on a perfectly bald head. He said that he had been for years carrying a bay window in front, and was given up to die at twenty-five years of age. He resurrected himself. He began by thinking, "If there is a God, He has no business in making me sick"; then he began to think it must be his own fault. You see, he was resurrecting himself from the disease that he had been constantly attracting to himself through his own fault. He found that sixteen elements are necessary to the body. So he altered his diet accordingly and got back his health completely. He kicks way up high in the air, and he successfully pitted his strength against mine. We are great friends. Much valuable health information I owe to him.

Since you have to eat, why not eat rightly? You can have a whole meal often, yet be on a starvation diet; whole meals of white bread and sugar and pies might satisfy one's hunger, but would kill in a few months. So resurrect yourself from the bad habit of eating wrongly. A rattlesnake gives you warning before it strikes, but rich gravy and white flour won't tell you; they look and taste so very nice. Everything white—refined flour, sugar, and grains—is not always good; sometimes brown

---

a large percentage of raw fruits and vegetables, he advised: "If your diet has consisted chiefly of cooked foods, introduce raw foods into it gradually, until your system becomes accustomed to the change. When cooking vegetables, it is better to steam than boil them. Vegetables cooked in water should be eaten with the broth in which they were prepared."

things—whole, unpolished grains, and natural sugar in fruits and honey—are very nice. We used to have unprocessed cereals until the mills came and we began to refine things; and now, by a roundabout way, the best is taken out of the grains. Colonic poisoning comes with white bread. You cannot afford to have constipation. The stomach exercise of Yogoda is marvelously efficient in promoting proper digestion and elimination.*

The Wisdom of Fasting

Another thing, every week you should fast one day on orange juice to rest the internal organs. You won't die—you will *live!* Once a month fast two or three days consecutively, living only on orange juice.† There is so much bondage to matter—of fear to miss a meal. It is so evident we are not living by the Spirit of God, as Jesus Christ spoke about living by the word of God: "Man shall not live by bread alone, but by every word that proceedeth out of the mouth of God."‡ Resurrect yourself from this bad mental habit of overeating and palate slavery. When you fast on orange juice it scrubs every cell. At least once every month you should give a thorough housecleaning to your body by fasting. Do not let poison accumulate in your system. When you suddenly become sick you hasten to pray to God for healing. Don't let yourself get sick. The greatest way to maintain health, and the simplest, is to fast on orange juice one day every week and for two or three days consecutively once a month. Resurrect your soul from the hypnosis of bad habits in eating.

You must do lots of resurrecting in order to get to God. To make the body spiritually fit, not only right eating but moderation in all things and sunlight and exercise are just as important.

---

* Taught as part of Paramahansaji's Energization Exercises in the *Yogoda Satsanga Lessons.*

† Persons in good health should experience no difficulty in fasting for two or three days; longer fasts should not be undertaken unless with competent medical advice and supervision. Anyone suffering from a chronic ailment or an organic defect should apply the dietary and health recommendations offered in this article only upon the advice of a physician.

‡ *Matthew* 4:4 (Bible).

Resurrect Yourself From the Consciousness of Disease

Then comes the question of resurrecting yourself from the *consciousness* of disease. That is more important than trying to use even meditation or physical means to seek a remedy when you are sick. According to experiments by German scientists, many people are better off because they do not constantly analyze their physical condition or suffer from mental discouragement because of their maladies. There is a close relation between the mind and the body, so destroying the consciousness of disease is vitally important. Many times diseases have left us, but our consciousness of disease brings them back again.

While meditating late one night, a certain saint saw the ghost of the dread smallpox disease entering the village where he lived. "Stop, Mr. Ghost!" he cried. "Go away. You must not molest a town in which I worship God."

"I will take only three people," the ghost replied, "in accordance with my cosmic karmic duty." At this the saint unhappily nodded assent.

The following day three persons died of smallpox. But the next day several more died, and each day thereafter more villagers were overcome by the fearful disease. Thinking that a great deception had been played on him, the saint meditated deeply and summoned the ghost. When it came, the saint rebuked it.

"Mr. Ghost, you deceived me and did not speak the truth when you said you would take only three people with your smallpox."

But the ghost replied, "By the Great Spirit, I did speak the truth to you."

The saint persisted. "You promised to take only three persons, and scores have succumbed to the disease."

"I took only three," said the ghost. "The rest killed themselves with fear."

You must resurrect your mind from the consciousness of disease—from the thought of disease. You are the invulnerable Spirit; but the body now rules the mind. The mind must rule the body. Then the body will not accept suggestions of environment and suggestions of heredity. Wrong ways of living on the physical plane have been handed down to posterity from our original ancestors who succumbed to mortal delusion. Often diseases appear only because you have stimulated the consciousness of disease inherited from your forefathers, and thereby reinforced your susceptibility. You should always remember that if Spirit were to withdraw the intelligent "radioed" energy that activates creation, you would drop dead, just like a bird that has been shot; despite all your prestige and all your money, you could not live. You must give the whole credit to God, remembering that you are living directly by His power. Resurrect yourself from the consciousness of physical disease. God did not create disease. Resurrect yourself from the disease consciousness that has been handed down by your forefathers. Do not mind difficulties; be unafraid. These are the truths that have been preached in India from ages ago. Truth that shall make you free!

Then comes resurrection from our mental habits. The silk-worm weaves threads around itself into a cocoon. Then, before it develops wings and slips out of the cocoon, the manufacturer gets hold of it, and the silkworm meets its death in its self-created prison. We all are similarly entrapped. Before the wings of spirituality grow, we foolishly weave threads of fear, worry, and ignorance around ourselves until disease and death come and destroy us. We find ourselves in bondage created by ourselves. What is most destructive? Our own misguided thoughts, our own wrong ways of living—thinking indiscriminately and then acting on it. We must resurrect ourselves from spiritually deadening anger thoughts, from the thoughts that engender selfishness, from the clamor of inharmonious living.

"Let the Dead Bury Their Dead"

Many people think they are awake, but they are not. Mostly they are walking dead. You have heard of people walking in their sleep, crying "fire" or lecturing. Most people are like that. I don't mean Yogoda students or those who are living the life of truth. Jesus said, "Let the dead bury their dead." *

------

*Luke 9:60 (Bible).

One was to be buried beneath the earthly sod by one who was already buried beneath the soil of ignorance. You should help to resurrect those who have buried themselves under their wrong living. In order to do that, you must be able to smile from your own resurrected soul. Not a smile like this: "I am DEElighted to meet you"—not that kind of smile. When you smile when God smiles through the heart, through the soul, and when the soul then smiles through the heart and the heart smiles through the eyes, then the Prince of Smiles is enthroned beneath the canopy of your celestial brow. Let no rebel hypocrisy ever destroy it. Smile though the storms of suffering shriek around you.

God knows that it is because you are beclouded by self-created ignorance that you are tossing on a sea of trials, unable to see the omnipresent Spirit pervading everything. He knows that you are adrift in the little bark of your life and must battle the storms around you. But He also knows that you are moving toward Him. When trials come, pray to the Father: "I have launched my boat on a dark sea, but I have heard Thy call. I know that Thou knowest I am coming." You must battle; even when the hands seem to break, you must battle, you must not give up. Then, when the clouds will vanish and the life of happiness and prosperity will be back again, you will forget your trials.

Trials do not come to destroy you, but to help you appreciate God better. God does not send those trials. They are of your own making—the effects of conscious or unconscious actions in the past, somewhere, sometime. You must blame yourself for these; but do not, as a result, allow yourself to develop an inferiority complex. All you have to do to overcome your trials is to resurrect your consciousness from the environment of spiritual ignorance. Ever affirm: "Heavenly Father, I know that Thou art coming to my aid, and that I will see Thy silver lining haloing the dark clouds. In this tumultuous sea of trial Thou art the polestar of my shipwrecked thoughts."

What are you afraid of? You are an immortal being. You are neither a man nor a woman, as you may think, but a soul, joyous, eternal. Do not identify your immortality with human habits; they are your deadliest enemies. Even as Jesus could manifest his love and say, when sorely tested: "Father, forgive them; for they know not what they do," so should you become able to forgive others, even in the midst of exacting trials, and say: "My soul is resurrected. My power to overcome is greater than all my trials, because I am a child of God." Those who receive God are those who develop their mental powers by serious application of spiritual laws. When your mental powers expand, your cup of realization will become big enough to hold the Ocean of Knowledge. Then you have resurrected yourself.

Give and Forget

Resurrection was celebrated last Easter, honoring Jesus whose life was such a great example. People to whom you do good may turn around and slap you. Expectation of recompense for doing good is meanness, is littleness. Give and forget. If your neighbor slaps you, just say he does not know any better; but don't say it loudly. Resurrect yourself from the littleness of life, the little things that disturb you.

Do you ever think that you have been completely unsettled by circumstances—ruffled, shattered, whipped, lacking power? Banish such thoughts! You have power; you do not use it. You have all the power you need. There is nothing greater than the power of the mind. Resurrect your mind from the little habits that keep you worldly all the time. Smile that perpetual smile—that smile of God. Smile that strong smile of balanced recklessness—that million-dollar smile that no one can take from you.

Several years ago, when I was on the train going to Los Angeles, I met a man whose manner and general appearance immediately attracted my attention. He was a well-dressed, prosperous-looking businessman, with every indication that he was blessed with all the good things of life and had every reason to be happy. But regardless of all these favorable outer impressions, I felt very sorry for him because he emanated deep gloom. I said to myself: "What is the matter with this man? He seems to have buried himself beneath this artificial habit of gloom. I must resurrect him."

Looking straight at him, I said: "Are you happy?" He tried to discourage me with a fierce look, but I returned his gaze squarely. I reasoned that by his glare he had already annihilated me in his mind, so he could not kill me again. Finally he spoke. "Is that your business?" "Yes," I replied. "I resurrect the walking dead."

Shortly, he said, "Yes, I am happy." "No," I insisted. "I can tell what is in the mind."

"Why shouldn't I be happy?" he retorted. "I put fifty to sixty thousand dollars a month in the bank." "Poor soul!" I thought, realizing that he believed that his happiness lay in depositing those large sums in the bank. But I said, "Tomorrow you may not be here to carry a cent. Have you opened your 'bank account' with God?"

Later he invited me to lunch, but he was still inwardly antagonistic to me. Then we talked again, and he became more reasonable. "Do not rely on riches," I advised. "You may die and not even have a chance to make a will. These material riches are not yours. Open your 'bank account' with God."

He had become interested, so he suggested, "Meet me in Boston." I countered with the proposal, "Meet me in Los Angeles." But he did not have time. Later, when in Boston, I was in the hotel where he had told me he stopped. When I inquired about him, the hotel manager said, "Don't you know what happened to him? He was coming from a hockey match and was struck down by a truck. He never regained consciousness." I felt very bad. He had awakened a little, but not enough.

The Lap of Immortality

If you have attunement with the Infinite, you will know that whether or not nature shatters your body you are still on the lap of Immortality, still on the lap of that infinite assurance. Resurrect yourself from the consciousness of human habits and the human thoughts thereof. Live every second in the consciousness of your relationship with the Infinite. That alone is everlasting; it is the one thing that will live forever. This I say not to frighten you, but to quicken your understanding, to quicken your efforts, so that you do not keep your soul buried under a false satisfaction.

Open your "bank account" with God—it will never be lost. You can use it through all your travels, now and in eternity, whether in an airplane or an astral plane. You should say to yourself: "From star to star I will fly; whether on this side of eternity, or the other side of eternity, or whether surging through the waves of life, from atom to atom—flying with the lights, whirling with the stars, or dancing with human lives—I am an immortal! I have resurrected myself from the consciousness of death."

Resurrect yourself from anger, from melancholy, from failures. You must succeed to know that you are God's child. Success is not limited to spiritual matters. Success must come in everything. Resurrect yourself from the consciousness of disease, from mental habits and weakness. Have a strong smile that will never be shattered by the trials of your circumstances.

Spiritual Resurrection

Then comes spiritual resurrection. Spiritual resurrection means metaphysical relaxation, to withdraw the consciousness from the tenacious habit of identification with your body. In meditation you release yourself from identification with your mental body by stilling the restless sensory mind. You must similarly relax the life force from the internal physical organs, and thus do away with body consciousness. In that relaxation of your hold on body consciousness you become free; your soul nature is revealed and you know that you can live without the body though living in the body; it is separate. Resurrection is not a change that takes place only after death. You must resurrect yourself while living in this body. You do it every night in sleep, which is unconscious resurrection. You must learn to do it in meditation, which is conscious resurrection. There were saints in India who, having entered a deathlike state, were buried, and later disinterred and brought back to life and consciousness after several days under the ground. They have proved that resurrection of the body is possible.* St. Paul, St. John, and other of Christ's disciples knew also the spiritual

---

* See story of Sadhu Haridas on page 316.

science of conscious relaxation of the life from the body in meditation and restoration of it at will—St. Paul thus declared, "I die daily."* To do without food and still live is another kind of conscious resurrection.

The resurrection of Jesus Christ is different. It is higher still. This higher resurrection means you understand creation—how to free the soul from the bondage of ignorance, the great delusive power of *maya.*

We have no physical existence except in the universal sense. The body you see is nothing but materialized energy. How could energy be sick? Sickness is a delusion. But simply saying that it is delusion is not enough. If in a dream you strike your dream head on a dream wall, you will have a dream skull fracture. Wake up and you are healed of your dream injury. Yogoda teaches that only by contacting God can one see that God has become the universe, and that the human body—and all things else—are naught but a mass of condensed energy; and energy is "frozen" Cosmic Consciousness, or God. We should not call it mind. Mind is different. To say that everything is mind is incorrect. It is Cosmic Consciousness that causes us to be aware of different things, to have a consciousness of so-called matter and a consciousness of Spirit.

I have written plainly in my *Scientific Healing Affirmations†* why it is we do not see Spirit in matter. Jesus Christ had the power to see it. Resurrection means not only to resurrect body and soul to another sphere of existence, as did Jesus, but to change the atoms of the body (as well as to spiritualize them and release them along with the mind). Everything—skin, hair, eyes—is nothing but frozen energy and frozen consciousness of God. When Peter cut off the ear of the centurion, Jesus restored it. How? The atoms obeyed him, because he *knew* that the atoms were controlled by the consciousness of God. They do not obey you because you are not attuned to that controlling power of Cosmic Consciousness, which is holding this flower together as a flower. You have the illusion of matter as a solid reality. By meditation you will be able to sepa-

---

* *I Corinthians* 15:31 (Bible).

† Published by Yogoda Satsanga Society of India.

rate the soul from the illusion of the solid body. You will know that the cosmic golden cord that binds the atoms is the tender consciousness of Spirit. It is with this cord that He binds the atoms to become the flower, or the human body. He takes myriad electrons, like a child modeling in clay, and throws them into eternity to become stars or universes. Imagine how very little we are to Him—I think nothing more than bacteria. Though we are so very small, yet as souls made in His image we are very big!

A little story—about bigness. We think our accomplishments are marvelous, but they are not so big to God at all. One day I saw a tiny ant crawling up a snowy mound of sand. I said, "To the ant this must be like scaling the Himalaya Mountains!" The pile no doubt seemed gigantic to the ant, but not to me. Similarly, a million of our solar years may be but a moment in the mind of God. We should train ourselves to think in grand terms: Eternity! Infinity!

The Crucifixion of Self-sufficiency

Last of all, resurrect your mind from formal faith—beliefs which may have given you a little satisfaction, but which you have outgrown; religions which you lived with under the conviction that you know—while you don't know. The greatest crucifixion of the soul is the crucifixion by the arrogant self-sufficiency of the ego—thinking how wonderfully big and wise we are. Your soul must be released from bondage to the littleness and limitations of the body and the suffering that the body is subject to. When you think of the devastation of disease, you think it an injustice of God; but *know* you are immortal—not to be crushed by mortal lessons, but to learn and manifest your immortality and *smile*. Say: "I am immortal, sent to a mortal school to learn and regain my immortality. Though challenged by all the purifying fires of the earth, I am the soul and cannot be destroyed. Fire cannot burn me; water cannot wet me; breezes cannot wither me; atoms cannot shatter me; I am the immortal dreaming the lessons of immortality—not to be crushed, but to be entertained." In the dreamland, sickness and health are the same, prosperity and failure are the same—only dream imaginings. But surely, a dream of prosperity is better than a dream of failure. So if you have to have dreams, why not have good dreams in this life? If you have too many bad dreams, you will be very busy crying and not have time to know that it is all a dream. Far better are the dreams of health and prosperity and wisdom.

Never Acknowledge Defeat

Resurrect your soul from all dreams of frailties. Resurrect your soul in eternal wisdom. What is the method? It includes many things: self-control, proper diet, fortitude, an undaunted mental attitude, and relaxation of the consciousness from body identification by faithful daily practice of scientific concentration and meditation principles. Refuse to be defeated. Do not acknowledge defeat; to acknowledge defeat is greater defeat. You have unlimited power; you must cultivate that power, that is all.

Meditation is the greatest way of resurrecting your soul from the bondage of the body and from the shackles of all your trials. Meditate at the feet of the Infinite. Learn to saturate yourself with the consciousness of God. Your trials may be heavy, may be great, but the greatest enemy of yourself is yourself. You are immortal; your trials are mortal. They are changeable; you are unchangeable. You can unleash infinite powers and shatter your finite trials.

Two frogs, one a big one and the other a small one, fell into a pail of milk. The sides of the pail were shiny and smooth, too slippery and steep for the frogs to climb out. They were battling to stay alive; but every time they lifted their mouths to catch a little oxygen, down they went. They paddled around and around. After a while, the big frog gave up and drowned. But the little frog said, "Life is too sweet. I don't want to die. I will keep paddling no matter if my little feet fall off." So it was battling for hours, when suddenly it found something solid under its feet—the milk was churned to butter! Out jumped the little frog! That is just how life is! After battling adversities insufficiently like the big frog, if you give up you deserve to succumb to your troubles; but if you keep on battling with determination, your difficulties will be overcome—some answer from the Infinite will emerge and you will hop out of your troubles. Be like the little frog. By all means keep battling. Determination! Resurrect yourself from weakness, disease, ignorance, consciousness of disease, and above all from the frailties of mortal habits that beset your life.

Oneness in the Infinite Christ

Self-Realization Fellowship International Headquarters,
Los Angeles, California, December 25, 1934

Evolution proceeds in a linear direction, one state evolving into the next. Thus does the individual soul progress upward through higher and higher forms of Nature until it finds perfect expression in the spiritually awakened divine man. The cosmic influence on this natural evolution is cyclical.* In the upward arc of the cycle, first comes material, then intellectual, and then spiritual development. Then the general trend of life again returns to the intellectual and the material planes. God's creation is in this manner constantly going on. We, the actors of many races, play again and again the drama of life on the stage of time. We should understand the purpose. We are here to play our parts well, but without becoming so enmeshed in and identified with our roles.

We have a distorted perception of life because we see with eyes of narrowness and selfishness. If only we would see instead with the eyes of God. When we open our inner eyes of soul wisdom, we behold the omnipresent Light of God. Within this Light is the consciousness of Christ, the "Son" or pure reflection of God present everywhere in the universe. This Christ Consciousness [*Kutastha Chaitanya*], the Infinite Christ, is God's intelligence and love knocking on the closed eyelids of our souls, urging us that all we have to do is look to this Light within and we shall see all ignorance and diversities vanish. To him who has opened his inner eye,† everything is One. Jesus referred to this universal consciousness

---

* Reference to the world cycles or *yugas* (see glossary).

† The single or spiritual eye of wisdom, or omniscient soul intuition. "If therefore thine eye be single, thy whole body shall be full of light" (*Matthew* 6:22, Bible). (See *spiritual eye* in glossary.)

when he said: "I and my Father are one."* Krishna spoke similarly from that state of divine oneness: "I am the Source of
everything; from Me all creation emerges....Behold as unified
in My Cosmic Body all worlds. ...But thou canst not see Me
with mortal eyes. Therefore I give thee sight divine."†

Seeing God as the underlying Reality is the way to solve the
problem of being caught up in the delusive distortions of our
material experiences. Stars, planets, plants, animals, and human
beings are all let loose on a beautiful cosmic stage, with each
one playing an assigned part. Very few people understand the
meaning of the play because they do not pause to think deeply
about it. To the unenlightened, the drama often seems chaotic
and unjust. But God purposely did not automatically make all
people poor or all people millionaires, because if everyone were
alike this drama could not go on. Diversity is the basis of
Nature, and self-evolution is one means of maintaining this
diversity. By the law of cause and effect, action and reaction, we
make of ourselves what we presently are and what we will be.
The result of this variety, created by both man and Nature, is
what we experience as the cosmic drama. However, God does not
want us to suffer because of these differences. He wants us to
know that whether one is currently playing the part of a king or
of a servant, he must do his best, but never forget that as a soul,
made in the image of God, he is only enacting a temporary role.

Therefore, it doesn't matter whether we scrub floors, or
whether we are the leaders of great nations; unless we know
that we are merely playing a part on the stage of time, we will
suffer from the dualities inherent in the consciousness of being
identified with these different stations and conditions. Stage
actors do not bemoan their particular parts, but enact their
roles to the best of their ability, knowing they are temporary
portrayals. Do you see? It is only when we take life too seriously that we suffer.

Realize the One Life Pervading Everything

While we recognize the relative existence of differences,
yet we must not only know intellectually, but realize spiritu-

---

* *John* 10:30 (Bible).   † Bhagavad Gita X:8, XI:7, 8.

ally, that One Life pervades everything. There is but one religion of God, one Truth underlying the different names of religion. That universal state of consciousness is very hard to attain unless one has Self-realization, the knowing that we are souls and that all souls are a part of the One God. The small waves and the big waves all arise from the same ocean. So, when we stand aside spiritually and view every person and every religion impersonally, we shall see that everything is made of God.

Until we see all waves of creation in this way, there will always be differences, with their accompanying troubles and difficulties. No man, no prophet, will ever be able to wipe away all the inequalities and divisions on this earth. But when you will find yourself in the consciousness of God, these differences will vanish and you will say:

> Oh, life is sweet and death a dream,
> When Thy song flows through me.
> Then joy is sweet, sorrow a dream,
> When Thy song flows through me.
> Then health is sweet, sickness a dream,
> When Thy song flows through me.
> Then praise is sweet and blame a dream,
> When Thy song flows through me.*

This is the highest philosophy. Do not be afraid of anything. Even when tossing on a wave in a storm, you are still on the bosom of the ocean. Always hold on to the consciousness of God's underlying presence. Be of even mind, and say: "I am fearless; I am made of the substance of God. I am a spark of the Fire of Spirit. I am an atom of the Cosmic Flame. I am a cell of the vast universal body of the Father. 'I and my Father are One.'"

Try to Live As Christ Lived

Realize the tremendous spiritual power and beauty of the life of Christ, and try to live as he lived. Christ had no nation-

---

* "When Thy Song Flows Through Me" in *Words of Cosmic Chants* by Paramahansa Yogananda.

ality. He loved all races as the children of God. Try to feel that brotherhood with all nationalities. Real brotherhood can never come unless we feel it in our hearts. Such feeling can be attained only through Self-realization and the actual contact of God in our hearts.

Everything will betray you if you betray God by forgetfulness of Him. So it is time to realize your unity with all by experiencing your oneness with God. Practice that feeling of unity in the vastness of your expanded consciousness in meditation. Be very determined in that respect. Shut out the world in the silence of meditation, lest the lesser things of God's creation attract your attention away from Him. Let naught else approach that inner temple. In the sanctum of your heart there must be enshrined one power, one joy, one peace—God. If you have that realization, you will find the Infinite Christ baptizing your consciousness in the unity of God's omnipresence.

Your outer life also must be clean—pure in word, thought, and action. Be kind to all; even if the greatest of sinners comes to you, consider him a brother—albeit a sleeping brother. Hurt no one; judge none else but yourself. Destroy moods; trample them to dust.

Learn to Guide Your Actions by the Inner Will of Conscience

Master [Swami Sri Yukteswar] used to say to me, "Learn to behave." That is the most difficult thing to do. You should learn to guide all of your actions by the inner will of your conscience attuned to the will of God, and not by your emotional feelings and instincts. When I first met my Guru, he said, "Allow me to discipline you." He did not mean that he was going to make a mechanical man out of me, a blind follower. He said, "I will give you divine sight." When I tuned my will with Master's, it became strengthened and guided by wisdom.

God's will is governed by wisdom and justice. Those who are in tune with Him are not bound by any dictates of whims and habits. They live in the freedom of God, their will governed by His wisdom and justice. So it is important for the spiritual novice to tune his will with those who are in tune with God. Such obedience is not negation of one's own will. It requires the cultivation of tremendous will power to become attuned to wisdom. It took all of my self-control to heed the counsel of my Guru rather than listen to my own prepossessed habits and instincts. Master never demanded anything from his disciples; each received according to his willingness and receptivity. By following him wholeheartedly, I gained complete control of myself—a freedom I might never have found on my own.

Neither God nor Satan—nor anyone—can influence you except by your own use or misuse of will. Use your God-given free choice to seek Him. Then you shall surely find freedom. And remember that it is of the utmost importance to surround yourself with the best company, those who will inspire you and strengthen your discrimination and will power.

Flies do not discriminate between filth and honey; they flit from one to the other. But the bee is attracted only to the sweetness of honey. Similarly, there are indiscriminate human beings who, like flies, are drawn to material desires, no matter how impure. Some may once in a while feel attracted to God and meditation; but as soon as another temptation comes, they are captivated again by material life. The devotee is like the honeybee. Devotees love only what is beautiful and pure. They see, hear, smell, taste, and touch only what is good. They will and feel goodness, and ever seek the sweet nectar of God's presence in meditation.

Above all, be sincere with God. Be humble as you try through inner receptivity to learn everything from the lips of God. Cast out of your life all that keeps you from God. "If thy hand offend thee, cut it off."* Remove all impediments in your path—anything that obstructs your spiritual development.

While There Is Yet Time, Meditate!

I hope you will all make the supreme effort to meditate. Your search for God cannot wait. Let all else wait, but do not keep God waiting for you. Tarry no more, lest old age and disease suddenly terminate your life. While there is yet time and opportunity, meditate!

---

* *Mark* 9:43 (Bible).

I am giving to you the living testimony of Christ that I feel in the joy of his presence since yesterday when he came to me during our meditation.* I had always thought that because he was Oriental his eyes were dark; I rejected the western concept that showed him with blue eyes. But strange to say, I saw him this time with blue eyes. They were so beautiful. Never have I seen such eyes! As I was beholding them, they then became wondrously dark; and the voice of Christ said, "Why do you want to see me in form? See me as Infinite!"

All saints who have merged in God have the power to don again the forms that they once had on earth. How few people realize the immanent presence of the angels and the great masters. Just as songs passing through the ether may be tuned in when you have a radio, so is it possible to tune in with saints, who are just behind the etheric veil of space, if only you will meditate.

When a great teacher comes on earth, his presence bestows power and inspiration, filling his disciples with much joy. But after he leaves, they may feel bereft and lost if they have no motivating spiritual power of their own. This is why meditation and divine attunement are necessary, that seekers may learn how to recharge themselves with inspiration and joy. All the wonders of God will be revealed in the ecstatic communion of deep meditation.

The contact of God is not oblivion of consciousness. Ecstasy is the awakening of consciousness, the extending of awareness from the limits of the body to the limitlessness of Eternity, whence you watch the little bubble of life dancing in the Ocean of Infinity.

I know I am but a figure in God's dream movie, as you are also. Some day, when we cease to be actors on the screen of life, we shall realize that our forms are but shadows interspersing the cosmic beam of God's omnipresence, and that the only thing in the manifested universe which is real is the light of the Infinite Christ. Let us send this thought to all who

---

* A reference to the annual all-day Christmas meditation, which Paramahansaji inaugurated at the Self-Realization Fellowship International Headquarters in 1931 and personally conducted for many years. This spiritual tradition has been continued by Yogodans/Self-Realizationists around the world.

are seeking happiness in any way, and who know not that what they are really seeking is God.

My greatest Christmas gift for you is the wish that the joy which Christ felt in his soul may come to you; and as you enter the portals of the new year, you may take with you into every day that ever new joy of Christ.

Again and again, pray in your soul: "O Christ, O Lord, come, clear away the dust of my indifference. Flood my consciousness, O Infinite Christ, with Thy divine consciousness!"

* * *

"Oh, What Joy!"

At the conclusion of the 1934 Christmas gathering, Paramahansaji poured out his heart to God in prayer. Sri Daya Mata, who recorded his words stenographically, noted on the transcription: "A very soul-stirring, devotional prayer that brought tears of intense longing for God to all present."

O beloved Spirit, Supreme Love Divine! we are held on Thy bosom of love in the omnipresent light and joy of the Infinite Christ. Before Thy love, my love is little; it is but borrowed from Thy love. O Christ, in ecstasy of happiness, our hearts are united into a vast altar whereon Thine effulgent presence is sparkling unceasingly.

Father, Mother, Friend, Beloved God, take away all things that I have, even the body. Naught else matters but that Thou art with me—Thy consciousness, Thy spirit, Thy love. No more fame, nor name, nor organization; only Thy Presence evermore. My only wish: May Thy love shine forever in my heart, and may I be able to awaken Thy love in all hearts.

Father, may we ever feel Thy joy. O Divine Ocean, vibrating beneath the wave of my consciousness, as a little wavelet I was tossed about in the storm of ignorance. Now I feel beneath every particle of my being the supporting presence of Thy vast ocean of joy.

Oh, what joy; oh, what peace; oh, what bliss of Thy Being. The fountain of Thy joy bursts forth in our souls, obliterating all consciousness of time. Joy! Joy! Joy! We bathe in the fountain of Thy happiness, in the bliss of Thy Presence.

O Father, Mother, Friend, Beloved God, I mean it, I mean it! Take away everything from me, if it be Thy will. Let me roll in joy in the dust at Thy feet. Thy love alone I would preach. Make me speak only of Thy love. No more sermons; no alluring people with the charm of words, but with the burning fervor of my love for Thee. Send to me devotees who love Thee, for I want naught else.

O Eternal Ecstasy, where is the end of Thy joy? Endless joy, eternal joy, takes my breath away; how can I talk, O blessed Presence?

O sacred God, our own Father, Mother, Beloved, Thou art the only reality. Be Thou enshrined in our hearts. Let us never wander away from Thee. Draw us to Thy warm bosom of immortality, O Mother, to drink the milk of Thy compassionate assurance.

Mother Divine, leave us not in the pit of temptation; strengthen our desire to desire Thee alone. O Spirit Divine, our own Beloved Holy of Holies, what joy, what happiness! Bless us always, wherever we may be. Teach us to drink Thy name in divine communion—all sermons and books I cast into the fire of Thy Presence. Send to me only those who, with me, want to drink of Thee.

My love walks the golden trail that leads to Thee. O Nearest of the near, yet Farthest of the far, I sought Thee everywhere, suddenly to find that Thou hadst been always in my heart. I offer my love to Thee within, without, everywhere. O Spirit Divine, I kneel at Thy feet; I am the humble dust at Thy feet.

Father, Mother, Friend, Beloved God, my own, receive my heart. Let me not waste time on anything. Wherever I go, wherever I may be, give me the joy of drinking Thy name with others. That is all I ask. Take away everything, but not my love for Thee. O Spirit, my own, my own, baptize us all with Thy love, that we truly feel Thy love.

O God, O Christ, O Guru, what shall I say to thank Thee for this joy? I am intoxicated with Thy joy! Eternal Ecstasy, I bow down again and again. Thou art in my every thought. What living joy, happiness everlasting. O Father, O Christ of eternal joy!

I bow to all of you, to the Infinite Christ who is present within you. O Christ, give to us the ecstasy of your joy, that it may be with us every hour, every minute, of every day. Joy! Joy! Joy!

Be One With
Christ Consciousness

December 24, 1938

An especially blessed annual occasion at Self-Realization Fellowship International Headquarters is the all-day Christmas meditation. Paramahansa Yogananda inaugurated these services in 1931, and personally conducted them each year. During these meditations, his words were sometimes an expression of his own divine ardor addressed directly to God; sometimes an appeal to the Lord on behalf of, or as one of, the assembled devotees; sometimes spiritual guidance for those present—the spontaneous inspirations of a soul in deep communion with God.

The call of life and the call of death are imperative, but *the call of God is the most important of all.* With utmost concentration, give your heart and soul unto God. Forget the consciousness of time. Today of all days you should use the full power of your soul to show God that you love Him more than anything in life. May you love the Giver of all gifts more than all His gifts! If you offer your reverence continuously, with ever-increasing intensity, you will see and feel the presence of God today as you have never experienced it before.

Forgetting time and space, let all of us expand the consciousness of our being. Be filled with peace and joy. Joy is the proof of the presence of God. As you go on meditating, a deep joy will come over your soul. Feel that joy. Feel expanded in the spirit of Christ. We are here to worship the Christ that was in Jesus, as well as Jesus the man who manifested Christ Consciousness *[Kutastha Chaitanya]*, and the Great Ones who are all one in that consciousness. God and Christ are one. All liberated masters, through their perfect attunement with the Son or Christ Consciousness, are united with God. So try, with greatest determination, to feel this consciousness of the Universal Christ.

If you dig with the pickax of attention, under the rocks of

restlessness you will find the gem of Christ Consciousness. This day may be the very day you succeed. This day may be for you the glorious dawn of turning from the land of matter to the greatest joy and freedom in God. Join in spirit with all your might and soul, with all your love, that we may all feel liberated in God. Place your hands, palms together, over your heart and say, *"Pranam."** Now pray with me:

"To the great God we bow. Jesus Christ, Bhagavan Krishna, Mahavatar Babaji, Lahiri Mahasaya, Sri Yukteswar, [our Gurupreceptor,] saints of all religions, we bow to the Christ Consciousness in each of you. *Aum. Aum. Aum.* Heavenly Father, charge our bodies with Christ Consciousness. Charge our minds with Christ Consciousness. Charge our souls with Christ Consciousness. We send forth this prayer to the world: that the birth of Christ be celebrated every year as we celebrate it today, by communion with Christ Consciousness. Wherever we go, let us speak of this day, that the world may come to observe each year a spiritual Christmas before the social Christmas on December 25th. For Christ was of God, and festivities are of the world; so by meditation we worship Christ in spirit, and by festivities we worship Christ in body. *Aum.* Peace. *Aum."*

Your meditation should not be an oblivion of wandering thoughts, but an attentive, constantly increasing devotion to God—a deep joy arising from contact with Spirit. In the silence within, implore His presence again and again, with the yearning you have felt when you have wanted something very badly. With that most urgent desire, pray to Him and tell Him that you want Him. No matter how your thoughts may be running here and there, pay no attention. Bring your mind back to God with the constant prayer: "Reveal Thyself. Come unto me; come unto me. O God, just as Thou dost reveal Thyself unto Christ, reveal Thyself unto me. Reveal Thyself. Come unto me." The concentration of your mind should be like a flood, gathering volume as it moves toward the ocean of God's presence. Again and again increase your fervor. "We bow at Thy

---

* From *pra*, "complete," and *nam*, "salutation" or "bowing down." This salutation, with the hands in the position of prayer, is an expression of reverence to God or to one in whom the Divine is manifest.

lotus feet of eternity, O Spirit! Reveal Thyself."

[A period of meditation followed. When Paramahansaji spoke again, he began with the following true story:]

A materialistic doctor once sought out a particular saint, thinking that he would set the master straight about a few matters. "If only I can meet this saint," he was thinking, as he walked along toward the master's hermitage, "I will twist his ear and show him that the world is real and that God is unreal."

Even as the doctor was thinking this, a disciple of the saint came running up to him and said, "My master wishes to see the physician who would twist his ear and teach him that God is unreal."

The doctor almost fainted with surprise. When he reached the saint, whom he found seated under a tree, he said, "For the first time I am penitent. I feel it was God who told you about me. Please tell me if I will ever meet this God who talks with you."

"Twice in your life," the saint replied, "if you pray very earnestly day and night."

"But the mind wanders," protested the doctor.

"It doesn't matter how many times the mind wanders," the saint answered. "If again and again you pray to God, He will answer."

One month after this incident, the wife of the doctor's brother became very ill. She was under the care of a naturopath who advised that recovery would depend on her having fresh grapes. But the fruit was out of season. When the doctor, her brother-in-law, heard this, he remembered the words of the saint: that God would hear his prayers. He whispered to his brother, "I will get some grapes."

The doctor sent a servant to the shops, but there were no grapes to be had. So the doctor prayed for a way to find some of the precious fruit. Day passed, and evening; at midnight he heard a knock on the door. He went to open it and there stood a man with a basket of grapes. Astounded, the doctor questioned him. "My employer sent this fruit to you," replied the stranger.

Next morning the servant's employer called and explained: "I had retired about ten o'clock last night when with inner

vision I saw you crying for grapes. My wife and I had just
returned from the north where this fruit grows, and had brought
some back with us. Again and again I saw you, always crying
for this fruit. At last a great Light appeared, and I heard a Voice
saying, 'Take those grapes to Dr.———.' I got up, but then I
thought I must have imagined it all, and so I went back to bed.
But though I dozed, still that Light and that Voice bothered
me. After a while I was awakened by the sound of my wife moving around. She told me that she also had seen a great Light
and had heard a Voice telling her to send our grapes to you at
once. And so I had my servant deliver them to you."

Thus the doctor knew that God had sent the fruit. He took
the grapes to his brother's wife, who with the aid of the blessed
fruit recovered quickly from her illness.

The doctor himself told me this story. The experience
had changed his life.

However, one should not seek God for the sake of such
experiences. As long as there is a desire for phenomena, God
Himself will not come. Let no one know what is in your heart,
what your soul feels. Inwardly you must continuously ask for
His presence. He will come. This is the day above all others that
you should try to receive Him. Forget the past. This can be the
greatest day of your life, if you will only make the effort. You
have passed so much time thinking of worldly pleasures. This
day you should pray with all your heart; this is the greatest
opportunity you have ever had to offer the bouquet of your
devotion to God.

Often, when I have least expected it, God has come. Many
times as I have walked by the ocean in Encinitas He has come.
Saint Francis and the Great Ones have come. Even now they are
all here with you. The astral heaven is just behind the gross
vibration of this world. Last night dear Seva Devi's spirit* in a
perfect astral form came to me and said, "I am free. I will be
with you tomorrow at the Christmas meditation." It is a great
joy to me that she also is with us, in truth and with great reverence. I see her as plainly as you see me.

---

* A devoted Western disciple of Paramahansaji to whom he had given this
Indian name. She had passed a month earlier after a serious illness.

We have to solve the great mysteries of life and death. They have one purpose—to make us seek with all the fervor of our souls until we find God, our eternal Beloved.

I know we miss our most beloved St. Lynn.* It was much against his will that he had to remain in Kansas City this time. But he is with us too, in spirit, right now.

I pray that you enjoy, every day of your life, the kind of communion with God you are having today. My heart is so thankful; it is overcome by His kindness. He has given me everything that I had wanted in this life; but, above all, He has given Himself. Such gratefulness I feel! He who played hide-and-seek in my heart—He is now ever near. He is hiding behind the audacity of all "real" manifestations. He is there, waiting for you. There is no need for you to wade through suffering. Run to Him. The Most Beloved is waiting; His arms are open to receive you and spiritualize you and immortalize you. There is no tiger of death or disease chasing you except in the dream of ignorance.

Be true in your heart. Do not make a display of your devotion for God before others. Be sincere. Be concentrated, be adamant in your effort in meditation today, for the Almighty is with us.

"Father, Mother, Friend, Beloved God, we thank Thee from our hearts that instead of wasting time on frivolities we are here to worship Thee and to show our gratefulness."

[A period of meditation followed.]

"The voice of the heart is Thy voice, O God! In our expressions of devotion we hear the echo of Thy voice. Seek not an excuse in our past karma or in our restlessness to punish us with Thine absence. Come unto us, for we are naught else but Thy children. We demand Thy presence! Let this day of our communion with Thee be a beacon light on the pathway of life, to lead us into Thine everlasting life. Lord, God, Heavenly Father, do Thou crown our day with the glory of Thy presence, so that this day with Thee may stand out in contrast to the other 364 days of the year that are spent in almost

---

* See *Sri Sri Rajarsi Janakananda* in glossary.

complete absorption in materiality.

"Bless us, O Lord! that we begin to love Thee so much that every day we become newly intoxicated with Thee, so much that on those days when we become restless for the world we abhor that state of mind.

"O Divine Spirit! bless us that every day be lived in Thy consciousness. Whenever we lapse into material consciousness, make us restless for Thee. Reverse the trend of our lives so that when bad habits try to hold our attention on matter, our minds will fly instead to Thee. We are restless when we are concerned with the world of matter, but peaceful when with Thee. In ecstatic communion we are all one with Thee. Thou art our life and our love and all the sweetness that we seek. With all our deepest devotion we bow to Thee. Thou art the Master of our hearts. It is up to Thee to surrender Thyself unto us. Even though our devotion is not sufficient, be Thou touched nevertheless by the romance of our sincerity and determination. Reveal Thyself unto us all.

"May Thy love shine forever on the sanctuary of our devotion, and may we be able to awaken Thy love in all hearts. Heavenly Father, leave us not in the pit of temptation wherein we fell through misuse of Thy gift of reason."

Again and again plunge within. Again and again bathe in the celestial joy of this precious moment, that all your life may be a recurrence of this divine experience. "Heavenly Christ, especially on this day we invoke thy presence, thy consciousness; may thy love shine on the sanctuary of our devotion. Heavenly Father, may Thy consciousness descend on us, and with Christ and the Great Ones may we ascend in Thee forever and forever. *Aum. Aum. Aum.*"

[Meditation]

It was the great Babaji, in conjunction with Christ, who sent this work of Self-Realization Fellowship [Yogoda Satsanga Society of India] to the world. Christ came to bring his consciousness to all, and it has grieved him deeply to see mankind growing away from worshiping him in spirit. The compassionate love of Christ for all men is real; communion with him is real; yet these truths mean so little to most people, because they have lost the true spirit of Christmas by celebrating the birth of Christ primarily in material ways. What is the purpose of celebrating, if not to experience the birth of Christ Consciousness in ourselves? Just realize what that means! It is wrong to deviate from the purpose of Christmas, which is to worship Christ in spirit. It was Christ who inspired me to hold these long meditations a day or two before Christmas. Many people in this country are now following this observance, and I hope that in time every church and family that honors Christ will observe a pre-Christmas day of silence and meditation.

Silence is the altar of God. We must not only silence our thoughts; we must commune with Christ. Christ is everywhere present, within you and without—a resplendent light. The baby Christ is born in the cradle of our love. Think of this today. Make every day a new birth of Christ Consciousness in your life. Spread this message everywhere. I hope each one of you will sponsor this idea in your home and in every other home.

You minimize your power. Awaken souls who have closed their eyes to God. God's omniscience is within both the wise man and the man who has closed his eyes to the light. It is up to you to see that light in yourself by long, deep communion— by a continuous expression of your love to the Almighty.

As in watching an engrossing movie one easily forgets all else, so the lover of God forgets everything but the Beloved. The ordinary man doesn't have enough devotion to feel God's presence, because his mind is habitually on material things rather than on Divinity. If movies and sex and worldly pleasures can hold one's attention for hours, then think how engrossing must be communion with God, the most entertaining Being in the universe! The trouble is that most people don't *try* to know Him. If you know Him, hours slip away in the greatest divine intoxication. I find no joy in anything else, no matter what I am doing, unless God is with me. And when I am disgusted with this world, I shut the doors of the senses and commune with God alone. I find there is no comparison in the world with the happiness that comes when one closes his eyes to the world and steadily marches on to God's blessed kingdom.

It seems very simple to me. It seems very difficult to you only because you think that in the darkness behind closed eyes there is no variety or entertainment. All possible variety is there; you don't find it because you don't wait for it. But after you cross the threshold of the subconscious mind, you begin to feel a great superconscious joy that intoxicates mind and body and soul. In that state hours and hours pass and the devotee is not conscious of the world.

There is a smile for the world on many a face, but it loses its luster if there is not behind it the smile of God. I see the end of everything; I see that all human pleasures lead down blind alleys. God doesn't want to impose Himself on you. You must seek Him out. He has given you the love you feel in your heart, and you misuse it to tie yourself to a few other human beings, whom you think of as your own. You forget, in binding yourself to your own little family, that they will all be snatched away from you. It is God you are loving in them, and it is you He is loving through them. No one can love God who has not love for his family and friends; but he who loses himself in human love will lose God. It is He who loves us as father, mother, children, and friends. When we forget the purpose of this drama we punish ourselves by our own ignorance. Don't be deluded by worldly goals. Even though I am ambitious for the work of Self-Realization [Yogoda Satsanga], I am free in my heart, knowing that the drama is being performed at God's will.

I know He loves me and I love Him. I love Him more than anything else. There is nothing else at all that enthralls my attention. I have found God more tempting than any worldly temptation.

"Night and day there is one longing in my heart, O Lord! Let me do what Thou dost want me to do, not follow my ambitions nor my desires. Teach me to do everything that Thou dost want me to do to make this earth a perfect one; that all my thoughts may declare Thee; that all the works I have done may remind others of Thee."

So, dear ones, meditate morning and night. Don't waste your time. Once in a while let your mind run here and there, but don't be bound by attachment to anything. Shut yourself in seclusion and meditate. At first your mind will rebel against your will; but if you are in earnest, you will eventually find that nothing else can satisfy you as meditation does. What freedom I find when I close my eyes! The joy of God possesses me. This is something real that is in my heart. What more in the way of miracles do you want to see than the miracle of the human body and of the cosmic body of Nature that God has created? The human body-battery is not sustained by food, but by every word (wave of cosmic energy) that is flowing through the medulla and brain and heart from the Creator Lord. Go to the source and feel God, and so find within that great bubbling Spring of joy and life.

I met a saint in India who had sat for eighteen years in meditation, seeking God, before he found Him. But think what he gained! God for all time to come, for eternity! Some time each day, take yourself away from everything and meditate. The best time to be with God is nighttime. Never go to bed unless you have communed with Him. And all the time, no matter what is happening, say to Him, "Lord, I want Thee above everything else. Thou mayest tempt me with all things, but naught else do I want but Thy presence."

When you say this from your heart, God will respond. You will realize there is no use spending your time detecting your faults or the faults of others. No matter how Satan tries to take me away (and he does try, even after years of my following this path), I see that I have God. He is always in my heart. My faults may have been extreme, but my love for God has drowned my faults. I am completely free in my heart; not a desire stalks me there. I love Him more than anything else. And, if He so desires, I am ready to scrub floors to express my love for Him.

"My body, my heart, my mind, my soul I dedicate to Thee, O Lord. I don't mind what Thou dost with my body. The little time I am here, I am wholly Thine, O Lord. May every muscle dance with Thy joy; every blood corpuscle be tinged with the glory of Thy light. The taste of matter is as poison in my mouth; I drink of Thy nectar now. There is nothing to compare to this experience, O Lord! I dedicate my life, my thoughts, my desires unto Thee. I found my desires to be but blind alleys, leading to infinite disappointments; but I have learned the lesson that in desiring the things that Thou dost wish me to have, Beloved God, I find all-fulfillment. May Thy presence be manifest to all, even as I feel Thee—and much more, for Thou art boundlessly entertaining. Reveal Thyself unto all.

"We are not here, O Lord, just to pray or chant. We are not here to observe mechanically this day in Jesus' honor, but to give consciously, at Thy feet of omnipresence, the bouquet of our love. Receive the fragrant joy of our hearts. It is very little, but all the joys and the love for Thee that grow in the garden of our hearts belong to Thee. Receive what is Thine. We are Thine. Naughty or good, we are Thy children. Thou art bound by this love to manifest and express Thyself unto us. Thou must come to us. We are ever free in Thee.

"The aurora dancing in the heavens, the mountains, the glowing furnaces of flame in the sun and stars—all are but expressions of Thy grace and Thine omnipresence. O Spirit, as our hearts wax more and more ardent for Thee, as our hearts rumble like an earthquake in their yearning for Thee, we speed our souls, caged in these earthly bodies, on to Thy shores of eternity. Thou art ours. Why shouldst Thou hide from us? Bless us that we close the doors of the senses and love Thee where Thou dost love to remain, on the tear-washed altars of our souls. Father, Mother, Friend, Beloved God! naughty or good, we are Thy children; we want Thee. All our discouragements, all our weaknesses, all our bad habits cannot anymore intimidate us; for our love for Thee is greater. Destroy the grafts of habits on the tree of our eternal life. We pluck the orchid of human pleasures from the tree of life and lay it at Thy feet. Thou art the one joy we are seeking in all human activities. We long for the effulgence of Thy glory, the luminosity of Thy being."

[Meditation]

"Father, we thank Thee. May this day shine forth in our lives as a beacon of Thy grace, Thy glory, and Thy remembrance to give us light in the darkness of this incarnation. Father, may Thy Light illumine this day and guide us throughout this life; and through many lives to come, if we must return to this world. Father, Mother, Friend, Beloved God, receive the unctuous fervor of our souls. Accept the pure love and devotion of our souls. What more can we say but that we love Thee? Manifest Thy consciousness in us as it was manifest in Christ. We are grateful for Thy bestowal of joy and Christ Consciousness today. We thank Thee eternally."

Make New Determinations: Be What You Want to Be!

Self-Realization Fellowship International Headquarters, December 31, 1934

"Heavenly Father, as we enter the New Year, may we behold through its open portals Thy glory, Thine ideals. May we feel with us always Thy power, Thy vitality, and Thy guidance to follow of our own accord, by continuous right activity, the direct path that leads to Thee."

Make new determinations as to what you are going to do and what you are going to be in this next year. Set a program for yourself; carry it through, and you will find how much happier you will be. Failure to keep to your schedule of improvement means you have paralyzed your will. You have no greater friend and no greater enemy than yourself. If you befriend yourself, you will find accomplishment.* There is no law of God preventing you from being what you want to be and accomplishing what you want to accomplish. Nothing detrimental that happens can affect you unless you sanction it.

It is your will power that is going to determine what you are able to do—nothing else: not your past habits, not your past karma, not your horoscope. Consulting astrological charts gives authority and strength to your past karma. It weakens your will. God is your will. You must absolutely let no prejudice of doubt or despondency come between the power of your will and your life. Doubt is disastrous. It paralyzes the motive power of hope and destroys the will. If will power is impaired, you have ruined your engine of accomplishment. Faith can accomplish anything; doubt can destroy everything. Under no circum-

---

* "Let man uplift the self (ego) by the self; let the self not be self-degraded (cast down). Indeed, the self is its own friend; and the self is its own enemy" (Bhagavad Gita VI:5).

stances allow yourself to become the victim of doubt.

Let nothing weaken your conviction that you can be whatever you want to be. There is no one obstructing you unless it be yourself. Though my master Swami Sri Yukteswarji again and again told me that, it was hard to believe it at first. But as I used the God-given gift of will power in my life, I found it to be my savior. Not to use the will is to be inert like a stone, an inanimate object—an ineffectual human being.

The Power of Thought

So many people are not only physically lazy but mentally idle as well. Constructive thought will absolutely, like a great hidden searchlight, show you the pathway to success. There is always a way to be found if you think hard enough. People who give up after a little while bedim their power of thought. In order to gain your end, you must do your utmost to use thought until it is luminous enough to reveal to you the way to your goal.

The power of suggestion is very strong. The ability to accomplish is all in the mind. Your body itself is virtually sustained by thought. Food is only incidental; the main power sustaining you is your mind, your consciousness. It is thought that brings energy into the body. When thought is neutralized, the body feels weak and begins to decay.

God's thought is the essence of everything. It is living, it is infinite. Out of the Infinite Vastness, everything has been drawn. God pulls a thought out of His consciousness and that thought becomes a living being. He pulls out another thought and tells it to become a flower, and it becomes a certain kind of blossom; other thoughts become mountains, or gems, or stars.

Cast away all negative thoughts and fears. Remember that as a child of God you are endowed with the same potentialities as the most excellent among men. As souls, none is greater than another. Attune your will to be guided by the wisdom of God as expressed in the wisdom of the sages. If your will is yoked to wisdom, you can achieve anything. Fear inhibits progress. Whatever shall come, be prepared to face it; have the mental preparedness to go through any change without succumbing to the inertia caused by suffering. To face death itself should not daunt you. Fear of death is ridiculous, because as long as you are not dead you are alive, and when you are dead there is nothing more to worry about! It is something we all have to go through, so it couldn't be so bad. We are waves on the surface of the sea; and for a time in death our consciousness becomes enwrapped in the Infinite Oneness whence we came. It is nothing to regret, but rather a rest, a pension, from the travails of life—a promotion to a greater freedom.*

Retain evenness of mind under all circumstances. In every situation be calmly active and actively calm. Banish all disillusionment, all disappointments you might have found in losses and suffering. These constraints on the power of thought and will must absolutely be done away with. Your trials did not come to punish you, but to awaken you—to make you realize that you are a part of Spirit and that just behind the spark of your life is the Flame of Infinity; just behind the glimmer of your thoughts is the Great Light of God; just behind your discriminative reason is the omniscience of Spirit; just behind your love is the all-fulfilling love of God. If you would just realize that! Do not disconnect yourself from God. He did not make anyone more privileged than another. All are made alike in His image; but not all reflect equally His Divine Light, due to their desires and bad habits. Your fulfillment lies not in obtaining the objects of your desire, but in the unfoldment of your soul qualities in making the effort to succeed in worthwhile endeavors. There is nothing to prevent you from feeling that great Power behind your life. It is your bad habits that tell you otherwise.

Bad Habits Are Your Worst Enemies

Bad habits are the worst enemies you can have. You are punished by those habits. They make you do things you do not want to do, and leave you to suffer the consequences. You must drop bad habits and leave them behind you as you move forward. Every day should be a transition from old habits to better habits. In this coming year make a solemn resolution to keep only those habits that are for your highest good.

The best way to get rid of your undesirable tendencies is not

---

* See *astral world* in glossary.

(*Left*) The author with the President of Mexico, Dr. Emilio Portes Gil, who was a great admirer of Sri Yogananda and his teachings, Mexico City, 1929. (*Right*) Greeting India's Ambassador to the U.S. Binay R. Sen, Madame Sen, and Consul General M. R. Ahuja; SRF International Headquarters, March 4, 1952.

Life is absolutely so ruthless; it makes a mockery of your self-imposed duties. Your engagements and striving to satisfy desires, even worthy ones, are canceled instantly when death comes. Why should you give so much importance to life? Nevertheless, you do have to keep busy just the same; but do not forget that this life is just a play. You must play well, but with the thought of God. Do your duties because you want to please God. Flying away from your dutiful activities will not save you, because that is not His plan. He Himself is eternally busy running His universe for our benefit. Nothing could be created or accomplished by anybody unless it was first born in the mind of God. We are only His instruments empowered to innovate changes and modifications for the betterment of ourselves and others. Use your God-given creative ability; that is the basis of success. Whatever has been done, try to improve upon it. The man of creative ability is among God's best instruments. He makes improvements on himself and on what evolution has thus far given to his earthly environment. God moves through such willing innovators.

Be active and use your will power and reason, all the time thinking that just behind your life is God's life, just behind your will is God's will. To find out what the Lord's will is, use your reason; don't just sit by and wait for things to come your way. Use your will; but ask God to guide you, and believe in His guidance. All around you, in so many ways, you will find conscious guidance. You won't have to worry anymore. Whatever part is given to you, if you do your best, that is all that matters.

All Roles Are Necessary in God's Drama

Be satisfied with your part. Do not bemoan your fate. In this life everyone has troubles which he thinks nobody else has. Never wish to be in the shoes of someone else who you think is better off than you are. It is best to wish for nothing, but to ask the Lord to give you what is for your highest good. You are a part of the Lord's creation; He needs everybody to carry on this drama. Never compare yourself with anybody else. You are what you are. Nobody is like you. Nobody can act your part as you can. Similarly, you should not try to play somebody else's part. What is important is to do the will of Him who sent you; that is what you want. While you do your part, think all the time that God is working through you.

Do not limit yourself with the narrowness of selfishness. Include others in your achievements and happiness, then you are doing the will of God. Whenever you think of yourself, think also of others. When you think of seeking peace, think of others who are in need of peace. If you do your utmost to make others happy, you will find that you are pleasing the Father.

To live in harmony, to live with strong will power to do the will of Him who sent you, is all you should be interested in. Never lose courage, and always be smiling. Have the smile of the heart and the smile of the face completely in harmony. If your body, mind, and soul register the smile of the inner consciousness of God, you can scatter smiles about you wherever you go.

The Joy of Meditation Is Your Best Company

Be always with people who inspire you; surround yourself with people who lift you up. Do not let your resolutions and positive thinking be poisoned by bad company. Even if you cannot find good company to inspire you, you can find it in meditation. The best company you can have is the joy of meditation. You sleep six or eight hours, and you don't feel that is difficult to do; you enjoy it because you are partially conscious of inner peace and joy. But when you are in meditation, you feel consciously the joy glimpsed in sleep. That joy is so much greater; hours slip away and you don't know it. That land of joy is just behind the subconsciousness of dreamland. In that state you realize: "I am not the ego; I have feeling, but I am not the feelings; I reason, but I am not the intellect; I have a body, but I am the Spirit."

Your devotion, like a plummet, must go deeper and deeper into the sea of divine perception. Those whose eyes of inner sight are opened in meditation will perceive the Presence of God right here, in the heart. As long as there will be a demon dance of restlessness and desires in the temple of the body, the Father will be away. But when there is persistence in devotion in calling to Him, He will come, just as a mother responds to the insistent crying of her infant. First, in the temple of silence He comes as peace. If you go deeper, then in the temple of *samadhi,* or Oneness, you meet Him, and touch Him, and feel His bliss within you and in omnipresence. Without the internal perception of God, it is very difficult to love Him. But when that Supreme Happiness permeates your thoughts and your whole being, you cannot help loving Him.

Life Is Filled With the Unseen Divine Presence

Your cup of life within and without is filled with the Divine Presence, but because of the lack of attention you do not perceive God's immanence. When you are in tune, as one tunes in a radio, then you receive Spirit. It is as if you take a bottle of sea water, cork it, and put it in the ocean; although the bottle floats in the waters, its contents do not mix with its oceanic surroundings. But open the bottle, and the water inside merges with the sea. We must remove the cork of ignorance before we can come in contact with Spirit.

Infinity is our Home. We are just sojourning awhile in the caravanserai of the body. Those who are drunk with delusion have forgotten how to follow the trail that leads to God. But when in meditation the Divine gets hold of the prodigal child, there is no dallying anymore.

Enter the portals of the New Year with new hope. Remember you are a child of God. It lies with you as to what you are going to be. Be proud that you are a child of God. What have you to fear? No matter what comes, believe it is the Lord who is sending that to you; and you must succeed in conquering those daily challenges. Therein lies your victory. Do His will; nothing can hurt you then. He loves you everlastingly. Think that. Believe that. *Know* that. And suddenly one day you will find you are immortally alive in God.

Meditate more and believe in that strong consciousness that God is always with you regardless of what happens. Then you will see that the veil of delusion will be taken away and you will be one with That which is God. That is how I found my greatest happiness in life. I am not looking for anything now because I have everything in Him. Never would I part with That which is the richest of all possessions.

This is my message to you for the New Year.

"Thy Love Alone Suffices"

An Evening of Divine Communion

A Thursday evening service led by Paramahansaji at Self-Realization Fellowship International Headquarters (Mt. Washington), shortly after his return from a year-long visit to India; December 6, 1936

"Beloved God and great Gurus, may Thine infinite grace bless this institution of Self-Realization Fellowship [Yogoda Satsanga Society of India], that it ever be as I have always wanted—as ordained by Thee.

"Heavenly Father, bless the child of my heart, St. Lynn. I thank Thee for sending to me such a soul to call my own, to represent Thee and Thy truth. I thank Thee also for all the wonderful souls who have come here to dedicate their lives, and for all those who will come in search of Thee. Manifest Thy Life in their lives. Bless us that through our love for Thee we make Mt. Washington a heaven on earth; and that in serving Thee we desire not our glory but Thine, O Father. May a portable heaven be established in the breast of each one who comes here to seek Thee. Mt. Washington, thou art hallowed by the beloved ones here. May this place bring forth those who love God.

"O Supreme Spirit, Father, Mother, Friend, Beloved God, we offer our unconditional devotion to Thee. May we love Thee with the love of all saints. Thou art the Fountain of all droplets of manifestation: the Power that creates the stars, the Vitality that sustains all creation and nurtures all life, the Beauty that makes all things beautiful, the Love that makes all hearts feel love. Thou art the Fountain of ever new joy, which gushes forth in sparkling display in the soul temples of all Thy meditative devotees. With my heart, my soul, my intelligence, mind, and devotion, I pray—I demand as Thy son—Thy presence amidst us. Naught else shall satisfy our hearts.

"I was never so happy as I am now, O Lord, because so many souls are calling unto Thee. I seek no power, no disciples, but only Thy love, O Spirit. Naught else shall occupy my heart. There is no room for anything but Thee. No more with words do I pray, but with my love, my heart, my soul.

"Divine Mother, last night Thou didst ask me what I want. Nothing do I crave but Thy love in my heart, and Thy love in those who love me and who seek Thee. That is all.

"Divine Spirit, hallowed be Thy kingdom which is within. With all the devotion of our beings we invoke Thee. Manifest Thy consciousness in us. Leave us not in the pit of temptation into which we fell through the misuse of Thy given reason. When we are stronger, if it is Thy will to test us, Father, make Thyself more tempting than temptation. On the balance scale of my mind I weighed Thee against all things else, and found Thee to be infinitely more attractive, more beautiful, more charming. Naught can compare with Thy matchless beauty. Before Thy beauty, all other enticements pale.

"O Prince Charmer, reveal Thyself unto us. Throughout all pathways of our lives, bless us, Thy devotees, that we be not deluded even for a moment to settle for anything less than Thy love in our hearts. Thou art our true Beloved. Such joy, such bliss; glories eternal. Where is desire, where is separation? They fade away before the brilliance of Thine ever new joy.

"O Spirit, what can match Thy love! Beloved of my heart, Beloved of all hearts, Lord of lords, God of gods, Father, Mother, Friend, Beloved God, Thy glory is great. I shun everything that does not remind me of Thee; I welcome everything that reflects Thee. O Spirit Divine, Thou hast brought Thy devotees here. No words shall I preach, but rather give to them Thy love with the bouquet of my heart.

"Spirit Divine, permeate our hearts with Thy glory, fill our souls with Thy spirit. Be Thou established within us forever. Thou alone, O Spirit, Thou alone. We bow to Thee again and again; we offer our love at Thy roseate feet. With Thy joy, O Spirit, pull our consciousness within. Absorb in Thy cosmic joy the distracting sensations of the flesh. Delude us not with the little body when Thy joy is waiting right behind the veil of silence. With Thy help we will tear the veil. Delude us no more with Thy cosmic delusion, but fill us with Thy love, that we may realize Thou art the One, the only One, we seek.

"All ambitions I lay at Thy feet, O Mighty Divine. Thy love alone suffices. Take even my life this instant if it is Thy wish. I want naught else but Thee, only Thee. In the hearts of Thy devotees I shall commune with Thee. I will waste no time, but use each moment to taste Thy name impressed in the consciousness of all hearts that love Thee. That is what I want— Thou who art the eternal Treasure of heaven. What more could I desire than the glory of Thy Spirit?

"O Spirit Divine, with my life, with my mind, with all the wisdom and perception I receive from Thee and from my beloved Guru, I take again and again this solemn vow in my heart: eternal allegiance to Thee, and all my love to the devotees who love Thee. Spirit, be with us, be with us. Such joy, such joy; oh, blessedness of Spirit, oh, blessedness of Thy glory! What shall I speak but of Thy love? Nay, fill our hearts with Thy love. That is all I want.

"O Infinite Lord, Thou art the illimitable sky; I am a drop of the sky. [Paramahansaji chants:] 'I am the sky, Mother, I am the sky....I am a little drop of the sky, frozen sky.'"*

The sky, infinite space, cannot be limited or hurt by anything; we are a droplet of that Infinity, a little nest cradling the omnipresent Spirit.

[Here Paramahansaji entered blissful *samadhi*. After a period of interiorized communion, he addressed the gathering of devotees:]

Never take the name of God in vain. When you sing to Him, feel what you are singing, and then sing what you are feeling. The God of heaven, the God of the clouds and stars, the God of gods, the God of the millions of souls that are come and those who are gone, the God of all devotees—to that Lord Eternal we give our undying allegiance. Why speak of Him with the dryness of words and from the limitation of thoughts? We shall feel Him in the temple of meditation, where He longs to come to us.

---

* From "I Am the Sky" in *Words of Cosmic Chants* by Paramahansa Yogananda.

As the ocean is just beneath the wave, so the ocean of Spirit is just beneath the wave of the body. In sleep you are not the body; you have no body. When you wake up, you limit yourself to the delusion of the flesh, but when you close your eyes you can feel your consciousness unbounded.

I see this little body as frozen sky; and as I meditate, the body becomes the vast sky, swept up in the infinitude of God. *Frozen sky* means frozen fancy, frozen imagination, as the images in a dream. In dreams you see people born and laugh and die, but when you wake up everything is gone. Similarly, this body is a condensation of the vastness of space. But that is not how it appears to you. When you are awake in ordinary consciousness, the body and its circumscriptions seem real, but you are actually dreaming. When you will forsake the dream of delusion in the true wakefulness of meditation, you will realize that your earthly experiences were frozen thoughts of God. Dreams in subconscious sleep are our own frozen thoughts, and we are the frozen dream-thoughts of God. To get out of this dream, you must wake up in Him. That wakefulness is reality. That is what I see every minute, every second; that consciousness remains always with me.

I am telling you these things as I am feeling them within. I don't want to lecture anymore. Divine Mother says, "Only drink My love with devotees." That is all I want to do. I have no other desire. Those who would come to me, come with that spirit.

Some of India's greatest teachers spoke very little. They taught their followers rather to go within and *feel*, and then asked them to explain what they experienced. Modern religion, on the contrary, stresses emotionalism or intellectual exposition. These do not give the seeker a real experience of God. Thirst for God is such that it can be satisfied by nothing less than God Himself.

In this ever-changing, uncertain world, you often feel very lonely. God alone will never disappoint you. Your joy in all other things grows stale, and you want something else. But God is That which, when you have Him, you want Him more and more.

The only real sermon is the contact of God—that great

power of God which is vibrating throughout this hall. It is very sacred. That is why I don't want to draw curiosity seekers with my words. I want only to give His love to thirsty souls everywhere. The glories of the masters have to be revived. They used to sit in the forest in divine communion—no talking, no trying to build a following—surrounded by true souls attracted by the magnetism of God-love. In the fields and among the trees, there God's light descends. Imagine! What joy! What glory! A place of divine communion—that is what Mount Washington is going to be. Day and night we shall drink His name. In this way we must seek Him, feel Him, and speak of Him, that those who come here may go away singing, feeling, and talking God.

Divine Mother came here. I talked to Her! "O Mother Divine, naught else do I want but communion with Thy consciousness, Thy glory, Thy power. Bless us, each one of us, that we may feel Thee and talk of Thee from the realization of our souls as we work to bring others away from the net of Satan.

"Father, Mother, Friend, Beloved God, awaken in all souls this love that I feel. Let there be no other desire, no other ambition but to receive and express Thy joy, Thy wisdom, Thy beauty eternal. We live, move, and have our being in Thee, O Lord. This body is worthwhile if on the soil of flesh, mind, and soul we sow the seeds of Thy love and reap the harvest of Thy bliss.

"Bless St. Lynn, again and again, that he carry on when I shall be gone. Never have I found anyone more honest, sincere, and prideless. May he ever be that way. No matter where he is, he shall be protected. May he live by the love of the Divine Spirit. May his life bear the testimony of my life.

"Mother Divine, the light of Thy love is eclipsed for a little while by the evils of the world. But we shall make manifest Thy love, that as a luminous divine flood it may burn darkness evermore. I feel Thy great power. With the cannons of Thy power we can destroy the world's evils; but Divine Mother, Thy greater power is the power of love. It is that power we shall have to establish to remove the wars and troubles that come upon the world. I feel the agony of the world, and I shall come on earth again and again to save Thy children.

"Bless us, Beloved God, that as a devoted band of Thy messengers we may traverse the earth to praise Thee and to spread Thy name and Thy glory—seeking all the while not the recognition of man, but Thy recognition, O Spirit.

"I want naught but to be with those who love Thee. I want to drink Thy name with Thy devotees. Come unto me, O Beloved, Thou first and last love of my heart. Let all feel Thy love and Thy glory that they may forsake all things, all fanciful dreams, and be filled with Thy love. Of naught else can I speak, but of Thy love, Thy joy! Instill in us the unceasing perception of Thy love, and the urgency of communing with Thee now. Teach us to forsake everything that keeps us from Thee.

"Thou alone art eternal and the only Reality. All things are enlivened and empowered by Thee. Thou art my food, my sleep, my strength, my joy. Oh, what freedom; what joy! Free all, as Thou hast freed me! Blessed art Thou who hast brought this joy to me.

Now pray with me, and let the yearning of your soul be behind your words: "Heavenly Father, Mother, Friend, Beloved God, I offer unto Thee the cries of my soul. Forgive my wanderings in the land of matter. Be with me now and forever, that I may feel unceasingly Thy blessed presence. I have not to acquire Thee, for Thou art already mine throughout eternity. Only bless me to revive my memory of Thy presence, the memory of my eternal possession of Thee. *Aum, Aum,* Amen."

Be a Conqueror of Hearts

*An informal talk to ashram residents and other members
at Self-Realization Fellowship International Headquarters,
Los Angeles, November 3, 1938*

If we look at life impersonally, we find it to be wonderful. We see it as a show; every day a different moving picture. We would not like to see the same film over and over again; it would be pointlessly monotonous. If life did not have its ups and downs, its victories and hard knocks, it would hardly be worthwhile. Only do not take it too seriously, for then it becomes extremely miserable. If you want to attain the unchangeable, imperturbable state of Spirit, be thou always of even mind. "O Arjuna! The relativities of existence have been overcome, even here in this world, by those of fixed equal-mindedness. Thereby are they enthroned in Spirit—verily, the taintless, the perfectly balanced Spirit."*

Personal desires are like an acid that corrodes the peace of our souls. Sometimes everything is going along nicely and we think the world and our place in it is all right; but then a time comes when everything seems to go against us. That is a lesson given to strengthen us, to bring out our hidden powers. But instead, the contradiction of desires causes anger. When desires are thwarted and we are caught in the paroxysm of anger, the mind becomes befogged and we forget our position and lose our discrimination; and when we act without discrimination, errors and unhappiness follow.† If you never get angry at life's

---

* Bhagavad Gita V:19.

† "Brooding on sense objects causes attachment to them. Attachment breeds craving; craving breeds anger. Anger breeds delusion; delusion breeds loss of memory (of the Self). Loss of right memory causes decay of the discriminating faculty. From decay of discrimination, annihilation (of spiritual life) follows" (Bhagavad Gita II:62–63).

reverses, or at their human instigators, you can see your way more clearly through whatever is going on around you.

That is why your peace is to be guarded above everything else. If you can retain your inner peace, therein lies your supreme victory. No matter how you are situated in life, never feel justified in losing your peace. When that is gone and you cannot think clearly, you have lost the battle. If you never lose your peace, you will find you are always victorious, no matter what the outcome of your problems. That is the way to conquer life. You have nothing to fear. If you have to be afraid at all, be afraid only of yourself. But if you do everything with sincerity and love in your heart, you do not have to fear anybody or anything. As you find your soul-reservoir of peace, less and less controversy will be able to afflict your life.

One who loves God lives in the soul, his true Self. He does everything for God, nothing for himself. He loves everybody, because he sees the world as the Lord's cosmic show. He can never be provoked to say or do anything in anger or with egotism, but only with desire to be of help to all. That is the attitude you must have. It has to be lived. It cannot come by any amount of pretense, but only when you see God in everyone—when you love everybody as a part of your love for God.

With each one of you that I am working for I feel that same tie that you feel with your families—I feel the same sense of oneness with all humanity as you feel with your closest relatives. No one can describe that feeling. When it comes, that is when you begin to understand the meaning and beauty of life.

Love People, but Not Their Faults

If you love God and therefore love everybody, that does not mean that you love the faults in people. Loving God makes you unwavering in His principles. When I knew for certain that I was only working for God alone, then the consciousness and the fear that I might be wrong in my convictions left me. I am ready to be corrected any time if I am wrong; but if I am right, the inner feeling never leaves me. It is not born of sentiment but of truth; and in that I stand firm.

Unshakable happiness in God is the right foundation of all activities, of everything you do. The man who wants to receive that secure understanding from God must be able to lay down his head at the feet of everyone; and yet also be prepared to stand resolute in truth, anchored in the happiness and assurance of God.

In the temple of the soul is the most beautiful perfect presence of God. Those who have complete love for God, who are floating in the love of God, can see His wonderful presence in all; but at the same time, they can see the blindness of those persons whose eyes are closed in error and ignorance. The lover of God thus sees both the darkness and the light in others. For example, there is a magnificent temple: those whose eyes are open see the beauty; but those who keep their eyes closed see not the temple but darkness. So it is that great souls are able to see God's glorious presence in all soul temples; but with that same light they see those who are stumbling in darkness because their eyes are closed.

I never wanted to be a teacher. I observed that that status often gives one the consciousness of knowing much when he knows very little. It was only when Master [Swami Sri Yukteswar] said to me, "You would not have received this wisdom if I had not given it to you," that I dedicated my life to teaching. As my Master gave this truth to me, so did he encourage me to give it unselfishly to others.

If you would be a teacher, you must be sincere. Whatever you say, you must feel from within. If you are upright and honest, your spirit can never be bribed to deviate from God's principles. You cannot be unkind because you are not activated by egotism or anger. What you do, you do with the utmost sincerity. Behave in that way—whether you are teaching from the pulpit or by the life you live—and see what happens to transform your life and the lives of those you seek to help. Be sincere and fearless in truth from this moment on. Wherever you go, let the Lord, not your ego, speak through you. You do not have to be shrewd with people; you have to be genuine. If you are genuine, everyone who is sincere will be harmonious with you— you will receive genuine feeling from them. If you approach others not with the attitude of bossing or anger but with sincere love, there are very few people who will misunderstand you. And God help them who misunderstand you, because by their own actions they place themselves in awkward situations.

If one loves the Father of all, and if he has the slightest thought of revenge toward anyone or desire to punish anyone, he falls a million miles away from God. One who loves God dares not entertain thoughts of doing injury to anyone. It would be wrong, of course, to support anyone blindly. But nonsupport of the wrongdoing in others does not mean that anyone should vengefully hurt others. A philosopher once said: "The best sort of revenge is not to be like him who did the injury." We should have respect for others' opinions as we wish others to respect our opinions; there is no room for ugliness. We should lovingly disagree as well as lovingly agree.

Judge Yourself Before God and Your Conscience

It is easy to be a master in words, but it requires a tremendous amount of strength to be a master living with people. Everyone sees and judges you according to his own mind. Years ago there was a young boy who traveled with us on a lecture tour from the East Coast to Los Angeles. He went out of his way to criticize everything. Before lecture time I used to comb my long hair. He was always analyzing me, but he didn't know that I had my mental camera on him also. After two weeks I said to him, "I would like to have a chat with you. What have you been writing about me in your letters?" He looked startled and said, "Someone has been opening my letters." I said, "Then you admit it. Since I knew you were doing so, I wanted to give you something to write about, so I have taken special pains to stand before the mirror and exaggerate the combing of my hair." He was ashamed.

What you are before God and your own conscience, that is what you are. Even if the whole world misunderstands you, nothing is lost; you are what you are. To stand criticism is a very effective way of becoming a better individual. Though it is easier to criticize others than to find fault in yourself, it is of prime importance to correct yourself first. I learned from Master to pick myself to pieces when criticized. If I find any flaw there, I correct myself; and when I do not find anything, I smile.

Conviction of truth is the paramount factor in satisfying your soul; never surrender or compromise that. When somebody criticizes or contradicts just to satisfy an egotistical desire to appear superior or dominant, that is wrong. Intelligent people can quickly find a level of agreement because they have a sympathetic attitude. My Master had such awesome wisdom that I used to enjoy engaging him in controversial discussions. When my understanding was faulty, he stood firm on his points. Sometime later I would understand and see where I was wrong. When your vision is guided by Divine Power, you do not swerve at all. You always feel the guiding hand of Spirit. That is the attunement you want to maintain in your life. Be fearless, sincere, and loving and you will be able to look everyone in the face, knowing that you have done your best, sincerely. If you want to prove to somebody your sincerity, let your actions speak for you.

God sends to you those experiences you need, that you might profit by them. If you run away from those lessons, you will still have to learn them sometime, somewhere else. Every experience is a good teacher if you learn from it; but it is a tyrant if you abuse that opportunity with resentment and nonunderstanding. With right attitude, life is very simple and very easy.

Only Spiritual Relationships Are Lasting

I hope all of you will understand my words. I have given myself entirely to God; and whatever He says to me I tell you. I believe that whatever God gives me has some practical value, and that it applies to all those who are near and dear to me. As I have said, I have no relatives. Each one of you who loves God is my own. The nature-ordained compulsion of the familial relationship is misleading; but the spiritual relationship is lasting, because God is our Father and we are His children. A mother loves her child now; but if that child dies and is reborn next door to her, she won't recognize that child in the same way. But the spiritual relationship is the strongest bond because it is continuous from one lifetime to another.

In the ultimate sense, as we are all the children of God we must learn to love everyone wholeheartedly and completely and impartially. I remember when my Master asked me, "Do you love everybody equally?" I said, "Yes." But he said, "Not yet, not yet." Then my youngest brother came to study in my school at Ranchi,* and I had that consciousness that he was mine. I realized then why my Master had said, "Not yet." Gradually that consciousness wore off, and I realized that my brother was but a part of all humanity which I loved. That is not an insensitive, inhuman attitude. You love all alike, as God does. Then you learn to do for others as you would do for your own. One day, again, Master asked me, "Do you love the whole world?" I just said, "I love." And he smiled and said, "Your work is finished."

It was the greatest joy when I went back to India in 1935–36 and found that my love for the land of my birth was not narrow, but that I felt that same love for all nations. When years earlier I was leaving my family home to follow this path, my father, who was the dearest to me after my mother's death, said, "Who will look after your brothers and sisters if I die?" I said, "Father, I love you more than anyone in the world; but He who has given you to me, I love greatest of all. I could not have appreciated you, nor could you appreciate me, if it were not for God. Someday, when I come to you with that Father's consciousness throbbing in my bosom, you will feel more that I was worthy of your love."

God's love is the supreme love. There is no love greater than that. The love that is born of instinct has its defects because it is compelled. That is why I sang to God as Divine Mother, "In this world, Mother, no one can love me; in this world they do not know how to love me."† Only the divine love of great ones is born of wisdom. That love is infinitely greater than parental or any other form of human love—Jesus gave up his life for the world.

Who cares for my soul but God and my Master. It was Master who guarded me always—guarded me from ignorance, actuated only by love. He showed infinite love to give me wisdom. I can see those eyes in which there was naught else than the Supreme Love.

---

* Yogoda Satsanga Vidyalaya, founded by Paramahansa Yogananda in 1918. (See *Ranchi school* in glossary.)

† From "Where Is There Love?" in *Words of Cosmic Chants* by Paramahansa Yogananda: "In this world, Mother, no one can love me. In this world they do not know how to love me. Where is there pure loving love? Where is there truly loving me? There my soul longs to be." Published by Yogoda Satsanga Society of India.

It is God who is loving us through our loved ones; there-fore, we should be all the more grateful to God who gives us a good mother and father, and good friends, and a guru who wants for us only our highest good. The love of the mother is close to the perfection of God's love, because she loves us when nobody else does; and she forgives when we are in error. But the ultimate expression of God's love is the love of a true guru. He loves us unconditionally; and out of that sublime love he instructs and disciplines us for the everlasting welfare of our souls. Though I shall always dearly love my mother, my love for my Master is supreme.

Real Love Versus Selfish Love

Do everything with the attitude of love—love for God and for God in all. It is hard for the ordinary person to tell the dif-ference between a desire for others' good and a desire to sat-isfy self-love. Often one who is well-intentioned in caring for others is carried away instead by self-love. When the desire for self-interest is gone completely from the consciousness, and the only desire is to serve others and do the highest good for all, that is wisdom. It is very difficult to do; but when selfish love completely goes, then one tastes divine love.

Real love is when you are constantly watching the prog-ress of the soul. As soon as you cater to someone's physical desires and bad habits you are not loving that soul anymore. You are just pleasing that person to avoid ill will. No matter how unpleasant it is to tell a friend that he is wrong, if you say it with love in your heart and stand firm on it, sometime that person will respect you if you are right. If you are wrong, even then he will know that you did it with sincerity, out of love. Never agree with anyone who is wrong, not even those who are nearest and dearest to you. To agree with wrongdoing is to bribe your soul in order to be looked upon favorably by the wrongdoer, and that will come out later on in some disastrous results. Do not fight; that is not the way to convince them. The way to influence others is by your love. Say what you have to say once or twice and then disband it from your mind. Be humble and free from anger. Just say, "Let us wait and see. Time will tell." Time brings out everything; and if there is a sympathetic understanding between friends, there will be no "I was right and you were wrong" attitude.

So this is my prayer to you, that all of you learn how to be true friends, how to be truly loving souls. If you have that divine attitude, you will be conquerors of hearts. There is nothing more satisfying than that. You will never be alone, for you will attract to yourself real souls. Even if you are left alone, you are with God.

You do not know how wonderful is that kind of love. It is sublime. At times you glimpse it when you are very happy and feel that oneness with God in others—when you love each other because God is your Father, irrespective of any human relation.

Attachment Cannot Form a Spiritual Bond; Love Can

We are gathered here to travel together for a little while. Then in diverse directions we have to go; but if we have divine love in our souls, no matter where we go we shall meet again in the kingdom of the Lord. We can never remain apart; we will be drawn to one another again. Attachment cannot form this spiritual bond; love can. Nature is dancing this *danse macabre,* the dance of death. Love outlasts death and the ravages of time. All those that I have loved before, in this or other lifetimes, I love the same now.

Attachment is disastrous, because it is that which is compulsive and limiting. As soon as a child is born the mother falls in love with it. That feeling is impressed on the mother by nature, otherwise she would not take care of the helpless infant. The compulsion to love our family members was given to us as our first lesson in learning to give love to all, unconditionally. But attachment spoils family love, and all forms of human relationships, because it excludes others and is blindly possessive. Disband attachment and learn to give true, sincere love to all. True love is impersonal and is not bound by anything. Our eyes bubble over with love, and we feel a wonderful togetherness; we feel we are one. Once in a while that is felt in ordinary life, but then it is so easily mutilated by familiarity and lack of respect.

We must learn to love our family purely, to love our friends purely, to love our country purely, and to love all mankind purely. Patriotism is wonderful; but if it leads to aggression, then it is wrong. Patriotic egotism is bad. Nations should beware of egotism. How many such nations have been destroyed by God. India was one of the greatest nations in the world. Karmically, her wealth and power were broken by foreign domination when under the influence of egotism the upper classes said, "We are Aryans," and began to exclude and demean others in the demarcations of the caste system.* But India will regain her former status because of her spirituality.

The perfected love of family, the perfected love of friends, the perfected love of nations, the perfected love of all mankind—that is the love of God, when impartially you are ready to live and to die for all. That is the reason I take this interest in all of you. As I enjoy God in Encinitas, He has made me feel that I have been neglectful of you.† It is that sense of spiritual duty, born of my love for God and for you all, that has brought me here to you. I have no other desire but the desire for God, and no other ambition than the ambition to work for God.

It is God who has brought us together. It is the greatest opportunity that anyone could have—to be able to serve God. When we will be gone from this earth, many souls shall come and feel our vibrations here. Whenever we leave good vibrations behind, we leave a part of our eternal lives. Shakespeare is gone, Lincoln is gone, but they have left some immortal part of their lives here. So have my Master and *Paramgurus.*‡ As long as the name of this earth shall last, vibrations left by great souls shall last; and whenever this earth shall go, that record shall rest in the bosom of the Father.

So shall we leave "footprints in the sands of time"—spiritual footprints of good vibrations, which those who come after us will feel. If we increase those vibrations by our love for God and service to His work, think how wonderful will be what we leave behind us.

---

* See *caste* in glossary.

† Since his return from India in 1936, Paramahansaji had been spending much time at the Self-Realization Fellowship Hermitage in Encinitas, where he could work on his writings in relative seclusion.

‡ See glossary.

Cooperate With One Another for the Good of All

In an institution the law of freedom depends on a common law. In a community—be it a hermitage, a meditation center, a family, a business—everyone should sacrifice his own desires and egoity for the good of all. When you are together, the laws of doing things together should be respected. It is not a question of who is greater or lesser—the ideal is to cooperate with one another. In this I hope you will do your part. To be able to follow the common laws of an institution is the way to create strength and harmony.

The opinion of God is written on the parchment of eternity, and it shall never be erased, not for all time to come. Try first and foremost to please God, then man. To try to please man is also pleasing to God, but your effort to please man must be with wisdom. Try not to displease people, but think always of your duty to God first.

It is so wonderful to be good and to be humble. Egotism repulses; humility attracts. When man behaves in a humble way, he strikes a beautiful chord in the hearts of others. A man of humility easily exercises a spiritual influence on others. Such a one has the satisfaction that he has done his best on this earth. That is what the avatar King Rama said: "I am Rama whose throne is the hearts of all." Those who reign in true hearts, they are the real kings. No one can feel egotism if God is in the heart. The more humble you are, the stronger you will be in Spirit.

As Self-Realization [Yogoda Satsanga] is marching on, I hope all of you will always say in your hearts, "Where is there pure loving love?" The power of love is the greatest of all powers. No power of authority is greater than that. Love can conquer all. There is so much love and understanding here. Sister Gyanamata* and Saint Lynn are most understanding, more than I have ever seen. Sister, unasked, quietly moves out of her room when guests come so that they will have a place to stay; she

---

* Sri Gyanamata ("Mother of Wisdom") was one of the first *sannyasinis* of Yogoda Satsanga Society of India/Self-Realization Fellowship. Paramahansa Yogananda often praised her saintly spiritual stature. Her life and inspiring spiritual counsel is presented in *God Alone: The Life and Letters of a Saint* (published by Yogoda Satsanga Society of India).

sleeps in the laundry room. If we all have God's love in our hearts, we shall one day reach that land where all the screens of misunderstandings will be gone—when our souls and our thoughts shall be crystal clear.

We came on earth to love each other with God's perfect love, free from any selfish desires. We all feel that way sometimes, but then it is taken away by Satan. Satan is inharmony and misunderstanding. God is Love and Love is God. Do not take it too seriously if anyone says unkind things about you. Just give love in return. Whoever does not understand you, just look at that person with love in your eyes, love that is born of complete understanding, and you will see how that person changes.

"Whatever I Have Said, I Have Said From My Heart"

What I say is not merely words, but what I feel for all of you. It would be the easiest thing to remain silent, or to go away and live under a tree with God alone. If ever I have offended through ignorance, I ask your forgiveness. My conscience is clear. I have nothing to fear. Whatever I have said, I have said from my heart. If you follow, you shall please God; and if you do not, it shall grieve God. But nothing you could do could cause me to feel anger toward you, because I have no desire of my own; my only desire is to please God and serve you all for your own sake.

Let us pray: "Heavenly Father, give us true love for all; and help us especially to practice that love with sincerity toward one another. Let us feel and manifest that love that we may enjoy eternity with all liberated souls, for Thou, O God, art that Love."

The Lord gave me a vision of the entire world, just now as I am talking to you. He said, "I love all and have given freedom to all to cast Me away or accept Me. If they follow My wishes or go against Me, still I love them all. Though I gave the world My love, heedlessly they are destroying one another with hatred, killing each other with bombs—still I love them all. They shall feel My love if they seek it in the temples of hearts. This love I have for all nations and all civilizations, irrespective of their wrongdoings, is the love thou must have—that thou mayest be able to feel and understand My love for all." This is the message of the Lord to you. He loves us all regardless of our wrong and evil actions—though the hurt we do to ourselves by bad actions saddens Him. If we would be God's true children, we must become unconditionally loving like Him.

So everything that you do, do for God. As long as you live, spread truth and love—be like little children, unafraid, simple, and kind. Never mind how others behave. There was a time when I felt some resentment, some hurt, if anybody slapped my hand when I raised it to help them; but I feel that no more. My heart is brimful with love for God and His tremendous love for all.

How to Quicken
Your Spiritual Progress

Self-Realization Fellowship Hermitage,
Encinitas, California, August 22, 1943

The path to God has been described as being only as broad as a razor's edge—and sometimes it is also as sharp. If by free choice one walks that narrow path with single-heartedness, and doesn't flinch or give up because of its incisiveness, he will reach God. It sounds difficult; but I maintain that the path is very simple if one makes up his mind to go all the way for the love of God. Whosoever loves God can never think of turning back.

Though the right attitude makes the path simple, that does not mean one will not encounter any conflicts and troubles along the way. But they do not dismay the true devotee.

Among the tests that might be faced, doubt is a devastating obstacle. So many people get caught in the indecisiveness of doubt—in speculation about God; in wondering if it is really possible to know Him, and if so, whether they themselves have the capability to find Him. Several incarnations are often wasted in such irresolute thinking.

I see how many seekers come and go on the path, giving in to the ways of delusion. I look at their karma from the past; and though I am saddened by their lack of determination, I understand. That is why I am never overencouraged when devotees come, and never discouraged by those who leave. I know exactly where the karma of each person is leading. But that pattern need not remain an absolute. If one listens to a master, he can change that self-created blueprint; he can overcome his karma.

If one is in doubt about proper diet, he doesn't give up eating. Yet when confronted with doubts in the search for God, some people give up their spiritual nourishment as though they could live without it. In doing so, they suffer. Therefore, when doubts come, they should be abolished by faith and will. Cling to one who has found God. That is the sure way to succeed on the spiritual path.

The Blind Cannot Lead the Blind

There are many who are trying to lead others, but who have no right to lead. The blind cannot lead the blind. No one can take you to God unless he himself has found God. Societies develop around charismatic personalities, but they die out with those personalities. A true guru has no personal ambition for name or fame; his one desire is to serve others with the realization of God.

I sought all over India to find a true master. I searched in books; I journeyed from temple to temple, from one holy place to another; but my doubts followed me everywhere. But when I found that one who had realization—my guru, Sri Yukteswarji—and saw that spirit divine in his eyes, all doubt went away. Through his blessing my whole life changed. That is why I stress to you the importance of following a true guru and his teachings. I told Master I would never teach about God unless I had tasted Him. By following Guru unconditionally, I found God.

When you are steadfast in the principles of the guru-disciple relationship, the spiritual path becomes very easy. You cannot then go astray. No matter how delusion tries to pull you away, the master who has experienced God knows your trouble and will help you to steady yourself on the path again. That is what the guru does for you if you are in tune with him. Even though you and the guru may be thousands of miles apart, his help will reach out to you. I feel Master with me all the time, even though he is no longer incarnate on this earth plane. To have the guidance and grace of guru with you—that is the easiest way to move along on the spiritual path.

God Is Already Yours

God is not to be acquired; He is to be realized, for He is already yours. This I say to Him all the time: "Lord, why do You hide Yourself? You have no right to do so, because everyone is Yours and You belong to everyone—permanently and everlastingly. So why this seeming separation?" Haphazard seekers excuse their spiritual lethargy by rationalizing: "My mind is too restless," or, "I am too sensual," and so on. Never concentrate on your faults. By doing so you identify yourself with them. You are the one who puts the veil of delusion in front of your wisdom's eyes. Whatsoever you think, that is what you are.

During the day you are tied to the remembrance of your weaknesses, but every night when you forget the world in sleep you also forget your limitations. In deep sleep you are pure Spirit, one with your Infinite Self. Why can't you realize that in the daytime? Every night God shows you what you are; why doubt it? You are not the bundle of bones and flesh at all. Consciously or unconsciously you are with God. Beyond the dream state, the true Self is manifest. "Beyond the flights of fancy, formless am I."* Your consciousness is expanded in the omnipresent Spirit. Hold on to the thought that every night you are with Spirit; only temporarily do you forget Him in the daytime.

Of all the things God has given to man, it could be said that His greatest gift is sleep, because it is the forgetting of this mortal dream, a respite from mortal consciousness. The ordinary man has no other escape, but even the crudest man has spiritual refreshment in the unconscious *samadhi†* of sleep. Yet in contrast to conscious *samadhi*, sleep is a sort of narcotic. I have played with sleep. I have approached the sleep state, and then remained in between wakefulness and somnolence. And sometimes I do sleep deeply, and can at the same time watch myself sleeping. By the control of these states of consciousness, different realizations of the workings of the soul and ego came to me.

Tonight when you drift into deep sleep you shall forget all of your weaknesses gathered through countless incarnations. You will be locked in the embrace of the Spirit. Learn to do that consciously in the daytime; hold on to the unruffled inner calmness of deep sleep. Then you can know God, for in calm-

---

* A line from a Sanskrit chant by Adi Shankaracharya, part of which is included in *Words of Cosmic Chants* by Paramahansa Yogananda under the title "No Birth, No Death."

† See footnote on page 17.

ness you are with the Infinite. *Kriya Yoga* meditation helps you to establish your consciousness in that state.

Regain Your Divine Nature

It isn't only meditation that I emphasize. Meditation plus keeping your mind with God during activity is what is necessary. Half the battle will be won by meditation, for the soul power that you bring out by meditation will influence your thoughts and behavior during activity. When you meditate deeply, that gives substantiation to your spiritual thoughts. The longer and deeper you meditate on a regular basis, the more you will find there is no difference between work and meditation. That is to say, whether you are working or meditating, you remain immersed in the divine consciousness of the blissful Spirit. You no longer identify yourself with the activities and aches and pains of a mortal body; you realize you are pure Spirit.

The body is a nest of delusion. It makes us believe in the reality of this finite world. But when we are with God, that seeming reality is gone. It is that simple. In the *samadhi* state of meditation, we consciously enjoy the blissful awareness of God as the Sole Reality.

Why do you give up your divine nature? Why do you put on all kinds of moods and emotions, which distort the expression of what you really are? Practice evenminded calmness all the time. Become a king, an absolute monarch, of your own mental realm of calmness. In calmness, the mind is wholly free of emotional agitations. Unless the mind is calm, God will be obscured. So let nothing disturb your peaceable kingdom of calmness. Night and day carry with you the joy of "the peace of God, which passeth all understanding."*

Moods are your greatest enemy. Don't indulge in them; destroy them, for they are a formidable stumbling block in the path of your progress. With the relentless might of watchfulness guard yourself against moods. No matter what trials come, I never permit moods to enter my consciousness. And I prefer not to mix with anyone who is moody. I won't give heed to their moods, because they are very contagious. Somebody

---

* *Philippians* 4:7 (Bible).

is grouchy; you go around him and you will feel grouchy too. Mix with those who have a positive, cheerful disposition. Somebody is smiling; you go around that person and you will feel like smiling.

Never get angry. Never try to get even with anyone. And don't find fault with others; correct yourself. The whole world may mistreat you, but why should you mistreat yourself by wrong behavior?

Do Not Accept Limiting Influences

Remember that all of your troubles are only grafts on your consciousness. They do not belong to your soul. So why accept their limiting influence? Why be fearful or doubtful? Why say that you are restless or moody, or that you can't meditate? Such statements are a lie, for they contradict the truth of your real Self. Rather, inwardly affirm, "I am a child of God. I am with Him; He is with me." For these many years since childhood, even though sometimes my mind might have been restless, still I do not remember a week or a day, or even a minute, that I have not been inwardly with Him—night and day. That is the way to live your life. In the beginning—and perhaps for years—you have to make constant effort; and then the need for effort is past, for you are always with God. The would-be concert pianist must practice and practice, until finally the music becomes a part of him. As the writer is always thinking of his compositions, and as the inventive engineer is always thinking of mechanics, so the divine man is all the time thinking of God. To have that constant remembrance of God is to be intensely happy. Nothing can describe that divine joy.

Yesterday I was busy all day with people, and it was late before I could get to my time of silence. But when I sat in my room to meditate, my mind was instantly with God. I prayed, "Lord, You are myself." And as soon as I said that, the world floated away from my consciousness and I was in complete ecstasy with God. The time will come when you will have that experience if you make the effort.

God has already given Himself to you, but you have not accepted Him. That you do not make the necessary effort to know Him is the underlying cause of all your sorrow. You bring it on yourself. "Lord, Thou didst make me a prince, but I willfully wandered away from my divine realm; and like a prodigal son, I chose to be a beggar."

Of course, I also blame God, and say that He is primarily responsible for our difficulties because He created us. Every day I scold Him. I say, "Lord, haven't You gathered much bad karma for creating this troublesome world?" But I know He has no karma. And when you realize your oneness with Him, that you are made in His image, you have no karma either. That is why I do not stress too much the theory of karma. The more you hold on to the concept of limitation, the more you bind yourself. Jesus said, "Is it not written in your law, I said, Ye are gods?"* The advanced attitude is not to dwell on the idea of sin, for it is a lie. When a sleeping prince is dreaming that he is a beggar and cries out in anguish at his poverty and hunger, you do not say to him, "Beggar, wake up!" You say, "Prince, wake up!" Similarly, why should anyone call himself or another a sinner? Forget that notion. No matter what mistakes you have made, hold constantly to the thought, "Lord, I am made in Thine image." You have within you the power to be good!

Want Naught Else but God

What is the use of just crying and bewailing your lot? Make up your mind that you can have God in this lifetime. To Him you must go, because in Him is your home. As long as you stay away from God, there will be no end to your troubles—physical, moral or mental, or spiritual. You do not know what you may have to go through. But you have enough intelligence to know your Self and to realize that you must go back to God whence you came.

Your love for God should be so great that you want naught else but Him. I cannot think of any desire to ask of Him. Sometimes I do ask for something in connection with His work, and He grants it—often immediately. But I can never ask for anything for myself except, "Be Thou with me always. It doesn't matter what trials come to me; just give me the strength to meet them with Thy consciousness. But never test me, Lord, with Your absence."

---

* *John* 10:34 (Bible).

Often I tell the Lord: "I am on to Your tricks now. You have created this world enticing to the senses to find out whether we love You or Your creation. I want only You, my Lord. There is no one who can help me or fill my heart but You—only You."

Talk to God in that way. He will make you think He is not responding. But when you are least looking for it, if you have complete love and trust, He will answer you. Even when you think God is away from you, if still you are continuously longing for Him—"Why isn't He coming?"—He is with you. Remember that. He is watching you. He knows every thought you think, every feeling you feel. To keep the mind full of rubbish is foolish. Fill your mind with thoughts of God. Pray for the unceasing remembrance of God. Think of Him before you act, while you are acting, and after you have finished your duties. "He who perceives Me everywhere and beholds everything in Me never loses sight of Me, nor do I ever lose sight of him."* He is nearest of the near, dearest of the dear, closer than the closest.

Hold on to the truth that God is the most important thing in your life. So long as you cling to human love, or life, or beauty, or fame, or money, or anything else as more important, He will not come to you.

You were sent on earth to experience God's cosmic show and then return to your abode in Him, but you have made this movie-house your home. This is no longer a home for me. To the worldly person, that seems very strange to say; but it is the most wonderful consciousness. What else could you want when you have established yourself in never-ending happiness? When you are in that ever new joy, how can you be in a mood or angry or crave this or that? You have no time for such mortal entanglements. I find that I am inwardly aloof from everything now, locked in oneness with God. I am not interested in anything else—except in those who are interested in God. The idea of joining a religious congregation in order to acquire health or wealth or power is nonsense. These are diverting ideas. Of course health is better than sickness, and success is better than failure, but the purpose of religion is to take you to God. Somehow you must get back to Him.

---

* Bhagavad Gita VI:30.

The only way we know to please God is to cast away all desires, even the desire for health. Inwardly be a perfect renunciant. Look after the needs of the body and mind, and fulfill your God-given duties, but with desireless nonattachment. Flying away from the world is not necessary. Neither should you become too engrossed in the world, because then you will not be able to remain inwardly nonattached. Those who out of laziness forsake all duties on the pretext of seeking God in seclusion multiply their troubles. Their moods, their passions, their weaknesses accompany them wherever they go. Dutiful action combined with meditation is the surer way to conquer the little self.

Why Should God Amuse Us With Powers and Miracles?

Another flaw common to unsettled spiritual seekers is that they begin to feel spiritually stale when the Lord doesn't give them phenomenal demonstrations. Why should God amuse us with powers and miracles? If you are inclined toward these, you do not want God; and you will not find Him. When you truly desire God, you do not crave anything else, and that includes powers. The attainment of the ability to perform miraculous feats is not necessarily an indication that one knows God. The divine man doesn't care for such capabilities; he worships the Sole Power—God. When you know God, you may not yourself possess miraculous powers, but at your command lies all the power of the universe if you need it. God gave me many powers in this life, but I gave them back to Him; I use them only if He tells me to do so.

There is a story of the mystic Madhusudan, and his meeting with Gorakhnath, the saint of Gorakhpur, where my body was born. When I heard this story, that cured me of any wish for miraculous powers. Gorakhnath had attained all the eight powers, or *aiswaryas*, of a fully enlightened yogi.* At the time of his departure from the body, he wanted to bestow his powers on some worthy soul. The masters can do that, even as

---

* The *aiswaryas* or *siddhis*, divine powers that manifest as the yogi advances through the highest stages of spiritual evolution, are discussed by Patanjali in his *Yoga Sutras*, section III; and by Swami Sri Yukteswar in chapter 4 of *The Holy Science* (published by Yogoda Satsanga Society of India).

the mantle of Elijah's power was passed to Elisha.* One day Gorakhnath saw in vision a young man, a very spiritual soul, standing by the Ganges in Banaras. Having the power to transport himself astrally from one place to another, Gorakhnath appeared before the young man, Madhusudan, who looked up and, seeing the saint, said, "Please do not stand in front of me. You are obstructing the sun."

The saint replied, "Do you not know who I am? I am Gorakhnath."

"I know," the young man said, "but I am busy now with my devotions." After some time the devotee inquired of the saint, "What is it you want of me?"

Gorakhnath explained, "I have eight powers; and the one to whom I give this *chintamani* [a mystical gem that grants all wishes] will have these powers. I wish to offer them to you."

Madhusudan said, "All right, give them to me." Whereupon, to the great astonishment of Gorakhnath, he took the mystical gem and threw it far out into the waters of the Ganges.

"Why did you do that?" Gorakhnath demanded.

Then the young man said, "Delusion still, delusion still. Those powers were given to me to do with as I wished, were they not? Well, that is the only use I have for them. Compared to That which I already have, they are nothing."

The great Gorakhnath bowed down to him and said, "You have rid me of the last delusion that was keeping me from God."

Even the great ones sometimes get distracted from the Goal. Gorakhnath was so enamored with his powers that he had not gone beyond them to God. But when at last he renounced attachment to that treasured possession, he attained God-union. You see, delusion takes many forms; but the divine devotee is like the single-hearted Madhusudan in this story. When you love God, you do not desire anything else, because God is the most lovable of anything you could possess. The devotee will accept no substitute for God. He knows that God is all in all, that He is ever present, and that He alone is a sure refuge from the travails of life.

---

* *II Kings* 2:9–14 (Bible).

Live in the Unchanging Reality

At one time, this world seemed so real to me. But I experience it now just like a motion picture. I see my mother sitting in Gorakhpur, peeling mangoes for me. It is as clear as if it were happening now, even though that mother whom I loved is no more. Those early scenes of my childhood are all coming to me. In the same way, this present motion-picture segment with all of you sitting here with me will one day be gone, replaced by new scenes and actors in the progressive film of time. Yet it will always remain in the cosmic movie archives.

Though I live in this world and behold it as a moving picture show that continuously comes and goes, still most of the time this earthly movie is away from my consciousness. I go within, into the Unchanging Reality. That is the way to seek God. Live in that eternal consciousness.

By searching the whole world, you will not find God. Intellectual discourses about the Creator will not give you God. But by seeking Him within, making the effort every day, you will find Him. The way to God is not through the intellect, but through intuition. Spirituality is measured by what you experience intuitively, from the communion of your soul with God. It is so simple if inside you are always talking to Him, "Lord, come to me!" Why do you put up a barrier of doubt between yourself and God? If you love Him and inwardly talk to Him, and *know* He is with you, you will get much more result than from hours of just sitting absentmindedly in silence, supposedly meditating, with your mind wandering over everything but God. Keep Him in your heart all the time. And when you meditate, go deep in divine communion.

Ultimately, you are wholly dependent upon God. You could not utter one word without the power of God. He throbs in your heart. He thinks through your brain. He knows your every thought and action even before you do. Why do you doubt Him? Talk straight to Him. Speak to Him. He will not disappoint you.

Conversation With God Requires Silence

Conversation with people requires audible voice. Conversation with God requires silence. People who talk too much are not with God; there is much less time in their thoughts for Him. Those who inwardly converse with God are outwardly more silent. No matter what their surroundings, they are habitually more quiet. Because the devotee has plenty to say to God, he has very little to say to others. When those who have much to say to God do speak, their words are of God, and are full of wisdom and understanding.

When the perception of God begins, you have no time for useless things. You want to remain by yourself—God and yourself. And you do not want to waste a precious moment that could rather be spent with Him. Even when such devotees are active, that activity never diminishes their perception of love for God.

Idle talking causes one to lose devotion for God. It feeds mental restlessness that takes the mind away from Him. Yesterday I was sitting by the pool here in Encinitas. There was a lot of chattering going on. But I was in that Infinite Light wherein the sky and everything was absorbed in divine radiance. I was practicing silence all the while. It isn't a forced state, but an inner stillness and peace that becomes a part of one's nature.

Try unceasingly to keep your mind on God. Be with Him all the time. Practice His presence. Don't waste your time. In this world of activity, the daytime is the devil's playground. The only way to outwit the devil is to keep your mind with God. And when night comes, forsake the world and all your cares of the day and meditate; be entranced with the love of God. To be with Him is a million times more joyous and strengthening than is sleep.

We Are Souls, Not Fleshly Beings

We are souls, individualized Spirit; that is why we must turn back toward God. We must think of ourselves as souls, not as fleshly beings. Now when I see the picture of my father and mother, I cannot believe my body was ever born from them, because I know they also were made by God. The Potter made the clay and fashioned out of it my father and mother and me. How shall I then say that my parents created me? My Father in Heaven was solely responsible for my coming. Similarly, Shankara said, "No birth, no death, no caste have I. Father,

Paramahansa Yogananda, New York, 1926

Yogoda Satsanga Society of India, Administration Building, Sakha Math and Ashram, Ranchi.

Self-Realization Fellowship Ashram Center, Encinitas, California, founded by Sri Yogananda in 1936. In the Hermitage (on the bluff high above the Pacific Ocean) he wrote *Autobiography of a Yogi* and other works. Today the site attracts visitors from all over the world, who come to stay at the SRF Retreat here or enjoy the beautiful clifftop meditation gardens.

Realizing God in Your Daily Life

Self-Realization Fellowship Temple,
Hollywood, California, October 4, 1942

If you have deep devotion for God, you can ask Him anything. Every day I bring new questions to Him, and He answers
me. He is never offended by any sincere query we put to Him.
Sometimes I even scold Him for starting this creation: "Who
is going to suffer the karma for all the evils in this drama?
You, the Creator, are free from karma. Why, then, did You subject us to this misery?"* I think He feels very sad for us. His
desire is to take us back, but He cannot do so without our cooperation and self-effort.

Though I blame God for creating delusion, that is nevertheless the state of affairs. That is not going to change. So rather
than blaming God for putting us in this mess, it is better to
blame ourselves for choosing to remain in it. We are the ones
who must free ourselves from delusion; and the only way is
through wisdom. The more you will deeply seek understanding from God, the more you will receive His answers. The true
devotee, even when enmeshed in many doubts, never loses his
devotion and determination.

Even true devotees think sometimes that God does not answer their prayers. He does answer silently, through His laws;
but until He is absolutely sure of the devotee He will not answer openly, He will not talk to the devotee. The Lord of Universes is so humble that He does not speak, lest in so doing
He influence the devotee's use of free will to choose or reject
Him. Once you know Him, there is no doubt that you will love
Him. Who could resist the Irresistible? But you have to prove
your unconditional love for God in order to know Him. You

---

* A particularly deep-felt sentiment in the context of the tragedies unfolding
as a result of the then raging World War II.

have to have faith. You have to *know* that even as you pray He is listening to you. Then He will make Himself known to you. He cannot then turn a deaf ear to your prayer.

Our relationship with God is not a cold impersonal one, like that between employer and employee. We are His children. He *has* to listen to us! There is no way that we can get away from the fact that we are His children. We are not merely creatures created by Him; we are a part of Him. He made us princes, but we have chosen to become slaves. He wants us to become princes once more, to return to our Kingdom. But no one, having renounced his divine heritage, will regain it without effort. We are made in His image, but we have somehow forgotten that truth. We have succumbed to the delusion that we are mortal beings, and we must sunder the veil of that delusion with the dagger of wisdom.

To attach any reality to the outward show of life expresses lack of true wisdom, but God has so impressed us with His *maya*—the cosmic illusion that causes us to see as real that which is only a play of light and shadows—that it is very hard not to be influenced by it. When you are hungry, it is *maya* that makes you think you will starve unless you eat. Yet, there are many persons who have fasted as long as seventy days. I have undergone long fasts, and after thirty days there is not even any sensation of hunger. But if your mind believes you cannot live without food, you will not live. That is a common delusion; its basis is solely in our minds. Because of the small number of exceptions to what appears to be a rule, science declares that human beings cannot live very long without food. There are cases, however, of people who live entirely without eating: Therese Neumann of Bavaria, and Giri Bala of Bengal, are two saints of the twentieth century who live without eating.[*]

We ordinarily think we cannot live without breath also, yet when in deep meditation we practice *Kriya Yoga*, we know it can be done. Saints of East and West have often entered the breathless *samadhi* state. Mortal life is simply a system of suggestions that makes us think we must conform to a certain pat-

---

[*] See chapters 39 and 46 in Paramahansaji's *Autobiography of a Yogi.*

tern of eating, breathing, and so on. But as soon as you meditate and permit your consciousness to retire within to its source, the immortal soul, you realize that you are not subject to these limiting patterns. You know then that fire cannot burn you, water cannot drown you, that both health and sickness are dreams. In the lusty heat of our desires and moods we have formed a conception of the world that is not true. The truth is embodied in the wisdom of the great ones that reveals to us the world as it really is. Had it not been for the training I received in this wisdom, I would not have liked to remain in this world.

"Get Away From This Ocean of Suffering"

The truth is, only fools are attached to this world. "Fools" are those who live in ignorance, those to whom the world is real because they think it is the only way of life. Ignorance is like an eczema. The more you try to get relief by indulging its demand to be scratched, the more it will itch; but the more you leave it alone, the less it will bother you. That is why Krishna tells Arjuna in the Bhagavad Gita: "Get away from this ocean of suffering."* Be in the world and do your part, but do not be caught up and bound by its delusions, or you will be enslaved.

Those who live on the sex plane all the time think they can't do without sex. But one who abstains and transmutes that energy never desires it. Smoking brings on the same delusion. People who have never smoked, or who have broken the habit, never miss tobacco.

God Is the Greatest Need of Your Life

You must cease to think you are a mortal being if you would find lasting happiness. Practice this truth in your daily life. It is a battle you have to fight throughout this life and incarnations to come, so it is better to start now! Do not put it off, thinking that you will start meditating tomorrow. Tomorrow will never come. Long ago I passed a whole year in this attitude, and still I was saying, "tomorrow." Then I made up my mind: "I will start meditating today." Since then I have never missed a day.

You must first resolve in your mind the importance of

---

* Paraphrase of XII:7.

God. You must realize inwardly that He is the greatest need of your life. First practice the presence of God in daily life by making your meditations very deep. It is better to meditate a little bit with depth than to meditate long with the mind running here and there. If you do not make an effort to control the mind it will go on doing as it pleases, no matter how long you sit to meditate.

Next, practice long meditation with depth. That is what takes you to His kingdom. Until you learn to practice meditation both long and deep, God will not reveal Himself to you. Gandhi devoted one day a week to silence and meditation. All saints who have found God sought that silence. I give my nights and mornings to Him. It is not possible to do exactly that in the business world, but if you will try, you will be surprised how much time you will find to devote to thoughts of God. We delude and deprive ourselves when we think we can wait until tomorrow to make that great effort to be with God.

Delusion is destroyed by good company, by the company of saints, and by devotion to the messengers of God. Even the thought of saints will help you to remove delusion. It is not personal association so much as attunement of thought with the messenger of God that destroys delusion. The true guru has no desire to place himself in the hearts of others, but rather to awaken in their consciousness the consciousness of God. Master [Swami Sri Yukteswar] was like that: he was one with us—never any show of his greatness. If anyone in the ashram wanted recognition or a high seat of authority, Master would give him that position. But I wanted the heart of Master, the divine consciousness he had within; and as a result, he is forever here in my heart. That is the attunement you want with the great ones.

Perform Your Duties With the Thought of God

Along with periods of meditation you should think day and night of God. "Door of my heart, open wide I keep for Thee....Night and day, night and day, I look for Thee night and day."* We must uplift our consciousness so that even the most worldly duties are performed with the thought of God.

---

* From "Door of My Heart" in *Words of Cosmic Chants* by Paramahansa Yogananda.

There are two kinds of duty: that which you do for yourself (which keeps you bound), and that which you do for God. Duty performed as an offering to God is as spiritually beneficial as meditation. God loves that devotion which makes of action as well as silence an oblation to Him. But you cannot find Him by good works alone: You must give your deepest love to Him. He wants you to surrender heart, mind, and soul. He wants to know that you love Him. You have to seek Him in both activity and meditation. When inwardly you walk with God, and also carry a heavy load of earthly duties on your shoulders, He loves you even more. So before you perform an action, while you are performing an action, and when you have finished that action, think of Him. The Gita says: "He who watches Me always, him do I watch. He never loses sight of Me, nor do I lose sight of him."*

Meditation must be practiced every day. Start now! Do not look to the future. Begin this very moment to think of God. In this thought you are a king. Why be a prisoner of mortal moods and habits? Is it not true that when you introspect you see that you have done things you did not want to do? To carry out one's resolutions is a constant battle. It is good to resolve to do a thing and then follow through. You must develop a strong, silent, cool will. Never give up your good resolutions.

Cultivate the will to think of God during activity. It is extremely important that you make this a part of your daily life. Don't follow this course a few days only and then forget all about it. Follow it as best you can every day. Even if you slip back into old habits, keep on trying. You will become spiritually strong and healthy in due time.

God Responds When We Make the Effort

God responds when we make the effort. Then you know that He *is*. He will no longer be a myth. He will respond invisibly to your desires, playing hide-and-seek with you. And after that He will come to you openly. Your past mistakes do not matter. But to continue in those mistakes is the greatest sin against yourself, for when you do wrong it deprives you of

---

* A paraphrase of Bhagavad Gita VI:30.

true happiness. You have the power to hurt yourself or to benefit yourself. It is up to you to keep away the ants of ignorance that bite your flesh. If you do not choose to be happy no
one can make you happy. Do not blame God for that! And if
you choose to be happy, no one can make you unhappy. If He
had not given us freedom to use our own will, we could blame
Him when we are unhappy, but He did give us that freedom.
It is we who make of life what it is.

You may ask, "Why, if we have free choice, do things not
turn out as we wish them to be?" It is because you have weakened your will, your consciousness of divine powers within
you. But if you strengthen your will by practicing self-control
and meditation, it becomes free; and as soon as your will is
free, you are master of your fate. But if you find that day by
day you are living a life against your conscience, you will never
be free. You must take time to do the things that are good for
your own welfare. No one stops you but yourself. You make
yourself a prisoner of your own moods and bad habits. That is
why you must train your will to be more elastic. Keep your
will under control by doing the best things in life—thinking
more of God, meditating more, practicing self-control, and so on.

The Dynamic Power of "Mental Whispers"

Of greatest help in your development is the habit of mental
whispering to God. You will see a change in yourself that you
will like very much. No matter what you do, God should be constantly in your mind. When you want to see a special show, or
to buy a dress or a car you have admired, is it not true that no
matter what else you may be doing your mind is continually
thinking how you can get those things? Until you fulfill your
strong desires, your mind will not rest; it ceaselessly works
toward fulfilling those desires. Your mind should be on God
night and day in the same way. Transmute petty desires into one
great desire for Him. Your mind should continually whisper,
"Night and day, night and day, I look for Thee night and day."

Mental whispers develop dynamic power to reshape matter into what you want. You do not realize how great is the
power of the mind. When your mind and will are attuned to the
Divine Will you do not have to move a finger in order to cre-

ate changes on earth. The divine law will work for you. All the salient accomplishments of my life have been achieved through that power of mind in tune with the will of God. When that divine dynamo is on, whatever I am wishing has to come to pass. When this new temple of ours came to my mind, there was a force behind it I knew could not be stopped. I saw the great will of God working. Things that the mortal mind could not even hope to expect were nevertheless done.*

Whatever you intensely believe in your mind will materialize. Jesus said, "Whosoever shall say unto this mountain, Be thou removed, and be thou cast into the sea; and shall not doubt in his heart, but shall believe that those things which he saith shall come to pass; he shall have whatsoever he saith."†

Do not discourage yourself by entertaining the thought that you are a sinner and that God will never come to you. You then paralyze your will. Sin is a temporary delusion, and what is done is finished. It doesn't belong to you anymore. But you should not commit the same error again.

Do Not Accept Your Bad Karma

Deny karma. Too many people misinterpret the meaning of karma, adopting a fatalistic attitude. You do not have to accept karma. If I tell you that somebody is standing behind you ready to hurt you because you once hit him, and you meekly say, "Well, it is my karma," and wait for him to strike you, of course you will get a blow! Why don't you try to mollify him? By pacifying him you may lessen his bitterness and remove his desire to strike you.

When you realize yourself as a child of God, what karma have you? God has no karma. And you have none, when you *know* you are His child. Every day you should affirm, "I am not a mortal being; I am not the body. I am a child of God." That is practicing the presence of God. God is free from karma. You

---

* Reference to the Self-Realization Fellowship Temple in Hollywood, dedicated August 30, 1942. The construction was undertaken during World War II, when restrictive guidelines were prevalent and building materials were scarce. All obstacles, one by one, were overcome.

† *Mark* 11:23 (Bible).

are made in His image. You also are free from karma.

The best way to remove your weaknesses is not to think about them; otherwise you will be overwhelmed. Bring the light in and you will feel that darkness never was. In that thought is one of the greatest inspirations of my life. If light is admitted into a cave where darkness has existed for thousands of years, darkness will vanish instantly. So will our faults and weaknesses vanish when we bring in the light of God. The darkness of ignorance can enter nevermore.

That is the philosophy of life by which we should live. Not tomorrow, but today, this minute. There cannot be any excuse for not thinking of God. Day and night, rolling in the background of your mind, God! God! God! instead of money or sex or fame. Whether you are washing dishes or digging a ditch or working in an office or a garden—whatever you may be doing—inwardly say, "Lord, manifest to me! You are right here. You are in the sun. You are in the grass. You are in the water. You are in this room. You are in my heart."

And when great love for God comes in your heart, you do not miss anything; no matter what you have or do not have in this world, you nevertheless feel fulfilled. Divine love transmutes all material desires—even the longing for human love, that mortal passion which so often brings pain either from its fickle nature or because it is snatched away by death. Loving the Lord, you can never turn back to being satisfied by lesser loves. In Him you will find all the love of all hearts. You will find completeness. Everything that the world gives you and then takes away, leaving you in pain or disillusionment, you will find in God in a much greater way, and with no aftermath of sorrow.

Every Minute Is Precious

Life seems such a tangible reality, and yet it is elusive. Every minute is precious. Today you are; tomorrow you are not. I remind myself of this every day. One by one we slip away. Others will come and we shall go. But the body is only a garment. How many times you have changed your clothing in this life, yet because of this you would not say that *you* have changed. Similarly, when you give up this bodily dress at death you do not change. You are just the same, an immortal soul, a child of

God. Reincarnation means merely a change of mortal dress. But your real self will never change. You must concentrate on your real self, not on the body, which is nothing but a garment.

I sometimes think that sense perceptions are the worst enemies of man, because they make us believe we are something we are not. The sensation of cold makes us think we are cold, and the sensation of heat makes us think we are hot. If we would but deny these sensations in our minds we would feel neither cold nor heat.

One night long ago in Duxbury, Massachusetts, I went to bathe in the ocean in the moonlight. Dr. M. W. Lewis and his son Bradford accompanied me. The water felt very cold, but I reminded myself that everything is made of electricity; that the same electricity that makes cold also makes heat, and the water itself is nothing more than a manifestation of electrical energies. Just as I was thinking these thoughts Bradford looked at me strangely, then turned to his father and exclaimed, "Swamiji* has a light around his body!" The light of God had come over me as I refused to accept the sensation of cold and reaffirmed instead the truth that everything is made of Divine Electricity.

Catch God in the Net of Unconditional Love

But if you speak about these things too much they are taken away from you. God is like a little child. He knows no guile. But if you play the slightest deceit or trick on Him He is gone. That is why it is so hard to get hold of Him. You have to catch Him in the net of your unconditional love. Love means craving for God. God appreciates love more than devotion: In devotion there is distance and awe, perhaps fear; in love there is unity, at-one-ment.

Do not despair if you do not yet feel an unconditional love for God. Salvation is for all. If you choose to delay on this path of evolution, it is your loss. You cannot stand still; you have to

---

* In 1935, Sri Yukteswar bestowed on his beloved disciple Yogananda the spiritual title *Paramahansa*. Prior to that time he was known as Swami Yogananda. (See *swami* in glossary.)

go forward or backward. But you must be redeemed sometime. To be redeemed is to drop the ignorance that covers the soul. You cannot see a nugget of gold if it is covered with mud. And so long as the mud of ignorance besmears the golden soul you cannot see it. You are unable to think of yourself as a soul because you know only the body. The human form is the mud that you have put over your soul, and that is why you do not know what you are. Wash away the mud, forget the body by meditation, and you will know what you are. How can you be anything but perfect, since you are God's child? But you have to realize your inherent divinity.

You must be very secret about your love for God. And you have to be very silent about His love; you must not speak about His being with you. Be like the great ones, who inwardly think constantly of the Beauty behind the flowers; the Light behind the sun; the Life that twinkles in all eyes, that beats in every heart; the Motion that walks in all feet, that works in all hands; the Mind that is working through all brains; the Love that is behind all loves.

God is so great, so marvelous! To live in the realm of divine consciousness is to see this mundane world—ignorant of God—as a nightmare, and to have eternal freedom from its terrors.

You waste precious time each day. Every little moment you spend with God will be spent to your best advantage; and whatever you achieve with the desire to please God in your heart will stand unto eternity. God is freedom from all misery. God is the wealth and the health you seek. God is the love you seek. The desire of the soul for God is behind all other desires. Worldly desires camouflage the longing of the soul to be reunited with God-Bliss. Only God can satisfy all the desires of this life and of past incarnations. I have found it so.

Nothing Can Match the Experience of God

So search for Him night and day. Nothing can match the experience you will have if you do this. God is the Goal you seek. You cannot live without Him. And all things you desire you will find in Him. He is playing hide-and-seek with His devotees, but some day, after this play is over, to each one of you He will say: "I hid from you long, not to torture you, but to make our reunion in the end bright and beautiful. After your search of incarnations you have come at last to Me, and I joyfully welcome you to your Home. I have been waiting long for you. You were not the only one who was seeking. Through all your life's experiences it was I, wearing disguises of different loves of family and friends, who pursued you. I have been watching and waiting for you more eagerly than you have sought Me. Many times you forgot Me, but I could not forget you, My child. Beloved, of your own free will you have at last come back to Me. We shall never again be parted."

Every human being is loved in that way by God. He is waiting for you. Don't give the world your attention. Do your duties, but be with God. It is worth it. Every moment of your life should be filled with the thought of God. Don't waste your time. I am anxious to go back to God; not only for myself, but to show others the way to that Eternal Safety. I want to go to Him, and to take others with me. Please pray with me:

"Glory to Thee, Lord of the universe, Lord of my soul! Thou dost love us and pursue us even when we do not love Thee. Lord of love, Lord of the world, occupy the temple of our lives! Be Thou the only King sitting on the throne of all our desires, for Thou art the only happiness, the only joy. Bless us that we find Thee, just behind our thoughts, every day, every minute of our existence. Take away from us the cup of mortal delusion; but if we must taste it for a little while, bless us that with greater joy and relish we shall taste the Eternal. *Aum.* Peace. *Aum.*"

PARAMAHANSA YOGANANDA:
A YOGI IN LIFE AND DEATH

Paramahansa Yogananda entered *mahasamadhi* (a yogi's final conscious exit from the body) in Los Angeles, California, on March 7, 1952, after concluding his speech at a banquet held in honour of H.E. Binay R. Sen, Ambassador of India.

The great world teacher demonstrated the value of yoga (scientific techniques for God-realization) not only in life but in death. Weeks after his departure his unchanged face shone with the divine luster of incorruptibility.

Mr. Harry T. Rowe, Los Angeles Mortuary Director, Forest Lawn Memorial-Park (in which the body of the great master is temporarily placed), sent Self-Realization Fellowship a notarized letter from which the following extracts are taken:

"The absence of any visual signs of decay in the dead body of Paramahansa Yogananda offers the most extraordinary case in our experience....No physical disintegration was visible in his body even twenty days after death....No indication of mold was visible on his skin, and no visible desiccation (drying up) took place in the bodily tissues. This state of perfect preservation of a body is, so far as we know from mortuary annals, an unparalleled one....At the time of receiving Yogananda's body, the Mortuary personnel expected to observe, through the glass lid of the casket, the usual progressive signs of bodily decay. Our astonishment increased as day followed day without bringing any visible change in the body under observation. Yogananda's body was apparently in a phenomenal state of immutability....

"No odor of decay emanated from his body at any time....The physical appearance of Yogananda on March 27th, just before the bronze cover of the casket was put into position, was the same as it had been on March 7th. He looked on March 27th as fresh and as unravaged by decay as he had looked on the night of his death. On March 27th there was no reason to say that his body had suffered any visible physical disintegration at all. For these reasons we state again that the case of Paramahansa Yogananda is unique in our experience."

AIMS AND IDEALS
of
Yogoda Satsanga Society of India

As set forth by
Sri Sri Paramahansa Yogananda, Gurudeva and Founder
Sri Sri Mrinalini Mata, Sanghamata and President

To disseminate among the nations a knowledge of definite scientific techniques for attaining direct personal experience of God.

To teach that the purpose of life is the evolution, through self-effort, of man's limited mortal consciousness into God Consciousness; and to this end to establish Yogoda Satsanga temples for God-communion, and to encourage the establishment of individual temples of God in the homes and in the hearts of men.

To reveal the complete harmony and basic oneness of original Yoga as taught by Bhagavan Krishna and original Christianity as taught by Jesus Christ; and to show that these principles of truth are the common scientific foundation of all true religions.

To point out the one divine highway to which all paths of true religious beliefs eventually lead: the highway of daily, scientific, devotional meditation on God.

To liberate man from his threefold suffering: physical disease, mental inharmonies, and spiritual ignorance.

To encourage "plain living and high thinking"; and to spread a spirit of brotherhood among all peoples by teaching the eternal basis of their unity: kinship with God.

To demonstrate the superiority of mind over body, of soul over mind.

To overcome evil by good, sorrow by joy, cruelty by kindness, ignorance by wisdom.

To unite science and religion through realization of the unity of their underlying principles.

To advocate cultural and spiritual understanding between East and West, and the exchange of their finest distinctive features.

To serve mankind as one's larger Self.

OTHER BOOKS BY
SRI SRI PARAMAHANSA YOGANANDA

Available at your local bookstores or from:
Yogoda Satsanga Society of India
Paramahansa Yogananda Path, Ranchi 834001, Jharkhand
Tel (0651) 2460071, 2460074, 2461578
www.bookstore.yssofindia.org

Autobiography of a Yogi

Paramahansa Yogananda's absorbing life story, regarded as a modern spiritual classic.

"These pages reveal, with incomparable strength and clarity, a fascinating life, a personality of such unheard-of greatness that from beginning to end, the reader is left breathless....We must credit this important biography with the power to bring about a spiritual revolution." —Schleswig-Holsteinische Tagespost, Germany

Also available in MP3 CD edition read by Sir Ben Kingsley.

God Talks With Arjuna: *The Bhagavad Gita—A New Translation and Commentary*

In this monumental two-volume work, Paramahansa Yogananda reveals the innermost essence of India's most renowned scripture. Exploring its psychological, spiritual, and metaphysical depths, he presents a sweeping chronicle of the soul's journey to enlightenment through the royal science of God-realization.

The Second Coming of Christ: *The Resurrection of the Christ Within You—A Revelatory Commentary on the Original Teachings of Jesus*

In this masterwork of inspiration, Paramahansa Yogananda takes the reader verse by verse through the four Gospels, illumining the universal path to oneness with God taught by Jesus to his immediate disciples: "how to become like Christ, how to resurrect the Eternal Christ within one's self."

Man's Eternal Quest

Volume I of Paramahansa Yogananda's lectures and informal talks, presenting many aspects of his "how-to-live" teachings and exploring little-known and seldom-understood aspects of meditation, life after death, the nature of creation, health and healing, the unlimited powers of the mind, and the eternal quest that finds fulfilment only in God.

The Divine Romance
Volume II of Paramahansa Yogananda's lectures, informal talks, and essays. Among the wide-ranging selections: *How to Cultivate Divine Love; Harmonizing Physical, Mental, and Spiritual Methods of Healing; A World Without Boundaries; Controlling Your Destiny; The Yoga Art of Overcoming Mortal Consciousness and Death; The Cosmic Lover; Finding the Joy in Life.*

Where There Is Light: *Insight and Inspiration for Meeting Life's Challenges*
Gems of thought arranged by subject; a unique handbook to which readers can quickly turn for a reassuring sense of direction in times of uncertainty or crisis, or for a renewed awareness of the ever present power of God one can draw upon in daily life.

Whispers from Eternity
A collection of Paramahansa Yogananda's prayers and divine experiences in the elevated states of meditation. Expressed in a majestic rhythm and poetic beauty, his words reveal the inexhaustible variety of God's nature, and the infinite sweetness with which He responds to those who seek Him.

The Science of Religion
Within every human being, there is one inescapable desire: to overcome suffering and attain a happiness that does not end. Paramahansa Yogananda explains how it is possible to fulfil these longings, and he examines the relative effectiveness of the different approaches to this goal.

In the Sanctuary of the Soul
Offering wisdom and insight selected from the writings of Paramahansa Yogananda, this inspirational book discusses ways by which we can deepen the power of our prayers and make them a daily source of love, strength, and guidance.

Inner Peace
Wise and inspiring selections from Yoganandaji's writings on inner peace, with practical applications to help us stay calm, happy, and evenminded, in spite of world conditions.

How You Can Talk With God
Defining God as both the transcendent, universal Spirit and the intimately personal Father, Mother, Friend, and Lover of all, Paramahansa Yogananda shows how close the Lord is to each one of us, and how He can be persuaded to "break His silence" and respond in a tangible way.

Metaphysical Meditations

More than 300 spiritually uplifting meditations, prayers, and affirmations that can be used to develop greater health and vitality, creativity, self-confidence, and calmness; and to live more fully in a conscious awareness of the blissful presence of God.

Scientific Healing Affirmations

Paramahansa Yogananda presents here a profound explanation of the science of affirmation. He makes clear why affirmations work, and how to use the power of word and thought not only to bring about healing but to effect desired change in every area of life. Includes a wide variety of affirmations.

Sayings of Paramahansa Yogananda

A collection of sayings and wise counsel that conveys Paramahansa Yogananda's candid and loving responses to those who came to him for guidance. Recorded by a number of his close disciples, the anecdotes in this book give the reader an opportunity to share in their personal encounters with the Master.

Songs of the Soul

Songs of the Soul, a collection of mystical poetry, is an outpouring of Paramahansa Yogananda's direct perceptions of God—in the beauty of nature, in humanity, in everyday life, and in ecstatic divine communion.

The Law of Success

Explains dynamic principles for achieving one's goals in life, and outlines the universal laws that bring success and fulfilment—personal, professional, and spiritual.

Words of Cosmic Chants

Words to 60 songs of devotion, with an introduction explaining how spiritual chanting can lead to God-communion.

AUDIO RECORDINGS OF PARAMAHANSA YOGANANDA

❖ Awake in the Cosmic Dream   ❖ Beholding the One in All

❖ Be a Smile Millionaire   ❖ In the Glory of the Spirit

❖ To Make Heaven on Earth   ❖ The Great Light of God

❖ One Life Versus Reincarnation

❖ Removing All Sorrow and Suffering

❖ Self-Realization: The Inner and the Outer Path

❖ Songs of My Heart (Chants, Poems, and Prayers)

भारत
INDIA
1977
परमहंस योगानंद 1893-1952
PARAMAHANSA YOGANANDA

In 1977, on the twenty-fifth anniversary of the *mahasamadhi* of Sri Sri Paramahansa Yogananda, the Government of India issued this commemorative stamp in his honour. With the stamp, the government published a descriptive leaflet, which read, in part:

"The ideal of love for God and service to humanity found full expression in the life of Paramahansa Yogananda.... Though the major part of his life was spent outside of India, still he takes his place among our great saints. His work continues to grow and shine ever more brightly, drawing people everywhere on the path of the pilgrimage of the Spirit."

ADDITIONAL RESOURCES ON THE KRIYA YOGA TEACHINGS OF PARAMAHANSA YOGANANDA

Yogoda Satsanga Society of India is dedicated to freely assisting seekers. For information regarding spiritual discourses and classes, meditation and inspirational services at our centres, a schedule of retreats, and our spiritual, as well as our medical, educational, emergency relief, and other charitable activities, we invite you to visit our website.

www.yssofindia.org

Yogoda Satsanga Society of India
Paramahansa Yogananda Path,
Ranchi 834001, Jharkhand
Tel (0651) 2460071, 2460074, 2461578

YOGODA SATSANGA LESSONS

The *Yogoda Satsanga Lessons* are unique among Sri Sri Paramahansa Yogananda's published works in that they give his in-depth instruction in the practice of the highest yoga science of God-realization. That ancient science is embodied in the specific principles and meditation techniques of *Kriya Yoga* (see glossary, and chapter 26 in *Autobiography of a Yogi*).

Lost to humanity for centuries during the dark ages, *Kriya Yoga* was revived in modern times by a line of enlightened masters—Mahavatar Babaji, Lahiri Mahasaya, Swami Sri Yukteswar, and Paramahansa Yogananda. To disseminate the liberating spiritual science worldwide through Yogoda Satsanga Society of India/Self-Realization Fellowship was the mission entrusted to Paramahansa Yogananda by his guru and *paramgurus.*

During his lifetime he traveled extensively, giving lectures and classes in India, the United States, and Europe. Yet he knew that many more than he could teach in person would be drawn to the yoga philosophy and practices. Thus he conceived "a series of weekly studies for the yoga seekers all over the world"—to perpetuate in their original purity, and in written form, the teachings handed down to him by his lineage of gurus.

The *Yogoda Satsanga Lessons* present the methods of concentration, energization, and meditation taught by Paramahansa Yogananda that are an integral part of the *Kriya Yoga* science. In addition, this comprehensive home-study series makes available the whole range of subjects covered by him in his lectures and classes offering his inspiring and practical guidance for attaining balanced physical, mental, and spiritual well-being.

After a preliminary period of study and practice, students of the *Yogoda Satsanga Lessons* may request initiation in the advanced *Kriya Yoga* meditation technique described in this book.

Further information about the *Yogoda Satsanga Lessons* is included in the booklet *Undreamed-of Possibilities*, available on request.

Those who have come to Yogoda Satsanga Society of India truly seeking inward spiritual help shall receive what they seek from God. Whether they come while I am in the body, or afterward, the power of God through the link of the YSS gurus shall flow into the devotees just the same, and shall be the cause of their salvation.

—Sri Sri Paramahansa Yogananda

GLOSSARY

Arjuna. The exalted disciple to whom Bhagavan Krishna imparted the immortal message of the Bhagavad Gita (*q.v.*); one of the five Pandava princes in the great Hindu epic, the *Mahabharata*, in which he was a key figure.

ashram. A spiritual hermitage; often a monastery.

astral body. Man's subtle body of light, *prana* or lifetrons; the second of three sheaths that successively encase the soul: the causal body (*q.v.*), the astral body, and the physical body. The powers of the astral body enliven the physical body, much as electricity illumines a bulb. The astral body has nineteen elements: intelligence, ego, feeling, mind (sense-consciousness); five instruments of knowledge (the sensory powers within the physical organs of sight, hearing, smell, taste, and touch); five instruments of action (the executive powers in the physical instruments of procreation, excretion, speech, locomotion, and the exercise of manual skill); and five instruments of life force that perform the functions of circulation, metabolization, assimilation, crystallization, and elimination.

astral light. The subtle light emanating from lifetrons (see *prana*); the structural essence of the astral world. Through the all-inclusive intuitive perception of the soul, devotees in concentrated states of meditation may perceive the astral light, particularly as the spiritual eye (*q.v.*).

astral world. The subtle sphere of the Lord's creation, a universe of light and colour composed of finer-than-atomic forces, i.e., vibrations of life energy or lifetrons (see *prana*). Every being, every object, every vibration on the material plane has an astral counterpart, for in the astral universe (heaven) is the blueprint of our material universe. At physical death, the soul of man, clothed in an astral body of light, ascends to one of the higher or lower astral planes, according to merit, to continue his spiritual evolution in the greater freedom of that subtle realm. There he remains for a karmically predetermined time until physical rebirth.

Aum (Om). The Sanskrit root word or seed-sound symbolizing that aspect of Godhead which creates and sustains all things; Cosmic Vibration. *Aum* of the Vedas became the sacred word *Hum* of the Tibetans; *Amin* of the Moslems; and *Amen* of the Egyptians, Greeks, Romans, Jews, and Christians. The world's great religions state that all created things originate in the cosmic vibratory energy of *Aum* or Amen, the Word or Holy Ghost. "In the beginning was the Word, and the Word was with God, and the Word was God....All things were made by him [the Word or *Aum*]; and without him was not any thing made that was made" (*John* 1:1, 3, Bible).

Amen in Hebrew means *sure, faithful.* "These things saith the Amen, the faithful and true witness, the beginning of the creation of God" (*Revelation* 3:14, Bible). Even as sound is produced by the vibration of a running motor, so the omnipresent sound of *Aum* faithfully testifies to the running of the "Cosmic Motor," which upholds all life and every particle of creation through vibratory energy. In the *Yogoda Satsanga Lessons* (*q.v.*), Paramahansa Yogananda teaches techniques of meditation whose practise brings direct experience of God as *Aum* or Holy Ghost. That blissful communion with the invisible divine Power ("the Comforter, which is the Holy Ghost"— John 14:26, Bible) is the truly scientific basis of prayer. See also *Sat-Tat-Aum.*

avatar. Divine incarnation; from the Sanskrit *avatara*, with roots *ava*, "down," and *tri*, "to pass." One who attains union with Spirit and then returns to earth to help mankind is called an avatar.

avidya. Literally, "non-knowledge," ignorance; the manifestation in man of *maya*, the cosmic delusion (*q.v.*). Essentially, *avidya* is man's ignorance of his divine nature and of the sole reality: Spirit.

Babaji. See *Mahavatar Babaji.*

Bhagavad Gita. "Song of the Lord." An ancient Indian scripture consisting of eighteen chapters from the *sixth book (Bhishma*

Parva) of the *Mahabharata* epic. Presented in the form of a dialogue between the *avatar* (*q.v.*) Lord Krishna and his disciple Arjuna on the eve of the historic battle of Kurukshetra, the Gita is a profound treatise on the science of Yoga (union with God) and a timeless prescription for happiness and success in everyday living. The Gita is allegory as well as history, a spiritual dissertation on the inner battle between man's good and bad tendencies. Depending on the context, Krishna symbolizes the guru, the soul, or God; Arjuna represents the aspiring devotee. Of this universal scripture Mahatma Gandhi wrote: "Those who will meditate on the Gita will derive fresh joy and new meanings from it every day. There is not a single spiritual tangle which the Gita cannot unravel."

Unless otherwise indicated, the quotations from the Bhagavad Gita in this volume are from Paramahansa Yogananda's own translations, which he rendered from the Sanskrit sometimes literally and sometimes in paraphrase, depending on the context of his talk. Paramahansaji's comprehensive translation and commentary is entitled *God Talks With Arjuna: The Bhagavad Gita—Royal Science of God-Realization* (published by Yogoda Satsanga Society of India).

Bhagavan Krishna. An *avatar* (*q.v.*) who lived in India ages before the Christian era. One of the meanings given for the word *Krishna* in the Hindu scriptures is "Omniscient Spirit." Thus, *Krishna,* like *Christ,* is a spiritual title signifying the divine magnitude of the *avatar*—his oneness with God. The title *Bhagavan* means "Lord." At the time he gave the discourse recorded in the Bhagavad Gita, Lord Krishna was ruler of a kingdom in northern India. In his early life, Krishna lived as a cowherd who enchanted his companions with the music of his flute. In this role Krishna is often considered to represent allegorically the soul playing the flute of meditation to guide all misled thoughts back to the fold of omniscience.

Bhakti Yoga. The spiritual approach to God that stresses all-surrendering love as the principal means of communion and union with God. See *Yoga.*

Brahma-Vishnu-Shiva. Three aspects of God's immanence in creation. They represent that triune function of the *Kutastha Chaitanya*/Christ Intelligence *(Tat)* that guides Cosmic Nature's activities of creation, preservation, and dissolution. See *Trinity*.

Brahman (Brahma). Absolute Spirit.

breath. "The influx of innumerable cosmic currents into man by way of the breath induces restlessness in his mind," Paramahansa Yogananda wrote. "Thus the breath links him with the fleeting phenomenal worlds. To escape from the sorrows of transitoriness and to enter the blissful realm of Reality, the yogi learns to quiet the breath by scientific meditation."

caste. Caste in its original conception was not a hereditary status, but a classification based on man's natural capacities. In his evolution, man passes through four distinct grades, designated by ancient Hindu sages as *Sudra, Vaisya, Kshatriya,* and *Brahmin.* The *Sudra* is interested primarily in satisfying his bodily needs and desires; the work that best suits his state of development is bodily labour. The *Vaisya* is ambitious for worldly gain as well as for satisfaction of the senses; he has more creative ability than the *Sudra* and seeks occupation as a farmer, a businessman, an artist, or wherever his mental energy finds fulfilment. The *Kshatriya,* having through many lives fulfilled the desires of the *Sudra* and *Vaisya* states, begins to seek the meaning of life; he tries to overcome his bad habits, to control his senses, and to do what is right. *Kshatriyas* by occupation are noble rulers, statesmen, warriors. The *Brahmin* has overcome his lower nature, has a natural affinity for spiritual pursuits, and is God-knowing, able therefore to teach and help liberate others.

causal body. Essentially, man as a soul is a causal-bodied being. His causal body is an idea-matrix for the astral and physical bodies. The causal body is composed of 35 idea elements corresponding to the 19 elements of the astral body plus the 16 basic material elements of the physical body.

causal world. Behind the physical world of matter (atoms, protons, electrons), and the subtle astral world of luminous life energy (lifetrons), is the causal, or ideational, world of thought (thoughtrons). After man evolves sufficiently to transcend the physical and astral universes, he resides in the causal universe. In the consciousness of causal beings, the physical and astral universes are resolved to their thought essence. Whatever physical man can do in imagination, causal man can do in actuality—the only limitation being thought itself. Ultimately, man sheds the last soul covering—his causal body—to unite with omnipresent Spirit, beyond all vibratory realms.

chakras. In Yoga, the seven occult centres of life and consciousness in the spine and brain, which enliven the physical and astral bodies of man. These centres are referred to as *chakras* ("wheels") because the concentrated energy in each one is like a hub from which radiate rays of life-giving light and energy. In ascending order, these *chakras* are *muladhara* (the coccygeal, at the base of the spine); *svadhisthana* (the sacral, two inches above *muladhara*); *manipura* (the lumbar, opposite the navel); *anahata* (the dorsal, opposite the heart); *vishuddha* (the cervical, at the base of the neck); *ajna* (traditionally located between the eyebrows; in actuality, directly connected by polarity with the medulla; see also *medulla* and *spiritual eye*); and *sahasrara* (in the uppermost part of the cerebrum).

The seven centres are divinely planned exits or "trap doors" through which the soul has descended into the body and through which it must reascend by a process of meditation. By seven successive steps, the soul escapes into Cosmic Consciousness. In its conscious upward passage through the seven opened or "awakened" cerebrospinal centres, the soul travels the highway to the Infinite, the true path by which the soul must retrace its course to reunite with God.

Yoga treatises generally consider only the six lower centres as *chakras*, with *sahasrara* referred to separately as a seventh centre. All seven centres, however, are often referred to as lotuses, whose petals open, or turn upward, in spiritual awakening as the life and consciousness travel up the spine.

chitta. Intuitive feeling; the aggregate of consciousness, inherent in which is *ahamkara* (egoity), *buddhi* (intelligence), and *manas* (mind or sense consciousness).

Christ (Kutastha) centre. The *Kutastha* or *ajna chakra* at the point between the eyebrows, directly connected by polarity with the medulla (*q.v.*); centre of will and concentration, and of *Kutastha Chaitanya*/Christ Consciousness (*q.v.*); seat of the spiritual eye (*q.v.*).

Christ Consciousness. "Christ" or "Christ Consciousness" is the projected consciousness of God immanent in all creation. In Christian scripture it is called the "only begotten son," the only pure reflection in creation of God the Father; in Hindu scripture it is called *Kutastha Chaitanya* or *Tat*, the cosmic intelligence of Spirit everywhere present in creation. It is the universal consciousness, oneness with God, manifested by Krishna, Jesus, and other *avatars*. Great saints and yogis know it as the state of *samadhi* (*q.v.*) meditation wherein their consciousness has become identified with the intelligence in every particle of creation; they feel the entire universe as their own body. See *Trinity*.

Concentration Technique. The Yogoda Satsanga Society of India Technique of Concentration (also *Hong-Sau* Technique) taught in the *Yogoda Satsanga Lessons*. This technique helps scientifically to withdraw the attention from all objects of distraction and to place it upon one thing at a time. Thus it is invaluable for meditation, concentration on God. The *Hong-Sau* Technique is an integral part of the science of *Kriya Yoga* (*q.v.*).

consciousness, states of. In mortal consciousness man experiences three states: waking consciousness, sleeping consciousness, and dreaming consciousness. But he does not experience his soul, superconsciousness, and he does not experience God. The Christ-man does. As mortal man is conscious throughout his body, so the Christ-man is conscious throughout the universe, which he feels as his body. Beyond the state of *Kutastha Chaitanya* is cosmic consciousness, the experience of oneness with God in His absolute consciousness beyond vibratory creation as well as with the Lord's omnipresence manifesting in the phenomenal worlds.

Cosmic Consciousness. The Absolute; Spirit beyond creation. Also the *samadhi*-meditation state of oneness with God both beyond and within vibratory creation. See *Trinity.*

cosmic delusion. See *maya.*

cosmic energy. See *prana.*

cosmic Intelligent Vibration. See *Aum.*

Cosmic Sound. See *Aum.*

dharma. Eternal principles of righteousness that uphold all creation; man's inherent duty to live in harmony with these principles. See also *Sanatan Dharma.*

diksha. Spiritual initiation; from the Sanskrit verb-root *diksh*, to dedicate oneself. See also *disciple* and *Kriya Yoga.*

disciple. A spiritual aspirant who comes to a guru seeking introduction to God, and to this end establishes an eternal spiritual relationship with the guru. In Yogoda Satsanga Society of India/Self-Realization Fellowship, the guru-disciple relationship is established by *diksha*, initiation, in *Kriya Yoga*. See also *guru* and *Kriya Yoga.*

Divine Mother. The aspect of God that is active in creation; the *shakti*, or power, of the Transcendent Creator. Other terms for this aspect of Divinity are Nature or *Prakriti*, Aum, Holy Ghost, Cosmic Intelligent Vibration. Also, the personal aspect of God as Mother, embodying the Lord's love and compassionate qualities.

The Hindu scriptures teach that God is both immanent and transcendent, personal and impersonal. He may be sought as the Absolute; as one of His manifest eternal qualities, such as love, wisdom, bliss, light; in the form of an *ishta* (deity); or in a concept such as Heavenly Father, Mother, Friend.

egoism. The ego-principle, *ahamkara* (lit., "I do"), is the root cause of dualism or the seeming separation between man and his Creator. *Ahamkara* brings human beings under the sway of *maya* (*q.v.*), by which the subject (ego) falsely appears as object; the creatures imagine themselves to be creators. By banishing ego consciousness, man awakens to his divine identity, his oneness with the Sole Life: God.

elements (five). The Cosmic Vibration, or Aum, structures all physical creation, including man's physical body, through the manifestation of five *tattvas* (elements): earth, water, fire, air, and ether (*q.v.*). These are structural forces, intelligent and vibratory in nature. Without the earth element there would be no state of solid matter; without the water element, no liquid state; without the air element, no gaseous state; without the fire element, no heat; without the ether element, no background on which to produce the cosmic motion picture show. In the body, *prana* (cosmic vibratory energy) enters the medulla and is then divided into the five elemental currents by the action of the five lower *chakras* (*q.v.*), or centres: the coccygeal (earth), sacral (water), lumbar (fire), dorsal (air), and cervical (ether). The Sanskrit terminology for these elements is *prithivi, ap, tej, prana,* and *akash.*

Encinitas, California. Encinitas, a seaside city in southern California, is the site of a Self-Realization Fellowship Ashram Center, Retreat, and Hermitage, founded by Paramahansa Yogananda in 1937. The spacious grounds and Hermitage building, which is situated on a bluff overlooking the Pacific Ocean, was a gift to Paramahansaji from Rajarsi Janakananda (*q.v.*).

Energization Exercises. Man is surrounded by cosmic energy, much as a fish is surrounded by water. The Energization Exercises, originated by Paramahansa Yogananda and taught in the *Yogoda Satsanga Lessons* (*q.v.*), enable man to recharge his body with this cosmic energy, or universal *prana.*

ether. Sanskrit *akash.* Though not considered a factor in present scientific theory on the nature of the material universe, ether has for millenniums been so referred to by India's sages. Paramahansa Yogananda spoke of ether as the background on which God projects the cosmic motion picture of creation. Space gives dimension to objects; ether separates the images. This "background," a creative force that coordinates all spatial vibrations, is a necessary factor when considering the subtler forces— thought and life energy (*prana*)—and the nature of space and the origin of material forces and matter. See *elements*.

evil. The satanic force that obscures God's omnipresence in creation, manifesting as inharmonies in man and nature. Also, a broad term defining anything contrary to divine law (see *dharma*) that causes man to lose the consciousness of his essential unity with God, and that obstructs attainment of God-realization.

gunas. The three attributes of Nature: *tamas, rajas,* and *sattva*— obstruction, activity, and expansion; or, mass, energy, and intelligence. In man the three *gunas* express themselves as ignorance or inertia; activity or struggle; and wisdom.

guru. Spiritual teacher. Though the word *guru* is often misused to refer simply to any teacher or instructor, a true God-illumined guru is one who, in his attainment of self-mastery, has realized his identity with the omnipresent Spirit. Such a one is uniquely qualified to lead the seeker on his or her inward journey toward divine realization.

When a devotee is ready to seek God in earnest, the Lord sends him a guru. Through the wisdom, intelligence, Self-realization, and teachings of such a master, God guides the disciple. By following the master's teachings and discipline, the disciple is able to fulfil his soul's desire for the manna of God-perception. A true guru, ordained by God to help sincere seekers in response to their deep soul craving, is not an ordinary teacher: he is a human vehicle whose body, speech, mind and spirituality God uses as a channel to attract and guide lost souls back to their home of immortality. A guru is a living embodiment of scriptural truth. He is an agent of salvation appointed by God in response to a devotee's demand for release from the bondage of matter. "To keep company with the Guru," wrote Swami Sri Yukteswar in *The Holy Science,* "is not only to be in his physical presence (as this is sometimes impossible), but mainly means to keep him in our hearts and to be one with him in principle and to attune ourselves with him." See *master.*

Gurudeva. "Divine teacher," a customary Sanskrit term of respect that is used in addressing and referring to one's spiritual preceptor; sometimes rendered in English as "Master."

Gurus of Yogoda Satsanga Society of India/Self-Realization Fellowship. The Gurus are Bhagavan Krishna, Jesus Christ, and a line of exalted masters of contemporary times: Mahavatar Babaji, Sri Sri Lahiri Mahasaya, Swami Sri Yukteswarji, and Sri Sri Paramahansa Yogananda. To show the harmony and essential unity of the Yoga precepts of Bhagavan Krishna and the teachings of Jesus Christ is an integral part of the YSS/SRF dispensation. All of these Gurus, by their sublime teachings and divine instrumentality, contribute to the fulfilment of the Yogoda Satsanga Society of India/Self-Realization Fellowship mission of bringing to all mankind a practical spiritual science of God-realization.

Hatha Yoga. A system of techniques and physical postures (*asanas*) that promotes health and mental calm. See *Yoga.*

Holy Ghost. See *Aum* and *Trinity.*

intuition. The all-knowing faculty of the soul, which enables man to experience direct perception of truth without the intermediary of the senses.

Jadava Krishna. *Jadava* refers to the clan of which Bhagavan Krishna was king, and is one of many names by which Krishna is known. See *Bhagavan Krishna.*

Jnana Yoga. The path to union with God through transmutation of the discriminative power of the intellect into the omniscient wisdom of the soul.

karma. Effects of past actions, from this or previous lifetimes; from the Sanskrit *kri*, to do. The equilibrating law of karma, as expounded in the Hindu scriptures, is that of action and reaction, cause and effect, sowing and reaping. In the course of natural righteousness, every human being by his thoughts and actions becomes the moulder of his own destiny. Whatever energies he himself, wisely or unwisely, has set in motion must return to him as their starting point, like a circle inexorably completing itself. An understanding of karma as the law of justice serves to free the human mind from resentment against God and man. A person's karma follows him from incarnation to incarnation until fulfilled or spiritually transcended. (See *reincarnation*.)

The cumulative actions of human beings within communities, nations, or the world as a whole constitute mass karma, which produces local or far-ranging effects according to the degree and preponderance of good or evil. The thoughts and actions of every human being, therefore, contribute to the good or ill of this world and all peoples in it.

Karma Yoga. The path to God through nonattached action and service. By selfless service, by giving the fruits of one's actions to God, and by seeing God as the sole Doer, the devotee becomes free of the ego and experiences God. See *Yoga*.

Krishna. See *Bhagavan Krishna*.

Krishna Consciousness. Christ Consciousness; *Kutastha Chaitanya*. See *Christ Consciousness*.

Kriya Yoga. A sacred spiritual science, originating millenniums ago in India. It includes certain techniques of meditation whose devoted practice leads to realization of God. Paramahansa Yoganandaji has explained that the Sanskrit root of *kriya* is *kri*, to do, to act and react; the same root is found in the word *karma*, the natural principle of cause and effect. *Kriya Yoga* is thus "union (*yoga*) with the Infinite through a certain action or rite (*kriya*)."*Kriya Yoga*, a form of *Raja* ("royal" or "complete") *Yoga*, is extolled by Bhagavan Krishna in the Bhagavad Gita and by

Patanjali in the *Yoga Sutras*. Revived in this age by Mahavatar Babaji (*q.v.*), *Kriya Yoga* is the *diksha* (spiritual initiation) bestowed by the Gurus of Yogoda Satsanga Society of India/Self-Realization Fellowship. Since the *mahasamadhi* (*q.v.*) of Sri Sri Paramahansa Yogananda, *diksha* is conferred through his appointed spiritual representative, the president of Yogoda Satsanga Society of India/Self-Realization Fellowship (or through one appointed by the president). To qualify for *diksha* Yogoda Satsanga/Self-Realization members must fulfil certain preliminary spiritual requirements. One who has received this *diksha* is a *Kriya Yogi* or *Kriyaban*. See also *guru* and *disciple*.

Kutastha Chaitanya. See *Christ Consciousness.*

Lahiri Mahasaya. *Lahiri* was the family name of Shyama Charan Lahiri (1828-1895). *Mahasaya*, a Sanskrit religious title, means "large-minded." Lahiri Mahasaya was a disciple of Mahavatar Babaji, and the guru of Swami Sri Yukteswar (Paramahansa Yogananda's guru). A God-realized master with miraculous powers, he was also a family man with business responsibilities. His mission was to make known a yoga suitable for modern man, in which meditation is balanced by right performance of worldly duties. He has been called a *Yogavatar*, "Incarnation of Yoga." Lahiri Mahasaya was the disciple to whom Babaji revealed the ancient, almost lost science of *Kriya Yoga* (*q.v.*), instructing him in turn to initiate sincere seekers. Lahiri Mahasaya's life is described in *Autobiography of a Yogi.*

Laya Yoga. This yogic system teaches the absorption of mind in the perception of certain astral sounds, leading to union with God as the cosmic sound of Aum. See Aum and *Yoga.*

Lessons. See *Yogoda Satsanga (Self-Realization Lessons) Lessons.*

life force. See *prana.*

lifetrons. See *prana.*

Lynn, James J. (St. Lynn). See *Rajarsi Janakananda.*

mahasamadhi. Sanskrit *maha*, "great," *samadhi*. The last meditation, or conscious communion with God, during which a perfected master merges himself in the cosmic *Aum* and casts off the physical body. A master invariably knows beforehand the time God has appointed for him to leave his bodily residence. See *samadhi*.

Mahavatar Babaji. The deathless *mahavatar* ("great *avatar*") who in 1861 gave *Kriya Yoga* (q.v.) initiation to Lahiri Mahasaya, and thereby restored to the world the ancient technique of salvation. Perennially youthful, he has lived for centuries in the Himalayas, bestowing a constant blessing on the world. His mission has been to assist prophets in carrying out their special dispensations. Many title signifying his exalted spiritual stature have been given to him, but the *mahavatar* has generally adopted the simple name of Babaji, from the Sanskrit *baba*, "father," and the suffix *ji*, denoting respect. More information about his life and spiritual mission is given in *Autobiography of a Yogi*. See avatar.

Mantra Yoga. Divine communion attained through devotional, concentrated repetition of root-word sounds that have a spiritually beneficial vibratory potency. See *Yoga*.

master. One who has achieved self-mastery. Paramahansa Yogananda has pointed out that "the distinguishing qualifications of a master are not physical but spiritual....Proof that one is a master is supplied only by the ability to enter at will the breathless state (*sabikalpa samadhi*) and by the attainment of immutable bliss (*nirbikalpa samadhi*)." See *samadhi*.

Paramahansaji further states: "All scriptures proclaim that the Lord created man in His omnipotent image. Control over the universe appears to be supernatural, but in truth such power is inherent and natural in everyone who attains 'right remembrance' of his divine origin. Men of God-realization... are devoid of the ego-principle (*ahamkara*) and its uprisings of personal desires; the actions of true masters are in effortless conformity with *rita*, natural righteousness. In Emerson's words, all great ones become 'not virtuous, but Virtue; then is the end of the creation answered, and God is well pleased.'"

maya. The delusory power inherent in the structure of creation, by which the One appears as many. *Maya* is the principle of relativity, inversion, contrast, duality, oppositional states; the "Satan" (lit., in Hebrew, "the adversary") of the Old Testament prophets; and the "devil" whom Christ described picturesquely as a "murderer" and a "liar," because "there is no truth in him" (*John* 8:44, Bible).

Paramahansa Yoganandaji wrote:

"The Sanskrit word *maya* means 'the measurer'; it is the magical power in creation by which limitations and divisions are apparently present in the Immeasurable and Inseparable. *Maya* is Nature herself—the phenomenal worlds, ever in transitional flux as antithesis to Divine Immutability.

"In God's plan and play (*lila*), the sole function of Satan or *maya* is to attempt to divert man from Spirit to matter, from Reality to unreality. 'The devil sinneth from the beginning. For this purpose the Son of God was manifested, that he might destroy the works of the devil' (*I John* 3:8, Bible). That is, the manifestation of Christ Consciousness (*Kutastha Chaitanya*), within man's own being, effortlessly destroys the illusions or 'works of the devil.'

"*Maya* is the veil of transitoriness in Nature, the ceaseless becoming of creation; the veil that each man must lift in order to see behind it the Creator, the changeless Immutable, eternal Reality."

meditation. Concentration upon God. The term is used in a general sense to denote practise of any technique for interiorizing the attention and focusing it on some aspect of God. In the specific sense, meditation refers to the end result of successful practise of such techniques: direct experience of God through intuitive perception. It is the seventh step (*dhyana*) of the eightfold path of Yoga described by Patanjali (*q.v.*), achieved only after one has attained that fixed concentration within whereby he is completely undisturbed by sensory impressions from the outer world. In deepest meditation one experiences the eighth step of the Yoga path: *samadhi* (*q.v.*), communion, oneness with God. (See also *Yoga.*)

medulla. The principal point of entry of life force (*prana*) into the body; seat of the sixth cerebrospinal centre, whose function is to receive and direct the incoming flow of cosmic energy. The life force is stored in the seventh centre (*sahasrara*) in the topmost part of the brain. From that reservoir it is distributed throughout the body. The subtle centre at the medulla is the main switch that controls the entrance, storage, and distribution of the life force.

Mt. Washington. Site of, and, by extension, a frequently used name for the Mother Centre and international headquarters of Self-Realization Fellowship in Los Angeles. The 12½-acre estate was acquired in 1925 by Paramahansa Yogananda. He made it a training centre for the Self-Realization monastics, and the administrative centre for disseminating worldwide the ancient science of *Kriya Yoga.* See also page 422.

paramahansa. A spiritual title signifying a master (*q.v.*). It may be conferred only by a true guru on a qualified disciple. *Paramahansa* literally means "supreme swan." In the Hindu scriptures, the *hansa* or swan symbolizes spiritual discrimination. Swami Sri Yukteswar bestowed the title on his beloved disciple Yogananda in 1935.

paramguru. Literally, "the preceding guru"; the guru of one's guru. To Yogodans/Self-Realizationists (disciples of Paramahansa Yogananda), *paramguru* refers to Swami Sri Yukteswarji. To Paramahansaji, it meant Lahiri Mahasaya. Mahavatar Babaji is Paramahansaji's *param-paramguru.*

Patanjali. Ancient exponent of Yoga, whose *Yoga Sutras* outline the principles of the yogic path, dividing it into eight steps: (1)

yama, moral conduct; (2) *niyama,* religious observances; (3) *asana,* right posture to still bodily restlessness; (4) *pranayama,* control of *prana,* subtle life currents; (5) *pratyahara,* interiorization; (6) *dharana,* concentration; (7) *dhyana,* meditation; and (8) *samadhi,* superconscious experience. See *Yoga.*

prana. Sparks of intelligent finer-than-atomic energy that constitute life, collectively referred to in Hindu scriptural treatises as *prana,* which Paramahansa Yogananda has translated as "lifetrons." In essence, condensed thoughts of God; substance of the astral world (*q.v.*) and life principle of the physical cosmos. In the physical world, there are two kinds of *prana:* (1) the cosmic vibratory energy that is omnipresent in the universe, structuring and sustaining all things; (2) the specific *prana* or energy that pervades and sustains each human body through five currents or functions. *Prana* current performs the function of crystallization; *Vyana* current, circulation; *Samana* current, assimilation; *Udana* current, metabolism; and *Apana* current, elimination.

pranam. A form of greeting in India. The hands are pressed, palms together, with the base of the hands at the heart and the fingertips touching the forehead. This gesture is actually a modification of the *pranam,* literally "complete salutation," from the Sanskrit root *nam,* "to salute or bow down," and the prefix *pra,* "completely." A *pranam* salutation is the general mode of greeting in India. Before renunciants and other persons held in high spiritual regard, it may be accompanied by the spoken word, *"Pranam."*

pranayama. Conscious control of *prana* (the creative vibration or energy that activates and sustains life in the body). The yoga science of *pranayama* is the direct way to consciously disconnect the mind from the life functions and sensory perceptions that tie man to body-consciousness. *Pranayama* thus frees man's consciousness to commune with God. All scientific techniques that bring about union of soul and Spirit may be classified as yoga, and *pranayama* is the greatest yogic method for attaining this divine union.

Raja Yoga. The "royal" or highest path to God-union. It teaches scientific meditation (*q.v.*) as the ultimate means for realizing God, and includes the highest essentials from all other forms of Yoga. The Yogoda Satsanga Society of India/Self-Realization Fellowship *Raja Yoga* teachings outline a way of life leading to perfect unfoldment in body, mind, and soul, based on the foundation of *Kriya Yoga* (*q.v.*) meditation. See *Yoga.*

Sri Sri Rajarsi Janakananda (James J. Lynn). Beloved disciple of Paramahansa Yoganandaji, and first successor to him as president and spiritual head of Yogoda Satsanga Society of India/Self-Realization Fellowship until his passing on February 20, 1955. Mr Lynn first received *Kriya Yoga* initiation from Paramahansaji in 1932; his spiritual advancement was so swift that the Guru lovingly referred to him as "Saint Lynn," until bestowing on him the monastic title of Rajarsi Janakananda in 1951.

Ranchi school. Yogoda Satsanga Vidyalaya, founded by Paramahansa Yogananda in 1918 when the Maharaja of Kasimbazar gave his summer palace and twenty-five acres of land in Ranchi, Jharkhand, for use as a boys' school. The property was permanently acquired while Paramahansaji was in India in 1935-36. More than two thousand children now attend Yogoda schools at Ranchi, from nursery school through college. See *Yogoda Satsanga Society of India.*

reincarnation. The doctrine that human beings, compelled by the law of evolution, incarnate repeatedly in progressively higher lives—retarded by wrong actions and desires, and advanced by spiritual endeavours—until Self-realization and God-union are attained. Having thus transcended the limitations and imperfections of mortal consciousness, the soul is forever freed from compulsory reincarnation. "Him that overcometh will I make a pillar in the temple of my God, and he shall go no more out" (*Revelation* 3:12, Bible).

The concept of reincarnation is not exclusive to Eastern philosophy, but was held as a fundamental truth of life by many ancient civilizations. The early Christian Church accepted the principle of reincarnation, which was expounded by the Gnostics and by numerous Church fathers, including Clement of Alexandria, Origen, and St. Jerome. It was not until the Second Council of Constantinople in A.D. 553 that the doctrine was officially removed from church teachings. Today many Western thinkers are beginning to adopt the concept of the law of karma (*q.v.*) and reincarnation, seeing in it a grand and reassuring explanation of life's seeming inequities.

rishis. Seers, exalted beings who manifest divine wisdom; especially, the illumined sages of ancient India to whom the Vedas were intuitively revealed.

sadhana. Path of spiritual discipline. The specific instruction and meditation practices prescribed by the guru for his disciples, who by faithfully following them ultimately realize God.

Saint Lynn (James J. Lynn). See *Rajarsi Janakananda*.

samadhi. The highest step on the Eightfold Path of Yoga, as outlined by the sage Patanjali (*q.v.*). *Samadhi* is attained when the meditator, the process of meditation (by which the mind is withdrawn from the senses by interiorization), and the object of meditation (God) become One. Paramahansa Yoganandaji has explained that "in the initial states of God-communion (*sabikalpa samadhi*) the devotee's consciousness merges in the Cosmic Spirit; his life force is withdrawn from the body, which appears 'dead,' or motionless and rigid. The yogi is fully aware of his bodily condition of suspended animation. As he progresses to higher spiritual states (*nirbikalpa samadhi*), however, he communes with God without bodily fixation; and in his ordinary waking consciousness, even in the midst of exacting worldly duties." Both states are characterized by oneness with the ever new bliss of Spirit, but the *nirbikalpa* state is experienced by only the most highly advanced masters.

Sanatana Dharma. Literally, "eternal religion." The name given to the body of Vedic teachings that came to be called Hinduism after the Greeks designated the people on the banks of the river

Indus as *Indoos*, or *Hindus*. See *dharma*.

Satan. Literally, in Hebrew, "the adversary." Satan is the conscious and independent universal force that keeps everything and everybody deluded with the unspiritual consciousness of finiteness and separateness from God. To accomplish this, Satan uses the weapons of *maya* (cosmic delusion) and *avidya* (individual delusion, ignorance).See *maya*.

Sat-Tat-Aum *Sat*, Truth, the Absolute, Bliss; *Tat*, universal intelligence or consciousness; *Aum*, cosmic intelligent creative vibration, word-symbol for God. See *Aum* and *Trinity*.

Self. Capitalized to denote the *atman* or soul, the divine essence of man, as distinguished from the ordinary self, which is the human personality or ego. The Self is individualized Spirit, whose essential nature is ever-existing, ever-conscious, ever-new Bliss. The Self or soul is man's inner fountainhead of love, wisdom, peace, courage, compassion, and all other divine qualities.

Self-realization. Paramahansa Yogananda has defined Self-realization as follows: "Self-realization is the knowing—in body, mind, and soul—that we are one with the omnipresence of God; that we do not have to pray that it come to us, that we are not merely near it at all times, but that God's omnipresence is our omnipresence; that we are just as much a part of Him now as we ever will be. All we have to do is improve our knowing."

Self-Realization. An abbreviated way of referring to Self-Realization Fellowship, the society founded by Paramahansa Yogananda, often used by him in informal talks; e.g., "the Self-Realization teachings"; "the path of Self-Realization"; "Self-Realization headquarters in Los Angeles"; etc.

Self-Realization Fellowship. The society founded by Sri Sri Paramahansa Yogananda in the United states in 1920 (and as Yogoda Satsanga Society of India in 1917) for disseminating worldwide, for the aid and benefit of humanity, the spiritual principles and meditation techniques of *Kriya Yoga* (*q.v.*). The international headquarters, the Mother Centre, is in Los Angeles, California. Paramahansa Yogananda has explained that the name Self-realization Fellowship signifies: "Fellowship with God through Self-realization, and friendship with all truth-seeking souls."

Self-Realization Fellowship Lessons. See *Yogoda Satsanga/Self-Realization Fellowship Lessons.*

Shankara, Swami. Sometimes referred to as Adi ("the first") Shankaracharya (Shankara + *acharya*, "teacher"); India's most illustrious philosopher. His date is uncertain; many scholars assign him to the eighth or early ninth century. He expounded God not as a negative abstraction, but as positive, eternal, omnipresent, ever new Bliss. Shankara reorganized the ancient Swami Order, and founded four great *maths* (monastic centres of spiritual education), whose leaders in apostolic succession bear the title of Jagadguru Sri Shankaracharya. The meaning of *Jagadguru* is "world teacher."

siddha. Literally, "one who is successful." One who has attained Self-realization.

soul. Individualized Spirit. The soul or Self (*atman*) is the true and immortal nature of man, and of all living forms of life; it is cloaked only temporarily in the garments of causal, astral, and physical bodies. The nature of the soul is Spirit: ever-existing, ever-conscious, ever-new joy.

spiritual eye. The single eye of intuition and omnipresent perception at the Christ (*Kutastha*) centre (*ajna chakra*) between the eyebrows. The deeply meditating devotee beholds the spiritual eye as a ring of golden light encircling a sphere of opalescent blue, and at the centre, a pentagonal white star. Microcosmically, these forms and colours epitomize, respectively, the vibratory realm of creation (Cosmic Nature, Holy Ghost); the Son or intelligence of God in creation (*Kutastha Chaitanya*/Christ Consciousness); and the vibrationless Spirit beyond all creation (God the Father).

The spiritual eye is the entryway into the ultimate states of divine consciousness. In deep meditation, as the devotee's consciousness penetrates the spiritual eye, into the three realms epitomized therein, the experiences successively the following states: superconsciousness or the ever new joy of soul-realization, and oneness with God as Aum (*q.v.*) or Holy Ghost; *Kutastha Chaitanya or* Christ consciousness, oneness with the universal intelligence of God in all creation; and cosmic consciousness, unity with the omnipresence of God that is beyond as well as within vibratory manifestation. See also *consciousness, states of; superconsciousness; Christ Consciousness.*

Explaining a passage from *Ezekiel* (43:1-2, Bible), Paramahansa Yoganandaji has written: "Through the divine eye in the forehead, ('the east'), the yogi sails his consciousness into omnipresence, hearing the word or Aum, the divine sound of 'many waters': the vibrations of light that constitute the sole reality of creation." In Ezekiel's words: "Afterwards he brought me to the gate, even the gate that looketh towards the east; and behold, the glory of the God of Israel came from the way of the east; and His voice was like the noise of many waters; and the earth shined with His glory."

Jesus also spoke of the spiritual eye: "When thine eye is single, thy whole body also is full of light.... Take heed therefore that the light which is in thee be not darkness" (*Luke* 11:34-35, Bible).

Sri Yukteswar, Swami. Swami Sri Yukteswar Giri (1855-1936), India's *Jnanavatar*, "Incarnation of Wisdom"; guru of Paramahansa Yogananda, and *paramguru* of Yogoda Satsanga Society of India/Self-Realization Fellowship *Kriyaban* members. Sri Yukteswarji was a disciple of Lahiri Mahasaya. At the behest of Lahiri Mahasaya's guru, Mahavatar Babaji, he wrote *The Holy Science*, a treatise on the underlying unity of Hindu and Christian scriptures, and trained Paramahansa Yoganandaji for his spiritual world-mission: the dissemination of *Kriya Yoga* (*q.v.*). Paramahansaji has lovingly described Sri Yukteswarji's life in *Autobiography of a Yogi.*

superconscious mind. The all-knowing power of the soul that perceives truth directly; intuition.

superconsciousness. The pure, intuitive, all-seeing, ever-blissful consciousness of the soul. Sometimes used generally to refer to all the various states of *samadhi* (*q.v.*) experienced in meditation, but specifically the first state of *samadhi*, wherein one transcends ego consciousness and realizes his self as soul, made in the image of God. Thence follow the higher states of realization: *Kutastha Chaitanya*/Christ consciousness and cosmic consciousness (*q.v.*).

swami. A member of India's most ancient monastic order, reorganized in the eighth or early ninth century by Swami Shankara (*q.v.*). A swami takes formal vows of celibacy and renunciation of worldly ties and ambitions; he devotes himself to meditation and other spiritual practices, and to service to humanity. There are ten classificatory titles of the venerable Swami Order, as *Giri, Puri, Bharati, Tirtha, Saraswati,* and others. Swami Sri Yukteswarji (*q.v.*) and Paramahansa Yoganandaji belonged to the *Giri* ("mountain") branch.

The Sanskrit word *swami* means "he who is one with the Self (*Swa*)."

Trinity. When Spirit manifests creation, It becomes the Trinity: Father, Son, Holy Ghost, or *Sat, Tat, Aum.* The Father (*Sat*) is God as the Creator existing beyond creation. The Son (*Tat*) is God's omnipresent intelligence existing in creation. The Holy Ghost (*Aum*) is the vibratory power of God that objectifies or becomes creation.

Many cycles of cosmic creation and dissolution have come and gone in Eternity (see *yuga*). At the time of cosmic dissolution, the Trinity and all other relativities of creation resolve into the Absolute Spirit.

Vedanta. Literally, "end of the Vedas"; the philosophy stemming from the *Upanishads*, or latter portion of the Vedas.

Shankara (eighth or early ninth century) was the chief exponent
of Vedanta, which declares that God is the only reality and
that creation is essentially an illusion. As man is the only
creature capable of conceiving of God, man himself must be
divine, and his duty therefore is to realize his true nature.

Vedas. The four scriptural texts of the Hindus: Rig Veda, Sama
Veda, Yajur Veda, and Atharva Veda. They are essentially a literature of chant, ritual, and recitation for vitalizing and spiriutal-
izing all phases of man's life and activity. Among the immense
texts of India, the Vedas (Sanskrit root *vid*, "to know") are the
only writings to which no author is ascribed. The Rig Veda
assigns a celestial origin to the hymns and tells us they have
come down from "ancient times," reclothed in new language. Divinely revealed from age to age to the *rishis*, "seers," the four
Vedas are said to possess *nityatva*, "timeless finality."

Yoga. From Sanskrit *yuj*, "union." Yoga means union of the individual soul with Spirit; also, the methods by which this goal is
attained. Within the larger spectrum of Hindu philosophy, Yoga
is one of six orthodox systems: *Vedanta, Mimamsa, Sankhya,
Vaisesika, Nyaya, and Yoga.* There are also various types of yoga
methods: *Hatha Yoga, Mantra Yoga, Laya Yoga, Karma Yoga,
Jnana Yoga, Bhakti Yoga,* and *Raja Yoga. Raja Yoga,* the "royal"
or complete yoga, is that which is taught by Yogoda Satsanga
Society of India/Self-Realization Fellowship, and which Bhagavan Krishna extols to his disciple Arjuna in the Bhagavad Gita:
"The yogi is deemed greater than body-disciplining ascetics,
greater even than the followers of the path of wisdom or of the
path of action; be thou, O Arjuna, a yogi!" (Bhagavad Gita VI:46).
The sage Patanjali, foremost exponent of Yoga, has outlined
eight definite steps by which the *Raja Yogi* attains *samadhi,* or
union with God. These are (1) *yama,* moral conduct; (2)
niyama, religious observances; (3) *asana,* right posture to still
bodily restlessness; (4) *pranayama,* control of *prana,* subtle life
currents; (5) *pratyahara,* interiorization; (6) *dharana,* concentration, (7) *dhyana,* meditation; and (8) *samadhi,* superconscious
experience.

yogi. One who practises Yoga (*q.v.*). Anyone who practises a scientific technique for divine realization is a yogi. He may be either married or unmarried, either a man of worldly responsibilities or one of formal religious ties.

Yogoda Satsanga Magazine. Four booklets published annually in English, Hindi, and Bengali by Yogoda Satsanga Society of India, featuring talks and writings of Sri Sri Paramahansa Yogananda, and containing other spiritual, practical, and informative articles of current interest and lasting value. *Satsangas* of Sri Sri Daya Mata and Sri Sri Mrinalini Mata, Sanghamata and President of Yogoda Satsanga Society of India/Self-Realization Fellowship, are also a regular feature.

Yogoda Satsanga Society of India. The name by which Sri Sri Paramahansa Yogananda's society is known in India. The Society was founded in 1917 by Paramahansa Yogananda. Its headquarters, Yogoda Satsanga Math, is situated on the banks of the Ganges at Dakshineswar, near Kolkata. Yogoda Satsanga Society has a branch math at Ranchi, Jharkhand, and Sakha Ashrams at Dwarahat, Uttarakhand and Noida, Uttar Pradesh. YSS has meditation centres in over 200 cities, towns, and villages throughout India. YSS also runs schools, colleges, hospitals, dispensaries, and medical camps; provides scholarships to deserving students all over India, and help to orphanages and leprosy colonies; and offers relief to those afflicted by natural disasters. "Yogoda," a word coined by Paramahansa Yogananda, is derived from yoga, union, harmony, equilibrium; and da, that which imparts. "Satsanga" is composed of sat, truth, and sanga, fellowship. For the West, Sri Yogananda translated the Indian name as "Self-Realization Fellowship." See also "Aims and Ideals of Yogoda Satsanga Society of India," Page 407.

The society publishes Paramahansa Yogananda's writings, lectures, and informal talks—including his comprehensive series of *Yogoda Satsanga Lessons* for home study; publishes audio and video recordings on his teachings; oversees its ashrams, kendras, and meditation centres, and the monastic community of the Yogoda Satsanga Order; conducts lecture and class series in